The Internal Geography of Trade

DIRECTIONS IN DEVELOPMENT
Trade

The Internal Geography of Trade

Lagging Regions and Global Markets

Thomas Farole, Editor

THE WORLD BANK
Washington, D.C.

1 2 3 4   16 15 14 13

ISBN (paper): 978-0-8213-9893-7
ISBN (electronic): 978-0-8213-9895-1
DOI: 10.1596/978-0-8213-9893-7

Cover photo: Marcia Mitsi; *Cover design:* Naylor Design

Library of Congress Cataloging-in-Publication Data

The internal geography of trade : lagging regions and global markets / Thomas Farole (editor).
    pages cm
ISBN 978-0-8213-9893-7 — ISBN 978-0-8213-9895-1
    1. Regional economic disparities. 2. Regional economics. 3. International trade. 4. Economic development. 5. International economic integration. 6. Developing countries—Commerce I. Farole, Thomas.
II. World Bank,
    HT388.I577 2013
    330.9—dc23   2013007863

Contents

Tables

Acknowledgments

This book was prepared by Thomas Farole (World Bank, International Trade Department), along with a team including Deborah Winkler (chapters 3, 4, 5, and 6), Andrés Rodríguez-Pose (chapters 2 and 5), Vassilis Tselios (chapter 5), Megha Mukim (chapter 7), Della Temenggung (chapter 8), and Aradhna Aggarwal and Prakash Singh Archa (chapter 9).

We are grateful for valuable comments and suggestions received by reviewers, including Somik Lall, Taye Mengistae, Kevin Carey, Vijay Tata, and Alexey Morozov.

Thanks also to Ana Margarida Fernandes, Federica Saliola, and Murat Seker for assistance in providing access to key datasets, and to Shienny Lie and Marinella Yadao for their administrative support.

The work was carried out under the overall supervision of Mona Haddad and Bernard Hoekman.

.

About the Contributors

Aradhna Aggarwal is a Senior Fellow at the National Council of Applied Economic Research in New Delhi, India.

Prakash Singh Archa is a Doctoral Candidate in the Department of Business Economics at Delhi University and ICSSR Doctoral Fellow at the Institute of Economic Growth University of Delhi, India.

Thomas Farole is a Senior Trade Specialist in the International Trade Department of the World Bank in Washington, DC.

Megha Mukim is an Economist in the Africa Region Finance and Private Sector Development Unit at the World Bank in Washington, DC.

Andrés Rodríguez-Pose is a Professor of Economic Geography at the London School of Economics and Political Science, U.K.

Della Temenggung is a Consultant Economist at the Multi-Donor Facility for Trade and Investment Climate in the World Bank, Jakarta, Indonesia.

Vassilis Tselios is a Lecturer in Economic Geography at the University of Southampton, U.K.

Deborah Winkler is a Consultant Economist in the International Trade Department of the World Bank in Washington, DC.

Abbreviations

AIFI	all-India financial institution
APINDO	Indonesia Employers Association (Asosiasi Pengusaha Indonesia)
ASEAN	Association of Southeast Asian Nations
ASI	Annual Survey of Industries (India)
BIDA	Batam Industrial Development Authority
BKPM	Investment Coordinating Board (Badan Koordinasi Penanaman Modal) (Indonesia)
BPS	Statistics Indonesia (Badan Pusat Statistik)
BRICS	Brazil, Russian Federation, India, China, and South Africa
CMIE	Centre for Monitoring the Indian Economy
DTA	domestic tariff area
EOUs	export oriented units
EPZ	export processing zone
EU	European Union
EU-15	15 countries that were members of the EU before May 1, 2004
FDI	foreign direct investment
GDP	gross domestic product
GIS	geographic information system
GMM	generalized method of moments
GRDP	gross regional domestic product
GSDP	gross state domestic product
HADP	Hill Area Development Program (India)
HDI	Human Development Index (Indonesia)
HHI	Herfindahl-Hirschman index
HUDCO	Housing and Urban Development Corporation (India)
IDBI	Industrial Development Bank of India
IDSMT	Integrated Development of Small and Medium Towns (India)
IEM	Industrial Entrepreneurs Memorandum (India)
IIDC	Integrated Infrastructure Development Centre (India)
ILPIC	Industrial Licensing Policy Inquiry Committee (India)

ISC   index of structural change
ISIC   International Standard Industrial Classification
IT   information technology
KADIN   National Trade and Industry Chamber (Kamar Dagang dan
              Industri) (Indonesia)
KAPET   Integrated Economic Development Zone (Kawasan Pengembangan
              Ekonomi Terpadu) (Indonesia)
LSDV   least squares dummy variable
MNE   multinational enterprise
MOI   Ministry of Industry (Indonesia)
MOSPI   Ministry of Statistics and Programme Implementation (India)
MP3EI   Master Plan for the Acceleration and Expansion of Indonesian
              Economic Growth (Master Plan Percepatan dan Perluasan
              Pembangunan Ekonomi Indonesia)
NAFTA   North American Free Trade Agreement
NCDBA   National Committee for the Development of Backward Areas
              (India)
NEDFI   North East Development Financial Corporation (India)
NEG   new economic geography
NEIP   North East Industrial Policy (India)
NIC   National Industrial Classification
NSSO   National Sample Survey Organisation (India)
OECD   Organisation for Economic Co-operation and Development
OLS   ordinary least squares
OSS   one stop services
PAD   Local Revenues (Pendapatan Asli Daerah) (Indonesia)
PPKTI   Acceleration of Eastern Indonesian Development
              (Percepatan Pembangunan Kawasan Timur Indonesia)
PPP   purchasing power parity
RBI   Reserve Bank of India
SEZs   special economic zones
SUSENAS   National Socioeconomic Survey (Survei Sosial Ekonomi Nasional)
              (Indonesia)
TFP   total factor productivity
UT   union territory (India)
WDR   World Development Report

Overview

Introduction: The Challenge of Lagging Regions

Globalization, Geography, and Emergence of Leading and Lagging Regions

Take a snapshot of the world at any time and it is clear that economic activity is unevenly distributed across places. In a dynamic context, however, neoclassical theory suggests that we should see convergence in per capita incomes over time, as factors move from high- to low-cost locations. The strong convergence in national incomes over the past 20 years seems to support this theory. Yet *within* many countries the opposite has been the case, with output and wealth increasingly being concentrated and cross-regional disparities apparently widening. This pattern of divergence appears to have become more acute in the recent era of globalization of trade and investment.

Economic theory, including endogenous growth, the role of institutions, and, most importantly, the "new economic geography" (NEG), have made significant progress in explaining the emergence of core-periphery patterns behind this divergence. They point to the critical role of agglomeration, which confers benefits to metropolitan cores that have the advantages of large markets, deep labor pools, links to international markets, and clusters of diverse suppliers and institutions. Regions relatively near the metropolitan core are likely to benefit from spillovers and congestion-related dispersion. Regions further outside the core (that is, the periphery), however, are not only less able to take advantage of spillovers, but also more likely to be far removed from key infrastructural, institutional, and interpersonal links to regional and international markets. As a result, they face significant challenges to becoming competitive locations to host economic activity. Thus the geographical pattern of core and peripheral regions is increasingly manifest in an economic pattern of "leading" and "lagging" regions.

The World Development Report Framework

The World Bank's *World Development Report 2009* (WDR 2009) brought the issue of economic geography strongly to the fore of the mainstream development agenda. The report argues that uneven patterns of economic activity and divergence in outcomes across regions are a natural consequence of processes of agglomeration: "Economic growth is seldom balanced. Efforts to spread it prematurely will jeopardize progress. Two centuries of economic development show that spatial disparities in income and production are inevitable. A generation of economic research confirms this" (World Bank 2009, 5–6). But the report also emphasizes that it is not simply structural factors such as poor location ("distance") or even lack of agglomeration potential ("density") that affect lagging regions. Other barriers, often resulting from government failures ("division"), can compound the situation, undermining integration and growth prospects.

Why Should We Care about Regional Disparities?

From an aggregate perspective, regional inequality is not necessarily a bad thing. Most evidence points to a positive association between the geographical concentration of economic activity and economic growth. Yet there are some important downsides to increasing disparities, and not simply for residents of lagging regions. Growing disparities across regions may threaten social and political cohesion, and at minimum will contribute to increasing demand for redistributive (versus productive) policies, which may have a dampening effect on overall growth. Of course, this depends on whether output inequality translates into income inequality. Where redistributive tax and transfer policies and fluid factor markets exist, entrenched regional inequalities can be significantly mitigated. However, in many if not most developing countries, both of these mechanisms are not yet effective.

In addition, many lagging regions are failing to make productive use of the resources available to them. Combined with self-reinforcing institutional failures, this leads to lagging regions getting caught in a "low growth trap" and acts as a drag on national growth potential. Finally, lack of economic opportunity in peripheral regions contributes to the massive rural-urban shifts that are already overwhelming the infrastructural, environmental, and institutional capacities of major metropolitan regions in many developing countries.

At the micro level, the prospects for individual firms to reap the benefits that accrue from globalization may depend as much on the neighborhood as on the country in which they operate. And as there is an endogenous relationship between income and many of the factors that contribute to firm success, firms in more advantageous geographical positions may become increasingly more competitive relative to those in lagging territories. Therefore, failing to address some of the root causes of regional disparities may condemn firms in these territories to operate on an increasingly unlevel playing field, which is likely to contribute to further widening of the gap in outcomes between leading and lagging regions.

The Trade and Location Nexus

The Role of Trade in Shaping Patterns of Leading and Lagging Regions

Trade plays a crucial role in the interaction between location, growth, and inequality. From the perspective of a regional economy, expanded market access through trade can have a quick and transformational impact on growth. For example, in the five years following the implementation of the North American Free Trade Agreement (NAFTA), Mexico's border regions grew real gross value added by 36 percent, more than three times faster than the average growth in other regions of the country (Baylis, Garduno-Rivera, and Piras 2009). But for regions that are already lagging—particularly those that are cursed both in terms of "distance" (remote) and "density" (sparsely populated)—the trends of global and regional trade integration can result in further isolation, as firms and consumers in the core increasingly engage outward at the expense of the domestic hinterland. Meanwhile, firms in remote regions may struggle to take advantage of the opportunities available from integration in global markets. Firms in the periphery lack local markets of significant size to facilitate scale economies that might condition them to compete globally; they face higher costs and time to reach export markets; they are often underserved by public goods (including both hard and soft infrastructure) that underpin access and competitiveness; and they tend to have less access to knowledge being produced at the technology frontier, resulting in less-competitive human capital and institutions.

A Firm-Level Perspective on Trade and Lagging Regions

Getting a clearer understanding of the relationship between trade and regional outcomes requires also looking at the question the other way round—that is, how places (locational factors) determine trade outcomes. From a policy perspective, it would be extremely valuable to identify if and how regional factors, including both regional endowments and the regional "investment climate" as well as the presence of spillovers from other firms, influence firms in their decision to trade and in their ultimate success in export markets. In the set of studies presented in this book, we combine a firm-level methodological approach (drawing from the burgeoning trade literature on heterogeneous firms) with traditional NEG approaches. In doing so, we aim for a richer understanding of the trade and location nexus in order to inform policies that address the challenge of lagging regions.

This book uses the WDR 2009 concept of *distance, density, and division* as a broad framework to investigate lagging regions. Using cross-country data and in-depth case studies in Indonesia and India, the analysis decomposes factors that depend on pure location ("first-order" geography), on agglomeration, and on the investment climate and other policy-induced regional determinants, as well as factors that are specific to firms and not to location.

Key Findings on the Relationship between Location and Trade

Trade Tends to Exacerbate Regional Inequalities, Especially in Developing Countries

In the analysis presented in chapter 2, we find that regional inequalities are growing in 18 of the 28 countries studied, with only three countries experiencing regional income convergence. The results from a comprehensive econometric model show that trade, *in combination with other factors*, may have a significant impact on regional inequality. In addition, trade openness is more likely to contribute to divergence in developing countries than in developed countries. This is not because trade inherently leads to regional inequality, but because developing countries tend to have a number of structural features that potentiate the polarizing effect of trade openness. These features include existing regional inequality, lower government expenditure, higher variations in regional sector structures, and a spatial structure dominated by high internal transaction costs coupled with a higher degree of coincidence between prosperous regions and foreign market access.

Evidence from our two case studies (Indonesia in chapter 4 and India in chapter 6) supports these findings, showing that greater trade openness seems to coincide with increasing regional inequality. However, export participation has grown substantially across almost all regions in both countries. Thus it is not the case that firms in lagging regions have been unable to access foreign markets at all; instead, they are expanding trade at a slower pace than in many of the leading regions. In fact, the findings show significant heterogeneity both in regional outcomes and in the regional response to trade openness in these countries, with winners and losers both in the core and in the periphery.

Another explanation for growing regional disparities may be found in the structural transformation of regional economies that is, in part, induced by trade integration. Evidence from both Indonesia and India shows that the relative change in sectoral output and export structures is much higher in peripheral regions than it is in the core. This is unsurprising, as these regions have been traditionally concentrated in a narrow set of natural resources sectors. This shift, however, brings with it adjustment costs and geographical shifts in production that may contribute to growing regional inequalities. On the other hand, there is little evidence of increasing concentration of export-oriented manufacturing output in both countries over the study period, suggesting that net agglomeration forces are weak. In fact, the geographical structure of sectors with preexisting clusters appears to have changed little during the period of growing trade openness, indicating territorial embeddedness of these clusters.

Firms in the Core Trade More, Despite Congestion Costs

The findings from the cross-country analytics as well as the case studies (chapters 3–7) provide clear evidence that firms located in core regions of countries are more likely to be exporters than those located outside the core regions. Even more so than exporting, we find that firms in the core make significantly greater use of imports than firms in more peripheral regions, highlighting the importance of imports in facilitating the competitiveness of firms in leading regions. On the other hand, firms in the core perceive a worse investment environment—particularly with respect to regulation, bureaucracy, and governance—than those in the periphery, indicating the presence of congestion costs. So what is it about the core that helps overcome these congestion costs?

Firms and Agglomeration Spillovers Matter Most

Apart from markets, the study finds that two things matter most: competitive firms and spillovers from agglomerations. We find striking differences in a number of firm-related factors that have, in previous research, been associated with exporting. Relative to firms in noncore regions, firms in the core are on average larger, have a greater share of foreign ownership, have a top manager with more experience, make greater use of technology, and are more likely to have an international quality certification and provide formal training for their workers. What is not clear is whether these firm characteristics are endogenous to the core, or whether it is a case of spatial sorting—that is, do core regions breed export-ready firms or do export-ready firms seek out core regions?

Agglomeration is also powerful. Firms are more likely to become exporters when located in regional economies where there is substantial diversity across sectors (urbanization economies) as well as density of firms and exporters in a specific sector (localization economies and export spillovers). These findings point to the potential importance of diverse industrial districts and more widely of the benefits of shared resources in overcoming the fixed-cost barriers to export entry.

On the other hand, the impacts of location and the investment climate are more nuanced. Location seems to matter more for facilitating export participation than export intensity, indicating that location and distance are important fixed-cost barriers to exporting. So-called "second-order geography"—regional endowments and the investment climate—appears to have relatively weaker, but still in some cases important, impacts on exporters, with infrastructure and access to finance being most important.

What Does It Mean for Peripheral Regions?

Taken together, the results from chapters 3–7 underline the power of agglomeration. The findings suggest that congestion costs and other forces of dispersion will not be sufficient to shift exporters (and export activity) to peripheral regions without very significant incentives, or at least without the existence of substantial endowments (such as natural resources) in these regions. On the other hand, for regions on the fringe of the core and in secondary cities, the potential to build export agglomerations is much more realistic. This is particularly the case in sectors that are in the stages of their industrial lifecycle in which the endowments of the metropolitan core are becoming less critical sources of comparative advantage.

The Failure of Traditional Lagging Region Policies

Overall, Regional Policy Has Had Little Success in Reversing or Even Slowing Divergence

Our two case studies illustrate how difficult and entrenched is the problem of lagging regions. Indonesia and India have spent decades and substantial sums to address the problem, yet divergence is growing in both countries. Indonesia's failure to tackle spatial inequality can in part be traced to an overemphasis on fiscal incentives for investment, too little focus on addressing the local investment climate and improving infrastructure, and almost no efforts to improve firm-level competitiveness. To make matters worse, the incentives offered to investors to locate in peripheral regions have been far too weak to make a significant impact on their location decisions, particularly in light of the relative differences in the locational competitiveness of regions. In contrast, India has tried virtually everything. This has included counterproductive and distortive policies like licensing restrictions and price equalization, but also more comprehensive programs that address the gaps pointed out previously for Indonesia. These findings suggest that addressing the problem of lagging regions requires not only designing good policies, but also implementing them effectively, and doing so over a long period of time.

Trade Integration Has Typically Not Been an Important Consideration of Lagging Region Policy

Facilitating trade or even exports typically is not a primary objective of regional industrial policies. Instead, the main objectives, rightly, tend to focus on relative growth in economic (and sometimes social and other human development) outcomes. The main channel through which regional policies usually hope to achieve these outcomes is *investment;* trade tends to be an implicit derivative of this. When national industrial policies became export-oriented in India and Indonesia, export objectives did filter through to regional policy, along with instruments like export processing zones (EPZs). But integration of trade and industrial policy objectives with regional policy remains limited.

Policy Implications

Principles of Policy Design for the Integration and Growth of Lagging Regions

Focus on the Core for Efficiency while Building Capacity in the Periphery

One of the clear findings from this set of studies is that interventions focused primarily on core regions are likely to have a bigger impact on aggregate competitiveness than interventions targeting peripheral regions. A related implication is that policies designed to improve the competitiveness of existing agglomerations, for example policies targeted to existing clusters, may be particularly effective in raising national competitiveness. Such policies will of course have consequences for regional inequalities, potentially exacerbating already growing disparities. But in the context of a spatially aware approach to competitiveness, more effective targeting of policies for peripheral areas, and, most important, a societal agreement on redistribution, the net result should be positive. On the other hand, it is also recognized that the unequal distribution of economic activity can constrain growth in the long run. Therefore, it remains critical that a balance is struck between improving aggregate competitiveness through interventions in the core and building the endogenous capacity for improved competitiveness and economic growth in peripheral regions.

Carving Out the Opportunities for Lagging Regions: Industrial and Regional Lifecycles

Truly peripheral regions, particularly those with low economic density, will likely struggle to attract investment away from core regions (except where investments are based on location-specific resource endowments, like in the tourism, mining, and agricultural sectors). However, the findings from these studies suggest that opportunities may emerge from industrial and regional lifecycles—that is, the process by which industrial activities shift from locations that offer advanced technological inputs and urbanization economies to those that offer low-cost production, scale, and possibly clusters of specialized inputs. From a policy perspective, this means that at least some noncore regions—those on the fringe of core regions, those with existing industrial specializations, and those with density and infrastructure to support agglomerations—might target investment in direct export-oriented manufacturing, or specialize in supplying less skill- and knowledge-intensive components to exporters in the core. In any case, intermediate regions, and certainly lagging, peripheral regions, should focus on the opportunities that are in line with their comparative advantage. This means avoiding attempts to build specialized clusters "from scratch" or to develop advanced sectors like high technology and life sciences without an existing base on which to anchor them.

Fiscal Incentives Should Only be a Complementary Tool

Although fiscal incentives may be effective at the margin, in most cases they are little more than a transfer of rents from lagging regions to private investors. The structural factors that determine the competitiveness of location have a far greater impact on a firm's long-run profits (and risks). The case of Indonesia shows that most countries' incentives fall far short of levels that would sway a firm's decision, and that incentive levels high enough to matter would in most cases be unaffordable. By implication, investment incentives should be considered as part of the policy arsenal only *after* structural and investment climate issues have been addressed to the point at which incentives can be cost effective.

A Framework for Different Types of Lagging Regions

Clearly not all lagging regions are the same. Some have greater potential to support agglomeration, others may benefit from cross-border integration, while others may have few realistic opportunities to integrate into global or even national production networks. Table O.1, inspired by the WDR 2009 and incorporating the findings of the studies in this book, provides a basic framework for the regional policies that may be most effective in addressing trade competitiveness and growth in different types of lagging regions.

Table O.1 Framework for Competitiveness Policies in Different Types of Lagging Regions

Region type	Nature of policies
Near the core	• Many of the traditional regional policies may be effective here, including investment incentives and export-oriented incentives • Promotion and facilitation of agglomeration, including industrial parks/special economic zones and cluster policies • Investment climate reforms
Peripheral but with economic mass	• Targeted foreign direct investment attraction (following comparative advantage and industry lifecycles) • Support to competitiveness of existing industry clusters • Transport connectivity and infrastructure • Investment climate reforms • Firm-level competitiveness interventions (training, finance, and so forth) • Critical importance of governance
Peripheral and without density	• Limited prospects for export-oriented investment; focus on endowment-based opportunities is applicable (mining, agriculture, tourism) • Focus on social infrastructure and connectivity • Firm-level competitiveness interventions

Targeting Factors of Production
The Importance of Firm-Level Interventions in Lagging Regions: Implications for Skills and Training, Access to Technology and Finance, and Export Promotion

The findings of this book show clearly that there is a gap in the competitiveness of firms in the periphery relative to those in the core. They also indicate that firm-level characteristics have a greater influence on trade outcomes for firms in noncore regions than regional investment climate characteristics and agglomeration (the opposite of the findings for firms in core regions). This suggests that efforts to raise the competitiveness of lagging regions and to expand their firms' export participation must go beyond the external environment to address firm-level competitiveness. Doing so will require introducing new tools and instruments into regional policy, including vocational development and training, improving access to technology, building management skills and capacity, and improving access to finance. In addition, where there is an explicit emphasis on export participation, export promotion programs will need to be retooled for more effective operation at the regional level.

Attracting and Linking Foreign and Domestic Capital
Foreign direct investment (FDI) tends to be a major driver of exports. However, foreign investors are much more likely to base themselves in the core. Therefore, efforts to attract FDI should consume a limited share of resources devoted to lagging regions and be highly targeted to those sectors in which a region has clear comparative advantage. Investment promotion efforts and incentives for investment should, at the very least, avoid bias against domestic investors. FDI attraction policies should be careful to target sectors and firms where there exist reasonable prospects for backward integration, particularly if fiscal incentives are being offered. Moreover, where FDI attraction is a fundamental component

of a regional development agenda, an explicit program designed to facilitate forward and backward linkages between investors and the local economy should be developed.

Developing and Empowering Labor

If too much attention has been paid to fiscal incentives, then too little has been paid to the local labor force. As recommended in the WDR 2009, policies to promote labor mobility are important. But it is also important for regional policy to focus on education and training to build local skills. Investment incentives under European Union (EU) regional policies, for example, tend to focus much more on supporting training and skills development rather than on underwriting risk.

Facilitating Connectivity

Facilitating Imports and Value Chain Integration

Competitiveness in exporting is also linked to importing. This is partly because having access to the highest-quality and most cost-effective imports allows firms to leverage dynamic gains of trade to improve competitiveness and profitability. It is also because, increasingly, becoming a competitive exporter is about participating in integrated regional and global value chains. This has two implications for regional policy. First, it raises yet another question mark over the practicality of aiming to attract export-oriented investment, at least in manufacturing, in peripheral regions. In the context of just-in-time global production networks, adding additional time and costs on both inbound and outbound legs of the production process will seriously impede the competitiveness of firms located in peripheral regions. Second, where the opportunity to attract (value-chain-oriented) investment to lagging regions is realistic, governments must identify and address location-specific barriers to importing. One of the main barriers is likely to relate to the transport infrastructure linking peripheral regions to both trade gateways and the metropolitan core. Addressing barriers to customs clearance of imports in lagging regions may also be an important part of the policy agenda. Among the solutions to address these barriers may be inland dryports, location of customs facilities within peripheral regions, and electronic clearance procedures.

Connecting and Integrating with Domestic and Regional Markets

Facilitating exports relies on improved connectivity of peripheral regions with not only global markets, but also *national* markets. The national market offers exporters access to agents and distributors, mainly based in the core, who can act as sources of indirect exporting. Furthermore, improved connectivity makes it more likely that a firm based in the core or abroad will locate part of their operation in a peripheral region to take advantage of a lower cost base or access to specific endowments.

Connectivity policies are particularly difficult when it comes to lagging regions. Indeed, one of the main lessons learned from the failed Mezzogiorno policies in Italy in the 1950s and 1960s is the problem of the "two-way road" and the risks of subsequent brain drain and hollowing out of local production. Despite these challenges, improving domestic connectivity must be central to the policy agenda to improve a region's competitiveness. This requires investment in hard infrastructure, such as roads, ports, and airports. But it also requires investment in soft infrastructure (such as customs) as well as efforts to address regulatory and competition barriers that hinder market access. For example, domestic trade in India has long been hampered by a wide range of interstate barriers, including standards and licensing requirements. Furthermore, barriers to competition in the transport sector raise the cost of domestic connectivity in many countries; this tends to hit peripheral regions hardest as they already suffer from lower levels of competition and lack of scale in transport markets. Finally, beyond domestic connectivity, addressing trade policy barriers that prevent integration with regional markets is also critical, particularly for border regions, which may be located much closer to the core of a neighboring country than their own domestic core.

Promoting Agglomeration

Leveraging Agglomeration—A Balancing Act

The powerful role of agglomerations in potentiating exports has important policy implications, but these must be considered carefully to avoid the inclination to attempt to build agglomerations where they have not developed organically. Both core and noncore regions should remove barriers to natural agglomeration. These include not only physical and social infrastructure, but also regulatory barriers, distorting land markets, and spatial planning, as well as poorly integrated goods and factor markets (particularly important for regions located along relatively closed international borders). Beyond the removal of these barriers, regional policies to support the development and competitiveness of existing clusters—but not to create them from scratch—may have a positive impact.

Special Economic Zones to Accelerate, Not to Catalyze

Special economic zones (SEZs) are increasingly being adopted by developing countries as tools of export-oriented development policy. In many if not most of these countries, they are also considered a tool for attracting investment into lagging regions. The international experience with using SEZs as a tool of regional development has been, almost without exception, a failure. On the other hand, the studies in this book highlight the importance of agglomeration, and in this sense SEZs, and industrial estates more broadly, may have a role to play. But SEZs are only likely to be effective for lagging regions with economic density and those located in close proximity to leading regions, where SEZs may offer the missing ingredients to accelerate slowly developing agglomerations. SEZs are far less likely to make a difference in low-density, geographically peripheral regions, where no agglomerations have emerged.

Coordination and Implementation

Spatially Aware Trade Policy and Trade-Aware Spatial Policy

Policies designed specifically to expand trade, as opposed to growth policies in general, may contribute to increasing spatial inequalities, particularly in developing countries. Thus, governments focusing on export-led growth and more broadly on policies designed to attract mobile capital should be aware up front of the potential spatial implications and should consider what policies may be required to mitigate their negative consequences. As discussed in this book, the degree to which trade policy will have significant spatial impacts will vary from country to country. Partly, this is because of different sectoral structures across countries. More importantly, it is because mechanisms that mitigate the development of widening spatial *income* disparities—tax and transfer policies and fluid factor markets—differ considerably from country to country.

Coordinating Regional Policies with National Trade and Industrial Policies

For regional policies to have an impact in the context of increasingly mobile factors of production, they must be comprehensive. This means combining simple measures to attract investment with policy interventions that actually make a territory an attractive investment location over the long term. Such interventions might address infrastructure, connectivity, the regulatory and bureaucratic environment, governance, and competitive firms, among others. The idea of intervening to create competitive firms in environments that are uncompetitive is a perhaps a catch-22, but the lesson is that the existence of clusters of competitive firms is among the most effective ways to attract other firms. Although many countries do have some or all of these elements in their national trade and industrial policies, they often do not translate effectively to regional policy. Coordination is difficult enough under top-down approaches to regional policy that could (in theory) derive from the national industrial policy. However, with increasing emphasis on locally developed solutions, coordination becomes more important to the success of both sets of policies.

Decentralization: Exploiting Opportunities and Addressing Challenges

The political responsibility for regional policy is increasingly shifting from the national to the regional or local level. This opens up the potential for more targeted, context-specific interventions and for greater policy innovation. Taking advantage of these opportunities, however, will require addressing three main challenges. First, regions must establish clear financial agreements with central governments on funding for regional policy. Second, they must improve coordination of policies among localities and between regions and the national government. Third, they must exploit the potential of innovative and active local political leadership in driving the regional development agenda, while also establishing a stable governance environment that is not dependent on any one individual. Addressing all of these challenges requires a multilevel approach to governance. This approach should combine incentives that promote experimentation among local actors with greater accountability, backed up by effective monitoring and evaluation.

The Internal Geography of Trade • http://dx.doi.org/10.1596/978-0-8213-9893-7

References

Baylis, K., R. Garduno-Rivera, and G. Piras. 2009. "The Distributional Effects of NAFTA in Mexico: Evidence from a Panel of Municipalities." Agricultural and Applied Economics Association, 2009 Annual Meeting, Milwaukee, WI, July 26–28.

World Bank. 2009. *World Development Report 2009: Reshaping Economic Geography.* Washington, DC: World Bank.

PART 1

Trade and Its Impact on Subnational Regions

CHAPTER 1

Trade, Location, and Growth

Thomas Farole

Globalization and Convergence: The Problem of Subnational Regions

Economic activity is unevenly distributed across places. Differences in the structure of economies, in the density of economic activity and population, and in wealth are clearly evident, whether comparing across nations or among regions within them. This is not only obvious to even the most casual observer, but it is also in line with economic theory, given that factor endowments are unlikely to be distributed evenly at any one point in time. But how is the spatial distribution of economic activity affected by the dynamic context of globalization, in which factors are increasingly mobile? Neoclassical theory suggests that we should see convergence in per capita incomes over time, as factors move from high- to low-cost locations.

Evidence from the most recent period of globalization seems to support this theory, as there has been strong convergence in national incomes over the past 20 years.[1] On the other hand, *within* many countries the opposite has been the case, with output and wealth increasingly being concentrated and cross-regional disparities widening (Puga 2002; Rodríguez-Pose 1999). For example, within the European Union (EU), the standard deviation of per capita gross domestic product (GDP) for member states (EU-15) as a whole declined from 12.5 to 11.4 in the 1990s; at the time, it increased from 26.5 to 28.5 for subnational regions within these member states (Farole, Rodríguez-Pose, and Storper 2011). Figure 1.1, which plots the Gini index[2] of regional inequality in OECD (Organisation for Economic Co-operation and Development) and BRICS (Brazil, Russian Federation, India, China, and South Africa) countries, shows increasing inequalities in about two-thirds of these countries.

In most cases, predominant urban regions have grown strongly, while many secondary regions—especially peripherally located, rural areas—have lagged further behind. This pattern of divergence can be seen across most middle-income and many low-income economies, and appears to have become more acute in the recent era of globalization of trade and investment. Indeed, patterns of divergence in regional productive output are particularly evident in many countries that have integrated rapidly into global or regional markets, including

Figure 1.1 Gini Index of Regional GDP per Capita in OECD and BRICS Countries, 2007 versus 1995

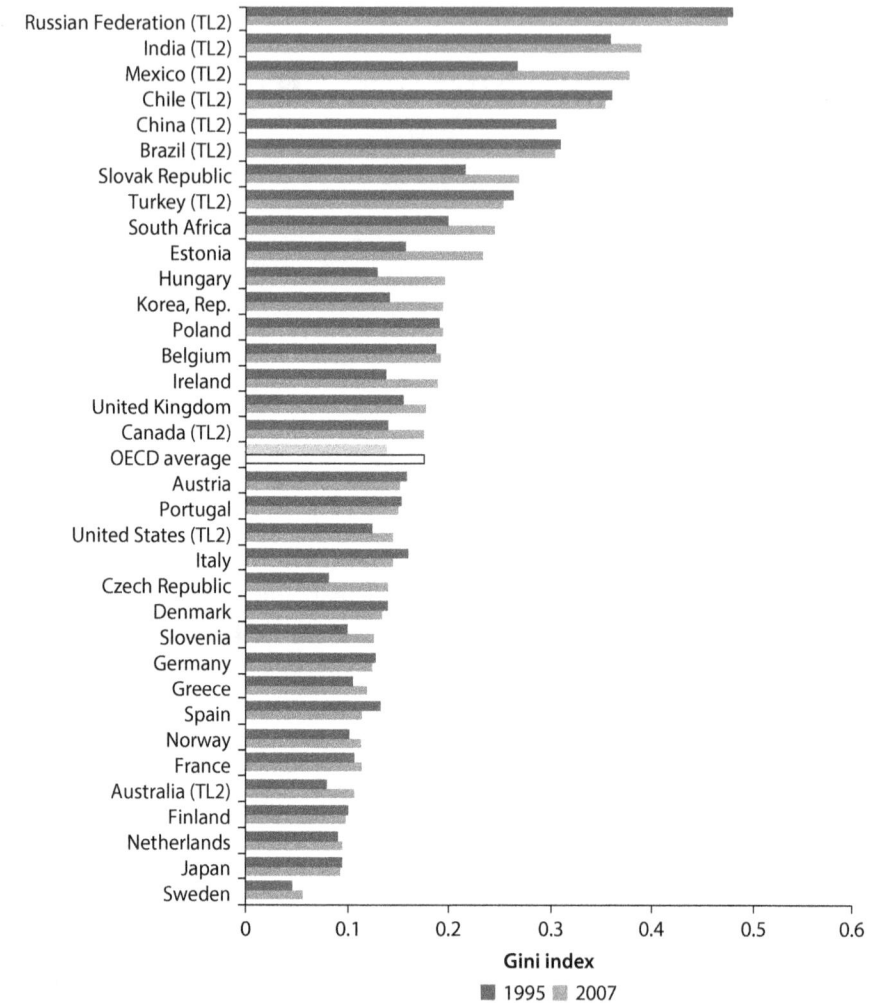

Source: OECD Regions at a Glance 2011 (http://www.oecd.org/gov/oecdregionsataglance2011.htm).
Note: BRICS = Brazil, Russian Federation, India, China, and South Africa, GDP = gross domestic product. TL2 refers to the Organisation for Economic Co-Operation and Development's (OECD's) macro-level definition of regions (that is, large regions). For all other countries, the analysis is at the TL3, or micro-level definition of regions (that is, small regions). Data for China are for mainland China only; New Zealand is excluded as data are unavailable after 2003.

East Asia, Mexico, and post-Communist transition countries; they are also prevalent in high-income economies, where formerly prosperous industrial regions increasingly lag behind the services sector–driven metropolitan regions (see Kanbur and Zhang 2005; Puga 1999; Rodríguez-Pose and Gill 2006; Sánchez-Reaza and Rodríguez-Pose 2002; Zhang and Zhang 2003). On the other hand, a number of studies in Brazil have pointed to a steady convergence in regional incomes over recent decades (see Azzoni 2001 and Ferreira 2000).

But noncore regions are far from homogenous in their development experiences and their economic outcomes. Within most OECD countries, there exist relatively peripheral regions—for example Navarre (Spain), Wales (the United Kingdom), and the west of Ireland—which have managed to link to national and international markets and maintain robust growth. Broadly similar experiences (with limitations) can be found in many middle-income and developing countries, including Chile, Argentina, and South Africa. In India, for example, the peripheral northeast lags far behind national averages on most economic and social indicators, whereas the arguably equally peripheral Kerala performs well on many of the same measures.

Why Regional Inequalities Matter

From a macro efficiency perspective, regional inequality is not necessarily a bad thing. Most evidence points to a positive association between the geographical concentration of economic activity and economic growth at a broader territorial scale (Bourguignon and Morrison 2002). This is partly because innovation, increasingly recognized as a fundamental determinant of growth, has been shown to be strongly affected by the concentration, or *agglomeration*, of economic agents. Indeed, innovation and agglomeration appear to be mutually reinforcing processes (Feldman 1994; Verspagen 1997).

Yet there are some important downsides to growing regional disparities, and not simply for residents of lagging regions. As intraregional inequalities grow, average figures of national income become increasingly meaningless, so that an apparently rising economy may actually mask economic stagnation and growing poverty in parts of a country. But in most cases, the primary concern is one of *relative* outcomes, or equity. Growing disparities across regions may threaten social and political cohesion. Most movements for secession or devolution are linked in part to issues of territorial income inequality.

Of course, there is a difference between output inequality and income inequality, and for purposes of cohesion the latter matters more. The degree to which output inequality translates to income inequality depends a lot on two factors: redistribution and factor mobility. Comprehensive tax and transfer programs in most OECD countries significantly narrow regional disparities. Sweden's extremely low regional Gini index (figure 1.1) does not reflect an even geographical spread of output, but rather a strong policy of income redistribution. Mobility of labor and capital across regions also represents a critical mechanism for addressing regional output disparities. In countries where workers and investors can easily move from areas of low to high demand, income disparities can be narrowed.

But even allowing for redistribution and fluid factor markets, there are reasons to be concerned about growing disparities in output across regions. First, these disparities may have direct impacts on economic efficiency. From a political economy perspective, even where growing spatial inequalities do not give rise to the territorial crises noted in the previous paragraph, they will almost certainly contribute to increasing demand for redistributive (versus productive) policies, which may have a dampening effect on overall growth (Aghion, Alesina, and Trebbi 2004). From a structural perspective, many lagging regions are not simply failing to keep pace, but also failing to make productive use of the resources available to them, leading to output that is significantly below the production possibilities frontier. This, combined with self-reinforcing institutional failures, leads to a problem of persistent underdevelopment at the regional level. Such underdevelopment is not just a problem for the lagging region caught in a low growth trap, but also acts as a drag on national growth potential (Farole, Rodríguez-Pose, and Storper 2011). Finally, while mobility should be encouraged to enable individuals to follow economic opportunities, this too has drawbacks. Most notably, labor mobility contributes to the massive rural-urban shifts that are already overwhelming the infrastructural, environmental, and institutional capacities of major metropolitan regions in many developing countries.

Whatever the aggregate picture may be, the prospect for an individual firm to reap the benefits that accrue from globalization may depend as much on the neighborhood as on the country in which they operate. An endogenous relationship exists between income and many of the factors that contribute to firm success, including both external factors, like education and infrastructure, and internal factors at the firm level, like innovation and productivity. Therefore, firms in more advantageous geographical positions may become increasingly more competitive relative to those in lagging territories. Failing to address some of the root causes of regional disparities may condemn firms in these territories to operate on an increasingly unlevel playing field, which is likely to contribute to further widening of the gap in outcomes between leading and lagging regions. Again, interregional mobility allows some possibility for individual firms to seek out those regions that best meet their needs (for skills, endowments, and so forth), but in many countries and for many firms such mobility is limited. Moreover, spatial sorting of firms is likely to contribute to further concentration in many developing countries.

Finally, regional inequalities matter because regions matter, more so than ever. Many authors have commented on the "hollowing out" of the nation-state, particularly in the context of trade and investment, as political power and resources are both transferred up to supraregional institutions (such as regional and preferential trading blocs and international regulatory bodies like the World Trade Organization) and devolved down to regional and local authorities.

Explaining the Emergence of Leading and Lagging Regions: The Economics of Place

New Economic Geography and Other Models

Significant progress has been made in recent decades in identifying the factors that shape the spatial configurations of economic growth, which result in the core-periphery patterns discussed previously. Three main explanatory models that predict agglomeration and growing cross-regional disparities can be highlighted here, none of which are mutually exclusive: new economic geography (NEG) models; endogenous growth and neo-Schumpeterian models; and institutional models.

The NEG models highlight the role of transport costs, economies of scale, and market size in determining agglomeration, and predicts increasing concentration of economic activity (Krugman 1991; Krugman and Livas-Elizondo 1996) resulting from this. For firms, the incentive to agglomerate, and in larger rather than smaller cities, increases with access to larger markets—the so-called "home market effect." Any reduction in the cost to access a larger market, whether through falling transport costs and opening up to trade, tends to increase this incentive for producers to agglomerate. This in turn creates incentives for workers and other firms in input-output relationships to locate in these same regions. From this, Marshallian economies—thick labor markets, thick supply markets, and knowledge spillovers—arise, acting as *centripetal* forces that reinforce the concentration of production in core areas (Fujita, Krugman, and Venables 1999), and leading to greater within-country disparities. There are of course limits to this process; land rents, congestion, and access to natural resources and other immobile factors act as *centrifugal* forces that disperse economic activity into the periphery (Fujuta, Krugman, and Venables 1999; Krugman 1991; Paluzie 2001).

Another set of models arise from endogenous growth theory and focus on innovation and the positions of territories relative to the technology frontier (Aghion and Howitt 2005; Grossman and Helpman 1991; Lucas 1988; Romer 1986). In these models, the potential to innovate and adapt is unevenly distributed across places. This has important spatial implications since the transaction costs of transmitting knowledge remain high, often involving long-established knowledge networks, face-to-face contact, and defined institutional channels (Farole, Rodríguez-Pose, and Storper 2011). Moreover, research has shown that knowledge spillovers tend to have very limited spatial bounds, falling off quickly with distance (Jaffe, Trajtenberg, and Henderson 1993; Rodríguez-Pose and Crescenzi 2008) tacit, rather than codified, knowledge is particularly location-bound (Gertler 2003; Morgan 1997). Innovation-based growth models also recognize the importance of scale economies in research and development and the appropriability (or absorption capacity) of technology. Again, the implications of these models is that there will be a tendency for knowledge and for innovation-intensive activities to agglomerate in existing core regions, with spillovers contributing to reinforce these regions relative to the periphery (Audretsch and Feldman 1996; Verspagen 1997). Offshoots of the innovation models of growth include metropolitanization theories such as the role of diversified cities (Duranton and Puga 2000; Jacobs 1969), of the "creative class" (Florida 2002), and of face-to-face contact in facilitating knowledge transfer (Storper and Venables 2004). These theories reinforce the importance of large cities as the drivers of economic growth.

Finally, institutional theories highlight the role of "appropriate" institutions in regional performance, and in underpinning the processes of cumulative causation that determine long-run patterns of regional growth or underdevelopment.

These institutional theories, which cover an eclectic range of approaches, including industrial districts (Kristensen 1992; Piore and Sabel 1984), "learning regions" (Gertler, Wolfe, and Garkut 2000; Henry and Pinch 2000), and regional systems of innovation (Cooke and Morgan 1998), identify a link between institutional conditions (both formal governance informal communities) and processes of agglomeration and growth. Conversely, where the institutional environment is plagued by weak governance, lack of capacity, and rent seeking, growth-supporting policies are unlikely to be sustained (Acemoglu 2006; Acemoglu and Johnson 2006). Institutional factors also tend to bias development outcomes in favor of agglomeration, as the quality of individual institutions is highly dependent on the availability and quality of human capital, and the effectiveness of institutions in the aggregate is strongly affected by scale and depth.

Taken together, all of this literature suggests that the trend toward agglomeration is likely to benefit the metropolitan cores. They have the advantages of large markets, deep labor pools, links to international markets, and clusters of diverse suppliers and institutions that combine to produce strong externalities and promote innovation. These advantages support internationally competitive domestic producers and create an attractive environment for foreign investors. Regions relatively near the metropolitan cores are likely to benefit from spillovers and congestion-related dispersion. Regions further outside the core, however, are less able to take advantage of spillovers and are more likely to be far removed from key infrastructural, institutional, and interpersonal links to regional and international markets. As a result, they face significant challenges to becoming competitive locations for hosting economic activity.

The World Development Report 2009 Framework

The *World Development Report 2009* (WDR 2009) brought the issue of economic geography strongly to the fore of the mainstream development agenda by emphasizing how processes of unevenness, spillovers, and circular causation (or reinforced path dependence) contribute to agglomeration and shape economic integration and growth. In particular, the report highlights unequivocally that uneven patterns of economic activity and divergence in outcomes across regions is a natural consequence of processes of agglomeration: "Economic growth is seldom balanced. Efforts to spread it prematurely will jeopardize progress. Two centuries of economic development show that spatial disparities in income and production are inevitable. A generation of economic research confirms this" (World Bank 2009, 5 and 6).

But in setting out its analytical framework, the WDR 2009 also emphasizes that it is not simply structural factors such as poor location ("distance") or even lack of agglomeration potential ("density") that affect lagging regions, but that other barriers, often policy induced or supported, ("division") can compound the situation, undermining integration and growth prospects (box 1.1).

The WDR 2009 also highlights the important fact of heterogeneity among lagging regions. Specifically, in setting out the proposed policy framework,

Box 1.1 Density, Distance, and Division

Density is the most important dimension locally. Distances are short, and cultural and political divisions are few and shallow. The policy challenge is getting density right by harnessing market forces to encourage concentration and promote convergence in living standards between villages and towns and cities. But distance can also be important because rapid urbanization leads to congestion, and divisions within cities can be manifest in slums and ghettos.

Distance to density is the most important dimension at the national geographic scale. Distance between areas where economic activity is concentrated and areas that lag is the main dimension. The policy challenge is helping firms and workers reduce their distance from density. The main mechanisms are the mobility of labor and the reduction of transport costs through infrastructure investments. Divisions within countries—differences in language, currency, and culture—tend to be small, though large countries such as India and Nigeria may be geographically divided because of religion, ethnicity, or language.

Division is the most important dimension internationally. But distance and density are also relevant. Economic production is concentrated in a few world regions—North America, Northeast Asia, and Western Europe—that are also the most integrated. Other regions, by contrast, are divided. Distance matters at the international level, but for access to world markets, divisions associated with the impermeability of borders and differences in currencies and regulations are a more serious barrier than distance. Having a large and dynamic economy within the neighborhood can help smaller countries, especially in regions distant from world markets. For economies in other regions, such as Central Africa and Central Asia, international integration is hardest.

Source: World Bank 2009.

Table 1.1 Typologies of the Lagging Region Challenge

	Type 1: Sparsely populated lagging areas	Type 2: Densely populated lagging areas in united countries	Type 3: Densely populated lagging areas in divided countries
Country examples	Chile, China, Ghana, Honduras, Pakistan, Peru, Russian Federation, Sri Lanka, Uganda, Vietnam	Bangladesh, Brazil, Colombia, Egypt, Arab Rep., Mexico, Thailand, Turkey	India, Nigeria
Dimension of the integration challenge	• Economic distance	• Economic distance • High populations in lagging areas	• Economic distance • High populations in lagging areas • Internal divisions

Source: World Bank 2009.

the report identifies three "country types" that help determine the nature of the challenge of lagging regions within the countries. These country types include: countries with sparsely populated lagging regions, united countries with densely populated lagging regions, and divided countries with densely populated lagging regions (see table 1.1). Of course, the report also acknowledges that even within

The Internal Geography of Trade • http://dx.doi.org/10.1596/978-0-8213-9893-7

countries heterogeneity exists. For example, in India, the majority of the poor live in densely populated lagging areas in the middle of the country, while the lagging northeast is sparsely populated. Thailand's lagging regions include a densely populated northeast and a sparsely populated and divided south (which is home to the country's Muslim minority).

Bringing Trade and Location into Sharper Focus

Trade plays a crucial role in the interaction between location, growth, and inequality. As such, it demands particular focus in trying to better understand and address the problem of lagging regions. Trade matters for several reasons. First, trade is increasingly an important driver of growth, both in the short and long term. From the perspective of a regional economy, expanded market access through trade can have a quick and transformational impact on growth. For example, in the five years following the implementation of the North American Free Trade Agreement (NAFTA), Mexico's border regions grew real gross value added by 36 percent, more than three times faster than the average growth in other regions of the country (Baylis, Garduno-Rivera, and Piras 2009). Trade allows regions to reap static benefits from deeper specialization than might be available in the domestic economy alone, and to gain the dynamic benefits of technology and knowledge spillovers. These, in turn, help drive improved productivity and contribute to long-term growth potential.

Critically, as trade integration (box 1.2) is also both a catalyst and an accelerator of agglomeration, it has the potential to deepen already-existing regional disparities. For regions that are already lagging—particularly those that are cursed both in terms of "distance" (remote) and "density" (sparsely populated)—the trends of global and regional trade integration can result in further isolation, as firms and consumers in the core increasingly engage outward at the expense of the domestic hinterland. Meanwhile, firms in remote regions may struggle to take advantage of the opportunities available from integration in global markets. They lack local markets of significant size to facilitate scale economies that might condition them to compete globally; they face higher costs and time to reach export markets; they are often underserved by public goods (including both hard and soft infrastructure) that underpin access and competitiveness; and they tend to have less access or exposure to knowledge being produced at the technology frontier, resulting in less competitive human capital and institutions. In addition, political economy and governance, endogenous in part to the challenges of geography and density, frequently aggravate these structural disadvantages; and where internal or cross-border conflicts exist, regions may suffer from the closure of critical trade links (Ahmed and Ghani 2008).

In fact, trade is inherent in the NEG models, which emphasize how changes in trading costs determine the location of production. Trade and its interaction with geography are also at the heart of the WDR 2009, which states, for example: "Cities, migration, and trade have been the main catalysts of progress in the developed world over the past two centuries..." (World Bank 2009, xx). Despite

Box 1.2 Trade, Trade Openness, and Trade Integration

Throughout this book, we use three different but closely related terms in discussing the interrelationship between trade and regions: trade, trade openness, and trade integration. To avoid confusion, each of these is explained briefly below.

Trade

Trade refers to the actual exchange of goods and services, both domestically and internationally. In this book, most of the discussion of trade is in the context of international, or cross-border, trade. There is analysis of how regional characteristics impact firms' participation and success in export markets, as well as discussion of importing.

Trade openness

Trade openness is a measure used to assess the relative importance of international trade to a country or region. The standard measure of trade openness is the total of imports and exports as a share of gross domestic product (GDP). Countries are generally considered to be more "open" the higher is their traded share of GDP. Country size and location (as well as other factors) have a significant impact on the level of trade openness that is observed in a country, which is why a country like the United States, with a large domestic market and few nearby trading partners, appears by this measure to be relatively closed, while smaller European Union countries appear highly open. In the context of this book, the importance of trade openness is to understand how significant increases in openness in countries affect different locations within countries.

Trade integration

Trade integration is variously used as both a concept and a measure. As a measure, it is an equivalent to trade openness—that is, it measures the relative level of a country's trade and its share of trade with certain partners. Often, trade integration refers specifically to the elimination of tariff and other barriers to trade among countries, and the subsequent growth in trade. As a concept, trade integration suggests that firms of a country or a region are becoming much more reliant on trade (as well as investment) with a set of regional or global trading partners, both in terms exports and imports. It may also suggest that firms are becoming part of regional or global value chains, linking them in input-output relationships with firms outside the domestic economy.

this, we still lack a clear and detailed understanding of the interaction between trade and economic geography *within* countries, and in particular of the factors that determine the relative capacity of different locations to support the competitiveness of export-oriented firms.

On the question of how trade shapes patterns of regional production and wealth, despite a substantial volume of research in recent years, both theory and empirics remain ambiguous (Brülhart 2009; Kanbur and Venables 2005). Depending on how centripetal and centrifugal forces are specified and how they interact NEG models have come to diametrically opposite conclusions on the outcomes for territories (see Krugman and Livas-Elizondo 1996;

The Internal Geography of Trade • http://dx.doi.org/10.1596/978-0-8213-9893-7

Paluzie 2001). Moreover, while transport costs are fundamental to NEG models, the U-shaped relationship between transport costs and agglomeration (Venables 2006) means that declining transport costs may herald either concentration or dispersion, depending on where in the (unobservable) curve one is situated. And in the likely scenario in which a firm is involved in a production chain with both domestic and foreign supply and domestic and foreign markets, the range of possible equilibrium outcomes complicates things still further (Monfort and Nicolini 2000). Empirical studies have been biased toward developed countries, and with the exception of the many studies of the spatial impacts of EU integration, most have been limited to single-country case studies. Again, the results have been ambivalent, with a majority of studies suggesting that integration contributes to regional divergence, but with quite a few studies pointing in the opposite direction (Brülhart 2009).

Perhaps more importantly, most of the existing research has focused on the impact of trade and investment on regional disparities, but very little looks at it the other way round—that is, how places (locational factors) determine trade outcomes. Places are not simply acted upon by processes of globalization, but they shape these very processes and therefore play an important role in determining the nature, extent, and outcomes of integration. Of course, places do not act; rather, individuals (workers and entrepreneurs), firms, and capital—mobile factors of production—act. What matters is the degree to which a regional environment establishes the conditions for competitiveness, and incentivizes firms to invest in growth and to engage in trade.

This link between location and firms highlights another gap in our understanding of the dynamics of location and trade. Virtually all the research on trade and location has focused on "macro-heterogeneity" across locations, ignoring the potentially important role "micro-heterogeneity"—the interaction of diverse firms with the regional environment (Ottaviano 2011). This heterogeneous firms approach, the so-called "new, new trade theory," has opened up a wealth of unique insights on trade dynamics in recent years. To date, it has not been employed in any comprehensive way to analyze regional determinants of trade performance.[3] Bringing together this firm-level methodological approach with a framework that emphasizes the impact of regions on trade outcomes (rather than the other way around) may offer a richer understanding of the trade and location nexus.

From a policy perspective, identifying if and how regional factors, including regional endowments and the regional "investment climate" as well as the presence of spillovers from other firms, influence firm trade competitiveness is important. Clearly, regional factors, including infrastructure, the skills endowments of workers, and regional institutions, affect firm productivity. Some regional factors may also have a direct impact on the fixed cost of exporting, which is particularly critical to facilitate export entry for firms.

This book, therefore, aims to contribute to a better understanding of the relationship between subnational regions and trade, and in particular to inform on the challenge of lagging regions, by bringing sharper focus to two issues discussed in the previous paragraphs:

1. How has trade openness affected the concentration of economic activity in developing countries, and what have been the main mediating factors determining this?
2. How does location determine trade participation and performance of firms?

In addition, chapters 8 and 9 of this book take a brief, qualitative look at how government policy has attempted to address the challenge of lagging regions, and the extent to which these policies target the factors that are likely to have a significant impact on firm competitiveness in regional and global markets. There are many examples of poor policy choices leading to inefficient or even perverse development outcomes at the subnational level—Italy's infrastructure and industrial policy in the Mezzogiorno, India's licensing and regulatory incentives for lagging regions, tax holidays in Thailand, targeted interest rate subsidies in Brazil (World Bank 2009). Indeed, for truly remote and sparsely populated regions, spatially targeted growth policies have for the most part been expensive failures, subsidizing inefficient investment, aggravating the leakage of the best firms and most talented workers, and contributing to unfavorable institutional environment.

An important hypothesis that sets the stage for the studies presented in this book is that, despite the powerful forces of agglomeration, regions located outside prime metropolitan cores are not consigned to become lagging regions, nor will they inevitably experience slower growth and divergence relative to core regions. Avoiding this fate, however, depends on how effectively they are able to integrate, both with regional and global markets, and on the economic core of their own country. This, in turn, is dependent on leveraging key regional assets and delivering on those specific regional factors that have the greatest impact on trade competitiveness. This is not to say that all regions have equal potential to be competitive. Regions that are geographically peripheral, are sparsely populated, and have few endowments will face a far more difficult task in becoming competitive locations for exporters. On the other hand, around the world there are many noncore regions for which global and regional trade integration offers substantial scope for moving to a higher and more sustainable growth path. This includes regions with access to key trade gateway infrastructure; regions with competitive clusters of economic activity; and regions rich in mineral, agricultural, or tourism resources. For these regions, taking advantage of trade opportunities often means addressing existing shortcomings in competitiveness.

Analytical Framework and Methodology

The WDR 2009 framework of *distance, density, and division* underlies the approach of the studies presented in this book. We attempt first to trace how trade has shaped regional outcomes, and then to understand the factors that mediate trade participation and performance across different regions. Specifically, we aim to decompose factors that depend on pure location (so-called "first-order" geography), on agglomeration, and on the investment climate and other policy-induced regional determinants, as well as factors that are specific to firms and not locations. Interestingly, this parallels the multinational enterprise (MNE) location choice framework set out by Dunning and Lundan (2008); they specify *endowment* factors (why economic activity would be "naturally" drawn to a particular location), *agglomeration* factors (which they define mainly as Marshallian externalities), and *policy-induced* factors.

Distance, Density, and Division

The first and most obvious potential source of locational advantage to firms is distance to markets. In terms of cross-border trade in particular, this means proximity to trade gateways like ports, airports, and land border crossings. Firms that are distant from ports will face higher costs, time, and risk in getting products to markets. The further they are from end markets, the higher the information barriers firms may face on market requirements and preferences, and the greater the challenges and transaction costs in the process of exchange (search, selection, and monitoring) (Fafchamps 2001).

Location also shapes competitiveness through "second-nature geography" effects. These include the interaction of firms within the spatial environment ("density") and through regional endowments and the regional policy environment ("division").

Density of economic agents in a territory has a potentially significant impact on firm competitiveness. Most critically, density helps firms to leverage scale economies, both internal and external. The "home market effects" described in NEG (Krugman 1991) allow firms with a larger accessible market to raise productivity by taking advantage of declining marginal costs of production. Density also produces external economies—often referred to as Marshallian externalities (Marshall 1890)—that enable firms to benefit from shared supply linkages, dense and specialized labor markets, and spillovers of knowledge and technology. Internal and external economies of scale help raise firm productivity and innovation, and may also lower the fixed costs that firms face in entering export markets (Baldwin and Krugman 1989). This may come through, for example, increased access to information on foreign markets or standards, lower transport costs, or greater interaction with suppliers, distributors, and other agents (Malmberg, Malmberg, and Lundequist 2000). On the other hand, density also may have offsetting effects on firms (Krugman 1991) through higher costs of inputs (bid up by competing demand) and congestion in accessing shared infrastructure (roads, energy, and so forth).

Distance and density are factors that cannot, at least in the short term, be changed. However, competitiveness is also the result of collective policy choices and implementation arrangements at the regional and national levels. The potential for firms in a territory to produce and export competitively is highly influenced by this policy environment, which in aggregate is often referred to as the "business climate" or the "investment climate." Competitiveness depends on the degree to which these policies support integration with national and regional markets, in terms of physical infrastructure, labor markets, capital flows, and knowledge and technology. Underpinning all of this is the institutional environment of regions, which has the potential to be either a major facilitator of or a barrier to competitiveness. Institutions have a critical influence on the provision of public goods, and the development and delivery of policies with respect to skills, innovation, and infrastructure.

In addition to both of these frameworks, we add *firm-specific* factors based on the heterogeneous firm perspective discussed previously. Distance, density, and division impact individual firms in different ways and to different degrees. Exporters have been shown to be more productive, innovative, and both capital and skill intensive than nonexporters (Bernard, Jensen, and Lawrence 1995). However, what is less clear is the degree to which this comes from "self-selection" of the most productive firms into exporting or is the result of learning-by-exporting. In either case, the regional context is likely to matter, as it will shape the fixed costs these exporters face (thus potentially raising or lowering the productivity barrier required for exporting) and possibly the productivity gains they can accrue from participating in exporting.

Methodology

The general framework of distance, density, and division is employed to analyze the issue of location and trade through two main methodological approaches: first, through an empirical analysis of large cross-country datasets; and second, through two individual country case studies, in Indonesia and India. Although the selection of the case study countries was made in part due to the availability of firm microdata data at the regional level, the two countries also represent useful lenses through which to assess issues of trade and regional development. Both are large, developing countries that opened to trade and investment relatively quickly around the same period (the early 1990s). Both countries also have long experienced significant "lagging region" problems and have launched a range of policy initiatives over decades to address them. Linked to this, both countries also have implemented major devolutions of political power toward the local level (India from the 1970s and 1980s; Indonesia much more recently with its "big bang" decentralization of 1999–2001). Substantial research has already been done on economic geography and lagging regions in both countries (see Akita and Lukman 1995; Bhattacharya and Sakthivel 2004; Gaur 2010; Ghosh 2008; Handa 2005; Hill, Resosudarmo, and Vidyattama 2007; Mathur 2001). This analysis can contribute to a stronger understanding of how the specific challenges in these countries shape and are shaped by issues of trade integration.

Details on the quantitative methodologies employed in the study are provided in the individual chapters.

Outline of the Book

This first part of the book focuses on how trade affects regions. Chapter 2 provides a new, dynamic look at the empirical evidence linking trade openness with regional convergence (or divergence, as it may be). We draw on a unique dataset of 28 countries (including 13 low- and middle-income countries) over several decades.

Part 2 provides a detailed analytical assessment of the relationship between location, exporting, and economic outcomes. In chapter 3, we use a large cross-country dataset to explore the nature and extent of regional factors that determine the entry and success of firms into exporting. Chapters 4 and 5 offer a case study of the Indonesian experience. Chapter 4 presents a descriptive analysis of the trends in regional divergence, structural change, and trade participation, followed by an assessment of how firm characteristics and the investment environment vary across regions within the country. Chapter 5 follows with an econometric investigation of the relationship between locational determinants and trade outcomes. To conclude part 2, chapters 6 and 7 provide an equivalent analysis, using the case study of India.

Part 3 of the book returns to the Indonesia and India cases, in chapters 8 and 9 respectively, to explore each of these countries' long history of policy interventions aimed at addressing the problem of lagging regions. The chapters provide a brief summary of the historical efforts made in the two case study countries to attract investment and promote growth and exports in lagging regions, exploring the nature of policies and how effective they have been in meeting their objectives.

Finally, in part 4, chapter 10 summarizes the main findings of the studies, and chapter 11 discusses implications of the findings on policies toward regions, particularly those located in peripheral areas.

Notes

1. This convergence is observed only when countries are weighted by population. Taking an unweighted measure actually shows divergence over this period. Indeed, the observation of convergence is almost fully explained by the rising incomes of China and India.

2. The Gini index is widely used in measuring inequality. An unweighted Gini index of regional inequality is taken as follows:

$$G_u = \left(\frac{1}{2\bar{y}_u}\right) \cdot \frac{1}{n(n-1)} \sum_i^n \sum_j^n |y_i - y_j|,$$

where y_i and y_j are the gross regional domestic products (GRDPs) per capita of regions i and j, respectively. The number of regions is n, and y_u is the unweighted mean of the per capita GRDPs. G_u varies from 0 for perfect equality to 1 for perfect inequality. An unweighted Gini index takes every region as one equal unit regardless of its population size; a weighted Gini index, by contrast, weights the regions' per capita GRDPs based on their respective population proportions.

The Internal Geography of Trade · http://dx.doi.org/10.1596/978-0-8213-9893-7

3. An exception is the limited use of regional dummies that are common in many of the trade studies using firm microdata. Although regional dummies may indicate the existence of regional differences in trade participation and performance, they provide no insight into the underlying factors.

References

Acemoglu, D. 2006. "Modeling Inefficient Institutions." NBER Working Papers 11940, National Bureau of Economic Research, Cambridge, MA.

Acemoglu, D., and S. Johnson. 2006. "De Facto Political Power and Institutional Persistence." *American Economic Review* 96 (2): 325–30.

Aghion, P., A. Alesina, and F. Trebbi. 2004. "Endogenous Political Institutions." *Quarterly Journal of Economics* 119 (2): 565–611.

Aghion, P., and P. Howitt. 2005. "Appropriate Growth Policy: A Unifying Framework." *Journal of the European Economic Association* 4: 269–314.

Ahmed, S., and E. Ghani. 2008. "Making Regional Cooperation Work for South Asia's Poor." Policy Research Working Paper Series 4736, World Bank, Washington, DC.

Akita, T., and R. Lukman. 1995. "Interregional Inequalities in Indonesia: A Sectoral Decomposition Analysis for 1975–92." *Bulletin of Indonesian Economic Studies* 31 (2): 61–81.

Audretsch, D., and M. Feldman. 1996. "Knowledge Spillovers and the Geography of Innovation and Production." *American Economic Review* 86: 630–40.

Azzoni, C. 2001. "Economic Growth and Income Inequality in Brazil." *Annals of Regional Science* 31 (1): 133–52.

Baldwin, R., and P. Krugman. 1989. "Persistent Trade Effects of Large Exchange Rate Shocks." *Quarterly Journal of Economics* 104 (4): 635–54.

Baylis, K., R. Garduno-Rivera, and G. Piras. 2009. "The Distributional Effects of NAFTA in Mexico: Evidence from a Panel of Municipalities." Agricultural and Applied Economics Association, 2009 Annual Meeting, Milwaukee, WI, July 26–28.

Bernard, A., J. Jensen, and R. Lawrence. 1995. "Exporters, Jobs, and Wages in U.S. Manufacturing: 1976–87." In *Brookings Papers on Economic Activity: Microeconomics*, 67–112. Washington, DC: The Brookings Institution.

Bhattacharya, B., and S. Sakthivel. 2004. "Regional Growth and Disparity in India." *Economic and Political Weekly* 39 (10): 1071–77.

Bourguignon, F., and C. Morrison. 2002. "Inequality among World Citizens: 1890–1992." *American Economic Review* 92 (4): 727–44.

Brülhart, M. 2009. "An Account of Global Intra-Industry Trade 1962–2006." *The World Economy* 32 (3): 401–59.

Cooke, P., and K. Morgan. 1998. *The Associational Economy: Firms, Regions and Innovation.* Oxford, U.K.: Oxford University Press.

Dunning, J., and S. Lundan. 2008. *Multinational Enterprises and the Global Economy.* 2nd ed. London: Edward Elgar.

Duranton, G., and D. Puga. 2000. "Diversity and Specialisation in Cities: Why, Where and When Does It Matter?" *Urban Studies* 37 (3): 533–55.

Fafchamps, M. 2001. "The Role of Business Networks in Market Development in Sub-Saharan Africa." In *Community and Market in Economic Development*, edited by M. Aoki and Y. Hayami, 186–215. Oxford, U.K.: Oxford University Press.

Farole, T., A. Rodríguez-Pose, and M. Storper. 2011. "Cohesion Policy in the European Union: Growth, Geography, Institutions." *Journal of Common Market Studies* 49 (5): 1089–111.

Feldman, M. 1994. *The Geography of Innovation.* Dordrecht, Netherlands: Kluwer Academic Publishers.

Ferreira, A. 2000. "Convergence in Brazil: Recent Trends and Long-Run Prospects." *Applied Economics* 32: 479–89.

Florida, R. 2002. *The Rise of the Creative Class, and How It's Transforming Work, Leisure, Community and Everyday Life.* New York: Basic Books.

Fujita, M., P. Krugman, and A. Venables. 1999. *The Spatial Economy: Cities, Regions and International Trade.* Cambridge, MA: MIT Press.

Gaur, A. 2010. "Regional Disparities in Economic Growth: A Case Study of Indian States." Paper prepared for the 31st General Conference of The International Association for Research in Income and Wealth, St. Gallen, Switzerland, August 22–28.

Gertler, M. 2003. "Tacit Knowledge and the Economic Geography of Context, or the Undefinable Tacitness of Being (There)." *Journal of Economic Geography* 3: 75–99.

Gertler, M., D. Wolfe, and D. Garkut. 2000. "No Place Like Home? The Embeddedness of Innovation in a Regional Economy." *Review of International Political Economy* 7: 688–718.

Ghosh, M. 2008. "Economic Reforms, Growth and Regional Divergence in India." *Margin: The Journal of Applied Economic Research* 2 (3): 265–85.

Grossman, E., and E. Helpman. 1991. "Quality Ladders in the Theory of Growth." *Review of Economic Studies* 58: 43–61.

Handa, S. 2005. "Regional Inequality and Human Capital in Indonesia." *Asia Keizai* 46 (6): 2–15.

Henry, N., and S. Pinch. 2000. "Spatialising Knowledge: Placing the Knowledge Community of Motor Sport Valley." *Geoforum* 31: 191–208.

Hill, H., B. Resosudarmo, and Y. Vidyattama. 2007. "Indonesia's Changing Economic Geography." Working Papers in Economics and Development Studies (WoPEDS) 200713, Department of Economics, Padjadjaran University, Bandung, Indonesia, revised Nov 2007.

Jacobs, J. 1969. *The Economy of Cities.* New York: Random House.

Jaffe, A., M. Trajtenberg, and R. Henderson. 1993. "Geographic Localization of Knowledge Spillovers as Evidenced by Patent Citations." *Quarterly Journal of Economics* 108: 577–98.

Kanbur, R., and A. Venables. 2005. *Spatial Inequality and Development.* Oxford, U.K.: Oxford University Press.

Kanbur, R., and X. Zhang. 2005. "Fifty Years of Regional Inequality in China: A Journey through Central Planning, Reform and Openness." *Review of Development Economics* 9 (1): 87–106.

Kristensen, P. 1992. "Industrial Districts in West Jutland, Denmark." In *Industrial Districts and Local Economic Regeneration*, edited by F. Pyke and W. Sengenberger. 122–73. Geneva, Switzerland: International Labour Organization.

Krugman, P. 1991. *Geography and Trade.* Leuven, Belgium: Leuven University Press; Cambridge, MA: MIT Press.

Krugman, P., and R. L. Elizondo. 1996. "Trade Policy and the Third World Metropolis." *Journal of Development Economics* 49 (1): 137–50.

Lucas, R. 1988. "On the Mechanics of Economic Development." *Journal of Monetary Economics* 22 (1): 3–42.

Malmberg, A., B. Malmberg, and P. Lundequist. 2000. "Agglomeration and Firm Performance: Economies of Scale, Localization, and Urbanization among Swedish Export Firms." *Environment and Planning A* 32 (2): 305–21.

Marshall, A. 1890. *Principles of Economics.* London: Macmillan.

Mathur A. 2001. "National and Regional Growth Performance in the Indian Economy: A Sectoral Analysis." Paper presented at the National Seminar on Economic Reforms and Employment in the Indian Economy, New Delhi.

Monfort, P., and R. Nicolini. 2000. "Regional Convergence and International Integration." *Journal of Urban Economics* 48 (2): 286–306.

Morgan, K. 1997. "The Learning Region: Institutions, Innovation and Regional Renewal." *Regional Studies* 31 (5): 491–503.

Ottaviano, G. 2011. "'New' Economic Geography: Firm Heterogeneity and Agglomeration Economies." *Journal of Economic Geography* 11 (2): 231–40.

Paluzie, E. 2001. "Trade Policy and Regional Inequalities." *Papers in Regional Science* 80 (1): 67–86.

Piore, M., and C. Sabel. 1984. *The Second Industrial Divide.* New York: Basic Books.

Puga, D. 1999. "The Rise and Fall of Regional Inequalities." *European Economic Review* 43 (2): 303–34.

———. 2002. "European Regional Policies in Light of Recent Location Theories." *Journal of Economic Geography* 2: 373–406.

Rodríguez-Pose, A. 1999. "Innovation Prone and Innovation Averse Societies: Economic Performance in Europe." *Growth and Change* 30: 75–105.

Rodríguez-Pose, A., and R. Crescenzi. 2008. "Research and Development, Spillovers, Innovation Systems, and the Genesis of Regional Growth in Europe." *Regional Studies* 42: 51–67.

Rodríguez-Pose, A., and N. Gill. 2006. "How Does Trade Affect Regional Disparities?" *World Development* 34: 1201–22.

Romer, P. 1986. "Increasing Returns and Long-Run Growth." *Journal of Political Economy* 94 (5): 1002–37.

Sánchez-Reaza, J., and A. Rodríguez-Pose. 2002. "The Impact of Trade Liberalization on Regional Disparities in Mexico." *Growth and Change* 33: 72–90.

Storper, M., and A. Venables. 2004. "Buzz: Face-to-Face Contact and the Urban Economy." *Journal of Economic Geography* 4: 351–70.

Venables, A. 2006. "Shifts in Economic Geography and Their Causes." *Economic Review, Federal Reserve Bank of Kansas City* Q IV 91 (4): 61–85.

Verspagen, B. 1997. *European 'Regional Clubs': Do They Exist, and Where Are They Heading? On Economic and Technological Differences between European Regions.* Maastricht, Netherlands: United Nations University and Maastricht University.

World Bank. 2009. *World Development Report 2009: Reshaping Economic Geography.* Washington, DC: World Bank.

Zhang, X., and K. Zhang. 2003. "How Does Globalisation Affect Regional Inequality within a Developing Country? Evidence from China." *Journal of Development Studies* 39: 47–67.

CHAPTER 2

Trade Openness and Regional Inequality

Andrés Rodríguez-Pose

Introduction

The World Bank's *World Development Report 2009* (WDR 2009) puts trade at the heart of the trinity of factors promoting growth. "Cities, migration, and trade have been the main catalysts of progress in the developed world over the past two centuries [and] these stories are now being repeated in the developing world's most dynamic economies" (World Bank 2009, 20). Although promoting trade is acknowledged to lead to greater territorial disparities (World Bank 2009, 6 and 12), this may not matter in the medium and long term as "evidence from today's industrial countries suggests that development has largely eliminated rural-urban disparities" (World Bank 2009, 62). Hence, from this perspective, the best way to deal with territorial inequality is not through "spatially balanced growth," which has been a "mantra of policy makers in many developing countries" (World Bank 2009, 73), but through the promotion of growth resulting from increases in trade and economic integration.

This approach rests, however, on three assumptions for which existing scholarly literature provides no firm answer, namely that (1) increases in trade lead to rising territorial inequalities; (2) these inequalities subsequently recede as a country develops; and (3) the emergence of spatial disparities does not represent a threat to future development, implying that developing countries should be more concerned about the promotion of growth than about inequalities (World Bank 2009, 12). However, the strength of these assumptions remains an open question, despite the surge of attention on the relationship between globalization, the rise of trade, and inequality.

Most of the work conducted so far on the link between trade and inequality has been concerned with the impact of increasing global market integration on interpersonal income inequality, in both the developed and the developing worlds (see, for example, Alderson and Nielsen 2002; Ravallion 2001; Williamson 2005; Wood 1994). The spatial dimension of inequality has attracted far less attention. This means that, as Kanbur and Venables (2005) underline, both the theoretical and empirical relationship between greater openness and spatial inequality remains ambiguous (see also Brülhart 2009). There are almost as many studies that point toward a link between trade and spatial convergence as those pointing toward spatial divergence (Brülhart 2009), and the direction and dimension of this relationship is far from uniform and varies from one country to another and according to the data and methods used.

Although the number of single-country case studies that have delved into this question has grown significantly in recent years, very scant cross-country evidence exists unveiling a general causal linkage between greater trade openness and market integration on the one hand, and intranational spatial inequality on the other.[1] This may be because the literature on the evolution of within-country spatial inequalities has tended—following the path opened by Williamson (1965) in his account of the relationship between spatial disparities and the stage of economic development—to focus on the internal and not the external forces of agglomeration and dispersion. From this perspective, economic development matters for the evolution of spatial inequalities, which tend to wane as a country develops. Hence, the factors that make a difference in explaining the evolution of regional inequality are considered to be internal to the country itself, while external factors are, at best, regarded as playing a supporting role in this process. When external factors are taken into consideration, the outcome is rather inconclusive. As Milanovic (2005, 428) puts it: "country experiences differ and [...] openness as such may not have the same discernable effects on countries regardless of their level of development, type of economic institutions, and other macroeconomic policies." Moreover, a large percentage of the literature dealing with the relationship between trade and spatial inequality has concentrated on developed countries—and in particular with the spatial effects of European Union (EU) integration (see, for example, Barrios and Strobl 2009; Niebuhr 2006). As a result, the findings, as inconclusive as they are, may be irrelevant in middle- and lower-income country environments.

Finally, it is far from certain that potential growth in intracountry regional disparities resulting from changes in trade patterns will be temporary and benign. The rise in inequalities may not just be a temporary stage, but rather one that becomes entrenched. This is especially likely in cases where (1) increasing polarization takes place during periods of low growth—meaning that not all regions within a country end up better off than before changes in trade patterns took place; (2) trade widens an already wide gap between rich and poor regions; and (3) new territorial inequalities resulting from trade reinforce preexisting social, political, cultural, or ethnic divides. Under these circumstances, increasing regional inequality may lead to a fragmentation of internal markets and to social, political, and/or ethnic tensions, which may threaten the very growth and prosperity that greater trade is supposed to bring about.

This chapter delves into the assumptions about the link between trade and regional inequality. More specifically, it focuses on the first two assumptions highlighted earlier: (1) whether changes in trade matter for the evolution of spatial inequalities and whether openness to trade affects developed and developing countries differently; and (2) whether there is a dynamic element to this association. The analysis covers the evolution of regional inequality across 28 countries—including 15 high-income and 13 low- and middle-income countries—over the period 1975–2005.[2]

In order to achieve this, the chapter combines the analysis of internal factors—in the tradition of Williamson—with that of change in real trade as a potential external factor that may affect the evolution of within-country regional inequality. Internal factors considered include Williamson's (1965) level of real economic growth and development, as well as a series of other factors, used as structural conditioning variables following the new economic geography (NEG) theory, which aims to account for apparent differences in the relationship between trade openness and spatial inequality. The analysis is conducted by running unbalanced static panels with country- and time-fixed effects, in order to address whether changes in trade patterns are connected with changes in spatial inequalities. This is followed by dynamic panel estimation, differentiating between short-term and long-term effects, as a way to assess whether this relationship changes with time.

The chapter is structured into five additional sections. The next section introduces a necessarily brief overview of the existing theoretical and empirical literature. The third section presents the data and their main trends. The fourth section outlines the theoretical framework and presents the variables included in the analysis, and the fifth section reports the results of the static and dynamic analysis, distinguishing between the differential effect of trade on regional inequality in developed and developing countries, and presents a series of robustness checks. The final section presents conclusions.

Trade and Regional Inequality in the Literature

As mentioned in the introduction, the link between changes in trade and the evolution of regional disparities has hardly captured the imagination of geographers and economists. In contrast with the growing literature on trade and interpersonal inequality, until recently there was a dearth of studies focusing on the within-country spatial consequences of changes in trade patterns. The emergence of the NEG theory has somewhat contributed to alleviate this gap in the literature, especially from a theoretical perspective. A string of NEG models concerned with the spatial implications of economic openness and trade (see, for example, Brülhart, Crozet, and Koenig 2004; Crozet and Koenig-Soubeyran 2004; Krugman and Livas-Elizondo 1996; Monfort and Nicolini 2000; Paluzie 2001) have appeared in recent years. In this literature, the causal effect of globalization on the national geography of production and income is conceptualized in terms of changes in cross-border market access that affect the interplay between agglomeration and dispersion forces. These forces, in turn, determine industrial location dynamics across domestic regions.

Because most of these models have a two-sector nature (agriculture/manufacturing), the central question has been whether increasing cross-border

The Internal Geography of Trade • http://dx.doi.org/10.1596/978-0-8213-9893-7

integration leads to a greater intranational concentration of manufacturing activity, and thereby growing regional inequality. However, due to the use of different sets of assumptions and because of the particular nature of the agglomeration and dispersion forces included in the models (Brülhart, Crozet, and Koenig 2004), contradictory and/or ambiguous conclusions have been derived from this type of analysis (compare, for example, Krugman and Livas-Elizondo 1996 to Paluzie 2001).

Empirical studies have not been better at resolving this conundrum. Most of the empirical analyses have tended to concentrate—in part as a result of the scarcity and lack of reliability of subnational comparable datasets across countries—on single-country case studies. Two countries feature prominently in empirical approaches. First and foremost is post-reform (post-1978) China, where an expanding number of studies have focused, among other things, on the trade-to-GDP (gross domestic product) ratio and/or foreign direct investment (FDI) inflows in order to explain either overall regional inequality or the growing coast-inland divide (see Jian, Sachs, and Warner 1996; Kanbur and Zhang 2005; Yang 2002; Zhang and Zhang 2003). Many of these studies have run time-series ordinary least squares (OLS) regressions with the measure of provincial inequality on the left-hand side and openness to trade and/or investment among a list of variables on the right. Most of these studies have found a significant positive effect of the rise in trade experienced by the country on regional inequality. Mexico has also featured prominently among those interested on the impact of trade on the location of economic activity. These studies use a number of measures, which range from changes in trade ratios (Rodríguez-Pose and Sánchez-Reaza 2005; Sánchez-Reaza and Rodríguez-Pose 2002), sometimes controlling for location and sector (Faber 2007), to FDI (Jordaan 2008a, 2008b), retail sales (Adkisson and Zimmerman 2004), or retail trade (Ford, Logan, and Logan 2009). They tend to find that increases in trade and greater economic integration in North American Free Trade Agreement (NAFTA) have resulted in important differences in the location of economic activity between border regions and the rest of Mexico, thus affecting the evolution of regional inequality.

Cross-country panel data analyses examining the link between changes in trade patterns and the evolution of regional disparities have been significantly fewer. A large number of these studies have concentrated on the impact of European integration on trade patterns and how these, in turn, influence regional inequality. Among these studies, the work of Petrakos, Rodríguez-Pose, and Rovolis (2005) and of Barrios and Strobl (2009) can be highlighted. Petrakos, Rodríguez-Pose, and Rovolis (2005) resort to a measure of relative intra-European integration for a sample of eight EU member countries, measured as national exports plus imports to and from other EU countries divided by total trade, rather than the overall trade-to-GDP ratios. Running a system of seemingly unrelated equations, they find mixed explanatory results for this variable and conclude that European integration affects countries differently. Barrios and Strobl (2009) run fixed-effects OLS analyses for the EU-15[3] over the period 1975–2000. Their aim is to explain how a measure of regional inequalities within each country is influenced by the trade-to-GDP ratio, as well as by trade over GDP in purchasing power parity (PPP) terms. For the latter, they find a significant positive effect on regional inequalities among EU-15 countries over 1975–2000.

Studies that focus on this topic and cover a more diverse sample of countries—involving both developed and developing ones—are rarer. Two such studies are Milanovic (2005) and Rodríguez-Pose and Gill (2006). Milanovic (2005) addresses the evolution of regional inequalities across the five most populous countries of the world: China, India, the United States, Indonesia, and Brazil, over varying time spans during the period 1980–2000. The results of his static fixed-effects and dynamic Arellano-Bover panel analyses point to an absence of a significant causal relationship between openness and regional inequalities. Rodríguez-Pose and Gill (2006) map two sets of binary relationships—first between nominal trade openness and regional inequality, and second between a trade composition index and regional inequality—for eight countries, including Brazil, China, Germany, India, Italy, Mexico, Spain, and the United States, over varying time spans between 1970 and 2000. They conclude that it is not trade openness per se that has any bearing on the evolution of regional inequality, but rather its combination with the evolution of the manufacturing-to-agriculture share of exports. This combination influences which regions gain and which lose from greater economic integration over time. As trade shifts from the primary sector to manufacturing, by virtue of manufacturing being more geographically concentrated—especially in emerging countries—than agriculture or mining, within-country regional disparities tend to increase; and they do so at a faster pace in the developing than in the developed world. Rodríguez-Pose and Gill (2006) find indicative support for this hypothesis based on the coincidence between changes in the evolution of their trade composition index and changes in regional inequalities across countries.

Given the diversity of results in both theoretical and empirical analyses, one would be hard pressed to generalize from the existing literature. The relationship between trade and regional inequalities thus remains wide open, from both a theoretical and an empirical perspective.

Overall Trade Openness and Regional Inequality: Empirical Evidence

We revisit the link between trade and regional inequality, using an unbalanced panel dataset comprising 28 countries over the period 1975–2005. The 28 countries included in the analysis are presented in table 2.1, which groups them according to whether they have experienced increasing, stable, or decreasing spatial disparities, using the evolution of the population-weighted coefficient of variation, over the time span covered by the data.

As can be seen, the majority of the countries included in the sample have experienced a rise in regional disparities over the period of analysis. In 18 out of the 28 countries, spatial inequalities have increased, while seven countries witnessed relative stability,[4] and only three—Belgium, Brazil, and South Africa—saw

Table 2.1 Increasing versus Decreasing Regional Inequality

Increasing regional inequality	Stable regional inequality	Decreasing regional inequality
Australia (1990–2005)	Austria (1988–2004)	Belgium (1977–96)
Bulgaria (1995–2004)	Canada (1981–2005)	Brazil (1989–2004)
Czech Republic (1995–2004)	China (1978–2004)	South Africa (1995–2005)
Finland (1995–2004)	Italy (1995–2004)	
France (1982–2004)	Japan (1975–2004)	
Greece (1979–2004)	Netherlands (1986–2004)	
Hungary (1995–2004)	United States (1975–2005)	
India (1993–2002)		
Indonesia (2000–05)		
Mexico (1993–2004)		
Poland (1995–2004)		
Portugal (1995–2004)		
Romania (1998–2004)		
Slovak Republic (1995–2004)		
Spain (1980–2004)		
Sweden (1994–2004)		
Thailand (1994–2005)		

a reduction in disparities. The rate of change varies enormously across countries (figure 2.1). Countries such as Bulgaria, China, Hungary, India, Poland, Romania, or the Slovak Republic have witnessed a very rapid rise in disparities, while the rate of increase has been more moderate in places such as Australia, Spain, the United Kingdom, or the United States. Rates of decline in inequalities have also varied hugely, with Belgium and Brazil experiencing the strongest decline in territorial inequalities. There is also no apparent difference between the trajectories of developed and of emerging countries. Some of the low- and medium-income countries included in the sample have seen spatial disparities increase—for example, Bulgaria, China, India, Indonesia, Mexico, and Thailand—while this has not been the case in Brazil and South Africa (figure 2.1). However, it is worth noting that the level of territorial inequalities differs widely among countries and especially between countries in the developed and developing worlds. Regional disparities in Thailand are eight times higher than those found in Australia or the United States (figure 2.1). The order of magnitude is four to one between China and Mexico and the former two high-income countries, and three to one in the case of Brazil and India.

The primary question that is asked is whether any general relationship between the evolution of trade openness and spatial inequalities across countries can be detected. In order to assess whether this is the case, a simple binary association between annual measures of real trade openness and regional inequality for each country separately is performed. Figure 2.2 maps the regression coefficient of the log Gini index of regional GDP per capita on the log of the share of exports plus imports in GDP adjusted to PPP by country. In figure 2.3, the same

Figure 2.1 Evolution of Regional Inequality in Sample Countries

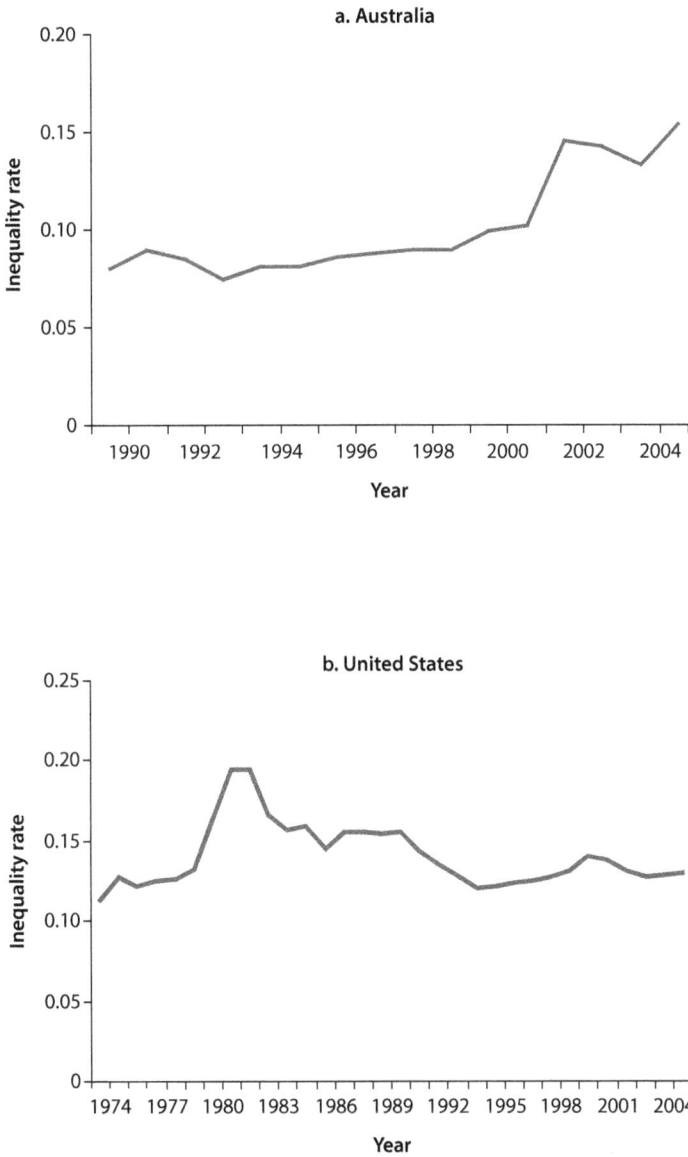

a. Australia

b. United States

figure continues next page

The Internal Geography of Trade • http://dx.doi.org/10.1596/978-0-8213-9893-7

Figure 2.1 Evolution of Regional Inequality in Sample Countries *(continued)*

c. Mexico

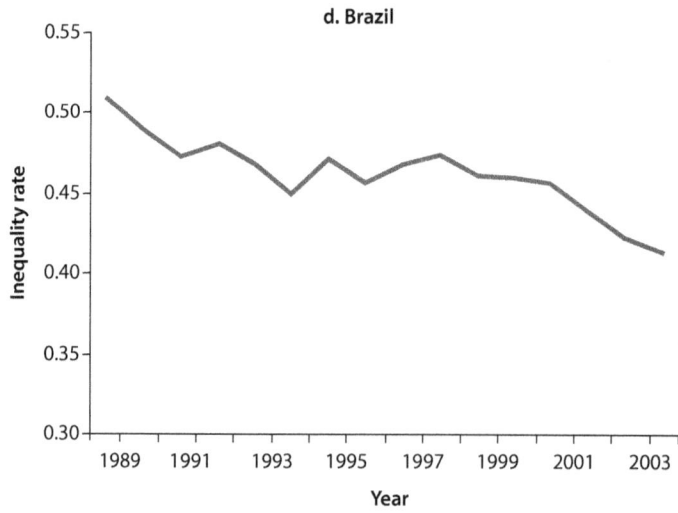

d. Brazil

figure continues next page

Figure 2.1 Evolution of Regional Inequality in Sample Countries *(continued)*

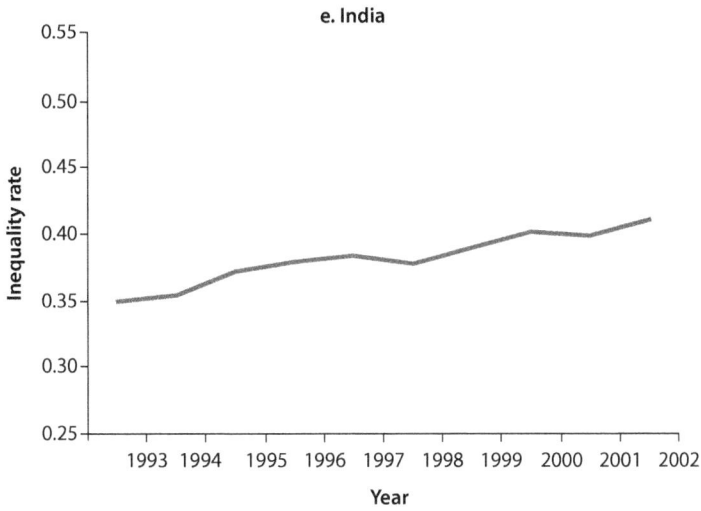

e. India

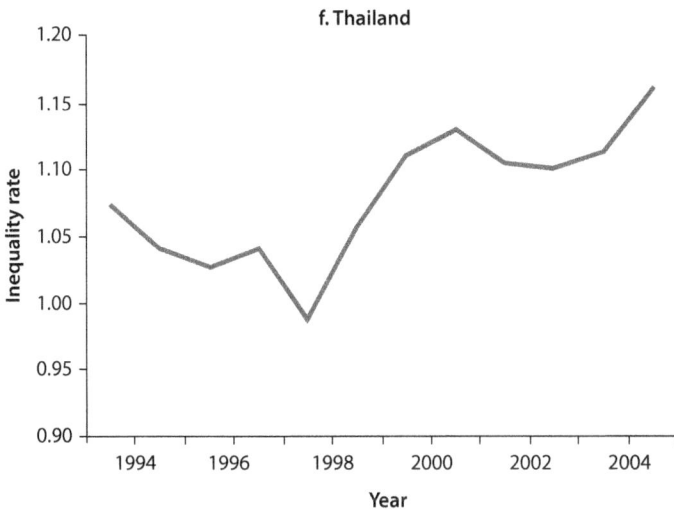

f. Thailand

figure continues next page

Figure 2.1 Evolution of Regional Inequality in Sample Countries *(continued)*

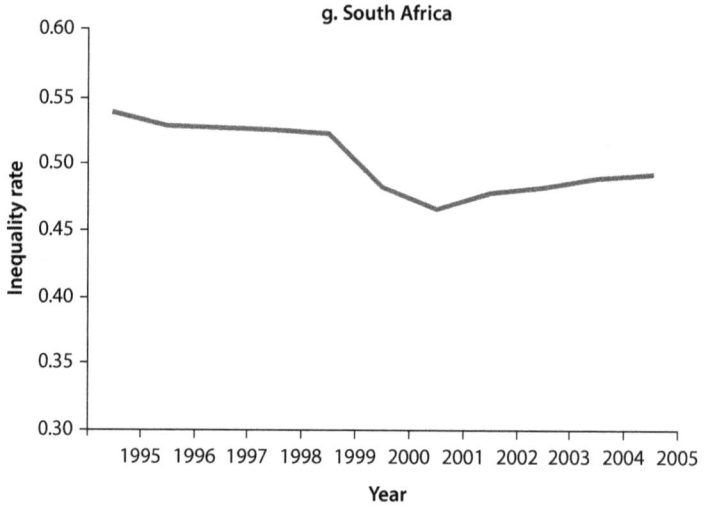

g. South Africa

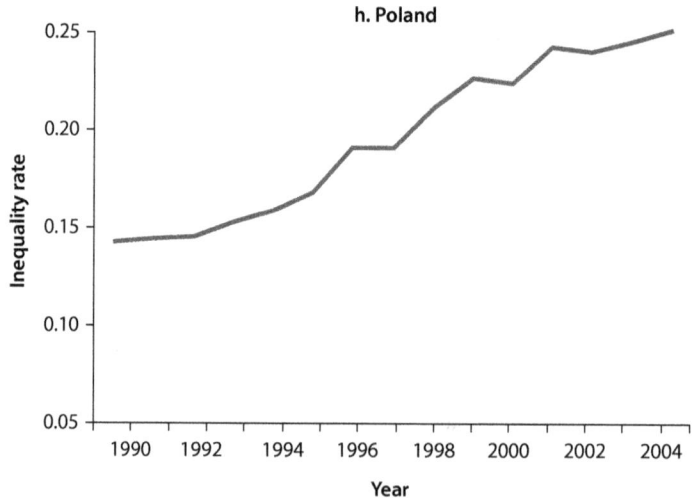

h. Poland

Note: Rate of inequality is measured by the population-weighted coefficient of variation.

Figure 2.2 Regression Coefficients of Regional Inequality on Real Trade Openness

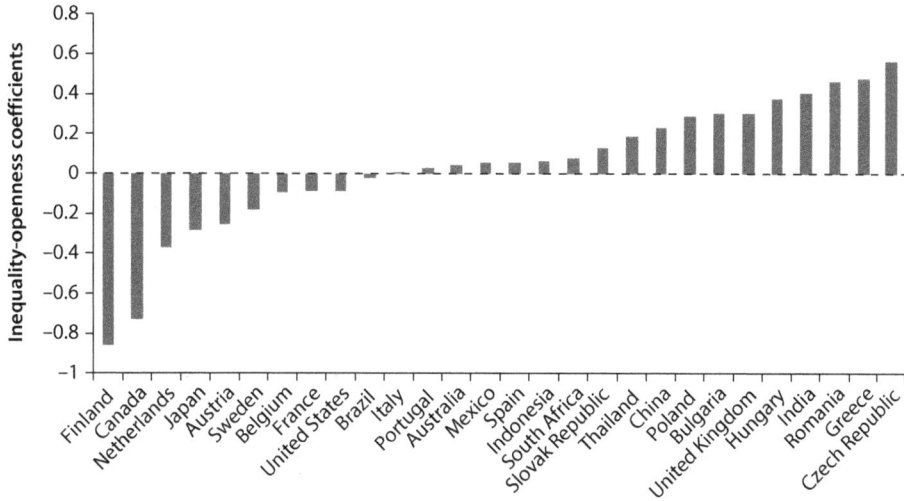

Figure 2.3 Regression Coefficients of Regional Inequality on Openness, Three-Year Average

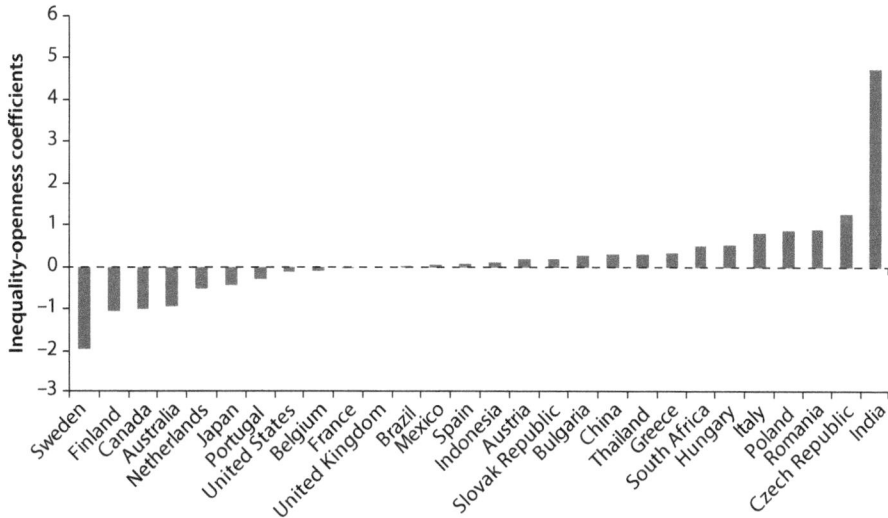

regression coefficients are presented, having replaced the annual measures by three-year averages, as multi-annual averages may be better than annual data at picking up any potential lagged effects, thus correcting for yearly fluctuations.

Figures 2.2 and 2.3 show no dominating pattern. There is a huge diversity in both the sign and the dimension of the coefficient, with some countries sporting a positive relationship between trade and the evolution of regional disparities and others a negative one. There consequently seems to be, as indicated by

Milanovic (2005) and Rodríguez-Pose and Gill (2006), no evidence of the presence of a simple linear relationship between the two variables that holds across different types of countries. A more subtle observation concerns the sequence of countries from left to right. On the whole, wealthier countries (Finland, Sweden, Canada, the Netherlands, Japan) tend to be located on the left-hand side of both figures, displaying a negative association between increases in trade and regional disparities, while poorer countries tend to be found toward the right-hand side of figures 2.2 and 2.3 (India, Romania, Poland). This relationship is, however, far from linear, with some high- and middle-income countries (Spain, Italy, the Republic of Korea, the United Kingdom, and Greece) displaying a positive binary association between trade and spatial inequality.

Model and Data

There are limitations, however, in what can be inferred from simple binary associations. They offer limited information about the mechanisms at play, and many other factors may be affecting the evolution of within-country regional disparities. To address this issue, we formulate in the following paragraphs a formal econometric specification with additional controls and conditioning variables. The specification is aimed at testing for a significant association between openness and spatial inequality and whether this association—if it exists—affects developed and developing countries in a different way.

The Basic Model

With very few exceptions (such as Milanovic 2005), the bulk of studies on the determinants of regional inequalities are based on static once-yearly specifications. However, regional inequality is bound to be a time-persistent phenomenon with a high degree of inertia. This makes overlooking time considerations problematic. Theory, however, provides no clear (if any) insights concerning the temporal dimension of internal spatial adjustments to changes in external market access. Hence, rather than guessing an appropriate adjustment timeframe, this chapter tackles potential inertia by formulating a dynamic model with past levels of spatial inequality on the dependent variable side. The use of dynamic panels—complementing static panels—has the advantage of introducing the distinction between short-term and long-term effects.

The general model is formulated as follows:

$$Inequality_{it}^* = \alpha + \sum \beta x_{it} + \varepsilon_{it} \qquad (2.1)$$

where $Inequality_{it}^*$ is the level of inequality in country i at time t corresponding to the spatial configuration that would arise if there was no inertia in the system and x_{it} is a vector of independent variables conditioning the spatial distribution of income in any given country i at time t. Using Brown's (1952) classical habit persistence model, equation 2.1 is transformed into equation 2.2:

$$Inequality_{it} - Inequality_{it-1} = \lambda(Inequality_{it}^* - Inequality_{it-1}), \ 0 < \lambda < 1 \qquad (2.2)$$

where the actual observed change of the spatial configuration ($Inequality_{it}$ − $Inequality_{t-1}$) is a fraction λ of the adjustment that would have taken place under instantaneous adjustment.

Parameter λ ranges between 0 and 1 and represents the speed of adjustment. If λ is close to 1, then the adjustment is almost instantaneous and the relationship between the theoretical determinants x_{it} and the actual observed spatial outcomes $Inequality_{it}$ is static. If λ is below 1, then the difference between the observed spatial outcomes and their inertia-free theoretical counterpart $Inequality^{*}_{it}$ becomes significant, creating the need to control for partial adjustment in a dynamic model. Rearranging and substituting for $Inequality^{*}_{it}$, we obtain:

$$Inequality_{it} = \lambda\,(\alpha + \Sigma\beta x_{it} + \varepsilon_{it}) + (1 - \lambda)\,Inequality_{it-1},\ 0 < \lambda < 1 \qquad (2.3)$$

Equation 2.3 presents the basic specification followed in the dynamic panel regressions. On the left-hand side of the equation is the dependent variable, representing the observed inequality. On the right, we find the theoretical determinants of the inertia-free spatial configuration plus the previous period's value of the dependent variable. The latter effectively controls for potential inertia and partial adjustment. By fixing the previous spatial outcome $Inequality_{it-1}$, the short-term effect of any independent variable x_{it} is given by its revealed regression coefficient when running equation 2.3. Conceptually, this coefficient represents the product $\lambda\beta$. The assumption for the long run is that a country's spatial configuration reaches a stable equilibrium, making the current and the previous year's inequality levels close to identical. Setting $Inequality_{it-1}$ equal to $Inequality_{it}$ in equation 2.3, the long-term effect of any independent variable on the spatial configuration can thus be derived by dividing the observed regression coefficient $\lambda\beta$ by the speed of adjustment parameter λ. The long-term effects can be derived by dividing the coefficients of the independent variables by 1 minus the coefficient of the lagged dependent variable.

The Conditioning Variables

Now that the basic model is set, the next task is to identify an appropriate set of conditioning variables capturing the relationship between trade openness and internal spatial inequality in the form of equation 2.1. This is done in two stages: the first one drawing on recent NEG models and the second reaching beyond the purely market access driven framework.

In an NEG core-periphery framework, distinguishing whether or not greater accessibility to foreign markets promotes economic growth is tricky. This is in part a consequence of the NEG's basic two-sector assumption and of the absence of intra-industry linkages. The introduction of cross-border intra-industry linkages and of a multisector industrial scenario in the analysis gives rise to an additional pull factor toward highly accessible regions. This pull factor comes into play once trade is liberalized and allows export market potential, intra-industry supply potential, and import competition to affect domestic sectors differently, depending on the comparative advantages revealed by market integration (Faber 2007). Sectors characterized by a revealed comparative advantage and/or cross-border, intra-industry linkages will thus grow faster in regions with good foreign market access, whereas import-competing sectors gain in relative terms in regions with higher "natural protection" related to poor market access. Faber (2007) finds empirical support for this trade-location linkage across 43 industrial sectors in post-NAFTA Mexico over the period 1993–2003.

This possible divergence of sector location patterns under cross-border market integration has important implications concerning whether and how market accessibility affects regional performance. Regions with high relative foreign market access that attract the winners of integration will also tend to shed declining sectors, resulting in higher medium- to long-term regional growth rates than in regions with limited and/or constrained foreign market access.

In conditions of increasing trade and economic integration, several additional country-specific factors may play a conditioning role in the evolution of regional inequalities. First is the degree of variation of foreign market accessibility among regions within any given country. If, given the previous discussion, we assume that relative foreign market access drives regional attractiveness for expanding sectors, then the locational pull will be strongest in countries characterized by high regional differences in cross-border market accessibility. Second, the degree of coincidence between the existing regional income distribution and the distribution of relative foreign market access affects the strength of the first factor. When relatively wealthy regions are also those with a greater degree of accessibility, increases in trade are likely to exacerbate previously existing inequalities. In contrast, when poorer regions have a market accessibility advantage relative to better-off regions, the net outcome of increases in trade is likely to be a reduction in regional disparities and within-country territorial convergence. Hence, it can be safely assumed that *greater trade openness will have a more polarizing effect in countries (1) characterized by higher differences in foreign market accessibility among its regions and (2) where there is also a high degree of coincidence between the regional income distribution and accessibility to foreign markets.* The presence of a strong coincidence between regional income distribution and accessibility to foreign markets is a sufficient, rather than a necessary, condition in order to generate greater inequality, as trade openness may also exacerbate previously existing inequality, even in cases when wealthier regions have less foreign market accessibility than poorer regions. It may be that differences in endowments or in adaptive capacity between rich and poor regions more than compensate for differences in accessibility.

Stepping outside the NEG framework, a third set of factors may come into play in determining the link between trade and regional inequality. For example, differences in the distribution of human capital and skills and infrastructure affect trade patterns as well as economic growth. It can therefore be envisaged that *the greater the regional differences in endowments and sector specialization, the greater the spatial impact of trade openness.*

Also outside the NEG framework, government policies are a fourth factor that may enhance or attenuate the spatial effects of changes in trade patterns. Governments with a greater social and territorial redistributive capacity through public policies will be in a better position to counter any potential tendency of increases in trade patterns leading to greater geographical polarization. Budgetary or regional policy transfers from prosperous to lagging regions will thus offset rises in regional inequality. *The effect of trade openness on spatial inequality will likely to be more severe in countries with a weaker redistributive capacity by the central government and/or with fewer provisions for interregional transfers.*

A fifth conditioning factor concerns the degree of labor mobility, especially within-country mobility. Depending on the conditions of any particular country, interregional worker mobility may contribute either to greater agglomeration, as workers concentrate in core areas offering higher salaries or greater job opportunities, or to greater territorial cohesion, if workers follow firms seeking lower costs in peripheral areas (Puga 1999). Hence, *the effect of trade on regional inequality will depend on the degree of interregional labor mobility and the specific conditions of the country.*

A final factor is the quality of institutions, which will vary significantly from one region to another. Poorer and/or lagging regions are likely to suffer the most from this situation. Problems of institutional sclerosis, clientelism, corruption, and pervasive rent seeking by durable local elites, which beset many lagging areas, are likely to contribute to trade bypassing these regions in favor of those with more "appropriate" institutions. "Informal institutions in these places are often similarly dysfunctional, resulting in low levels of trust and declining associative capacity, and restricting the potential for effective collective action" (Farole, Rodríguez-Pose, and Storper 2009, 11). *"Inappropriate" institutions will thus represent an important barrier for trade, leading to a spatial effect of trade more severe in countries with a significant gap in institutional capacity among its regions.*

Unfortunately, due to lack of comparable and reliable data on interregional labor mobility and institutions across the 28 countries covered in the analysis, the latter two hypotheses cannot be tested. We therefore have to assume that labor mobility and institutions are not systematically correlated with any of the other regressors, thus implying that there is no omitted variable problem in leaving out this conditioning interaction.

There is also a need to control for other factors that may affect the relationship between trade and spatial inequality. The key element in this realm relates to Williamson's (1965) classical account of the linkage between spatial disparities and the stage of economic development. In Williamson's account, the level of within-country spatial inequality is fundamentally the result of the level of national economic development (proxied in this case by real GDP per capita and its growth). As countries prosper, inequalities tend to diminish, making economic growth a primary driver of changes in spatial inequalities. Williamson's theory is built into the WDR 2009. There it is stated that not only has "development ... largely eliminated rural-urban disparities," but also that "high urban shares and concentrated economic density go hand in hand with small differences in rural-urban well-being on a range of indicators" (World Bank 2009, 62). As economic growth is also likely to be correlated with changes in trade (Sachs and Warner 1995), a control for real GDP per capita and its interaction with the country's development stage is included in the analysis.

The Empirical Model, Data, and Method

The previous discussion leads to the transformation of equation 2.1 into the following empirical specification (2.4). Table 2A.1 presents the actual values of the structural conditions across the 28 countries.

$$Inequality_{it}^* = \alpha + \beta1[\ln(GDPcap_{it})*Development_i] + \beta2[\ln(Trade_{it})$$
$$*\ln(MarketAccess_i)*\ln(Coincidence_i)] + \beta3[\ln(Trade_{it}) \qquad (2.4)$$
$$*\ln(Sectors_t)] + \beta4[\ln(Trade_{it})*\ln(Government_i)] + \varepsilon_{it}$$

where:

$Inequality_{it}$ represents the level of within-country regional inequality in country i in year t, measured using the Gini index of regional GDP per capita.

$GDPcap_{it}$ denotes real GDP per capita in PPP in constant US$ (2000) for country i in year t.

$Development_i$ is a dummy variable which takes the value of 1 if country i is a developing or transition economy and 0 otherwise. The categories were assigned on the basis of historical World Bank classifications. Each country was assigned to its most frequent classification over the time period covered in the dataset. This variable is, in turn, subdivided into three components:

1. *High income_i* is another dummy variable that takes the value of 1 if country i has been most frequently classified as a high-income country and 0 otherwise.
2. *Middle income_i* is a dummy variable that takes the value 1 of if country i has been most frequently classified as a middle-income country and 0 otherwise.
3. *Low income_i* is a dummy variable that takes the value of 1 if country i has been most frequently classified as a low-income country and 0 otherwise.

$Trade_{it}$ represents the total imports and exports in current U.S. dollars divided by GDP in PPP current U.S. dollars for country i in year t.

$Sectors_i$ is a variable aimed at capturing the degree of interregional sectoral differences that exist across countries, proxied by the standard deviation of the share of agriculture in regional GDP, averaged across the time periods under study for country i.[5]

$Government_i$ denotes the size of government in country i, proxied by the share of nonmilitary government expenditure in total GDP averaged across the time periods under study. It is assumed that interregional transfer programs and social expenditures are linearly related to the level of government expenditure in total GDP and that, in most countries, there will be a certain progressiveness built into the territorial distribution of investment.

MarketAccess$_i$ denotes the degree of interregional differences in foreign market access across countries. Taking into account existing data constraints in the countries covered in the sample, two alternative measures of market access are used. The first variable (*Surface*$_i$) is each country's surface area in square kilometers. However, the surface area of a country is a rather crude measure of market access, especially in view of the huge diversity in population density among countries. Hence an alternative composite measure of internal market access polarization (*MAPolarisation*$_i$) is constructed. In this measure, the surface area in square kilometers of a country is transformed into an index ranging between 0 and 100 and introduced as the first element. The second element is the ratio (adjusted by population density) of paved road and railway kilometers over the square root of the land area. The adjustment for population density is intended to account for the fact that some countries have vast unpopulated areas while others are much more densely populated. The infrastructure-to-land-area ratio is weighted by transforming each country's land area to the panel's mean population density. In the case of Australia, this transformation greatly reduces the country's adjusted land area, whereas in the case of the Netherlands it increases it. The paved road and railroad line kilometers relative to the square root of the adjusted land area is used as a population-density adjusted indicator of infrastructure quantity and quality across countries. As with the surface area, this composite measure is transformed into an index ranging between 0 and 100, where 100 represents the score for the country with the lowest endowment in infrastructure (in our panel Thailand, see table 2A.1). The two 0–100 scores are then combined into an aggregate score of possible values between 0 and 200, where increasing scores suggest increasing internal differences of foreign market access.

The main logic behind the use of the *MAPolarisation*$_i$ variable is that both the level of absolute internal distances (element 1) and the population-density-adjusted infrastructural endowments (element 2) determine the degree of interregional variation in access to foreign markets. The first concerns the internal transport distances, the second proxies for the average transportation costs of a country. A one-to-one weighting was chosen under the assumption that the proxy for quality and quantity of transport infrastructure will reflect not only average transport costs per kilometer of landmass, but also the number and availability of international transshipment and customs facilities along a country's coasts and borders.

Coincidence$_i$ reflects the degree of coincidence between relative regional market access positions and regional income per capita levels across countries. Once again, two alternative measures of coincidence between both factors are used. The first (*Coincidence25*$_i$) is the ratio of the average GDP per capita levels of the regions in the top 25 percent in terms of foreign market access over average regional GDP per capita. The second (*Coincidence50*$_i$) calculates the same ratio on the basis of the regions in the top 50 percent in terms of relative foreign market access. In order to ensure consistency with the dependent measure of regional inequality, which treats each region as one observation, the coincidence ratios are also computed disregarding regional population sizes.

The Internal Geography of Trade • http://dx.doi.org/10.1596/978-0-8213-9893-7

The question is how to determine relative market access positions. There is absence of adequate and comparable datasets of regional transport costs to an equivalent selection of international trade points in each country. Therefore, the method used in this analysis consists in first identifying the trade entry points that account for at least 70 percent of the country's total trade, as well as the top quarter or half of the regions (in terms of border or coast location) in closest proximity to the main trade routes. In the cases where two regions were close in terms of border/coast accessibility to the main trade routes, the region with the higher number of international ports or border crossings was chosen.

Beyond a mere response to limited data availability, this geography-based construction of the coincidence measures also addresses a potential endogeneity issue. Assuming that perfect data about each region's foreign market access in terms of actual transport-cost-weighted market potential are available, it is highly likely that high degrees of regional inequality are associated with higher degrees of coincidence, because regional prosperity tends to be a driver of market access when measured in terms of human-built infrastructure. Relying on physical proximity and border or coast location instead is not subject to this potential endogeneity issue. As in the case of the previous structural conditioning variables, the coincidence measures are averaged across periods for each country.

The data sources for each of the variables are presented in table 2A.2.

In order to assess the original questions of whether trade and the remaining variables included under equation 2.4 affect regional inequalities and whether this relationship changes over time, both static OLS with country and time-fixed effects, as well as dynamic panels are run. The static analysis aims at discovering the association (or lack of it) between trade and the evolution of regional disparities. In the case of the dynamic regressions, generalized method of moments (GMM) estimations are applied in order to distinguish between short- and long-term effects, following Arellano and Bond (1991), Arellano and Bover (1995), and Blundell and Bond (1998). The problem with running OLS on panels that include the lagged dependent variable is that it will be correlated with the error term even after getting rid of the unobserved country heterogeneity therein. To adjust for this bias, Arellano and Bond have proposed a first-difference GMM estimator that uses lagged values of the dependent and predetermined variables and differences of the strictly exogenous ones as instruments. Arellano and Bover and Blundell and Bond have proposed a system GMM estimator in which variables in levels are instrumented with lags of their own first differences to exploit additional moment conditions.

The Impact of Trade Openness on Regional Inequality

Static Analysis

In this section, the results of running the different specifications of equation 2.4 are presented. Table 2.2 introduces the results for the static OLS with country

Table 2.2 Static Panel with Country and Time-Fixed Effects

	1	2	3	4	5	6	7	8	9	10
GDPcap	0.1680	0.2433**	0.2766**	0.2657**	0.3049***	0.1799	0.1791	0.2251**	0.2418**	0.3607***
GDPcap*Development		−0.1223	−0.1721	−0.1523*	−0.1992**	−0.0540	−0.0404	−0.1025	−0.0998	−0.2363***
Trade	0.0725	0.1728***	0.1042*	−0.4840***	0.8620***	1.7055***	1.770***	1.1955**	1.2968***	2.1162***
Trade*Development			0.1237*							0.1160
Trade*Government				−0.3337***						−0.0932
Trade*Sectors					0.2081***					0.2358***
Trade*Coincidence50*MAPolarisation						0.7888				
Trade*Coincidence25*MAPolarisation							0.8889***			
Trade*Coincidence50*Surface								0.1544***		
Trade*Coincidence25*Surface									0.1351***	0.1272**
Constant	−1.510	−3.631	−3.811	−3.729	−3.968	−3.297	−3.317	−3.699	−3.841	−4.592
R^2 (within)	0.003	0.227	0.2327	0.2527	0.2577	0.2503	0.2622	0.2775	0.2885	0.359
Observations	435	435	435	435	435	435	435	435	435	435
F-test for country dummies	Prob > F = 0.640	Prob > F = 0.000	Prob > F = 0.000	Prob > F = 0.000	Prob > F = 0.000	Prob > F = 0.000	Prob > F = 0.000	Prob > F = 0.000	Prob > F = 0.000	Prob > F = 0.000

Note: GDP = gross domestic product. *, **, and *** correspond to 10, 5, and 1 percent significance levels, respectively, computed with heteroskedasticity adjusted standard errors. Time- and country-fixed effects are included.

and time-fixed effects. All unobserved invariant country and time heterogeneity has been eliminated from the model. Therefore, the coefficients can be interpreted as the partial effects that annual variations of independent variables around the country mean have had on annual variations of spatial inequality around the country mean.

When trade is considered as a free-standing variable (table 2.2, Regression 1), no association whatsoever is found between changes in trade patterns and the evolution of regional disparities. This coincides with the results of other studies that have looked at the simple association between trade and regional inequality (see, for example, Rodríguez-Pose and Gill 2006). This lack of association changes when, as specified in the diverse hypotheses, trade is considered in interaction with a series of country-specific factors. Here, the results of the static panel highlight, in contrast to most previous studies operating with international panels, the presence of a weak, but positive and highly significant, effect of the dimension of real trade on spatial inequality when pooling across all countries. Having controlled for the internal growth effect and its different slope across developed and developing countries, a 1 percent increase in real trade openness is on average associated with a 0.17 percent increase of the Gini index of regional inequality (table 2.2, Regression 2). The results also indicate that this effect is significantly stronger in developing countries than in developed ones (table 2.2, Regression 3), although the binary *Development* dummy interaction is only significant at the 10 percent level.

Regressions 4–9 in table 2.2 take us beyond the simple binary relationship between trade and inequality and introduce the conditioning structural variables identified in the previous section. All the coefficients have the expected sign. Rises in trade are associated with lower regional inequalities in countries with large government size and with higher inequalities in cases of strong interregional sector differences, when there are important differences in market access and when these coincide with geographical disparities in income per capita. And, with the exception of one particular combination of the spatial structure conditions in Regression 6, all are significant at the 1 percent level. Poorer countries with lower government expenditure, higher variations in regional sector structures, and a spatial structure dominated by high internal transaction costs coupled with a higher degree of coincidence between prosperous regions and foreign market access are thus bound to experience greater rises in regional inequality when opening to foreign trade.

Interestingly, when all conditioning interactions are added together (table 2.2, Regression 10), the binary *Development* dummy interaction effect becomes insignificant. The same is the case for the *Government* expenditure interaction. These changes could simply be the result of collinearity between the *Development* dummy and the *Government* variable. But this is not the case. The *Government* variable remains significant once the *Sectors* interaction is dropped, meaning that the problem of collinearity arises between the *Government* and *Sectors* interactions, but not between *Development* and *Government*. This suggests that the proposed structural variables account to a great extent for the apparent differences in the association between trade and within-country spatial inequalities across developed and developing countries.

In order to test whether the weak binary *Development* dummy interaction of the trade impact also holds at a less aggregate categorical level, the panel is divided into high-, middle-, and low-income countries, according to the World Bank's classification, using the high-income group as the reference category. Table 2.3 reports the results of this type of analysis.

Adding greater nuances to the developed/developing country division leads to an increase in the significance of development dummy interactions (Regression 2, table 2.3), in comparison to those reported in Regression 3 (table 2.2). The results suggest that variations in levels of trade openness have a significantly higher association with average variations in spatial inequality in middle- and low-income countries than in high-income ones in the short term. There is, in contrast, no significant difference between the impact of changes in trade on spatial inequality between low- and middle-income countries (Regression 2, table 2.3).

Besides testing for different slopes of the trade effect on spatial inequality across groups, we also examine whether the effect of trade has changed as countries progress in terms of economic development, by interacting trade openness with the countries' real GDP per capita (Regression 3, table 2.3). The resulting coefficient points toward a weakening of the positive association between increases in trade and within-country spatial inequalities as countries become wealthier. Overall, table 2.3 once again suggests that trade has had a higher impact on spatial inequality in developing countries, and that this effect tends to

Table 2.3 Trade Effect in Developed and Developing Countries

	1	2	3	4
GDPcap	0.2766**	0.4628***	0.1427	−0.0954
GDPcap*Development	−0.1721*	−0.3489***	−0.2438**	0.3507*
Trade	0.1042*	−0.0587	0.9534**	2.8924***
Trade*Development	0.1237*			−3.2878***
Trade*GDPcap			−0.0814**	−0.2888***
Trade*GDPcap*Development				0.3508***
Trade*Middle Income		0.3963***		
Trade*Low Income		0.3523***		
Constant	−3.811	−5.027	−2.262	−1.951
R^2 (within)	0.2327	0.2968	0.2347	0.2681
Observations	435	435	435	435
F-test for country dummies	Prob > F = 0.000	Prob > F = 0.000	Prob > F = 0.000	Prob > F = 0.000

Note: GDP = gross domestic product. *, **, and *** correspond to 10, 5, and 1 percent significance levels, respectively, computed with heteroskedasticity adjusted standard errors. Time- and country-fixed effects are included.

be diminishing with economic development at a slower pace than in developed countries.

An important final point concerns the striking difference between the coefficient results for the internal determinant of spatial inequality in the tradition of Williamson (1965), and the external trade–induced factor. Particularly surprising is the negative and frequently significant coefficient of the interaction term. This suggests that, after controlling for real trade openness, variations of real income per capita have on average had a less positive association with variations in spatial inequality in developing countries as opposed to developed ones. In other words, economic growth has on average been less polarizing in developing countries than in developed ones.

These findings indicate that the external effect of real trade openness on internal spatial inequality appears to have had a more polarizing effect in developing countries than economic growth. We next try to identify the underlying structural factors behind the observed differences in the trade effect in this context. As noted in Regression 9 in table 2.2, the diminishing size and lack of significance of the development dummy interaction (after controlling for spatial structure, government intervention, and sector differences) point to these structural factors as part of the reason. This line of reasoning is confirmed in table 2.4, in which the variable averages are collapsed across different country groups.

In table 2.4, all the identified conditioning country characteristics appear to be working against developing countries. This is quite pronounced after disaggregating countries into high-, middle-, and low-income clusters, especially when taking into account current existing degrees of global integration, on one side, and levels of spatial inequality, on the other. This implies that, as highlighted by Rodríguez-Pose and Gill (2006), the room for growth in spatial inequalities is much greater in the developing than in the developed world, for the following reasons: (1) developing countries tend to be characterized by structural features that potentiate the polarizing effect of trade openness; (2) they already have much higher existing levels of spatial inequality; and (3) their level of trade openness is, on average, still only a fraction of that among developed countries.

Table 2.4 Structural Factors across Groups of Countries

	Developed	Developing	Developing/ developed ratio	High income	Middle income	Low income	Low/high ratio
Inequality	0.11	0.25	2.27	0.11	0.18	0.28	2.57
Real trade openness	0.44	0.22	0.51	0.46	0.26	0.16	0.35
Government	0.17	0.13	0.79	0.18	0.15	0.11	0.61
Sectors	0.03	0.06	2.30	0.02	0.05	0.09	3.62
MAPolarisation	95.97	125.63	1.31	96.55	110.16	135.42	1.40
Coincidence50	1.03	1.09	1.06	1.03	0.97	1.23	1.19
Coincidence25	1.04	1.28	1.23	1.05	1.06	1.48	1.41

Dynamic Analysis

Table 2.5 presents the results of the dynamic panel regressions. The results were computed using the xtabond2 command in STATA (Roodman 2006). Reported results correspond to the first-difference Arellano-Bond GMM estimation. The reason for this is that the usually preferred Arellano-Bover system GMM was repeatedly rejected by the Sargan test of over-identification, indicating that its additional assumptions on the data generating process did not hold.

As could be expected, when switching to dynamic panels with the lagged level of inequality included on the right-hand side, most of the differences in current within-country spatial inequality levels are explained by previous levels of within-country inequality, meaning also that the effect of trade openness on regional inequality ceases to matter (table 2.5, Regression 1). The same is the case for the binary *Development* dummy interaction term in Regression 2 (table 2.5).

Regressions 3–9 introduce the structural conditions in the dynamic model. Here, the partial effects of the static fixed-effect model are confirmed in the cases of sector differences and government expenditure, which also render the *Trade* variable significant at the 5 percent level (Regressions 3 and 4, table 2.5). The introduction of the spatial variables, in contrast, while keeping the same coefficient signs of the static analysis, display insignificant coefficients with the exception of Regression 9, which substitutes the *Development* dummy by a relatively crude binary proxy of internal market access polarization.

The high degree of inertia inferred from the coefficient of the lagged level of regional inequality comes as no surprise, with the speed of adjustment parameter lying around 0.3. This coefficient suggests the presence of a strong difference between short-term and long-term effects of all included independent factors (table 2.5).

Robustness Tests

In order to check whether these results are robust to differences in specifications, the Gini index of regional inequality is replaced by alternative inequality measures. The specifications in tables 2.2–2.4 are thus run replacing the Gini coefficient of within-country regional inequality as the dependent variable with two alternative measures: the Theil index and the population-weighted coefficient of variation. The results are robust to the change in specification and can be provided upon request.

Another robustness check, given the limited number of observations in a panel including 28 countries relative to the time of the analysis, is to use a bias-corrected least squares dummy variable (LSDV) estimator (Bun and Kiviet 2003; Kiviet 1995), instead of a instrumental variable GMM estimation. This approach also allows accommodating for unbalanced panels (Bruno 2005). By resorting to this method, the aim is to check whether the results from the Arellano-Bond GMM estimation in table 2.3 prove robust

Table 2.5 Dynamic Panel with First-Difference Arellano-Bond GMM

	1	2	3	4	5	6	7	8	9	10
Lagged inequality	0.7132***	0.7188***	0.6917***	0.6917***	0.7126***	0.7154***	0.7112***	0.7090***	0.7099***	0.6917***
GDPcap	−0.0102	0.0002	0.006	0.0216	−0.0165	−0.0106	−0.0168	−0.0137	0.0040	0.0037
GDPcap*Development	0.0303	0.0243	0.0141	−0.0038	0.0289	0.0261	0.0338	0.0311	0.0166	0.0133
Trade	0.0158	0.0200	−0.2429**	0.2631**	−0.1196	−0.0803	0.0862	0.1187	0.0232	0.1172
Trade*Development		−0.0116								−0.0486
Trade*Government			−0.1384**							−0.0636
Trade*Sectors				0.0726**						0.0596
Trade*Coincidence50*MAPolarisation					−0.0110					
Trade*Coincidence25*MAPolarisation						0.0694				
Trade*Coincidence50*Surface							0.0009			
Trade*Coincidence25*Surface								0.0174		
Trade*Coincidence25*Development									0.7210**	0.5898*
Observations	379	379	379	379	379	379	379	379	379	379
Sargan test	Prob > chi2 = 0.9355	Prob > chi2 =0.9407	Prob > chi2 = 0.8894	Prob > chi2 = 0.9147	Prob > chi2 = 0.9493	Prob > chi2 = 0.9484	Prob > chi2 = 0.9541	Prob > chi2 = 0.9461	Prob > chi2 = 0.9530	Prob > chi2 = 0.9395
2nd order autocorrelation	Pr > z = 0.5032	Pr > z = 0.4920	Pr > z = 0.5262	Pr > z = 0.5343	Pr > z = 0.5011	Pr > z = 0.4886	Pr > z = 0.5333	Pr > z = 0.5252	Pr > z = 0.4877	Pr > z = 0.4958

Note: GDP = gross domestic product, GMM = generalized method of moments. *, **, and *** correspond to 10, 5, and 1 percent significance levels, respectively, computed with heteroskedasticity adjusted standard errors. Trade, sectors, government, and spatial variables entered the instrument matrix as strictly exogenous. Time-fixed effects are included.

to an alternative estimator. The results are displayed in table 2.6. Standard errors have been derived by setting the number of bootstrap repetitions to 200.

Table 2.6 reveals that the size and sign of the coefficients of interest remain similar to those presented in table 2.5. The speed of adjustment parameter slightly decreases to below 0.25 as indicated by the higher coefficient of the lagged level of regional inequality. However, none of the previously found significance levels is confirmed. This makes it difficult to draw any firm conclusions on the dynamic adjustment process between openness and regional inequality from our data. Beyond the highly significant static associations that we found, the data do not support any robust partial relationship in the dynamic setting that introduces short-term and long-term effects.

Conclusions

The aim of this chapter has been to improve our understanding of the relationship between changes in trade patterns linked to global market integration, on the one hand, and within-country spatial inequalities, on the other, from both a theoretical and an empirical perspective. This is particularly relevant given the recent emphasis of the WDR 2009 that increases in trade may lead to greater growth at the expense of increases in territorial disparities, but that this is a temporary condition as greater development would eventually weaken within-country spatial inequality.

The chapter is based on a model that combines regional spatial characteristics with a series of country features. The spatial characteristics include the degree of interregional variation in access to foreign markets and whether these differences in foreign markets coincide with differences in income. The conditioning country features include the degree of interregional sector variation, the level of government expenditure, the degree of labor mobility, and institutions. Lack of data on the two latter categories allows testing for the former two conditions only. In the theoretical tradition of Williamson (1965) and in order to test whether development weakens spatial inequalities, the chapter also controls for the internal growth effect and its interaction with the country's development stage. The influence of these variables on the evolution of within-country regional inequality is then tested using both static fixed effects and dynamic panels.

The results show that trade—when considered in combination with country-specific factors—matters for the evolution of regional inequalities. There is a weak association between both factors in static panel analyses, which improves significantly as the conditioning variables are included in the analysis. This implies that, while changes in trade make a difference for the evolution of spatial disparities, the impact of changes in trade is more polarizing in countries with higher interregional sector differences, lower shares of government expenditure, and a combination of higher internal transaction costs with higher

Table 2.6 Dynamic Panel with Bias-Corrected LSDV (Arellano-Bond as Initiating Estimator)

	1	2	3	4	5	6	7	8	9	10
Lagged inequality	0.7695***	0.7732***	0.7625***	0.7562***	0.7717***	0.7712***	0.7658***	0.7637***	0.7688***	0.7601***
GDPcap	-0.0042542	-0.0114254	-0.0057356	0.0018603	-0.0016792	-0.0032934	-0.0006512	0.0003451	-0.010194	-0.0076126
GDPcap*Development	0.0447277	0.0553157	0.0543923	0.0366075	0.0393897	0.0413365	0.0422675	0.0414348	0.0539687	0.0507196
Trade	0.0072552	0.0171614	-0.0514281	0.1724832	-0.1523919	-0.094782	0.0582092	0.1016657	0.0197978	0.3415041
Trade*Development		-0.0231123								-0.0508706
Trade*Government			-0.030624							0.0416388
Trade*Sectors				0.0488378						0.0697132
Trade*Coincidence50*MAPolarisation					-0.0674853					
Trade*Coincidence25*MAPolarisation						0.1046937				
Trade*Coincidence50*Surface							-0.0081276			
Trade*Coincidence25*surface								0.0143537		
Trade*Coincidence25*DevDum									0.5699036	0.5615131
Observations	379	379	379	379	379	379	379	379	379	379

Note: GDP = gross domestic product. *, **, and *** correspond to 10, 5, and 1 percent significance levels, respectively, computed with 200 bootstrap repetitions. Trade, sectors, government, and spatial variables entered the instrument matrix as strictly exogenous. Time-fixed effects are included.

degrees of coincidence between wealthier regions and foreign market access. However, the spatial country variables cease to be significant once controlling for lagged levels of inequality in dynamic panels, meaning that no firm conclusions can be extracted regarding the dynamic timeframe of spatial adjustments and the distinction between short-term and long-term effects of trade openness.

The key result is that changes in trade patterns seem to affect the evolution of regional inequality in developing countries to a much greater extent than in developed ones. The spatially polarizing effect of trade also decreases at a significantly slower pace in developing countries than in developed ones. And trade, in contrast to what was suggested by Williamson (1965), seems to have a greater sway on the evolution of regional inequality than economic growth. This means that economic growth—whether directly provoked by changes in trade or not—cannot offset the potentially negative effects for territorial equality of increases in trade in the developing world.

By and large, countries in the developing world are characterized by a series of features that are likely to potentiate the spatially polarizing effects of greater openness to trade. Their higher existing levels of regional inequality, their greater degree of sector polarization, the fact that their wealthier regions often coincide with the key entry points to trade, and their weaker state all contribute to exacerbate regional disparities as trade with the external world increases. And countries in the developing world have a much greater scope for increases in spatial polarization, as their level of international market integration, while growing rapidly, is still a fraction of that of developed countries.

Policy makers may thus need to tread carefully when thinking about the potential implications of greater market openness for their countries. While greater openness to trade is likely to yield rewards in terms of growth and the absolute welfare of a country's citizens, it may also bring the unwelcome consequence of greater territorial polarization. As pointed out in the WDR 2009, this dynamic may not necessarily be bad in the short term. However, increasing territorial inequality can be destabilizing in countries with already high levels of spatial polarization and where territorial differences may pile on top of preexisting social, cultural, ethnic, and/or religious grievances. More spatial inequality could ultimately undermine the very economic benefits that trade is supposed to bring about. Hence, it is convenient to bring the territorial implications of trade into the trade policy equation. This may suggest trade policies aimed at promoting growth broadly, rather than just focused on generating greater agglomeration, as these can have unintended effects that may ultimately limit their influence on development. A return to "spatially balanced" growth policies is not advisable, but many growth policies based on trade may benefit from including a "spatially sensitive" dimension, if the potential economic benefits of greater openness to trade for countries in the developing world are to be maximized.

Annex 2A Structural Conditions and Data

Table 2A.1 Structural Conditions by Country

Country	DevDum	DevDumHigh	DevDumMid	DevDumLow	Government	Sectors	MAPol	Coin25	Coin50
Australia	0	1	0	0	0.16	0.02	145.09	1.00	1.05
Austria	0	1	0	0	0.18	0.02	83.72	1.06	1.07
Belgium	0	1	0	0	0.20	0.01	87.77	0.95	1.10
Brazil	1	0	1	0	0.17	0.07	182.44	0.59	0.65
Bulgaria	1	0	0	1	0.14	0.06	98.83	1.15	1.12
Canada	0	1	0	0	0.20	0.03	174.58	1.00	0.91
China	1	0	0	1	0.13	0.07	182.86	1.73	1.32
Czech Republic	1	0	1	0	0.20	0.03	95.42	0.88	1.15
Finland	0	1	0	0	0.21	0.02	96.04	1.18	1.13
France	0	1	0	0	0.20	0.02	57.36	0.97	0.99
Greece	0	0	1	0	0.11	0.06	90.30	0.93	1.00
Hungary	1	0	1	0	0.09	0.04	93.96	1.10	0.76
India	1	0	0	1	0.09	0.11	118.73	1.17	0.97
Indonesia	1	0	0	1	0.06	0.11	116.06	1.18	1.29
Italy	0	1	0	0	0.17	0.02	87.69	1.25	1.22
Japan	0	1	0	0	0.15	0.02	74.53	1.02	1.03
Mexico	1	0	1	0	0.10	0.05	117.73	1.41	1.04
Netherlands	0	1	0	0	0.21	0.02	91.47	1.07	1.00
Poland	1	0	1	0	0.18	0.04	88.10	1.06	1.01
Portugal	0	1	0	0	0.16	0.07	96.02	1.41	1.13
Romania	1	0	0	1	0.08	0.07	97.60	0.97	0.95
Slovak Republic	1	0	1	0	0.19	0.02	96.40	1.85	1.33
South Africa	1	0	1	0	0.17	0.02	104.42	1.03	1.00
Spain	0	1	0	0	0.16	0.03	84.48	1.02	1.07
Sweden	0	1	0	0	0.25	0.02	83.10	0.97	0.95
Thailand	1	0	0	1	0.08	0.13	104.80	1.92	1.46
United Kingdom	0	1	0	0	0.17	0.03	83.34	1.10	1.05
United States	0	1	0	0	0.12	0.02	96.43	1.05	0.98

Table 2A.2 Variables and Sources of Data

Variable	Source of data
Inequality	National statistical offices, and Eurostat Regio database
GDPcap	Word Development Indicators
Development	Historical Series of World Bank Classifications
High income	Historical Series of World Bank Classifications
Middle income	Historical Series of World Bank Classifications
Low income	Historical Series of World Bank Classifications
Trade	UN Comtrade and World Development Indicators
Government	World Development Indicators
Coincidence	UN Comtrade, World Port Database, own calculations

Note: GDP = gross domestic product, UN = United Nations.

Notes

1. Brülhart (2009) limits the number of cross-country analyses to 11, virtually all using urban primacy data, rather than regional data (see, for example, Ades and Glaeser 1995; Brülhart and Sbergami 2008; Nitsch 2006).

2. The analysis of the evolution of regional disparities requires good subnational data series, which imply a degree of sophistication by national statistical offices. Thus, using the most recent World Bank classification, no country included in the sample can be considered as low income, *sensu stricto*, while only China, India, Indonesia, and Thailand are classified as lower-middle-income countries.

3. Austria, Belgium, Denmark, Finland, France, Germany, Greece, Ireland, Italy, Luxembourg, the Netherlands, Portugal, Spain, Sweden, and the United Kingdom.

4. It is often the case that overall stability trends during the period of analysis hide significant variations in the evolution of regional inequality. Two such cases are Canada and China. In both countries, albeit for very different reasons, regional disparities decreased during the 1980s, but have tended to grow—and in the case of China, particularly rapidly—since the early 1990s.

5. Ideally, we could have used a finer sectoral disaggregation in order to capture in a more precise way the variation of modern sector endowments between domestic regions, perhaps including the subsectors of the service sector for the developed world. But given the diversity of countries included in the panel, the share of agriculture in regional GDPs over time was the best comparable indicator available.

References

Ades, A. F., and E. L. Glaeser. 1995. "Trade and Circuses: Explaining Urban Giants." *Quarterly Journal of Economics* 110 (1): 195–227.

Adkisson, R., and L. Zimmerman. 2004. "Retail Trade on the U.S.-Mexico Border during the NAFTA Implementation Era." *Growth and Change* 35 (1): 77–89.

Alderson, A., and F. Nielsen. 2002. "Globalisation and the Great U-Turn: Income Inequality Trends in 16 OECD Countries." *American Journal of Sociology* 107: 1244–99.

Arellano, M., and S. Bond. 1991. "Some Tests of Specification for Panel Data: Monte Carlo Evidence and an Application to Employment Equations." *Review of Economic Studies* 58: 277–97.

Arellano, M., and O. Bover. 1995. "Another Look at the Instrumental-Variable Estimation of Error-Components Models." *Journal of Econometrics* 68: 29–52.

Barrios, S., and E. Strobl. 2009. "The Dynamics of Regional Inequalities." *Regional Science and Urban Economics* 39 (5): 575–91.

Blundell, R., and S. Bond. 1998. "Initial Conditions and Moment Restrictions in Dynamic Panel Data Models." *Journal of Econometrics* 87: 115–43.

Brown, T. M. 1952. "Habit, Persistence and Lags in Consumer Behaviour." *Econometrica* 20 (3): 355–71.

Brülhart, M. 2009. "The Spatial Effects of Trade Openness: A Survey." Unpublished paper, University of Lausanne, Switzerland.

Brülhart, M., M. Crozet, and P. Koenig. 2004. "Enlargement and the EU Periphery: The Impact of Changing Market Potential." *World Economy* 27 (6): 853–75.

Brülhart, M., and F. Sbergami. 2008. "Agglomeration and Growth: Empirical Evidence." *Journal of Urban Economics* 65 (1): 48–63.

Bruno, G. S. F. 2005. "Approximating the Bias of the LSDV Estimator for Dynamic Unbalanced Panel Data Models." *Economics Letters* 87: 361–66.

Bun, M. J. G., and J. F. Kiviet. 2003. "On the Diminishing Returns of Higher Order Terms in Asymptotic Expansions of Bias." *Economics Letters* 79: 145–52.

Crozet, M., and P. Koenig-Soubeyran. 2004. "EU Enlargement and the Internal Geography of Countries." *Journal of Comparative Economics* 32 (2): 265–78.

Faber, B. 2007. "Towards the Spatial Patterns of Sectoral Adjustments to Trade Liberalisation: The Case of NAFTA in Mexico." *Growth and Change* 38 (4): 567–94.

Farole, T., A. Rodríguez-Pose, and M. Storper. 2009. "Cohesion Policy in the European Union: Growth, Geography, Institutions." Background paper for the Barca Report, An Agenda for a Reformed Cohesion Policy, DG Regio, Brussles.

Ford, T. C., B. Logan, and J. Logan. 2009. "NAFTA or Nada? Trade's Impact on U.S. Border Retailers." *Growth and Change* 40 (2): 260–86.

Jian, T., J. Sachs, and A. Warner. 1996. "Trends in Regional Inequality in China." NBER Working Paper 5412, National Bureau of Economic Research, Cambridge, MA.

Jordaan, J. A. 2008a. "Intra- and Inter-Industry Externalities from Foreign Direct Investment in the Mexican Manufacturing Sector: New Evidence from Mexican Regions." *World Development* 36 (12): 2838–54.

———. 2008b. "Regional Foreign Participation and Externalities: New Empirical Evidence from Mexican Regions." *Environment and Planning A* 40 (12): 2948–69.

Kanbur, R., and A. J. Venables, eds. 2005. *Spatial Inequality and Development*. Oxford, U.K.: Oxford University Press.

Kanbur, R. and X. Zhang. 2005. "Fifty Years of Regional Inequality in China: A Journey through Central Planning, Reform and Openness." *Review of Development Economics* 9 (1): 87–106.

Kiviet, J. F. 1995. "On Bias, Inconsistency, and Efficiency of Various Estimators in Dynamic Panel Data Models." *Journal of Econometrics* 68: 53–78.

Krugman, P., and R. Livas-Elizondo. 1996. "Trade Policy and the Third World Metropolis." *Journal of Development Economics* 49 (1): 137–50.

Milanovic, B. 2005. *Worlds Apart: Measuring International and Global Inequality*. Princeton, NJ: Princeton University Press.

Monfort, P., and R. Nicolini. 2000. "Regional Convergence and International Integration." *Journal of Urban Economics* 48 (2): 286–306.

Niebuhr, A. 2006. "Market Access and Regional Disparities. New Economic Geography in Europe." *Annals of Regional Science* 40: 313–34.

Nitsch, V. 2006. "Trade Openness and Urban Concentration: New Evidence." *Journal of Economic Integration* 21: 340–62.

Paluzie, E. 2001. "Trade Policies and Regional Inequalities." *Chapters in Regional Science* 80 (1): 67–85.

Petrakos, G., A. Rodríguez-Pose, and A. Rovolis. 2005. "Growth, Integration, and Regional Disparities in the European Union." *Environment and Planning A* 37 (10): 1837–55.

Puga, D. 1999. "The Rise and Fall of Regional Inequalities." *European Economic Review* 43: 303–34.

Ravallion, M. 2001. "Growth, Inequality and Poverty: Looking Beyond Averages." *World Development* 29 (11): 1803–15.

Rodríguez-Pose, A., and N. Gill. 2006. "How Does Trade Affect Regional Disparities?" *World Development* 34: 1201–22.

Rodríguez-Pose, A., and J. Sánchez-Reaza. 2005. "Economic Polarization through Trade: Trade Liberalization and Regional Growth in Mexico." In *Spatial Inequality and Development*, edited by R. Kanbur and A. J. Venables. Oxford, U.K.: Oxford University Press.

Roodman, D. 2006. "How to Do xtabond2: An Introduction to 'Difference' and 'System' GMM in Stata." Working Paper 103, Center for Global Development, Washington, DC.

Sachs, J. D., and A. M. Warner. 1995. "Economic Reform and the Process of Global Integration." *Brookings Chapters on Economic Activity*, 26 (1): 1–118.

Sánchez-Reaza, J., and A. Rodríguez-Pose. 2002. "The Impact of Trade Liberalization on Regional Disparities in Mexico." *Growth and Change* 33: 72–90.

Williamson, J. G. 1965. "Regional Inequality and the Process of National Development: A Description of the Patterns." *Economic Development and Cultural Change* 13 (4): 3–45.

———. 2005. "Winners and Losers over Two Centuries of Globalization." In *Wider Perspectives on Global Development*, 136–74. Hampshire, U.K.: Palgrave Macmillan.

Wood, A. 1994. *North-South Trade, Employment, and Inequality: Changing Fortunes in a Skill-Driven World*. Oxford, U.K.: Clarendon Press.

World Bank. 2009. *World Development Report 2009: Reshaping Economic Geography*. Washington, DC: World Bank.

Yang, D. T. 2002. "What Has Caused Regional Inequality in China?" *China Economic Review* 13: 331–4.

Zhang, X., and K. H. Zhang. 2003. "How Does Globalisation Affect Regional Inequality within a Developing Country? Evidence from China." *Journal of Development Studies* 39: 47–67.

How Does Location Determine a Firm's Prospects for Trade Integration?

Introduction

Part 2 represents the heart of this book. Having established in part 1 that trade may contribute to widening regional inequalities in developing countries, mediated through a number of structural and policy features, part 2 of the book explores the mechanics through which this may happen. Specifically, part 2 attempts to trace the relationship between firm location within a country and trade participation. It takes a firm-level approach to this analysis, analyzing how location-specific determinants shape the competitiveness of individual firms in export markets. Chapter 3 makes use of a unique dataset of firms across 126 countries to analyze the determinants of firm export competitiveness, including factors that are firm specific and those that are location specific (including geography, agglomeration, and the regional investment climate). Chapters 4 and 5 explore the case of Indonesia, starting with a descriptive analysis of the relationship between trade, regional characteristics, and regional outcomes in chapter 4, and following up with an econometric exercise (broadly in line with the approach taken in chapter 3) in chapter 5. Finally, chapters 6 and 7 carry out the same exercise in India.

Methodological Note

The econometric analysis presented in chapters 3, 5, and 7 is focused on linking observed export outcomes (firm-level export participation and export intensity) to a set of explanatory factors that are firm- and location-specific. The presumed causality of the exercise is, of course, that these firm and location factors determine export outcomes. In this context, it is important to bear in mind two potential limitations of the empirical analysis.

First, the analysis assumes implicitly that firms are not mobile across regions—they emerge, grow, and export (or not) within the same region throughout their life. In practice, firms, like workers, may move across regions. And, indeed, they may do so systematically—it is possible that exporting firms move into locations that are the best fit for them based on local endowments, which results in a spatial sorting of industries. This could lead to cases of reverse causality where regional characteristics do not influence exporting behavior, but where exporters instead self-select into certain locations. Due to data limitations (most regional data were not available on a time-series basis), only one of the three empirical studies is able to include lagged regional variables, which to some extent addresses the concern of potential endogeneity related to reverse causality.

Second, it may be possible that regional variables are correlated with unobserved regional endowments. Although we believe that our regional variables already cover important time-varying regional characteristics including agglomerations, the investment climate, and institutions, such unobserved effects would be picked up by the error term and could lead to an omitted variable bias, influencing the coefficient size and possibly sign of some independent variables. Adding regional fixed effects could at least control for unobserved regional effects that are constant over time. However, adding regional dummies in most cases did not yield significant results for the regional variables, as such dummies seem to have a higher explanatory power than other regional characteristics. Our econometric results should therefore be interpreted with some caution.

CHAPTER 3

Firm Location and the Determinants of Exporting in Developing Countries

Thomas Farole and Deborah Winkler

Theoretical Background

Introduction

This chapter addresses the following three research questions: (1) Are there significant differences in export participation and performance, and in the firm capabilities and the perceived investment climate, for exporting in core versus noncore regions? (2) What is the effect of firm characteristics versus regional determinants—including the investment climate and agglomeration economies—on exporting behavior? (3) Do the determinants of exporting have a differential effect if firms are located in core versus noncore regions? To answer these questions, the analysis combines two strands of literature that have been particularly vibrant in recent years, namely on spatial agglomeration and on the firm-level determinants of exporting.

Firm-Level and Regional Determinants of Exporting

There has been a growing body of trade literature on the determinants of exporting at the firm level. Econometrically, exporting in such studies is modeled as a dummy variable equal to one if there is some exporting and zero otherwise. At the latest, since the seminal chapter by Bernard and Jensen (1995), researchers have recognized that exporters outperform nonexporters in the same sector and country in terms of skills, wages, productivity, technology, and capital intensity (see literature review in Wagner 2007). Consequently, researchers started to ask whether exporters perform better because of self-selection into the exporting market and because of learning-by-exporting. Self-selection refers to ex ante differences across firms, while learning-by-exporting refers to ex post gains of exporters versus nonexporters. Self-selection refers to the fact that exporting involves additional costs of exporting, including transportation, marketing, and distribution costs; hiring of employees with specific skills; and production costs for necessary adjustment that only more productive firms are able to absorb. Learning-by-exporting refers to knowledge flows that exporting firms absorb from international buyers and competitors, which renders them more productive (Wagner 2007).

Researchers in the field of international marketing have identified several internal and external determinants that increase the probability of exporting at the firm level. Zou and Stan (1998), for instance, review 50 studies on the determinants of export performance between 1987 and 1997. In a more recent paper, Sousa, Martínez-López, and Coelho (2008) review 52 studies in the international marketing literature between 1998 and 2005. Export market characteristics, domestic market characteristics, and industry characteristics were the most frequently examined external determinants. Internal determinants include controllable factors, such as export marketing strategy and management perception, and uncontrollable factors, such as management and firm characteristics.

Firm-level determinants of exporting in the international trade literature generally include firm size, firm age, productivity, ownership, worker skills, and sunk entry costs of exporting (see, for example, Aitken, Hanson, and Harrison 1997, Bernard and Jensen 1999, Clerides, Lach, and Tybout 1998, Greenaway and Kneller 2004, and Roberts and Tybout 1997). This strand of literature typically adds regional dummies along with industry dummies to the firm-level determinants of exporting, since location might account for most of the differences between exporters and nonexporters.

Although such regional dummies might indicate regional differences, they do not reveal which specific characteristics determine the propensity of exporting. From a policy perspective, identifying such regional determinants is very important, because regional characteristics (such as availability of skills, transport costs, infrastructure, or institutions) influence the costs of exporting and, thus, self-selection into exporting. Regional characteristics might also have an indirect effect on learning-by-exporting. The lower the regional skills level, the less likely it is that a firm will absorb knowledge flows from international buyers and competitors. Institutions might also influence absorption capabilities of firms across regions.

Several studies have examined regional determinants of firm-level foreign direct investment (FDI). (See, for example, Deichmann, Karidis, and Sayek 2003, for Turkey, and Amiti and Javorcik 2008, for China.) However, there are no international trade studies to our knowledge that explicitly integrate regional determinants of exporting. In this chapter, regional determinants do not refer to agglomeration economies, which we focus on in the next section. Even in the field of international marketing, only four out of 50 studies reviewed by Zou and Stan (1998) and only six out of 52 studies reviewed by Sousa, Martínez-López, and Coelho (2008) address domestic market characteristics, which are measured at the national rather than regional level. This chapter aims to contribute to regional research by incorporating regional determinants of exporting.

Agglomeration Economies and Exporting

Our study includes four measures of regional agglomeration economies: (1) a region's number of firms as percentage of a country's total number of firms (urbanization effects); (2) the Herfindahl-Hirschman index (HHI)[1] by region, defined as the sum of squares of an industry's output share (sector diversity); (3) a region's number of firms within the same industry as a percentage of a country's total number of firms within the same industry (localization effects); and (4) a region's number of exporters[2] as a percentage of the region's total number of firms (export spillovers).

Agglomeration economies can have a particularly favorable influence on a firm's propensity to export as they can reduce the sunk entry costs of exporting (Aitken, Hanson, and Harrison 1997). Agglomeration economies can lower (1) production costs through sharing of resources, mainly social and physical infrastructure, and (2) transportation and transaction costs through increased interaction between suppliers and customers on site (Malmberg, Malmberg, and Lundequist 2000). Hence, an agglomeration can increase the probability of self-selection into exporting.

On the other hand, agglomerations may be characterized by congestion costs (Krugman 1991), which can increase (1) production costs through the sharing of resources (leading, for example, to power outages), and (2) transportation and transaction costs through increased waiting times (for example, for intermediate inputs or licenses). These effects can counterbalance the gains from agglomerations as described previously. The net effect may therefore be ambiguous.

Studies in the field of international marketing have long acknowledged the role of agglomeration economies on exporting, and international trade studies have followed to recognize their importance. Malmberg, Malmberg, and Lundequist (2000) analyze the impact of localization and urbanization economies on export performance for Swedish firms in 1994. The authors find that traditional-scale economies combined with urbanization economies have a much larger positive effect on export performance than localization economies. Mittelstaedt, Ward, and Nowlin (2006) confirm that urbanization and localization economies increase the probability of exporting for small manufacturing firms in the southeastern United States. In a recent study, Antonietti and Cainelli (2009) show a positive effect of local knowledge spillovers on export propensity and export share for Italian manufacturing firms between 1998 and 2003, using several measures of urbanization and localization economies.

Other studies have focused on the role of export spillovers for the likelihood of exporting. Aitken, Hanson, and Harrison (1997) find that while the presence of multinational firms in a region was beneficial for a Mexican firm's export decision between 1986 and 1990, the proximity to other exporters in a region was not. Bernard and Jensen (2004) find that the presence of exporters (outside a firm's industry) and the presence of exporters within the same industry (outside a firm's region) had no impact on U.S. manufacturing firms' exporting behavior between 1984 and 1992. Surprisingly, the number of exporters within the same region and industry show a negative effect on a firm's entry into exporting.

While the studies mentioned previously reject the existence of positive export spillovers, other studies find evidence for a positive impact of export spillovers on exporting. Lovely, Rosenthal, and Sharma (2005) focus on the perspective of U.S. firms' headquarters in 2000. The authors find that the spatial concentration of headquarter activity of exporters relative to that of nonexporters at different regional levels rises with the industry share of exports to countries with a diffi-cult trading environment. The explanation is that exporting requires specialized knowledge of foreign markets, which contributes to a spatial concentration among exporters. Greenaway and Kneller (2008) find that for a sample of manu-facturing firms in the United Kingdom between 1988 and 2002, the presence of exporters in the same region or industry was favorable for exporting. Koenig (2009) also confirms that a higher share of local exporters exporting to the same destination increased the probability of exporting for French manufacturers between 1986 and 1992, but this effect was destination-specific. Koenig, Mayneris, and Poncet (2010) show evidence that the presence of local product- and/or destination-specific exporters encouraged the probability of exporting for French manufacturers between 1998 and 2003. However, the authors do not find export spillovers on the firms' export volume.

The Role of Firm Location for the Determinants of Exporting

So far, our focus has been on how location characteristics (such as regional determinants and agglomeration economies) can influence export performance. Another important question is how firm location influences the determinants of exporting. In the second part of this chapter, we apply regression analysis to evalu-ate whether firm-level and regional determinants of exporting and agglomeration economies have a differential effect if firms are located in core versus noncore regions of a country. We use a cross-section of more than 35,000 manufacturing and services firms in 77 developing countries. We hypothesize that traditional firm-level characteristics matter less for firms located in core regions, since a firm's business environment will explain a larger share of a firm's export behavior.

The remainder of this chapter is structured as follows. In the next section, we compare firms located in the core with firms located in noncore regions to detect significant differences in export performance. We also analyze other performance indicators related to a firm's business and business environment. In the third section, we perform an econometric exercise where we first study the impact of firm-level and regional determinants as well as agglomeration economies on exporting. We then examine the role of location, assessing whether the determinants of exporting are different for firms located in core versus noncore regions. Based on the results of the empirical analysis, we derive some policy conclusions in the last section.

Descriptive Analysis: Core versus Noncore Regions

Data

The World Bank Enterprise Analysis Unit recently published the Enterprise Surveys Indicator Database.[3] This publication covers 215 enterprise surveys for 126 countries from 2002 to 2010. Enterprise surveys represent a comprehensive source of firm-level data in emerging markets and developing economies. One major advantage of the enterprise surveys is that the survey questions are the same across all countries. Moreover, the Enterprise Surveys represent a random sample of firms using three levels of stratification: sector, firm size, and region.

The Enterprise Surveys Indicator Database covers a wide range of indicators—on firm characteristics, business environment, innovation and technology, workforce and skills, permits and licenses, infrastructure, finance, and corruption, among others. In making use of this dataset, we apply the following rules: (1) we include only the most recent Enterprise Surveys for each country into the analysis; (2) we drop high-income countries to cover only emerging or developing countries[4]; and (3) in order to be able to detect differences between a country's core and its noncore regions, we consider countries with at least three regions.[5]

As a next step, we had to determine which regions to consider as core regions. We define these as follows:

- We determine a region's relative size, defined as the number of firms in a region divided by the total number of firms in the country. This exercise is representative for each country, since Enterprise Surveys represent a stratified random sample with regard to regions. Note that this procedure includes both manufacturing and services firms. We set the core dummy CORE = 1 for the region with the largest relative size.
- In some cases, the Enterprise Surveys defined regions around the country's capital very narrowly, resulting in a relatively small relative size of such regions. In such cases, we bypass the first rule and define these as core regions.

We set CORE = 0 for all other regions. The procedure above results in 77 countries covering 430 regions, 87 of which are core regions. One downside of the database is that the definition of regions is not harmonized across countries. The list of countries, year of most recent survey, number of regions by country as well as the number of firms (total and for manufacturing and services firms separately) can be found in table 3A.1. Table 3A.2 shows the names of the core regions for each of these countries.

Manufacturing Firms

In a next step, we calculate weighted averages of selected indicators per firm in the core and compare these averages with noncore regions. We use sampling weights as provided by the Enterprise Survey Indicator Database. We also perform a t-test for the null hypothesis that there is no significant difference between the core and noncore regions for a given indicator.[6] We do this separately for manufacturing and services firms. Our analysis covers 29,451 manufacturing firms, which represent almost 84 percent of the overall sample (table 3A.3). The sectoral distribution in table 3A.3 shows that food, garments, and metals and machinery alone make up 40 percent of all manufacturing firms. On average, around 45 percent of all manufacturing firms are located in core regions as defined above. However, the extent of concentration in the core varies across the sectors. For example, over 56 percent of firms in the leather sector are located in core regions, but only 30 percent of firms in the wood and furniture sector are in the core.

Table 3.1 summarizes the indicators for manufacturing firms. Regarding firm characteristics, manufacturing firms in the core are on average three years

Table 3.1 Manufacturing Firms in Core versus Noncore Regions

Firm characteristics	Core	Noncore	p-value[a]	Core/noncore
Export and trade outcomes				
Direct exports (% of sales)	5.0	4.6	0.374	1.09
% of firms that export directly	18.1	13.1	0.058**	1.38
% of firms that use material inputs and/or supplies of foreign origin	44.5	34.3	0.010***	1.30
Firm characteristics				
Age and ownership				
Average age (years)	20.6	17.7	0.003***	1.17
Private domestic ownership (%)	90.9	89.0	0.467	1.02
Private foreign ownership (%)	8.0	3.3	0.047*	2.46
Technology				
% of firms with internationally recognized quality certification	24.0	17.1	0.047*	1.41
% of firms using technology licensed from foreign companies	13.2	8.9	0.127	1.48
% of firms using their own website	55.5	36.4	0.000***	1.52
% of firms using email to communicate with clients/suppliers	73.0	56.6	0.000***	1.29
Workforce				
% of firms offering formal training	37.5	32.0	0.170	1.17
Average number of seasonal/temporary, full-time employees	5.4	4.5	0.226	1.19
Average number of permanent, full-time employees	96.6	66.8	0.117	1.45
Average share of skilled production workers (% of production workers)	66.0	74.2	0.004***	0.89
Average experience of the top manager working in the firm's sector (years)	19.9	17.8	0.037**	1.11
% of firms identifying labor regulations as a major constraint	33.0	19.1	0.001***	1.72
% of firms identifying labor skill level as a major constraint	39.0	27.6	0.002***	1.41
Investment climate				
Infrastructure				
Number of power outages in a typical month	10.3	6.8	0.001***	1.51
Duration of power outages (hours)	3.7	3.0	0.157	1.25
Value lost due to power outages (% of sales)	4.3	3.2	0.014**	1.34
Delay in obtaining an electrical connection (days)	37.8	26.6	0.338	1.42
Average electricity from a generator (%)	2.7	1.6	0.001***	1.70
Average number of incidents of water insufficiency in a typical month	7.2	6.0	0.362	1.20
Delay in obtaining a water connection (days)	20.0	19.0	0.897	1.05
Delay in obtaining a mainline telephone connection (days)	13.2	12.1	0.652	1.09
Transport and trade facilitation				
Average time to clear direct exports through customs (days)	9.1	8.0	0.573	1.14
Average time to clear imports from customs (days)	13.6	10.4	0.137	1.31
Average time of inventory of most important input (days)	27.2	21.2	0.031**	1.28
% of firms identifying customs & trade regulations as a major constraint	18.8	11.6	0.045**	1.63
% of firms identifying transportation as a major constraint	19.7	19.8	0.981	1.00
Regulations and tax				
Senior management time spent in dealing with requirements of government regulation (%)	14.3	7.5	0.000***	1.91
Average number of visits or required meetings with tax officials	1.3	1.0	0.011**	1.29

table continues next page

Table 3.1 Manufacturing Firms in Core versus Noncore Regions *(continued)*

Firm characteristics	Core	Noncore	p-value[a]	Core/noncore
% of firms identifying tax rates as major constraint	49.2	40.3	0.024**	1.22
% of firms identifying tax administration as major constraint	42.1	29.7	0.003***	1.42
Permits and licenses				
Average time to obtain operating license (days)	55.3	50.3	0.693	1.10
Average time to obtain import license (days)	40.8	28.1	0.341	1.45
Average time to obtain construction-related permit (days)	145.7	61.3	0.112	2.38
% of firms identifying business licensing and permits as major constraint	30.7	20.1	0.016**	1.53
Corruption				
% of firms expected to pay informal payment to public officials	24.8	13.3	0.000***	1.87
% of firms expected to give gifts to get an operating license	18.2	8.5	0.007***	2.13
% of firms expected to give gifts in meetings with tax officials	20.9	11.6	0.042**	1.81
% of firms expected to give gifts to secure a government contract	19.4	17.3	0.710	1.12
% of firms identifying corruption as a major constraint	47.4	38.7	0.029**	1.22
Access to finance				
Finance from internal sources (%)	58.6	55.7	0.593	1.05
Finance from banks (%)	25.1	27.1	0.702	0.93
Finance from trade credit (%)	11.1	9.1	0.63	1.21
% of firms with line of credit or loans from financial institutions	47.5	40.4	0.066**	1.17
% of firms using banks to finance investments	36.7	40.7	0.487	0.90
% of firms using banks to finance expenses	42.5	32.1	0.020**	1.32
% of firms identifying access to finance as a major constraint	42.5	26.4	0.000***	1.61

Source: Calculations from Enterprise Survey Indicators, World Bank.

a. *t*-test of difference in means.

$*p < 0.1, **p < 0.05, ***p < 0.01$

older and have an average foreign ownership share of 8 percent, which is more than twice as high as their incumbents in noncore regions. Although there seems to be no significant difference between the average export shares of core and noncore regions, the percentage of manufacturing firms that export is 38 percent higher in the core. This finding is important as it suggests that the difference lies in export participation, but once the threshold of export participation is reached, there is no difference in export intensity. Other trade-related indicators show that on average, firms in the core are more strongly involved in offshoring (that is, use material inputs and/or supplies of foreign origin) and more often identify customs and trade regulations as a major constraint, but this is more likely a function of them being exporters than of their location.

Regarding technology, the percentage of manufacturing firms with internationally recognized quality certification, that use their own website, and that use email to communicate with clients and/or suppliers is between 29 and 52 percent higher in the core. In terms of workforce, the average share of skilled production workers in total production workers is unexpectedly smaller in the core, while managers have on average two years more of sector experience. More than a third of all manufacturing firms in the core identify labor regulations and labor skill levels as a major constraint, compared to a fifth and a quarter in noncore regions, respectively.

One of the biggest surprises is that almost across the board, firms in the core perceive a worse business climate than those in noncore regions. Infrastructure-related indicators reveal the existence of congestion costs in agglomerations, especially with regard to electricity. The number of power outages, value lost due to the latter, and the average electricity from a generator are all higher in the core compared to noncore regions.

The percentage of manufacturing firms in the core identifying business licensing and permits as major constraints is 53 percent higher. On average, senior management has to spend more time dealing with requirements of government regulation and the average number of visits or required meetings with tax officials is also higher. The percentage of manufacturing firms identifying taxes and tax administration as a major constraint is more than 20 and 40 percent higher in the core, respectively. There is also a stronger perception of corruption in the core, measured as the percentage of manufacturing firms expected to pay informal payments or gifts to public officials or tax officials and to give gifts to obtain an operating license. All these indicators are about twice as high as in noncore regions. Regarding finance, the percentage of manufacturing firms in the core with a line of credit or loans in the core is 17 percent higher. In addition, the share of manufacturing firms using banks to finance expenses is more than 30 percent higher. Nevertheless, the perception of manufacturing firms regarding access to finance is more pessimistic in the core.

Services Firms

The analysis of services covers 5,790 firms, which represent 16 percent of the overall sample (see table 3A.3). We dropped retail or wholesale trade firms and hotels and restaurants as these do not represent typical firms for which cross-border trade would be significant. Around 60 percent of the remaining services firms focus on business services including information technology (IT) services, telecommunications, accounting & finance, advertising & marketing, and other business services. Another third of the firms is in construction or transportation. On average, almost 52 percent of services firms are located in the core. Table 3.2 shows the indicators for services firms. Fewer indicators show a statistically significant difference between core and noncore regions than is the case with manufacturing firms, which might be due to the low number of observations for some indicators.

Regarding firm characteristics, services firms in the core have a higher share of exports in sales than services firms in noncore regions, which is statistically insignificant. Export participation also does not show a significant difference. Contrary to the findings in manufacturing, this implies that differences in both export participation and export intensity are more difficult to achieve for services firms in the core. Other trade-related indicators show that the average

Table 3.2 Services Firms in Core versus Noncore Regions

	Core	Noncore	p-value[a]	Core/noncore
Export and trade outcomes				
Direct exports (% of sales)	4.9	3.5	0.224	1.41
% of firms that export directly	12.1	10.4	0.515	1.17
% of firms that use material inputs and/or supplies of foreign origin	6.5	25.1	0.468	0.26
Firm characteristics				
Age and ownership				
Average age (years)	14.6	14.5	0.974	1.00
Private domestic ownership (%)	93.3	93.0	0.901	1.00
Private foreign ownership (%)	5.7	4.7	0.591	1.21
Technology				
% of firms with internationally-recognized quality certification	14.5	16.8	0.560	0.86
% of firms using technology licensed from foreign companies	4.1	4.1	0.989	0.99
% of firms using their own website	52.3	55.6	0.639	0.94
% of firms using email to communicate with clients/suppliers	80.3	79.2	0.822	1.01
Workforce				
% of firms offering formal training	47.5	37.1	0.387	1.28
Average number of seasonal/temporary, full-time employees	4.7	5.8	0.596	0.82
Average number of permanent, full-time employees	71.9	45.1	0.091*	1.60
Average experience of the top manager working in the firm's sector (years)	16.8	15.9	0.436	1.06
% of firms identifying labor regulations as a major constraint	21.7	30.6	0.220	0.71
% of firms identifying labor skill level as a major constraint	35.0	54.0	0.006***	0.65
Investment climate				
Infrastructure				
Number of power outages in a typical month	6.4	4.0	0.019**	1.59
Duration of power outages (hours)	3.3	2.1	0.038**	1.58
Value lost due to power outages (% of sales)	4.4	5.4	0.430	0.81
Delay in obtaining an electrical connection (days)	80.9	24.9	0.114	3.24
Average electricity from a generator (%)	1.3	0.3	0.008***	5.12
Average number of incidents of water insufficiency in a typical month	4.4	4.9	0.716	0.90
Delay in obtaining a water connection (days)	43.9	14.7	0.099*	2.98
Delay in obtaining a mainline telephone connection (days)	15.1	13.2	0.563	1.14
Transport and trade facilitation				
Average time to clear direct exports through customs (days)	6.4	9.9	0.246	0.64
Average time to clear imports from customs (days)	11.2	18.7	0.170	0.60
Average time of inventory of most important input (days)	19.8	11.4	0.036**	1.73
% of firms identifying customs & trade regulations as a major constraint	15.1	19.7	0.412	0.77
% of firms identifying transportation as a major constraint	23.9	20.5	0.501	1.17
Regulations and tax				
Senior management time spent in dealing with requirements of government regulation (%)	12.3	13.6	0.315	0.90
Average number of visits or required meetings with tax officials	1.3	1.3	0.955	0.99
% of firms identifying tax rates as major constraint	38.9	56.5	0.011**	0.69
% of firms identifying tax administration as major constraint	28.6	45.8	0.020**	0.62

table continues next page

Table 3.2 Services Firms in Core versus Noncore Regions *(continued)*

	Core	Noncore	p-value[a]	Core/noncore
Permits and licenses				
Average time to obtain operating license (days)	43.2	42.7	0.969	1.01
Average time to obtain import license (days)	15.6	23.2	0.152	0.67
Average time to obtain construction-related permit (days)	93.6	71.7	0.341	1.31
% of firms identifying business licensing and permits as major constraint	19.0	30.8	0.079	0.62
Corruption				
% of firms expected to pay informal payment to public officials	20.6	19.4	0.786	1.06
% of firms expected to give gifts to get an operating license	16.6	13.8	0.616	1.20
% of firms expected to give gifts in meetings with tax officials	10.7	13.5	0.572	0.80
% of firms expected to give gifts to secure a government contract	14.6	20.4	0.488	0.71
% of firms identifying corruption as a major constraint	40.0	56.3	0.015**	0.71
Access to finance				
Finance from internal sources (%)	72.3	58.5	0.032**	1.24
Finance from banks (%)	13.9	22.9	0.075*	0.61
Finance from trade credit (%)	6.6	11.1	0.153	0.60
% of firms with line of credit or loans from financial institutions	42.7	41.3	0.828	1.04
% of firms using banks to finance investments	26.1	32.9	0.384	0.79
% of firms using banks to finance expenses	29.4	43.1	0.182	0.68
% of firms identifying access to finance as a major constraint	28.8	35.3	0.386	0.82

Source: Calculations from Enterprise Survey Indicators, World Bank.
a. *t*-test of difference in means.
*$p < 0.1$, **$p < 0.05$, ***$p < 0.01$

time of inventory of the most important input is more than 20 days in the core compared to 11 days in noncore regions. Although ownership variables show no significant difference, it is worth pointing out the generally lower FDI share of services versus manufacturing firms.

Unlike manufacturing firms, there seem to be no significant differences between core and noncore regions with regard to technology. Regarding the workforce, the average number of permanent full-time employees is 60 percent higher in core regions than noncore regions. The percentage of firms identifying labor skill levels as a major constraint is lower in the core for services firms.

Infrastructure-related indicators confirm the existence of congestion costs in agglomerations for services firms, especially with regard to electricity. The number and duration of power outages per month is higher in the core. Moreover, the time to obtain a water connection is three times higher for services firms in the core compared to firms in noncore regions. The same holds for the time to obtain electrical connection, which narrowly misses the 10 percent significance level. As a result, the percentage of electricity from a generator is more than four times higher for services in the core. Services firms show no significant locational differences with regard to permits.

Surprisingly, the percentage of firms identifying taxes and tax administration as well as corruption as a major constraint is lower in the core. Regarding finance, a higher percentage of firms in noncore regions uses finance from banks, while services firms in the core tend to depend more strongly on internal sources, which seems surprising.

Conclusions

Overall, as expected, we find that both manufacturing and services firms in the core have higher levels of export participation and higher shares of exported output than firms in noncore regions. For manufacturing firms, the differences in export participation are significant, while for services firms there are no significant differences with regard to export intensity and participation. Manufacturing firms in core regions also make significantly greater use of imported inputs, a factor that may contribute to their productivity and thus export participation.

We also find significant differences in the regional investment climate reported by firms operating in core versus noncore regions. In this respect, some of the findings were surprising. Results from both manufacturing and services firms indicate a generally poorer investment climate in the core, suggesting the possible existence of congestion costs. For firms in the manufacturing sector in particular, almost all aspects of the investment climate were identified as more problematic by firms located in the core, including reliability of electricity, customs and trade facilitation, regulatory burdens on management, business licensing, and corruption. On the other hand, the finding of greater access to finance (at least for manufacturing firms) and the potential of technology spillovers in the core may offset some of these congestion costs.

The results suggest there may be different dynamics affecting export performance for firms in the core and firms outside it. Moreover, the fact that export performance is generally better in the core, despite what is reported to be a worse investment climate, indicates that other factors, such as first-order geography and the potential benefits of agglomeration, may play an important role.

Econometric Analysis

In the following section, we examine the role of location for export participation using regression analysis. In particular, we study whether the determinants of exporting are different if firms are located in core versus noncore regions.[7]

Econometric Model

We follow the theoretical model of exporting of Roberts and Tybout (1997). A firm i's export propensity at time t depends on a firm's expected revenues R and costs c plus sunk entry costs of exporting, S:

$$\Pr(ex_{it} = 1) = \Pr(R_{it} > c_{it} + S(1 - ex_{it-1})) \tag{3.1}$$

where ex denotes an export dummy at the firm-level. Sunk entry costs of exporting, S, are 1 if a firm exported in period $t - 1$ and 0, otherwise. In other words, a firm exports if expected profits $\pi > 0$.

A firm's expected profits π are affected by firm-level characteristics, regional characteristics, and agglomeration economies, which can generate or lower revenues R and/or costs c. Equation 3.1 translates into:

$$\Pr(ex_{it}=1) = \Pr(\pi_{it} = \beta firm_{it} + \gamma reg_{rt} + \delta agg_{rt} + S(1 - ex_{it-1}) > 0) \qquad (3.2)$$

where subscript r designates regions, *firm* designates firm-level determinants of exporting, *reg* designates regional determinants of exporting, and *agg* designates agglomeration economies.

Sunk entry costs of exporting S might explain a large part of export activity. Since our data sample only covers the most recent Enterprise Surveys for each country, we cannot capture sunk entry costs of exports by adding lagged exports as an explanatory firm-level variable. We propose an alternative way to account for sunk entry costs of exporting. We make the following assumptions:

1. Exporters that haven't exported in the previous period (new exporters) export a share of their output that is below threshold ζ. Ruhl and Willis (2008) show that for a sample of Colombian manufacturing firms between 1982 and 1986, new firms export on average 3–4 percent of sales upon entry into the export market, and export intensity increases with every additional year exporters stay on the export market. Ma and Zhang (2008) show the distribution of export intensities for new Chinese manufacturing exporters between 1999 and 2005. In 2005, 58 percent of domestic new exporters reported an export intensity of between 0 and 10 percent, while this percentage was 36 percent for foreign new exporters. Although these percentages were somewhat lower in the preceding years, at least a third of domestic new exporters and at least a quarter of foreign new exporters export 10 percent or less in their first year. We assume that a similar distribution holds for our sample. Given that the average export intensity of all direct exporters in our sample is 48.3 percent, this reflects that old exporters usually export a larger share of their sales.

2. Firms that exported in the previous period and stop exporting now (exiting exporters) have an export intensity below threshold ζ. Using Colombian customs data from 1996 to 2005, Eaton et al. (2007) find that almost half of all exporters did not export in the previous year, but their contribution to export revenues is extremely small and most new exporters leave the export market in the following year. Although firms exiting the export market do not necessarily have to be new exporters, it is much more likely that firms with a smaller export intensity will stop exporting as opposed to firms with a high export share.

3. We relax the assumption that new exporters have to carry the whole burden of sunk costs upon entry into the export market. This assumption is in line with Eaton et al. (2007), who suggest that new exporters and their buyers undergo a period of learning about one another before locking in major exporting contracts. Surviving exporters typically start to export into a single foreign

market and gradually expand into additional markets, suggesting that "the costs of 'testing the waters' may be substantially less than the cost of locking in major exporting contracts" (Eaton et al. 2007, 17).

We attribute an export dummy to firms only that exceed a certain threshold ζ of export intensity. Assumptions (1) and (3) ensure that applying a threshold ζ only covers established exporters that have paid the bulk of sunk entry costs, but not new exporters. Assumption (2) makes sure that exiting exporters wouldn't fall under the category exporter if their export intensity is below the threshold ζ. If all three assumptions hold, lagged exports—the measure for sunk entry costs— and the dependent variable would be identical. Since lagged exports would perfectly predict exports in such a case, lagged exports as a measure of sunk entry costs couldn't be included into the regression analysis. Equation 3.2 then translates into:

$$Pr(ex_{it} = 1) = Pr(\pi_{it} = \beta firm_{it} + \gamma reg_{rt} + \delta agg_{rt} > 0) \tag{3.3}$$

where $ex_{it} = 1$ if a firm's export share $\geq \zeta$ and 0 otherwise.

Empirical Specification

We focus on the following equation:

$$ex_i = \alpha_0 + \beta firm_i + \gamma reg_r + \gamma agg_r + D_c + D_s + \varepsilon_i \tag{3.4}$$

where α_0 designates the constant, D_c designates country-fixed effects, D_s designates sector-fixed effects, and ε_i designates the idiosyncratic error term.

Following the literature on the firm-level determinants of exporting described above, we include firm size, firm age, foreign ownership, as well as measures of workers' skills and productivity. This leads to the following version of equation 3.4:

$$\begin{aligned} ex_i = \alpha_0 &+ \beta_1 \ln emp_i + \beta_2 \ln age_i + \beta_3 fdi_i + \beta_4 \ln comp_i + \beta_5 \ln tfp_i \\ &+ \beta_6 \ln tech_i + D_c + D_r + D_s + \varepsilon_i \end{aligned} \tag{3.5}$$

where D_r denotes region-fixed effects.

The firm-level indicators from the Enterprise Surveys Indicator Database combined with data from the Enterprise Analysis Unit[8] are defined as follows:

- *emp* = total number of permanent and temporary employees in logarithms
- *age* = years of operation in logarithms
- *fdi* = 1 if foreign private ownership $\geq$ 10 percent and 0 otherwise
- *comp* = average real compensation per worker (including wages, salaries, and bonuses) in logarithms
- *tfp* = total factor productivity (TFP) in logarithms
- *tech* = *iso* + *tech_for* + *website* + *email* $\in \{0, 1, 2, 3, 4\}$, where *iso* = 1 if firm has internationally recognized quality certification and 0 otherwise, *tech_for* = 1 if firm uses technology licensed from foreign firms and 0 otherwise, *website* = 1

if firm uses own website to communicate with clients or suppliers, and *email* = 1 if firm uses email to communicate with clients or suppliers. This technology indicator captures both worker skills and productivity.

In a second step, we substitute regional determinants of exporting and agglomeration economies for regional dummies. Following the economic geography literature, we include variables related to investment climate, which yields equation 3.6:

$$ex_i = \alpha_0 + \beta_1 \ln emp_i + \beta_2 \ln age_i + \beta_3 fdi_i + \beta_4 \ln comp_i + \beta_5 \ln tfp_i + \beta_6 tech_i$$

$$+ \gamma_1 \ln customs_r + \gamma_2 \ln electr_r + \gamma_3 \ln license_r + \gamma_4 credit_r + \gamma_5 corrup_r \qquad (3.6)$$

$$+ D_c + D_s + \varepsilon_i$$

where the regional determinants of exporting are defined as follows:

- *customs* = average number of days to clear imports from customs in logarithms by region
- *electr* = hours of power outages per month in logarithms by region
- *license* = average number of days to obtain either operating license, import license, or construction-related permit in logarithms by region
- *credit* = the percentage of firms with a credit line by region
- *corrup* = the percentage of firms expected to pay informal payment to public officials by region.

The calculation of these regional indicators is based on all firms in the sample, regardless of a firm's specific industry. We used weights provided by the Enterprise Analysis Unit to calculate regional averages. Note that we only include some regional determinants of exporting due to data limitations of our available regional investment climate indicators (see tables 3.1 and 3.2). Thus, we only use one variable to capture infrastructure (*electr*), transport and trade facilitation (*customs*), permits and licenses (*license*), corruption (*corrup*), and access to finance (*credit*), respectively. We do not capture regulation and tax, and by focusing on regional investment climate, it might be possible that we omit other regional determinants of exporting, such as those related to average skills and productivity. However, we believe that these are indirectly captured by agglomeration economies.

Finally, we include four types of regional agglomeration economies, namely (1) a region's number of firms as percentage of a country's total number of firms (*agg_size*); (2) the HHI by region, defined as the sum of squares of an industry's output share (*agg_hhi*)[9]; (3) a region's number of firms within the same industry as percentage of a country's total number of firms within the same industry (*agg_ind*); and (4) a region's number of direct and indirect exporters as percentage of a region's total number of firms (*agg_ex*).

The first effect refers to *urbanization economies* that are not industry specific and, thus, capture spillovers due to a geographical concentration of different economic activities.[10] The second effect measures *sector diversity* within a region. The third measure captures *localization economies* due to a geographical concentration of firms in the same industry in an agglomeration. We will refer to the fourth measure as *export spillovers*. This leads to equation 3.7:

$$ex_i = \alpha_0 + \beta_1 \ln emp_i + \beta_2 \ln age_i + \beta_3 fdi_i + \beta_4 \ln comp_i + \beta_5 \ln labprodp_i$$

$$+ \beta_6 tech_i + \gamma_1 \ln customs_r + \gamma_2 \ln electr_r + \gamma_3 \ln license_r + \gamma_4 credit_r$$

$$+ \gamma_5 corrup_r + \delta_1 agg\_size_r + \delta_2 agg\_hhi_r + \delta_3 agg\_ind_r \tag{3.7}$$

$$+ \delta_4 agg\_ex_r + D_c + \varepsilon_i$$

We run three types of estimations: (1) on the whole sample, (2) on core regions only as defined previously and (3) on noncore regions only. This allows us to detect how the firm-level determinants of exporting change if firms are located in core versus noncore regions. We would hypothesize that traditional firm-level characteristics matter less for firms located in core regions, since a firm's business environment will explain a larger share of a firm's export behavior. That is, we expect smaller regression coefficients in the specifications where only core regions are included.

We apply a threshold ζ of export intensity to define exporters as follows:

$ex = 1$ if a firm's export share $\geq \zeta = 10$ percent and 0 otherwise, where export share is defined as a firm's direct exports as percentage of sales.

This threshold not only serves as an alternative way to deal with sunk entry costs due to the unavailability of lagged export data (see discussion earlier in this section), but also lowers the risk of occasional exporters biasing the results. Moreover, we include only direct exporters in our analysis.

Due to the different nature of manufacturing and services firms, we focus first in the next subsection on manufacturing firms, and then follow with a focus on services firms.

Regression Results: Manufacturing Firms

In the following discussion, we estimate a probit model as described in equation 3.5. All specifications are robust to heteroscedasticity and include sector and region-fixed effects. We cluster standard errors at the regional level to allow for the possibility that ε_i are correlated across firms within regions. The summary statistics are shown in table 3.3. The estimation results for manufacturing firms are shown in table 3.4. Columns 1–4 show the results for all firms, columns 5–8 for firms in core regions only, and columns 9–12 for firms in noncore regions only.

For each of these three groups, we run four specifications (see table 3.4): (1) firm-level determinants of exporting plus country, region, and sector-fixed effects as specified in equation 3.5; (2) firm-level and regional determinants of exporting plus country and sector-fixed effects as specified in equation 3.6; (3) firm-level determinants of exporting and agglomeration economies only plus country-fixed effects; and (4) firm-level and regional determinants of exporting including agglomeration economies plus country-fixed effects as specified in equation 3.7.

In a first step, we focus on the overall sample, regardless of firm location (columns 1–4). Regarding firm-level determinants of exporting, employment,

Table 3.3 Summary Statistics, Manufacturing Firms

Variable	Observations	Mean	Standard deviation	Minimum	Maximum
ex_i	29,137	0.2211	0.4150	0	1
$lnempl_i$	28,989	3.7281	1.4318	0	8.8537
$lnage_i$	25,854	2.6594	0.8235	0	5.2470
fdi_i	28,683	0.1206	0.3256	0	1
$lncomp_i$	23,346	10.9104	2.5921	1.4411	23.1763
$lntfp_i$	18,062	0.0026	0.5006	−3.4143	5.1795
$tech_i$	29,451	1.4489	1.2069	0	4
$lncustoms_r$	22,100	2.2195	0.7579	0	4.3807
$lnoutage_r$	22,421	2.6303	1.4676	−2.6593	6.8638
$lnlicense_r$	22,194	3.4059	0.8278	0.6931	5.8278
$credit_r$	21,310	39.0862	24.2962	0	100
$corrup_r$	22,586	29.4013	25.0620	0	100
agg_size_r	29,451	30.2287	24.2924	0.0755	92.8144
agg_hhi_r	26,802	0.3497	0.1588	0	1
agg_ind_r	29,451	33.8674	26.4016	0	100
agg_ex_r	29,451	30.0196	18.4930	0	100

FDI, compensation per worker, TFP, and technology increase a firm's propensity of exporting, which is significant across all specifications. Age seems to have a negative effect on a firm's propensity to export, but is only significant in two specifications.

Regarding the regional determinants of exporting (columns 2 and 4), most variables show the expected signs. A region's longer waiting time to clear imports at customs, a longer monthly duration of power outages, a longer waiting time to obtain licenses, and corruption have a negative coefficient sign. A region's percentage of firms with a credit line shows a negative effect, indicating congestion costs. However, only the electricity and credit line variables are significant.

Finally, we focus on the agglomeration economies (columns 3 and 4). Urbanization economies (that is, an agglomeration of firms of all types) appear to hamper the probability of exporting, while localization economies (that is, an agglomeration of firms in the same industry) as well as an agglomeration of others exporters encourages exporting. The negative effect of general agglomeration may indicate the presence of congestion costs, while the positive results on other types of agglomeration suggests the possibility of industry and export spillovers.

In a second step, we focus on the effect of firm location on the determinants of exporting. Columns 5–8 report the results for firms located in core regions, while columns 9–12 show the results for firms located in noncore regions. Regarding location, all firm-level determinants of exporting seem to matter more for firms located in noncore regions, especially FDI and technology, but also compensation per worker and TFP. The negative effect of age can only be confirmed for manufacturing firms in noncore regions. This implies that other non-firm-level determinants of exporting—for example, those related to the investment climate—explain a bigger share of export behavior in the core.

Table 3.4 Probit Regressions, Manufacturing Firms

Dependent variable: ex_i	All regions					Core regions			Noncore regions			
	(1)	(2)	(3)	(4)	(5)	(6)	(7)	(8)	(9)	(10)	(11)	(12)
$lnemp_i$	0.3182***	0.3286***	0.2995***	0.3133***	0.3153***	0.3243***	0.3095***	0.3142***	0.3240***	0.3228***	0.2958***	0.3174***
	[0.000]	[0.000]	[0.000]	[0.000]	[0.000]	[0.000]	[0.000]	[0.000]	[0.000]	[0.000]	[0.000]	[0.000]
$lnage_t$	−0.0417**	−0.0241	−0.0415*	−0.0234	−0.0065	−0.0049	−0.0079	−0.0031	−0.0729**	−0.0257	−0.0657**	−0.0311
	[0.046]	[0.237]	[0.053]	[0.284]	[0.818]	[0.866]	[0.797]	[0.924]	[0.017]	[0.375]	[0.030]	[0.322]
fdi_i	0.4423***	0.4293***	0.4240***	0.4204***	0.3133***	0.3214***	0.3050***	0.3073***	0.6514***	0.5998***	0.5780***	0.6040***
	[0.000]	[0.000]	[0.000]	[0.000]	[0.000]	[0.000]	[0.000]	[0.000]	[0.000]	[0.000]	[0.000]	[0.000]
$lncomp_i$	0.0661***	0.0593***	0.0410***	0.0458***	0.0572***	0.0626***	0.0454**	0.0522**	0.0802***	0.0677***	0.0508**	0.0537**
	[0.000]	[0.000]	[0.009]	[0.005]	[0.008]	[0.003]	[0.039]	[0.014]	[0.001]	[0.007]	[0.013]	[0.030]
$lntfp_i$	0.0704**	0.0670**	0.0640**	0.0641**	0.0596	0.0716*	0.0599	0.0707*	0.0794*	0.0687*	0.0667*	0.0631
	[0.018]	[0.021]	[0.021]	[0.026]	[0.129]	[0.082]	[0.132]	[0.094]	[0.076]	[0.088]	[0.087]	[0.114]
$lntech_i$	0.3014***	0.2594***	0.2768***	0.2501***	0.2768***	0.2634***	0.2644***	0.2524***	0.3269***	0.2694***	0.2923***	0.2570***
	[0.000]	[0.000]	[0.000]	[0.000]	[0.000]	[0.000]	[0.000]	[0.000]	[0.000]	[0.000]	[0.000]	[0.000]
$lncustoms_r$		−0.0691		0.0132		1.8335***		0.2742***		0.0158		0.0207
		[0.212]		[0.793]		[0.000]		[0.000]		[0.813]		[0.730]
$lnelectr_r$		−0.1015***		−0.0968***		0.4652***		0.4979***		−0.1010**		−0.0783**
		[0.002]		[0.000]		[0.000]		[0.000]		[0.032]		[0.038]
$lnlicense_r$		−0.0451		−0.0157		−2.9167***		2.1293***		−0.0150		0.0234
		[0.349]		[0.701]		[0.000]		[0.000]		[0.802]		[0.644]
$credit_r$		0.0004		−0.0028*		0.0185***		0.0913***		0.0002		−0.0047***
		[0.851]		[0.074]		[0.000]		[0.000]		[0.916]		[0.004]
$corrup_r$		0.0001		−0.0022		0.0328***		0.0446***		0.0000		−0.0006
		[0.944]		[0.228]		[0.000]		[0.000]		[0.992]		[0.828]
agg_size_r			−0.0055**	−0.0054**			−0.0083	−0.1259***			−0.0175***	−0.0260***
			[0.023]	[0.042]			[0.452]	[0.000]			[0.007]	[0.000]

table continues next page

Table 3.4 Probit Regressions, Manufacturing Firms *(continued)*

Dependent variable: ex_i	All regions					Core regions				Noncore regions		
	(1)	(2)	(3)	(4)	(5)	(6)	(7)	(8)	(9)	(10)	(11)	(12)
agg_hhi_r			−0.2114	−0.1169			−3.9669*	−22.3927			−0.1514	−0.0528
			[0.243]	[0.539]			[0.079]	—			[0.454]	[0.807]
agg_ind_r			0.0030	0.0025			0.0030	0.0021			0.0052*	0.0050
			[0.219]	[0.349]			[0.415]	[0.596]			[0.055]	[0.105]
agg_ex_r			0.0191***	0.0184***			0.0056	0.1746***			0.0229***	0.0217***
			[0.000]	[0.000]			[0.811]	[0.000]			[0.000]	[0.000]
$constant_i$	−1.1347***	−1.4245*	−2.8918***	−2.1357***	−2.7600***	0.5269	−2.1192	−4.6891***	−3.0521***	−0.6152	−3.5559***	−1.8039***
	[0.000]	[0.091]	[0.000]	[0.004]	[0.000]	[0.120]	[0.161]	[0.000]	[0.000]	[0.246]	[0.000]	[0.000]
Country fixed effects	Yes	Yes	Yes	Yes	Yes	Yes	Yes	Yes	Yes	Yes	Yes	Yes
Region fixed effects	Yes	No	No	No	Yes	No	No	No	Yes	No	No	No
Sector fixed effects	Yes	Yes	No	No	Yes	Yes	No	No	Yes	Yes	No	No
McFadden's adjusted pseudo R^2	0.270	0.264	0.287	0.263	0.251	0.244	0.243	0.234	0.290	0.282	0.321	0.286
Observations	14,021	12,457	14,969	12,454	6,921	6,317	6,929	6,317	7,100	6,093	7,981	6,090

Note: — = not available. Standard errors are clustered at the regional level.
*$p < 0.1$, **$p < 0.05$, ***$p < 0.01$ (p-values in parentheses)

Interestingly and in line with these findings, the coefficients of regional determinants are larger and more significant for firms located in core regions. That is, the investment climate has a stronger influence on a firm's propensity of exporting for firms located in the core as opposed to noncore regions (columns 6 and 10). In fact, only electricity and access to finance plays a role in noncore regions. However, most regional variables in the core do not show the expected coefficient signs. We believe that these inverse signs reflect an endogeneity problem—that is, manufacturing firms that are located in regions with higher congestion costs (urban agglomerations) are more likely to export. Analogously, urbanization economies and export spillovers are larger in the core than in noncore regions.

Tables 3A.5–3A.7 report the regression results by firm size, where large firms are firms with at least 100 employees, medium firms are firms with 20–99 employees, and small firms are firms with less than 20 employees. We will not go into detail here, but simply point out some interesting findings.

- Firm-level determinants seem to matter more for smaller firms. That is, the coefficient signs of firm-level determinants of exporting are larger for medium and small firms and smaller for large firms. This is in line with observations of greater variation in productivity performance across small firms.
- Most firm-level determinants are more important in noncore regions, in particular FDI ownership.
- Urbanization economies show a significant negative association with exporting across large and medium firms, particularly in core regions.
- We detect positive export spillovers across all firm sizes in all locations. This positive effect is stronger in the core.
- Localization economies only matter for exporting for medium firms in noncore regions.
- A higher sector diversity increases exporting only for small firms in noncore regions.
- Regional determinants do not appear to have any clear impact related to firm size.

Regression Results: Services Firms

We repeat the exercise above for services firms only. As compensation per worker and labor productivity are only available for manufacturing firms, we cannot include these measures. Summary statistics are shown in table 3.5, with the regression results shown in table 3.6. First, we focus on the overall sample in columns 1–4. As expected, employment, FDI, and technology increase a firm's propensity to export, which is significant across all specifications. Age shows no effect on a firm's propensity to export.

Regarding the regional determinants of exporting (columns 2 and 4), the coefficient signs are mostly as expected, but only the customs variable is significant. That is, regional determinants seem to matter less for services firms than they do for manufacturing firms. Finally, we focus on agglomeration economies (columns 3 and 4). Export spillovers increase the likelihood of exporting, confirming

Table 3.5 Summary Statistics, Services Firms

Variable	Observations	Mean	Standard deviation	Minimum	Maximum
ex_i	3,447	0.0908	0.2874	0	1
$lnempl_i$	3,362	3.2132	1.3339	0	8.4764
$lnage_i$	3,425	2.4036	0.8361	0	4.9558
fdi_i	3,439	0.1163	0.3206	0	1
$tech_i$	3,471	1.4690	1.0200	0	4
$lncustoms_r$	2,998	2.3181	0.8308	0	4.3807
$lnoutage_r$	3,078	2.6401	1.4566	−2.6593	6.8638
$lnlicense_r$	3,042	3.4694	0.7831	0.6931	5.8278
$credit_r$	3,087	37.8542	24.0435	0	100
$corrup_r$	3,105	28.1838	22.3384	0	100
agg_size_r	3,471	36.6389	27.5236	0.1511	92.8144
agg_hhi_r	2,951	0.3772	0.1611	0	1
agg_ind_r	3,471	40.2982	29.1207	0	100
agg_ex_r	3,471	23.8894	15.7467	0	75

the results for manufacturing firms. Localization economies show a positive impact in column 4.

Regarding regional determinants, the coefficient signs are somewhat ambiguous. Almost none of these effects is significant in noncore regions. In core regions, only electricity, credit, and corruption show the expected coefficient signs, while customs and license show inverse effects, indicating an endogeneity problem. As in the manufacturing sample, regional determinants matter more for firms in core regions.

Tables 3A.8–3A.10 report the regression results by firm size. Many variables now show ambiguous results. Due to the low number of observations, the results should be interpreted with caution.

Conclusions

In this chapter, we addressed the following three research questions: (1) Are there significant differences in export participation and performance, and in the firm characteristics and perceived investment climate for exporting in core versus noncore regions? (2) What is the effect of regional determinants, including the investment climate and agglomeration economies, on exporting behavior? (3) Do the determinants of exporting have a differential effect if firms are located in core versus noncore regions? We used a cross-section covering more than 35,000 manufacturing and services firms in 77 developing countries.

We find that the average share of exporting firms is higher in core regions for manufacturing firms, while there is no significant difference in export intensity. This finding is important as it suggests that the difference lies in export participation, but once the threshold of export participation is reached, there is no difference in the experiences of firms in core versus noncore regions. In services, on the other hand, export participation and intensity do not show a significant difference between core versus noncore regions.

Table 3.6 Probit Regressions, Services Firms

Dependent variable: ex_i	All regions				Core regions				Noncore regions			
	(1)	(2)	(3)	(4)	(5)	(6)	(7)	(8)	(9)	(10)	(11)	(12)
$lnemp_i$	0.0600	0.0635*	0.0581*	0.0590*	0.0044	0.0259	0.0253	0.0271	0.1817***	0.1389**	0.1204**	0.1275**
	[0.137]	[0.067]	[0.079]	[0.093]	[0.927]	[0.587]	[0.588]	[0.581]	[0.009]	[0.014]	[0.023]	[0.031]
$lnage_i$	0.0651	0.0204	0.0135	0.0136	0.0115	−0.0140	−0.0421	−0.0426	0.2028	0.1071	0.1180	0.0801
	[0.343]	[0.745]	[0.826]	[0.844]	[0.885]	[0.872]	[0.623]	[0.658]	[0.138]	[0.354]	[0.271]	[0.524]
fdi_i	0.5801***	0.5624***	0.5903***	0.5768***	0.3534**	0.2611**	0.3022**	0.2947**	1.4035***	1.3022***	1.1528***	1.2768***
	[0.000]	[0.000]	[0.000]	[0.000]	[0.017]	[0.038]	[0.018]	[0.025]	[0.000]	[0.000]	[0.000]	[0.000]
$lntech_i$	0.3061***	0.3038***	0.3138***	0.3373***	0.2875***	0.2958***	0.3142***	0.3265***	0.3701***	0.3474***	0.3673***	0.3961***
	[0.000]	[0.000]	[0.000]	[0.000]	[0.000]	[0.000]	[0.000]	[0.000]	[0.002]	[0.000]	[0.000]	[0.000]
$lncustoms_r$		−0.2289***		−0.1779*		1.7966***		5.0104***		−0.2530**		−0.1518
		[0.006]		[0.092]		[0.001]		[0.000]		[0.034]		[0.241]
$lnelectr_r$		−0.0038		−0.0151		0.1245		−1.3549***		−0.0069		0.0500
		[0.925]		[0.746]		[0.183]		[0.000]		[0.927]		[0.533]
$lnlicense_r$		−0.0250		−0.0056		0.4275		3.5485***		−0.0842		−0.0691
		[0.717]		[0.947]		[0.209]		[0.000]		[0.440]		[0.547]
$credit_r$		0.0009		0.0002		0.0868***		0.2352***		0.0009		−0.0046
		[0.783]		[0.947]		[0.002]		[0.000]		[0.813]		[0.253]
$corrup_r$		0.0029		0.0013		−0.1480***		−0.3660***		0.0051		0.0017
		[0.523]		[0.801]		[0.000]		[0.000]		[0.334]		[0.778]
agg_size_r			0.0051	−0.0045			0.0072	−0.0260***			−0.0081	0.0004
			[0.368]	[0.359]			[0.604]	[0.000]			[0.561]	[0.976]
agg_hhi_r			0.3586	0.2865			−33.2314**				0.2210	−0.0051
			[0.380]	[0.486]			[0.016]				[0.655]	[0.992]
agg_ind_r			−0.0036	0.0088**			−0.1210***	0.2764***			0.0031	0.0321***
												[0.000]

table continues next page

Table 3.6 Probit Regressions, Services Firms (continued)

Dependent variable: ex_i	All regions				Core regions					Noncore regions		
	(1)	(2)	(3)	(4)	(5)	(6)	(7)	(8)	(9)	(10)	(11)	(12)
agg_ex_r			[0.583]	[0.050]			[0.003]	[0.000]			[0.819]	[0.006]
			0.0273***	0.0201***			0.0903**	0.0810***			0.0295***	0.0172**
			[0.000]	[0.000]			[0.023]	[0.000]			[0.001]	[0.011]
$constant_i$	−1.9083***	−1.0532**	−1.9693***	−2.5648***	−1.6431***	−13.8835***	3.0479*	−42.2142	−2.2371***	−1.5122*	−2.7663***	−2.8350***
	[0.000]	[0.024]	[0.000]	[0.000]	[0.000]	[0.000]	[0.061]	—	[0.000]	[0.089]	[0.000]	[0.002]
Country fixed effects	Yes	Yes	Yes	Yes	Yes	Yes	Yes	Yes	Yes	Yes	Yes	Yes
Region fixed effects	Yes	No	No	No	Yes	No	No	No	Yes	No	No	No
Sector fixed effects	Yes	Yes	No	No	Yes	Yes	No	No	Yes	Yes	No	No
McFadden's adjusted pseudo R^2	0.041	0.101	0.129	0.120	0.069	0.074	0.077	0.083	0.029	0.093	0.118	0.107
Observations	1,948	2,218	2,376	2,012	1,259	1,139	1,112	990	689	880	989	850

Note: — = not available. Standard errors are clustered at the regional level.
*$p < 0.1$, **$p < 0.05$, ***$p < 0.01$ (p-values in parentheses)

Our econometric findings affirm the importance of firm-specific characteristics in determining export performance. But they also highlight the role of locational factors, including the investment climate, and most importantly the role of agglomeration.

Regarding regional determinants of exporting, our overall results for manufacturing firms show that only electricity and credit are determinants of export participation. All regional determinants are significant in the core, but show ambiguous coefficient signs, which we relate to an endogeneity problem. Regarding the regional determinants for services firms, the signs are mostly as expected in the overall sample and in noncore regions. Only customs in the overall sample is significant, suggesting that regional determinants are less important for services firms. In core regions, electricity, credit, and corruption show the expected coefficient signs.

We also included four measures on agglomeration economies, namely urbanization economies, sector diversity, localization economies, and export spillovers. Urbanization economies appear to reduce the likelihood of exporting, across virtually all firm sizes and locations, whereas export spillovers increase it. The urbanization economies measure holds for manufacturing firms only, while the latter measures hold for both manufacturing and services firms. Sector diversity has a positive impact on exporting for manufacturing and services firms located in core regions. Localization economies tend to be positive for manufacturing and services firms, but are less significant.

Regarding firm location, our findings for manufacturing and services firms confirm that firm-level determinants of exporting seem to matter more for firms located in noncore regions. This implies that other non-firm-level determinants of exporting—those related to the investment climate—explain a bigger share of export behavior in the core. As a result, both regional determinants of exporting and agglomeration economies play a larger role in core regions for both manufacturing and services firms.

While these results present just a broad cross-country picture, several findings may be of use in considering policy interventions to promote trade or regional development. First, the fact that firms in core regions are more likely to export, despite what appear to be significant congestion costs, suggests that interventions to improve the investment climate in the core are likely to have a much bigger impact than interventions in noncore regions, where firm-specific characteristics are of greater importance. This is particularly true for services firms.

Second, the importance of export spillovers and—to a lesser extent—of localization economies highlights the potential value of efforts to remove barriers to natural agglomeration both in core and noncore regions, for example through investments in infrastructure, the provision of social services, and regional integration arrangements. Third, efforts to address the investment climate should be targeted to ensuring broad access to finance and improved hard and soft trade infrastructure (such as customs and electricity). Again, the impacts on exports are likely to be greater if these are targeted first in the core.

Finally, expanding the export participation of smaller firms, particularly those based outside the core, is likely to require interventions that address firm-level competitiveness, for example targeting management skills and access to finance.

Annex 3A Countries, Regions, and Firms

Table 3A.1 Number of Firms and Regions by Country

Country	Survey year	Total number of firms	Number of manufacturing firms	Number of service firms	Number of regions
Afghanistan	2008	355	119	73	6
Albania	2007	173	110	33	8
Algeria	2007	481	385	55	11
Angola	2010	188	141	35	3
Argentina	2010	887	793	69	5
Armenia	2009	195	115	51	4
Azerbaijan	2009	202	118	50	4
Bangladesh	2007	1,368	1,276	17	6
Belarus	2008	146	104	24	7
Benin	2009	89	50	32	3
Bhutan	2009	179	87	27	4
Bolivia	2010	203	142	46	3
Brazil	2009	1,670	1,342	308	15
Bulgaria	2009	147	96	33	6
Cambodia	2007	278	134	57	5
Cameroon	2009	174	116	44	3
Cape Verde	2009	95	65	10	3
Chile	2010	849	775	62	4
Colombia	2010	778	706	52	4
Côte d'Ivoire	2009	334	193	126	3
Croatia	2007	457	411	13	6
Congo, Dem. Rep.	2006	276	192	74	4
Ecuador	2010	142	119	12	3
Egypt, Arab Rep.	2008	1,324	1,141	119	25
Eritrea	2009	131	99	26	3
Estonia	2009	155	90	27	5
Ethiopia	2006	374	359	9	15
Macedonia, FYR	2009	201	122	34	4
Gabon	2009	124	37	83	3
Georgia	2008	216	125	36	6
Ghana	2007	353	292	60	4
Honduras	2010	189	150	32	3
India	2006	2,220	2,218	1	16
Indonesia	2009	1,246	1,157	59	9
Jordan	2006	480	353	93	3
Kazakhstan	2009	291	184	42	5
Kenya	2007	475	396	24	4

table continues next page

Table 3A.1 Number of Firms and Regions by Country (continued)

Country	Survey year	Total number of firms	Number of manufacturing firms	Number of service firms	Number of regions
Kosovo	2009	154	103	18	7
Kyrgyz Republic	2009	160	97	33	5
Lao PDR	2009	171	143	15	4
Latvia	2009	146	89	29	6
Liberia	2009	112	73	36	3
Lithuania	2009	163	104	26	4
Madagascar	2009	298	204	68	4
Malawi	2009	98	70	17	3
Malaysia	2007	1,115	1,115	0	6
Mali	2010	199	125	45	4
Mauritius	2009	294	183	88	6
Mexico	2010	1,287	1,157	110	8
Moldova	2009	195	108	45	4
Mongolia	2009	218	130	31	5
Montenegro	2009	49	37	8	3
Morocco	2007	576	457	59	4
Mozambique	2007	351	341	4	4
Nepal	2009	174	128	45	3
Nigeria	2007	1,223	948	84	11
Pakistan	2007	784	783	0	13
Peru	2010	805	760	43	4
Philippines	2009	1,052	957	70	5
Poland	2009	254	158	48	6
Romania	2009	305	184	63	8
Russian Federation	2009	826	706	62	7
Senegal	2007	340	259	78	4
Serbia	2009	223	136	43	6
South Africa	2007	722	680	27	4
Swaziland	2006	138	106	0	3
Tajikistan	2008	212	115	41	4
Tanzania	2006	307	286	5	4
Thailand	2006	1,043	1,043	0	7
Turkey	2008	965	903	49	5
Uganda	2006	365	334	7	5
Ukraine	2008	671	581	65	5
Uzbekistan	2008	200	121	42	3
Venezuela, RB	2010	135	85	48	3
Vietnam	2009	867	782	30	5
Yemen, Rep.	2010	280	244	30	6
Zambia	2007	319	304	11	4
Total		35,241	29,451	3,471	430

Source: Enterprise Survey Indicators, World Bank.

Table 3A.2 Core Regions

Country	Core regions	Country	Core regions
Afghanistan	Kabul	Lao PDR	Vientiane Capital
Albania	Tirana	Latvia	Riga
Algeria	Alger	Liberia	Montserrado
Angola	Lunada	Lithuania	Vilniaus
Argentina	Buenos Aires	Madagascar	Antananarivo
Armenia	Yerevan	Malawi	Southern
Azerbaijan	Baku and Apsheronski	Malaysia	Central
Bangladesh	Dhaka	Mali	Bamako
Belarus	Grodnenskaya, Minsk	Mauritius	Port Louis
Benin	Cotonou	Mexico	Distrito Federal, Guadalajara
Bhutan	Phuentsholing	Moldova	Centre
Bolivia	La Paz	Mongolia	Ulaanbaatar Capital City
Brazil	São Paulo, Rio de Janeiro	Montenegro	Centre and South
Bulgaria	Yuzhen Tsentralen, Yugozapaden	Morocco	Casablanca
		Mozambique	Maputo
Cambodia	Phnom Penh	Nepal	Central
Cameroon	Douala	Nigeria	Lagos
Cape Verde	Santiago	Pakistan	Karachi
Chile	Santiago	Peru	Lima
Colombia	Bogota	Philippines	National Capital Region (excl. Manila), Manila
Côte d'Ivoire	Abidjan	Poland	Central Region
Croatia	Zagreb and Surroundings	Romania	Bucharest-Ilfov
Congo, Dem. Rep.	Kinshasa	Russian Federation	Central
Ecuador	Pichincha	Senegal	Dakar
Egypt, Arab Rep.	Cairo	Serbia	Belgrade
Eritrea	Maekel	South Africa	Johannesburg
Estonia	North-Estonia	Swaziland	Matsapha, Manzini
Ethiopia	Addis Ababa	Tajikistan	Capital (Dushanbe)
Macedonia, FYR	Skopje Region	Tanzania	Dar Es Salaam
Gabon	Libreville	Thailand	Bangkok And Vicinity
Georgia	Tbilissi	Turkey	Marmara
Ghana	Accra-Temin	Uganda	Kampala
Honduras	Tegucigalpa	Ukraine	North, Kiev
India	Maharashtra, Karnataka, Tamil Nadu, Gujarat	Uzbekistan	Samarkandskaya
Indonesia	Java Barat, DKI Jakarta	Venezuela, RB	Caracas
Jordan	Amman	Vietnam	South East
Kazakhstan	South	Yemen, Rep.	Sana'A
Kenya	Nairobi	Zambia	Lusaka
Kosovo	Prishtine		
Kyrgyz Republic	Bishkek		

Source: Enterprise Survey Indicators, World Bank.

Table 3A.3 Number of Total Firms and Core Firms by Sector

	Number of firms	% distribution	% distribution by broad sector	Number of firms in core	% of firms in core
Manufacturing	29,451	83.6	100.0	13,352	45.3
Textiles	2,477	7.0	8.4	1,125	45.4
Leather	573	1.6	1.9	323	56.4
Garments	4,039	11.5	13.7	2,060	51.0
Food	5,719	16.2	19.4	2,325	40.7
Metals and machinery	4,563	12.9	15.5	1,969	43.2
Electronics	954	2.7	3.2	392	41.1
Chemicals and pharmaceuticals	2,502	7.1	8.5	1,318	52.7
Wood and furniture	956	2.7	3.2	289	30.2
Non-metallic and plastic materials	3,136	8.9	10.6	1,314	41.9
Auto and auto components	502	1.4	1.7	188	37.5
Other manufacturing	4,030	11.4	13.7	2,049	50.8
Services	5,790	16.4	100.0	2,985	51.6
Business services[a]	3,471	9.8	59.9	1,880	54.2
Other: construction, transportation, and so on	2,319	6.6	40.1	1,105	47.6
Total	35,241	100.0	n.a.	16,337	46.4

Source: Enterprise Survey Indicators, World Bank.
Note: n.a. = not applicable.
a. Business services include information technology services, telecommunications, accounting and finance, advertising and marketing, and others.

Table 3A.4 Number of Total Firms and Core Firms by Firm Size

Firm size	Number of firms	% distribution	Number of firms in core	% of firms in core
Small (< 20 employees)	13,374	38.0	5,700	42.6
Medium (20–99 employees)	12,433	35.3	5,929	47.7
Large (≥100 employees)	9,171	26.0	4,556	49.7
Unknown	263	0.7	152	57.8
Total	35,241	100.0	16,337	46.4

Source: Enterprise Survey Indicators, World Bank.

Table 3A.5 Regression Results, Large Manufacturing Firms

Dependent variable: ex$_i$	All regions		Core regions		Noncore regions	
	(1)	(2)	(3)	(4)	(5)	(6)
lnemp$_i$	0.1258***	0.1440***	0.1277***	0.1564***	0.1348**	0.1449**
	[0.000]	[0.000]	[0.002]	[0.002]	[0.017]	[0.011]
lnage$_i$	−0.0680*	−0.0493	−0.0299	−0.0693	−0.0939*	−0.0311
	[0.074]	[0.198]	[0.556]	[0.244]	[0.097]	[0.563]
fdi$_i$	0.4168***	0.3892***	0.3397***	0.2865***	0.5315***	0.5518***
	[0.000]	[0.000]	[0.000]	[0.001]	[0.000]	[0.000]
lncomp$_i$	0.0321	−0.0143	−0.0077	−0.0270	0.0764**	0.0134
	[0.193]	[0.533]	[0.837]	[0.421]	[0.038]	[0.676]
lntfp$_i$	−0.0079	0.0278	−0.0504	−0.0650	0.0236	0.0872
	[0.858]	[0.550]	[0.415]	[0.331]	[0.716]	[0.193]
lntech$_i$	0.2645***	0.1838***	0.2910***	0.2256***	0.2450***	0.1626***
	[0.000]	[0.000]	[0.000]	[0.001]	[0.000]	[0.003]
lncustoms$_r$		0.1254		1.5682***		0.1721*
		[0.130]		[0.000]		[0.063]
lnelectr$_r$		−0.0777**		−0.3751***		−0.0361
		[0.050]		[0.000]		[0.463]
lnlicense$_r$		−0.0823		−0.4746***		−0.1025
		[0.243]		[0.000]		[0.234]
credit$_r$		0.0022		0.0594***		0.0052**
		[0.284]		[0.000]		[0.015]
corrup$_r$		−0.0018		0.0407***		−0.0020
		[0.626]		[0.000]		[0.676]
agg_size$_r$		−0.0100**		−0.0398***		−0.0090
		[0.023]		[0.000]		[0.270]
agg_hhi$_r$		−0.1044		−21.9949		−0.0051
		[0.682]		—		[0.987]
agg_ind$_r$		0.0067		0.0104		0.0018
		[0.126]		[0.135]		[0.649]
agg_ex$_r$		0.0195***		0.1165***		0.0167***
		[0.000]		[0.000]		[0.000]
constant$_i$	−0.4696	−1.4597**	−0.5061	−1.4271**	−1.1032**	−1.0182
	[0.137]	[0.023]	[0.379]	[0.024]	[0.013]	[0.328]
Country fixed effects	Yes	Yes	Yes	Yes	Yes	Yes
Region fixed effects	Yes	No	Yes	No	Yes	No
Sector fixed effects	Yes	No	Yes	No	Yes	No
McFadden's adjusted pseudo R^2	0.078	0.081	0.102	0.073	0.052	0.067
Observations	3,471	2,937	1,745	1,561	1,726	1,355

Note: — = not available. Large: ≥ 100 employees. Standard errors are clustered at the regional level.
*$p < 0.1$, **$p < 0.05$, ***$p < 0.01$ (*p*-values in parentheses)

Table 3A.6 Regression Results, Medium Manufacturing Firms

Dependent variable:	All regions		Core regions		Noncore regions	
ex_i	(1)	(2)	(3)	(4)	(5)	(6)
lnemp_i	0.4331***	0.3837***	0.3726***	0.3437***	0.5213***	0.4390***
	[0.000]	[0.000]	[0.000]	[0.000]	[0.000]	[0.000]
lnage_i	0.0017	0.0280	0.0055	0.0263	0.0133	0.0328
	[0.963]	[0.433]	[0.913]	[0.602]	[0.800]	[0.555]
fdi_i	0.5487***	0.5539***	0.3743***	0.4551***	0.8792***	0.6448***
	[0.000]	[0.000]	[0.003]	[0.000]	[0.000]	[0.000]
ln$comp_i$	0.0883***	0.0899***	0.1110***	0.1096***	0.0753	0.0969**
	[0.001]	[0.001]	[0.000]	[0.001]	[0.108]	[0.021]
lntfp_i	0.1118**	0.0971**	0.1222*	0.1515**	0.1055	0.0649
	[0.023]	[0.044]	[0.064]	[0.037]	[0.167]	[0.315]
ln$tech_i$	0.3141***	0.2604***	0.2560***	0.2519***	0.3850***	0.3039***
	[0.000]	[0.000]	[0.000]	[0.000]	[0.000]	[0.000]
ln$customs_r$		−0.0360		0.6799***		−0.0183
		[0.651]		[0.000]		[0.856]
ln$electr_r$		−0.0912**		2.0348***		−0.1459**
		[0.017]		[0.000]		[0.019]
ln$license_r$		0.0685		1.1315***		0.1034
		[0.238]		[0.000]		[0.195]
$credit_r$		−0.0061**		0.0609***		−0.0091***
		[0.024]		[0.000]		[0.001]
$corrup_r$		−0.0004		0.0389***		0.0043
		[0.893]		[0.000]		[0.313]
agg_size_r		−0.0023		−0.0555***		−0.0483***
		[0.498]		[0.000]		[0.000]
agg_hhi_r		0.0192		−20.1826		0.3315
		[0.952]		—		[0.375]
agg_ind_r		−0.0008		−0.0068*		0.0128**
		[0.804]		[0.076]		[0.013]
agg_ex_r		0.0186***		0.0365***		0.0268***
		[0.000]		[0.000]		[0.000]
$constant_i$	−2.6468***	−5.1313***	−3.7972***	−13.1709***	−3.0298***	−3.8098***
	[0.000]	[0.000]	[0.000]	[0.000]	[0.000]	[0.000]
Country fixed effects	Yes	Yes	Yes	Yes	Yes	Yes
Region fixed effects	Yes	No	Yes	No	Yes	No
Sector fixed effects	Yes	No	Yes	No	Yes	No
McFadden's adjusted pseudo R^2	0.141	0.145	0.120	0.104	0.159	0.163
Observations	4,828	4,527	2,607	2,350	2,221	2,106

Note: — = not available. Medium: 20–99 employees. Standard errors are clustered at the regional level.
*$p < 0.1$, **$p < 0.05$, ***$p < 0.01$ (p-values in parentheses)

Table 3A.7 Regression Results, Small Manufacturing Firms

Dependent variable: ex$_i$	All regions		Core regions		Noncore regions	
	(1)	(2)	(3)	(4)	(5)	(6)
lnemp$_i$	0.5013***	0.4558***	0.5108***	0.4742***	0.5044***	0.4542***
	[0.000]	[0.000]	[0.000]	[0.001]	[0.000]	[0.000]
lnage$_i$	−0.0518	−0.0180	0.0184	0.0344	−0.1512**	−0.0801
	[0.293]	[0.684]	[0.780]	[0.621]	[0.047]	[0.234]
fdi$_i$	0.6564***	0.4580***	0.2206	0.1247	1.2780***	0.9435***
	[0.000]	[0.000]	[0.225]	[0.487]	[0.000]	[0.000]
lncomp$_i$	0.1481***	0.1174**	0.1382**	0.1553**	0.1704**	0.1343**
	[0.003]	[0.014]	[0.037]	[0.026]	[0.013]	[0.018]
lntfp$_i$	0.2217***	0.1262**	0.1786**	0.1770*	0.2473**	0.0829
	[0.001]	[0.042]	[0.045]	[0.057]	[0.017]	[0.378]
lntech$_i$	0.3489***	0.3143***	0.3239***	0.3485***	0.4175***	0.3349***
	[0.000]	[0.000]	[0.000]	[0.000]	[0.000]	[0.000]
lncustoms$_r$		−0.1021		−0.3620*		−0.1687
		[0.194]		[0.077]		[0.227]
lnelectr$_r$		−0.0824		−0.5637***		0.0118
		[0.138]		[0.000]		[0.873]
lnlicense$_r$		−0.0412		−4.9731***		0.0575
		[0.561]		[0.000]		[0.540]
credit$_r$		−0.0063*		0.3421***		−0.0173***
		[0.093]		[0.000]		[0.000]
corrup$_r$		−0.0053*		0.1939***		−0.0059
		[0.099]		[0.000]		[0.230]
agg_size$_r$		0.0006		0.0435***		−0.0188
		[0.898]		[0.000]		[0.247]
agg_hhi$_r$		−0.4974				
		[0.186]				
agg_ind$_r$		−0.0034		0.0002		−0.0071
		[0.445]		[0.970]		[0.440]
agg_ex$_r$		0.0171***		0.1662***		0.0308***
		[0.000]		[0.000]		[0.000]
constant$_i$	−2.4606***	−1.8900**	−3.6742***	−16.8984	−2.8044***	−4.9694***
	[0.000]	[0.034]	[0.000]	—	[0.005]	[0.000]
Country fixed effects	Yes	Yes	Yes	Yes	Yes	Yes
Region fixed effects	Yes	No	Yes	No	Yes	No
Sector fixed effects	Yes	No	Yes	No	Yes	No
McFadden's adjusted pseudo R^2	0.138	0.172	0.120	0.121	0.116	0.206
Observations	3,583	4,625	2,238	2,232	1,340	2,200

Note: — = not available. Small: 5–19 employees. Standard errors are clustered at the regional level.
*$p < 0.1$, **$p < 0.05$, ***$p < 0.01$ (p-values in parentheses)

Table 3A.8 Regression Results, Large Services Firms

Dependent variable:	All regions		Core regions		Noncore regions	
ex_i	(1)	(2)	(3)	(4)	(5)	(6)
lnemp_i	−0.0068	−0.0651	−0.1899	−0.3007	0.3604	0.2891
	[0.966]	[0.628]	[0.376]	[0.169]	[0.212]	[0.225]
lnage_i	0.1939	0.1170	0.1506	0.3123	0.0839	−0.2901
	[0.354]	[0.460]	[0.600]	[0.295]	[0.817]	[0.389]
fdi_i	0.4949*	0.5868***	0.1659	0.2173	1.3952**	1.5139***
	[0.090]	[0.008]	[0.613]	[0.533]	[0.039]	[0.001]
ln$tech_i$	0.2877*	0.4859***	0.3211*	0.3511*	0.0788	0.5698**
	[0.069]	[0.000]	[0.087]	[0.059]	[0.777]	[0.013]
ln$customs_r$		0.0714		0.5744**		0.5732
		[0.739]		[0.025]		[0.125]
ln$electr_r$		−0.0815		−0.3461***		0.0433
		[0.341]		[0.000]		[0.787]
ln$license_r$		−0.0396		7.9047***		0.0402
		[0.824]		[0.000]		[0.916]
$credit_r$		0.0036		0.0096		0.0120
		[0.576]		[0.433]		[0.308]
$corrup_r$		−0.0011		−0.4506***		0.0101
		[0.884]		[0.000]		[0.420]
agg_size_r		−0.0210**		−0.2189***		−0.1252**
		[0.017]		[0.000]		[0.012]
agg_hhi_r		−0.1891				−2.1165*
		[0.798]				[0.054]
agg_ind_r		0.0180**		0.2749***		0.0813***
		[0.042]		[0.000]		[0.001]
agg_ex_r		0.0186*		−0.0221		0.0067
		[0.066]		[0.104]		[0.701]
$constant_i$	−7.4805***	−2.1635*	−6.3055	−24.7191***	−3.0709*	−4.0269
	[0.000]	[0.079]	—	[0.000]	[0.078]	[0.182]
Country fixed effects	Yes	Yes	Yes	Yes	Yes	Yes
Region fixed effects	Yes	No	Yes	No	Yes	No
Sector fixed effects	Yes	No	Yes	No	Yes	No
McFadden's adjusted pseudo R^2	−0.241	−0.048	−0.200	−0.136	−0.318	−0.115
Observations	278	412	176	176	102	152

Note: — = not available. Large: ≥ 100 employees. Standard errors are clustered at the regional level.
*$p < 0.1$, **$p < 0.05$, ***$p < 0.01$ (p-values in parentheses)

Table 3A.9 Regression Results, Medium Services Firms

Dependent variable: ex_i	All regions		Core regions		Noncore regions	
	(1)	(2)	(3)	(4)	(5)	(6)
lnemp_i	0.1564	0.1303	0.2865	0.4149*	−0.5329	−0.2778
	[0.390]	[0.413]	[0.126]	[0.059]	[0.301]	[0.404]
lnage_i	0.1097	0.0198	−0.1198	−0.2838	0.9960***	0.5251*
	[0.448]	[0.887]	[0.426]	[0.127]	[0.004]	[0.057]
fdi_i	0.7627***	0.7990***	0.5581**	0.3596	1.6696**	1.4979***
	[0.002]	[0.001]	[0.045]	[0.212]	[0.013]	[0.004]
lntech_i	0.2972***	0.3023***	0.2305**	0.2250	0.8060***	0.5031***
	[0.005]	[0.006]	[0.039]	[0.165]	[0.008]	[0.004]
lncustoms_r		−0.2156		1.3946***		−0.1899
		[0.296]		[0.000]		[0.518]
lnelectr_r		0.0051		−0.6314***		0.0571
		[0.963]		[0.000]		[0.791]
lnlicense_r		−0.2682*		−2.9945***		−0.5176*
		[0.078]		[0.000]		[0.075]
credit_r		−0.0102		−0.0045***		−0.0163
		[0.113]		[0.000]		[0.112]
corrup_r		−0.0023		−0.1955***		−0.0042
		[0.776]		[0.000]		[0.776]
agg_size_r		0.0116		0.0033		0.0346
		[0.262]		[0.316]		[0.197]
agg_hhi_r		0.7951				1.6619
		[0.238]				[0.171]
agg_ind_r		−0.0036		0.1794***		−0.0021
		[0.673]		[0.000]		[0.931]
agg_ex_r		0.0280***		0.1131***		0.0272**
		[0.000]		[0.000]		[0.049]
constant_i	−2.4474***	−1.6742	−2.5638***	−0.2428	−2.7501	−0.2637
	[0.000]	[0.150]	[0.000]	[0.793]	[0.158]	[0.904]
Country fixed effects	Yes	Yes	Yes	Yes	Yes	Yes
Region fixed effects	Yes	No	Yes	No	Yes	No
Sector fixed effects	Yes	No	Yes	No	Yes	No
McFadden's adjusted pseudo R^2	−0.070	0.042	−0.046	−0.035	−0.074	0.011
Observations	482	601	352	267	130	229

Note: Medium: 20–99 employees. Standard errors are clustered at the regional level.
*$p < 0.1$, **$p < 0.05$, ***$p < 0.01$ (p-values in parentheses)

Table 3A.10 Regression Results, Small Services Firms

Dependent variable:	All regions		Core regions		Noncore regions	
ex_i	(1)	(2)	(3)	(4)	(5)	(6)
lnemp_i	0.2488	0.2972*	0.2291	0.2416	0.2551	0.1828
	[0.215]	[0.086]	[0.307]	[0.346]	[0.587]	[0.642]
lnage_i	−0.0292	−0.0609	0.0126	−0.0710	−0.1373	−0.0551
	[0.784]	[0.517]	[0.917]	[0.691]	[0.531]	[0.781]
fdi_i	0.8023***	0.8260***	0.5651*	0.6180*	2.2730**	2.5945**
	[0.004]	[0.001]	[0.069]	[0.062]	[0.034]	[0.037]
ln$tech_i$	0.3254***	0.2870***	0.3004***	0.3019**	0.4487	0.4978*
	[0.000]	[0.004]	[0.002]	[0.037]	[0.106]	[0.053]
ln$customs_r$		−0.8189***		1.2429***		−0.7327*
		[0.000]		[0.000]		[0.087]
ln$electr_r$		−0.0849		−0.8085***		0.5222**
		[0.297]		[0.000]		[0.044]
ln$license_r$		0.4877***		1.1837***		0.2064
		[0.002]		[0.000]		[0.599]
$credit_r$		0.0128**		0.2979***		−0.0178*
		[0.038]		[0.000]		[0.095]
$corrup_r$		0.0132		−0.0267***		−0.0397*
		[0.193]		[0.000]		[0.053]
agg_size_r		0.0063		0.1774***		0.0135
		[0.616]		[0.000]		[0.746]
agg_hhi_r		0.2605				−2.6471**
		[0.715]				[0.025]
agg_ind_r		0.0050		−0.1863***		0.1014***
		[0.657]		[0.000]		[0.001]
agg_ex_r		0.0141		−0.2150***		0.0540***
		[0.128]		[0.000]		[0.007]
$constant_i$	−1.8445***	−5.4891***	−1.8625***	−7.6369	−2.2956*	−4.7845**
	[0.000]	[0.000]	[0.000]	—	[0.055]	[0.028]
Country fixed effects	Yes	Yes	Yes	Yes	Yes	Yes
Region fixed effects	Yes	No	Yes	No	Yes	No
Sector fixed effects	Yes	No	Yes	No	Yes	No
McFadden's adjusted pseudo R^2	0.034	0.064	0.051	0.044	−0.070	−0.119
Observations	514	617	403	301	111	184

Note: — = not available. Small: 5–19 employees. Standard errors are clustered at the regional level.
*$p < 0.1$, **$p < 0.05$, ***$p < 0.01$ (p-values in parentheses)

Notes

1. The Herfindahl-Hirschman index (HHI) is an inverse measure of sector diversity and is defined as the sum of a region's squared output shares across sectors. A HHI of 1 reflects perfect sector concentration, that is, a region produces only one product. A lower HHI reflects higher product diversity within a region.

2. Exporters include direct exporters and "indirect exporters," defined as exporters who sell domestically to third parties that then export the products or services without modification. Goods sold domestically as intermediates to an exported product are not considered indirect exports.

3. See http://www.enterprisesurveys.org/~/media/FPDKM/EnterpriseSurveys/Documents/Misc/Indicator-Descriptions.pdf for a description of the indicators. Our analysis is based on the October 2011 release of the Enterprise Survey Indicator Database.

4. We dropped these, since the database only included nine high-income countries that were not representative of high-income countries (the Czech Republic, Germany, Greece, Hungary, Ireland, Portugal, the Slovak Republic, the Republic of Korea, and Spain).

5. We applied a threshold of three and not two regions, because in many countries with only two regions, these had similar relative sizes, rendering the determination of core regions very difficult.

6. Since some strata only had one observation, we did not use stratification. This affects the standard errors, which in general should be larger than when the strata is specified, or in other words, this should result in a more conservative test.

7. Besides location, we also take into account firm size. Results are shown in annex 3A.

8. We obtained firm-level compensation and total factor productivity (TFP) data from Frederica Saliola and Murat Seker from the Enterprise Analysis Unit of the World Bank. Total factor productivity has been calculated using a transcendental logarithmic (trans-log) production function, which allows for increasing or decreasing returns to scale and possible interactions between factor inputs. All local currencies have been converted into U.S. dollars and deflated using a gross domestic product (GDP) deflator in U.S. dollars (base year 2000). Exchange rates and GDP deflators have been obtained from the World Development Indicators.

9. We obtained firm-level output data from Frederica Saliola and Murat Seker from the Enterprise Analysis Unit of the World Bank. We aggregated the data to obtain output shares by industry. Output has been converted into U.S. dollars and deflated using exchange rates and a GDP deflator in U.S. dollars (base year 2000) from the World Development Indicators.

10. The literature typically adds GDP or population by region firms to capture urbanization effects. Using number of firms for this measure instead would only take into account absolute differences, whereas our study is concerned with relative differences in regional sizes. Moreover, the database has only stratified the survey sample across regions within a country, but not across countries.

References

Aitken, B., G. Hanson, and A. Harrison. 1997. "Spillovers, Foreign Investment, and Export Behavior." *Journal of International Economics* 43 (1–2): 103–32.

Amiti, M., and B. Javorcik. 2008. "Trade Costs and Location of Foreign Firms in China." *Journal of Development Economics* 85 (1–2): 129–49.

Antonietti, R., and G. Cainelli. 2009. "The Role of Spatial Agglomeration in a Structural Model of Innovation, Productivity and Export: A Firm-Level Analysis." *Annals of Regional Science* 46 (3): 577–600.

Bernard, A. B., and J. B. Jensen. 1995. "Exporters, Jobs, and Wages in US Manufacturing: 1976–87." *Brookings Papers on Economic Activity: Microeconomics*: 67–112.

———. 1999. "Exceptional Exporter Performance: Cause, Effect or Both?" *Journal of International Economics* 47 (1): 1–25.

———. 2004. "Why Some Firms Export." *Review of Economics and Statistics* 86 (2): 561–69.

Clerides, S. K., S. Lach, and J. R. Tybout. 1998. "Is Learning by Exporting Important? Micro-Dynamic Evidence from Colombia, Mexico, and Morocco." *Quarterly Journal of Economics* 113 (3): 903–47.

Deichmann, J., S. Karidis, and S. Sayek. 2003. "Foreign Direct Investment in Turkey: Regional Determinants." *Applied Economics* 35 (16): 1767–78.

Eaton, J., M. Eslava, M. Kugler, and J. Tybout. 2007. "Export Dynamics in Colombia: Firm-Level Evidence." NBER Working Paper 13531, National Bureau of Economic Research, Cambridge, MA.

Greenaway, D., and R. Kneller. 2004. "Exporting and Productivity in the United Kingdom." *Oxford Review of Economic Policy* 20 (3): 358–71.

———. 2008. "Exporting, Productivity, and Agglomeration." *European Economic Review* 52 (5): 919–39.

Koenig, P. 2009. "Agglomeration and the Export Decisions of French Firms." *Journal of Urban Economics* 66 (3): 186–95.

Koenig, P., F. Mayneris, and S. Poncet. 2010. "Local Export Spillovers in France." *European Economic Review* 54 (4): 622–41.

Krugman, P. 1991. "Increasing Returns and Economic Geography." *Journal of Political Economy* 99: 483–99.

Lovely, M., S. Rosenthal, and S. Sharma. 2005. "Information, Agglomeration and the Headquarters of US Exporters." *Regional Science and Urban Economics* 35 (2): 167–91.

Ma, Y., and Y. Zhang. 2008. "What's Different about New Exporters? Evidence from Chinese Manufacturing Firms." Unpublished paper, Department of Economics, Lingnan University, Hong Kong SAR, China.

Malmberg, A., B. Malmberg, and P. Lundequist. 2000. "Agglomeration and Firm Performance: Economies of Scale, Localization, and Urbanization among Swedish Export Firms." *Environment and Planning A* 32 (2): 305–21.

Mittelstaedt, J., W. Ward, and E. Nowlin. 2006. "Location, Industrial Concentration and the Propensity of Small US Firms to Export—Entrepreneurship in the International Marketplace." *International Marketing Review* 23 (5): 486–503.

Roberts, M. J., and J. R. Tybout. 1997. "The Decision to Export in Colombia: An Empirical Model of Entry with Sunk Costs." *American Economic Review* 87 (4): 545–64.

Ruhl, K., and J. Willis. 2008. "New Exporter Dynamics." Unpublished paper. New York: NYU Stern School of Business.

Sousa, C., F. Martínez-López, and F. Coelho. 2008. "The Determinants of Export Performance: A Review of the Research in the Literature between 1998 and 2005." *International Journal of Management Reviews* 10 (4): 343–74.

Wagner, J. 2007. "Exports and Productivity: A Survey of the Evidence from Firm-level Data." *World Economy* 30 (1): 60–82.

World Bank, n.d. *Enterprise Survey Indicators.* Online database. Washington, DC: World Bank. http://www.enterprisesurveys.org.

Zou, S., and S. Stan. 1998. "The Determinants of Export Performance: A Review of the Empirical Literature between 1987 and 1997." *International Marketing Review* 15 (5): 333–56.

CHAPTER 4

Trade and Regional Characteristics in Indonesia

Deborah Winkler

Introduction

This chapter, and the three that follow, move from the cross-country regularities discussed in chapter 3 to delve more deeply into the economic geography of exporting in specific developing countries. In this chapter and in chapter 5, the example is Indonesia, while chapters 6 and 7 take up the case of India. As noted in chapter 1, both these countries followed import substitution policies during the 1970s and 1980s, and then shifted to a more open, export- and investment-oriented strategy by the late 1980s and early 1990s. Both are also large, developing countries with significant population densities in peripheral regions, and a long history of "lagging region" problems.

In this chapter, we focus on a descriptive analysis of the relationship between trade and regions in Indonesia. This includes analyzing regional outcomes (for example, the convergence or divergence of per capita gross regional domestic product). In addition, it involves looking in more detail at the location of economic activity and the changes in sectoral output and export in the regions, as these are likely to be related to the observed variation in regional outcomes. Finally, we present some descriptive statistics on the differences in the regional investment climate in core versus noncore regions of Indonesia, in line with what was presented on a global basis in the section "Descriptive Analysis" of the previous chapter. Following this, in chapter 5, we carry out an econometric exercise to identify the factors that are associated with exporting in Indonesia's provinces, again broadly in line with the approach taken in chapter 3.

Data

We make use of two main data sources: the Indonesia Manufacturing Census and the World Bank Enterprise Surveys (see table 4.1). While the Manufacturing Census provides a more comprehensive data source than the Enterprise Surveys due to the broader geographical coverage and the much larger sample size, the Enterprise Surveys cover a wider range of indicators, most importantly

Table 4.1 Overview of Main Data Sources

Data source	Description/coverage	Main drawbacks
Manufacturing Census	Firm-level survey with data on manufacturing sector; data available by province	Only covers firms with > 20 staff; limited data on firm characteristics and no data on regional characteristics
World Bank Enterprise Surveys	Firm-level survey with data on manufacturing and services sector[a]; data available by province	Limited sample size, particularly at provincial level; limited data on firm characteristics; largely perception-based

Sources: BPS-Statistics Indonesia 2012; Enterprise Survey Indicators, World Bank.
a. For comparability with the Manufacturing Census, we make use only of the manufacturing sample in the Enterprise Surveys.

on the business environment in which firms operate (including such factors as infrastructure, finance, corruption, and business regulations). Therefore, we make use of the Manufacturing Census to assess trade participation and performance, but rely on the Enterprise Surveys to get a richer understanding of firm characteristics and perceptions of the regional and national business environment.

The Manufacturing Census is a survey of manufacturing establishments (at the plant level) with at least 20 workers, conducted annually by the Indonesian Bureau of Statistics (Badan Pusat Statistik[1]). The Manufacturing Census Data cover data on a firm's inputs, output, and trade. Our available database covers the period 1990–2008 (1990 was the first year in which the Census provided information on a firm's export activity).[2] The census data classify firms into 5-digit International Standard Industrial Classification (ISIC) Rev. 2 industries. Currently, Indonesia consists of 33 provinces, seven of which have been created since 2000. The manufacturing census data cover all provinces except for Sulawesi Barat. In order to make the provinces comparable over the period 1990–2008, we grouped all newly created provinces back to their original provinces. In addition, we also aggregated provinces into five island groups for some of the analysis. For a list of provinces and province codes, as well as province groups and island groups used, see table 4A.1. Table 4A.2 shows the number of firms by island group. Input and output data, including exports, were deflated using a value added deflator, while net investment flows were deflated using an investment price deflator. The value added deflator was constructed by dividing manufacturing value added in current prices by manufacturing value added in 2000 constant prices.

Enterprise Surveys are published by the World Bank and represent a comprehensive source of firm-level data in emerging markets and developing economies. They comprise a random sample of firms using three levels of stratification: sector, firm size, and region. The latest Enterprise Survey for Indonesian firms was conducted between August 2009 and January 2010 and covers nine provinces: Bali, Banten, DKI Jakarta, Java Barat, Java Tengah, Java Timur, Lampung, Sulawesi Selatan, and Sumatra Utara. Although the whole sample includes around 1,400 firms, we only focus on the 1,176 manufacturing firms. Table 4A.3 shows the distribution of firms across sectors and regions.[3]

Economic Geography and the Evolution of Regional Inequalities in Indonesia

In this section, we provide a very a brief introduction to the economic geography of Indonesia. Specifically we intend to show (1) the extent of regional inequality (in economic activity and outcomes) and how this has evolved over time; and (2) the relationship between "lagging" regions and geographical factors, including location and density. A number of studies provide more detailed background on regional inequalities and the geography of production structures in Indonesia; see, for example, Deichmann et al. (2005), Handa (2005), Hill (1987), and Sjöholm (1999).

Snapshot of Indonesia's Economic Geography

The Gini coefficient of regional inequality in Indonesia stands above 0.3, which is relatively high by international standards, although not out of line with many large, developing countries (see figure 4.1). Inequality is driven by relative concentration in three very different types of regions (see table 4.2). First are the areas of dense population around the geographical "core" of the country—Jakarta, West Java, and Southern Sumatra. Second are some geographically peripheral regions with small populations and substantial natural resources, and third are the Riau islands, with their free trade zones and location near Singapore. By contrast, economically "lagging" regions include the peripheral provinces that are less

Figure 4.1 Gini Index of Regional Income Inequality in Selected Countries, 2005

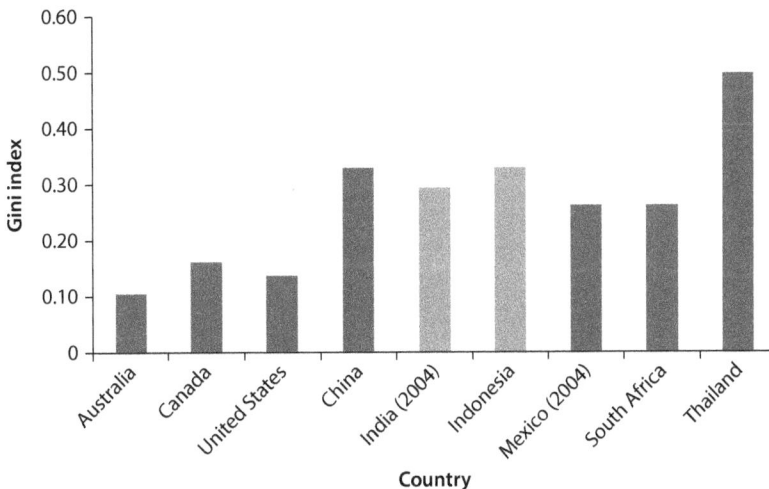

Source: Calculations based on dataset from Rodríguez-Pose 2011.

Table 4.2 Comparison of Indonesia's Provincial Economic Output, 2008

	GRDP current price (m Rupiah)	Population ('000)	GRDP per capita (current Rupiah)	Index vs. IDN average
Prov. Kalimantan Timur	315,220,363	3,095	101,848,259	5.532
Prov. DKI Jakarta	677,411,092	9,146	74,066,378	4.023
Prov. Riau	276,400,130	5,189	53,266,550	2.893
Prov. Kepulauan Riau	59,207,618	1,453	40,748,533	2.213
Prov. Papua	54,733,628	2,057	26,608,473	1.445
Prov. Bangka Belitung	21,720,598	1,123	19,341,583	1.050
Prov. Sumatera Selatan	133,358,882	7,122	18,724,920	1.017
Prov. Nanggroe Aceh Darussalam	73,530,750	4,294	17,124,068	0.930
Prov. Papua Barat	12,471,606	730	17,084,392	0.928
Prov. Jawa Timur	621,581,955	37,095	16,756,489	0.910
Prov. Sumatera Utara	213,931,697	13,042	16,403,289	0.891
Prov. Kalimantan Tengah	32,350,804	2,057	15,727,177	0.854
Prov. Sumatera Barat	71,232,992	4,763	14,955,489	0.812
Prov. Jawa Barat	602,420,555	40,918	14,722,630	0.800
Prov. Jambi	39,665,345	2,788	14,227,168	0.773
Prov. Bali	49,922,604	3,516	14,198,693	0.771
Prov. Kalimantan Selatan	45,515,623	3,447	13,204,416	0.717
Prov. Banten	122,497,457	9,602	12,757,494	0.693
Prov. Sulawesi Utara	27,842,985	2,208	12,610,048	0.685
Prov. Sulawesi Tengah	28,151,502	2,438	11,546,966	0.627
Prov. Kalimantan Barat	48,415,521	4,249	11,394,568	0.619
Prov. Jawa Tengah	364,895,438	32,626	11,184,192	0.607
Prov. DI Yogyakarta	38,102,133	3,469	10,983,607	0.597
Prov. Sulawesi Selatan	85,143,191	7,805	10,908,801	0.592
Prov. Sulawesi Tenggara	22,173,885	2,075	10,686,210	0.580
Prov. Lampung	74,490,599	7,391	10,078,555	0.547
Prov. Bengkulu	14,446,964	1,642	8,798,395	0.478
Prov. Nusa Tenggara Barat	35,261,677	4,364	8,080,128	0.439
Prov. Sulawesi Barat	7,778,001	1,032	7,536,823	0.409
Prov. Gorontalo	5,899,787	972	6,069,740	0.330
Prov. Nusa Tenggara Timur	21,621,835	4,534	4,768,821	0.259
Prov. Maluku	6,269,710	1,321	4,746,185	0.258
Prov. Maluku Utara	3,856,362	960	4,017,044	0.218

Sources: Calculations based on data from Badan Pusat Statistik (http://www.bps.go.id/eng/index.php).
Note: GRDP = gross regional domestic product, IDN = Indonesia, Prov. = Province.

endowed with natural resources, as well as some relatively densely populated areas in Central and East Java. This contrast is illustrated even more starkly in table 4.3, which compares provincial measures of remoteness,[4] population, and infrastructure[5] with per capita output. In this table, the organization by island group highlights that each group (with the notable exception of Sulawesi) includes at least one "leading" and several "lagging" provinces. On the whole, the most "remote" provinces tend to also have smaller populations and worse infrastructure. This suggests that distance, density, and division (induced by poor

Table 4.3 The Links between Distance, Density, and Lagging Regions in Indonesia

	Remoteness	Population (2008)	Infrastructure	GRDP per capita vs. IDN average
Sumatra				
Prov. Nanggroe Aceh Daruss	0.5301	4,294	0.45	0.9
Prov. Sumatera Utara	0.4736	13,042	0.49	0.9
Prov. Sumatera Barat	0.4094	4,763	0.71	0.8
Prov. Riau	0.3907	5,189	0.35	2.9
Prov. Jambi	0.3063	2,788	0.58	0.8
Prov. Sumatera Selatan	0.2085	7,122	0.53	1.0
Prov. Bengkulu	0.1948	1,642	0.72	0.5
Prov. Lampung	0.0794	7,391	0.49	0.5
Java				
Prov. DKI Jakarta	0.0035	9,223	0.98	4.0
Prov. Jawa Barat	0.0102	40,918	0.70	0.8
Prov. Jawa Tengah	0.0318	32,626	0.64	0.6
Prov. DI Yogyakarta	0.0341	3,469	0.76	0.6
Prov. Jawa Timur	0.0017	37,095	0.58	0.9
Prov. Bali	0.0932	3,516	0.97	0.8
Kalimantan				
Prov. Kalimantan Barat	0.4011	4,249	0.31	0.6
Prov. Kalimantan Tengah	0.1272	2,057	0.15	0.9
Prov. Kalimantan Selatan	0.0577	3,447	0.56	0.7
Prov. Kalimantan Timur	0.3059	3,095	0.21	5.5
Sulawesi				
Prov. Sulawesi Utara	0.4736	2,208	0.72	0.7
Prov. Sulawesi Tengah	0.3019	2,438	0.54	0.6
Prov. Sulawesi Selatan	0.1243	7,805	0.51	0.6
Prov. Sulawesi Tenggara	0.2793	2,075	0.45	0.6
Eastern Islands				
Prov. Maluku	—	1,340	—	0.3
Prov. Papua	1.0000	2,098	0.15	1.4
Prov. Nusa Tenggara Barat	0.1740	4,364	0.76	0.4
Prov. Nusa Tenggara Timur	0.3599	4,534	0.40	0.3

Correlation coefficient	Remoteness	Population	Infrastructure	Output per capita vs. IDN average
Remoteness	1	−0.4185*	−0.5212**	0.0474
Population		1	0.1948	−0.0554
Infrastructure			1	−0.1568
Output per capita vs. average				1

Sources: Calculations based on data from Badan Pusat Statistik (http://www.bps.go.id/eng/index.php); World Bank 2011.
Note: — = not available, GRDP = gross regional domestic product, IDN = Indonesia, Prov. = Province. Provinces in bold are those covered in the Enterprise Surveys (including Banten, which is covered in the Enterprise Surveys separately from Java Barat).
* indicates significance at 0.05 level; ** indicates significance at 0.01 level.

connectivity) may conspire to hold back regions in Indonesia. On the other hand, the relationship between these factors and per capita output is actually (weakly) positive, reflecting the strong bias of the Indonesian economy toward sectors based on natural resources. This may mask lack of jobs and poverty at the household level in many of these peripheral, resource-rich provinces. Whether this relationship between economic output and location holds within the manufacturing sector alone is something we will explore further in chapter 5.

Evolution of Regional Inequalities

In the context of the economic geography described above, we next ask how regional inequalities have evolved in the two decades since Indonesia became a more open, trade-integrated economy. Figures 4.2 and 4.3 indicate that regional inequalities in Indonesia have grown quite considerably, rising 25 percent between 1990 and 2008. Although inequality hardly changed in the initial period of opening between 1990 and 1996, it grew rapidly during the Asian crisis period, and continued to rise in the decade since. The data on trade openness seem to suggest that trade openness grew rapidly only after 1996, precisely the period in which inequalities increased most significantly. However, the apparent rapid increase in trade openness is a function not so much of major trade growth but of substantial contraction of the Indonesian domestic economy during the Asian crisis (gross domestic product [GDP] declined by over 13 percent in 1998). Inequality continued to rise when the trade share of GDP returned to more "normal" levels after the crisis. This suggests that while trade openness may play a part in the evolution of regional inequalities in Indonesia, there may well be other important factors contributing to it, such as the growing reliance of the economy on natural resources–based sectors.

Figure 4.2 Gini Index of Regional Income Inequality and Trade Openness in Indonesia, 1990–2008

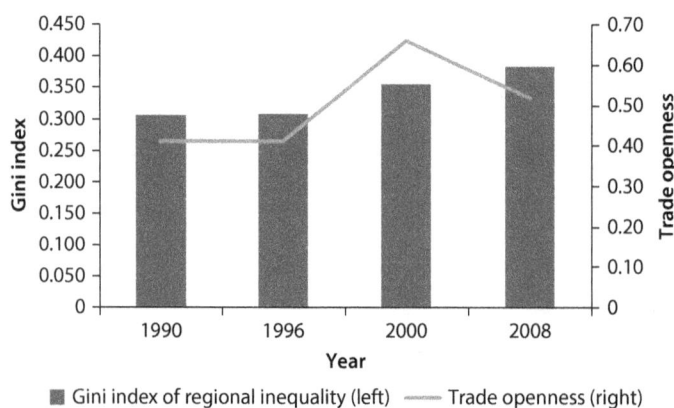

Sources: Calculations based on data from Badan Pusat Statistik (http://www.bps.go.id/eng/index.php); World Bank 2010.
Note: Data based on gross regional domestic products per capita in current prices. Data weighted by provincial population. Trade openness calculated as the merchandise trade share of gross domestic product.

Figure 4.3 GDP per Capita Relative to the Indonesia Average by Major Island Group, 1990–2008

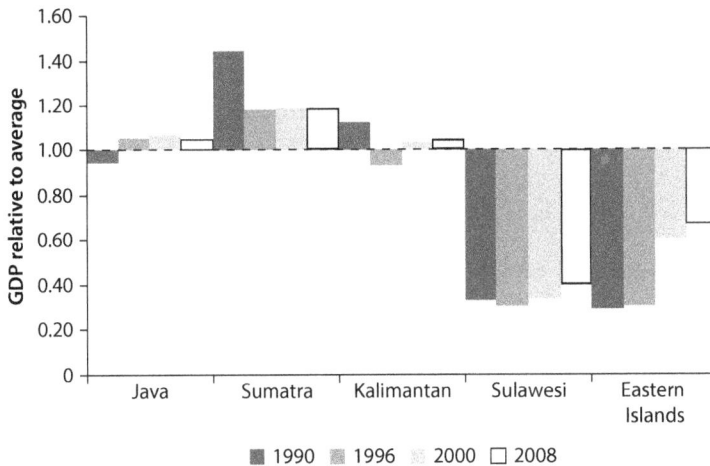

Sources: Calculations based on data from Badan Pusat Statistik (http://www.bps.go.id/eng/index.php); World Bank 2010.
Note: GDP = gross domestic product. Data based on gross regional domestic products per capita in constant 2000 prices. Data weighted by provincial population. Bali is included in the Java island grouping.

Indeed, figure 4.3, which starts to give a better picture of the regional winners and losers over the past two decades, hints at this. Overall, the picture is one of relatively minor changes—all island groups remained in 2008, by and large, in the same relative positions they were in 1990. This is noteworthy in a country that grew so rapidly and underwent so many changes during this period. Kalimantan remains far and away the "leading" island group, with particularly strong growth relative to the rest of the country since 1996. The Sumatra and the Eastern Islands can be described as the two regional "losers" over this period. Sumatra experienced much slower growth than the rest of the country during the 1990–96 manufacturing boom period, bringing it much closer to the national average in terms of output per capita. Two important factors behind this slow growth were the conflict in Aceh and the relative (short-term) decline in the Riau islands, whose free zones had been particularly attractive when Indonesia's trade policy was more closed. Both provinces have since rebounded, however, supporting the stabilization of Sumatra's position. The Eastern Islands comprise, along with Sulawesi, the main lagging regions in Indonesia. Despite a period of strong gains in the first half of the 1990s, they have been unable to keep pace with the growth of the rest of the country and have fallen further behind during the last decade. With the bulk of the population and economic activity, Java remains more or less stable at the national average output per capita.

But even these island groupings mask substantial variation in the experiences of individual provinces. Within Java, Jakarta's GDP per capita grew from 2.6 times the national average in 1990 to over four times the national average just 10 years later (and maintained this level through 2008), while Central Java declined from 0.72 to 0.61 times the national average over the two decades.

Bali, one of the most trade-dependent economies in Indonesia, rose to 11 percent above the national average in 1996, but has since declined rapidly to fall 23 percent below the national average by 2008. GDP per capita in East Kalimantan is almost nine times higher than it is in West Kalimantan, a gap that has doubled between 1996 and 2008. In Maluku, GDP per capita declined steadily from 77 percent of the national average in 1990 to only 24 percent by 2008 (and is now 23 times lower than in the leading province of East Kalimantan). See table 4A.4 for a summary of performance across all provinces.

Trade Participation and Structural Change in Indonesian Provinces

Trade Participation

According to the data from the World Bank Enterprise Surveys (see table 4.4 in the next section), firms in Indonesia's "core" (Jakarta and Java Barat) are twice as likely to be exporters as those outside the core; this is powerful evidence to indicate that centrality matters for exporting in Indonesia. Looking at this in more detail, however, shows that the picture is heterogeneous. Figures 4.4 and 4.5 give some perspective on the relative export participation and intensity of firms across geographies in Indonesia. Figure 4.4, focused on a much narrower set of provinces that are not major natural resources–based exporters, gives a much stronger indication that firms in more centrally located provinces are much more likely to export. Across the country, the share of manufacturing firms that export varies widely across provinces, from less than 5 percent (in Nusa Tenggara Timur and Bara) to more than 40 percent in Riau, Bali, and Kalimantan Tengah. In Java, Jakarta and Java Timur have firm export participation rates of only 10 percent and 11 percent, respectively, while 36 percent of Yogyakarta's manufacturing firms export.

Figure 4.4 Share of Direct Exporter Firms in Enterprise Survey Provinces

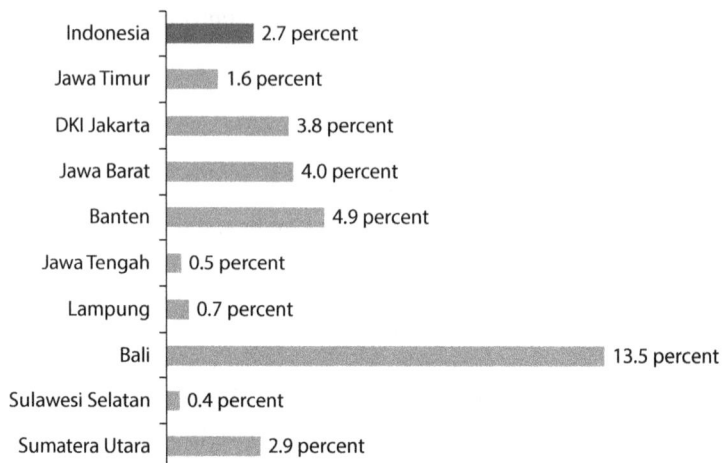

Indonesia	2.7 percent
Jawa Timur	1.6 percent
DKI Jakarta	3.8 percent
Jawa Barat	4.0 percent
Banten	4.9 percent
Jawa Tengah	0.5 percent
Lampung	0.7 percent
Bali	13.5 percent
Sulawesi Selatan	0.4 percent
Sumatera Utara	2.9 percent

Source: World Bank 2009.

Figure 4.5 Export Location Quotient by Island Group

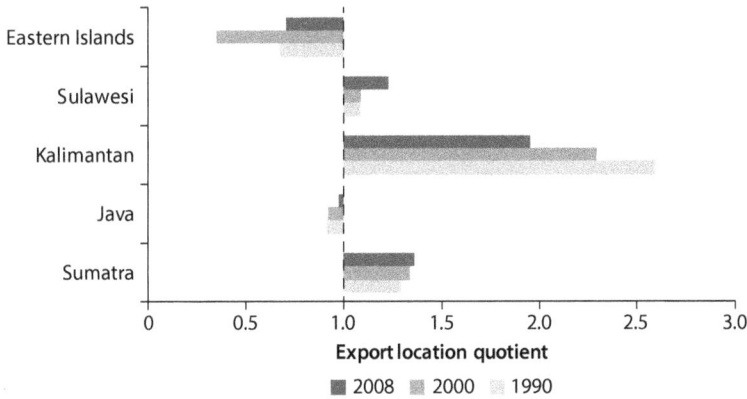

Export location quotient

■ 2008 ■ 2000 ▓ 1990

Source: Calculations based on BPS-Statistics Indonesia 2012.

Figure 4.5 presents a location quotient by island group, which measures manufacturing export share to population share (a result greater than 1.0 means that share of national manufacturing exports is greater than the population share of the island group; less than 1.0 means that it is less than the population share). This indicates that export participation is particularly high in Kalimantan, but also relatively high in Sumatra and Sulawesi. By contrast, export participation is far below expected levels in the Eastern Islands, despite its relatively low population. This result is likely to be biased, however, by the strong natural resources base in some provinces (particularly in Kalimantan, but also in Sulawesi and Sumatra), which are almost exclusively exported. In addition, manufacturing firms in Kalimantan, Sulawesi, and Sumatra tend to be much larger and more capital-intensive, on average, than those in the rest of the country.

Provinces located in the core also tend to be more trade integrated than peripheral provinces, when imports are taken into account. Figures 4.6 and 4.7 show the offshoring intensity (that is, the share of material inputs that are imported) of island groups and select provinces. It shows that firms in Java and Sumatra make much greater use of imported inputs than those in Kalimantan, Sulawesi, and the Eastern Islands. Firms in Jakarta and Java Barat make the greatest use of imported inputs (firms in Jakarta import more than 15 percent of inputs),[6] while firms in Nusa Tenggara Barat, Kalimantan Tengah, Kalimantan Selatan, and Sulawesi Tenggara import almost nothing.

Changes in Sectoral Specialization

Even if we take as a given that trade has a significant impact on the nature of regional inequalities, the relationship is not likely to be a direct one—that is, trade affects regional outcomes through other channels. The most important of these, at least in the medium term, is how trade impacts the output structure of regions. For regions that were previously relatively closed to international trade, openness may alter significantly the sectoral structure of the region, as the combination

Figure 4.6 Imported Inputs as a Percentage of Total Material Inputs

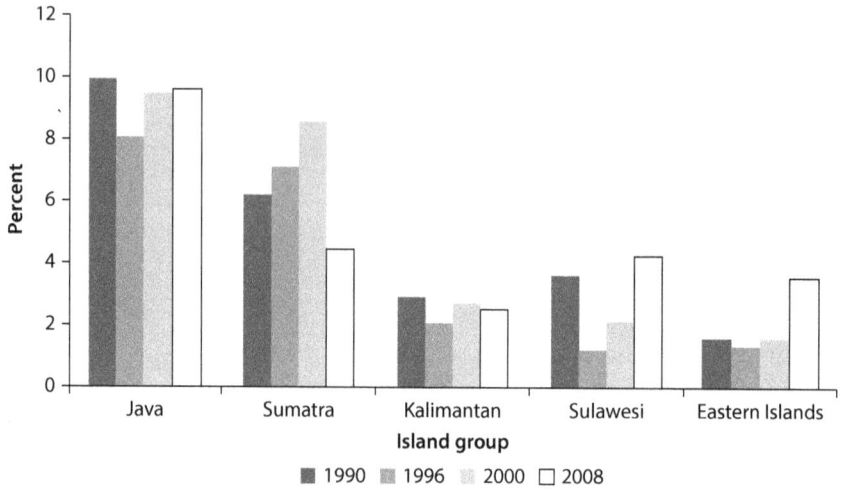

Source: Calculations based on BPS-Statistics Indonesia 2012.

Figure 4.7 Material Inputs of Foreign Origin as a Percentage of Total Material Inputs

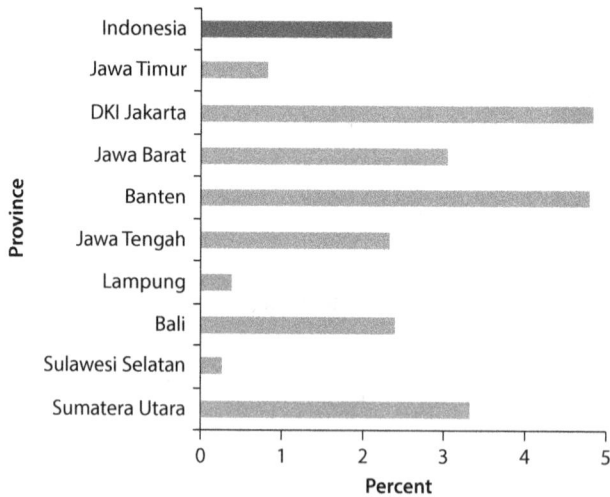

Source: World Bank 2009.

of export opportunities and import competition leads to regions deepening their specialization in sectors in which they have a comparative advantage. This changing sectoral structure may bias outcomes in favor of regions that are comparatively advantaged in sectors that are faster growing, offer greater potential to reap the benefits of value addition, and/or contribute to greater employment (directly and through multiplier effects). By contrast, regions whose lack of competitiveness would have been shielded under a closed trade regime may face significant adjustment costs.

With this in mind, in this section we look briefly at the structural changes in the regional economies of Indonesia over the past two decades. To do so, we apply an index of structural change (ISC) in employment, output, and exports. We use the measure by Stoikov (1966), which has been widely used in economic research and computed by Dietrich (2011) in equation 4.1:

$$ISC_{rst} = 0.5 \sum_{i=1}^{N} \left| \frac{x_{irt}}{X_{rt}} - \frac{x_{irs}}{X_{rs}} \right| \qquad (4.1)$$

where subscript i denotes sectors, r regions, and s and t two points in time. x_{irt}/X_{rt} is the sectoral share of employment, output, or exports by region r at time t in a region's total sectoral employment, output, or exports, and x_{irs}/X_{rs} is the sectoral share of employment, output, or exports by region r at time s. In a first step, this index requires calculating first differences of the sectoral shares between the two points in time. In a second step, one sums up the absolute amounts of these sectoral differences. Since all changes are counted twice (because an increase in a sectoral share means a decrease of other sectoral shares), one needs to multiply the measure by 0.5. The ISC ranges between 0 and 1. It can be interpreted as the sectoral change as a percentage of the whole economy. If the sectoral structure does not change over the period, the index is equal to 0. If all sectors change completely—that is, existing sectors discontinue and new sectors are created—then the index is equal to 1.

Figure 4.7 shows the ISC for manufacturing output and exports by main island group. As a robustness check, we calculated the ISC at the 2-digit (9 sectors), 3-digit (29 sectors), and 4-digit (109 sectors) industry level using the ISIC Rev. 2 classification. In figure 4.7, we show just the results from the 3-digit calculation—details for individual provinces at 2-, 3-, and 4-digit levels are provided in table 4A.5.

The results indicate a fairly strong correlation between output and export structural change across all provinces, with structural change in exports significantly greater than change in output. In fact, every single province experienced greater structural change in exports than in output, suggesting that trade openness contributed significantly to changing regional export structures. They also show, not surprisingly, that the regions with the highest output shares (see table 4.2) experienced relatively lower structural change in output and exports. Interestingly, these same regions—specifically the island groups of Java and Sumatra (but also Sulawesi)—experienced a much greater structural change in exports versus output than did the more peripheral regions, like Kalimantan and the Eastern Islands. In fact, four provinces that make up the country's main manufacturing core—Jakarta, Java Barat, Java Timur, and Yogyakarta—experienced the highest ratio of change of exports over output.

At a provincial level, the highest structural changes in output were in Muluku, Kalimantan Tengah, Sulawesi Tenggerah, Jambi, and Riau (including Kepulauan Riau); the first three of these (along with Nusa Tenggara Timur and Kalimantan Selatan) also show the highest change in export structure. The lowest structural changes in output can be found for Bengkulu, Sulawesi Utara (including Gorontalo), Java Timur, Java Tengah, and Java Barat (including Banten). The first four of these (along with Lampung) were also the five provinces with the lowest structural change in exports.

As noted above, provinces that experienced the greatest structural change were almost all in peripheral areas. This may, however, be more a reflection of the lack of diversification in their economies than of the impact of trade openness. Most provinces in the outer islands were almost fully concentrated in a single export commodity in the early 1990s (in almost all cases, wood). Over the period under study, these provinces usually added a second export commodity (typically food). This single change of course has a dramatic impact on the structural change statistic, whereas a province that was already diversified across a number of products would be unable to achieve such significant changes. One provincial experience of structural change is worthy of note. As a result of its free trade zones, Riau's export structure shifted substantially—from wood, rubber, and food at the beginning of the period to electrical machinery by the end. Finally, provinces with the least change in export and output structure include not just the already-integrated core provinces, but also peripheral ones like Sulawesi Tenggara, Sulawesi Barat, and Bengkulu. Thus, even the affects of trade failed to have a significant impact on some peripheral regions.

Finally, while the emphasis in this book is on the manufacturing sector, it may well be the case that significant trade-induced structural changes are happening to regions outside the manufacturing sector, particularly in those peripheral regions that had (and perhaps still have) limited participation in manufacturing. Therefore, in figure 4.8, we look at total economy structural change by island group. Due to limited data, we are only to measure at a highly aggregated level (nine broad sectors[7]). Therefore, shifts in products and even broad product groups would not be captured. We are also unable to measure output or exports directly, but can at least proxy this with employment data. Overall, the results suggest substantially less structural change, as would be expected with this broad level of aggregation, particularly for peripheral regions that show substantial change in manufacturing output and exports. By far, the greatest structural change in the overall economy appears to be in Sumatra. Probing this in more detail with province-specific data, we see this change is driven particularly by Riau, Aceh, and Lampung, but that most provinces in Sumatra experienced higher than average structural change. Interestingly, the provinces that experienced substantial structural change based on manufacturing output and exports show contrasting results in the total economy analysis. Provinces like Riau and Jambi showing some of the highest overall structural change, while Maluku, Kalimantan Tengah, and Nusa Tenggara Timur are among the five provinces with the lowest overall structural change in Indonesia.

Industrial Relocation: Changing Spatial Patterns of Industry

Finally, in this subsection, we take an alternative approach to understanding structural change—this time from the perspective of where industry locates

Figure 4.8 Index of Structural Change in Manufacturing Output and Exports by Island Group, 1990–91 to 2007–08

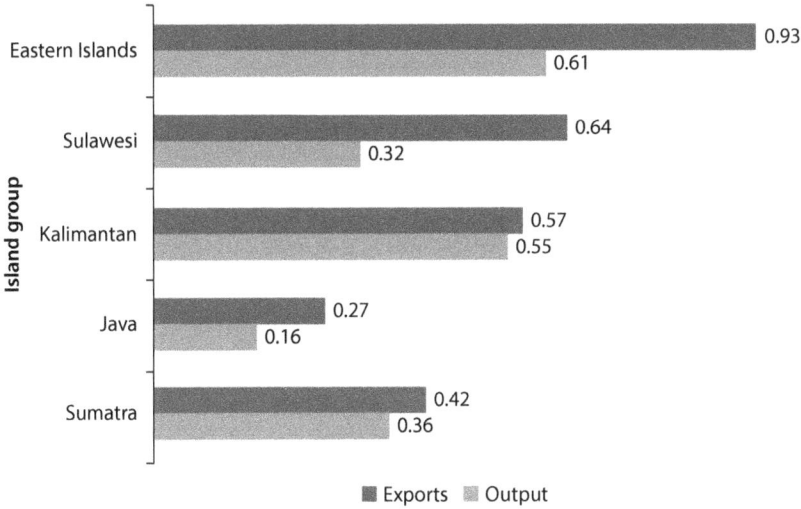

Source: Calculations based on BPS-Statistics Indonesia 2012.
Note: Output and exports are at 2000 prices. Index for output is based on 1990/91 and 2007/08 averages. Index for exports is based on 1990/91 average and 2008. ISIC Rev. 2 classifications are used. We used the averages of 1990/91 and 2007/08 as the two points in time to smooth any abnormal annual figures.

(that is, looking at things through an industry rather than a regional lens). Here we present high-level, descriptive data on the regional location patterns of manufacturing in order to support further understanding of the determinants of regional divergence observed in Indonesia.

In figure 4.9, we use a modified version of the Herfindahl-Hirschman index (HHI) calculated for each product category by taking the total sum of the squared market shares of all regions producing that good (equation 4.2):

$$HHI_j = \sum_i (S_{ij})^2 \qquad (4.2)$$

where S_{ij} is the share of region i expressed as a percentage of a country's total output of product j.[8] The HHI can range between $1/n$ (if each of the n regions has the same output share), and 1, if one region produces all, where n designates the total number of regions producing this good. A decline reflects a greater degree of spatial dispersion of output in that sector, while an increase reflects a greater degree of regional concentration.

Not only is the level of change relatively high in many sectors, but also, as was the case with the geographical ISCs, structural change of exports is much greater, in most cases, than that of output. In fact, taking an unweighted average across manufacturing sectors shows that export geographical structural change was twice that of output structural change. This suggests that the export-oriented

Figure 4.9 Index of Structural Change in Employment for Total Economy by Island Group, 1990–91 to 2007–08

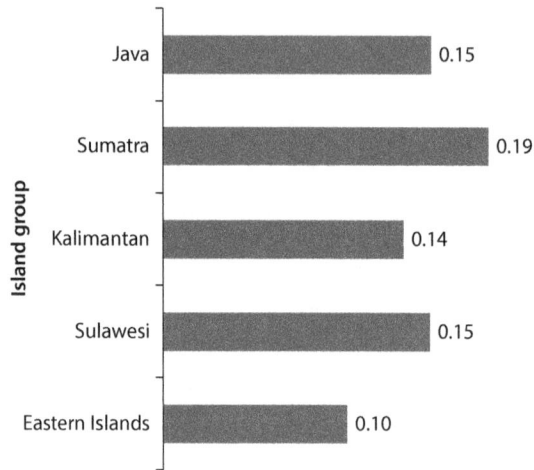

Source: Calculations based on data from Badan Pusat Statistik (http://www.bps.go.id/eng/index.php).
Note: Index is based on nine sectors covering the whole economy. Employment is defined as number of working people (15 years and above).

production shifted its geographical position within the country substantially, and substantially more than did domestic-oriented production. Figure 4.10 shows that the biggest structural changes in export-oriented production took place in relatively capital-intensive sectors, like iron and steel, other chemicals, tobacco, and other food and animal feeds. Combined with the significant gap between exports and output ISC in these product groups, the results suggest that the figures may be skewed by one or several large, export-oriented units. By contrast, some of the traditional export-oriented manufacturing sectors, like apparel, textiles, furniture, and footwear, showed low to moderate levels of geographical relocation. This may reflect that territorializing power of established clusters.

Firm and Regional Characteristics: Descriptive Analysis Using Enterprise Survey Data

As discussed throughout this book, much research has an association between firm characteristics and export performance; similarly, characteristics outside the firm—specifically the local business environment—also play an important mediating role. In this section, we provide a descriptive overview of the relationship between trade participation and firm and regional characteristics. It relies mainly on the Enterprise Survey data discussed previously, which restricts our coverage to a relatively narrow range of provinces, with particularly limited coverage of the truly peripheral provinces. Table 4.4 follows the same analytical approach used in chapter 3 (see the section "Descriptive Analysis") by comparing the differences in mean outcomes of various indicators for firms based in core versus noncore

Figure 4.10 Index of Geographical Change in Output and Exports by Industry, 1990–91 to 2007–08

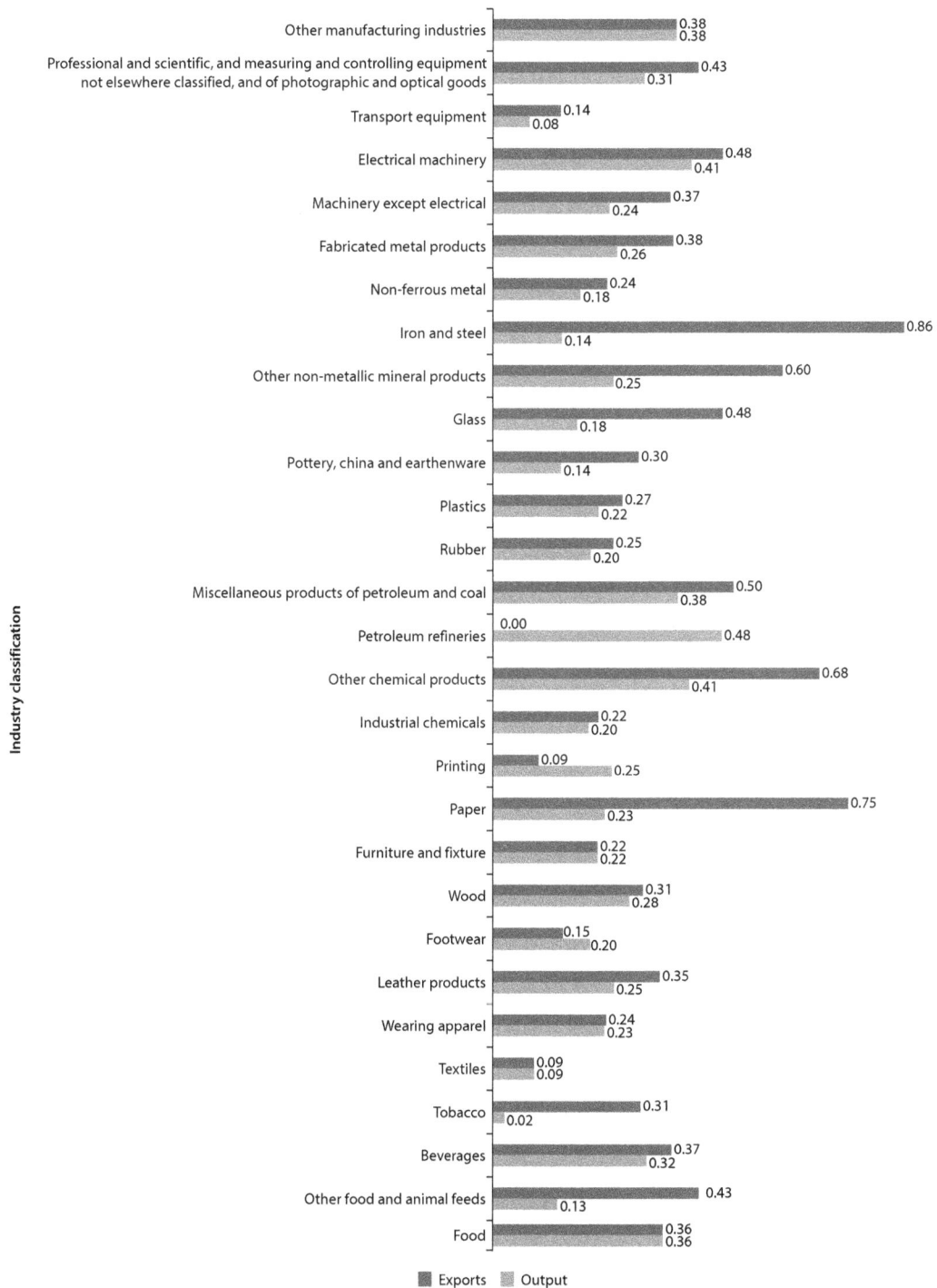

Industry classification	Exports	Output
Other manufacturing industries	0.38	0.38
Professional and scientific, and measuring and controlling equipment not elsewhere classified, and of photographic and optical goods	0.43	0.31
Transport equipment	0.14	0.08
Electrical machinery	0.48	0.41
Machinery except electrical	0.37	0.24
Fabricated metal products	0.38	0.26
Non-ferrous metal	0.24	0.18
Iron and steel	0.86	0.14
Other non-metallic mineral products	0.60	0.25
Glass	0.48	0.18
Pottery, china and earthenware	0.30	0.14
Plastics	0.27	0.22
Rubber	0.25	0.20
Miscellaneous products of petroleum and coal	0.50	0.38
Petroleum refineries	0.00	0.48
Other chemical products	0.68	0.41
Industrial chemicals	0.22	0.20
Printing	0.09	0.25
Paper	0.75	0.23
Furniture and fixture	0.22	0.22
Wood	0.31	0.28
Footwear	0.15	0.20
Leather products	0.35	0.25
Wearing apparel	0.24	0.23
Textiles	0.09	0.09
Tobacco	0.31	0.02
Beverages	0.37	0.32
Other food and animal feeds	0.43	0.13
Food	0.36	0.36

■ Exports ▨ Output

Source: Calculations based on BPS-Statistics Indonesia 2012.
Note: Output and exports are at 2000 prices. Index for output is based on 1990/91 and 2007/08 averages. Index for exports is based on 1990/91 average and 2008. ISIC Rev. 2 classifications is used.

Table 4.4 Comparison of Firm and Regional Characteristics in Core and Noncore Provinces of Indonesia

	Core	Noncore	p-value	Core/noncore
Export and trade outcomes				
Direct exports (% of sales)	2.3	0.8	0.063*	2.93
% of firms that export directly	4.1	2.1	0.096*	1.92
% of firms that use material inputs and/or supplies of foreign origin	5.8	4.0	0.255	1.46
Firm characteristics				
Age and ownership				
Average age (years)	13.4	16.5	0.000***	0.81
Private domestic ownership (%)	96.9	84.0	0.000***	1.15
Private foreign ownership (%)	3.1	0.9	0.034**	3.32
Technology				
% of firms with internationally recognized quality certification	3.1	1.4	0.08*	2.25
% of firms using technology licensed from foreign companies	4.4	4.1	0.839	1.08
% of firms using their own website	3.2	3.0	0.883	1.05
% of firms using email to communicate with clients/suppliers	13.3	5.0	0.000***	2.64
Workforce				
% of firms offering formal training	6.3	4.3	0.307	1.45
Average number of seasonal/temporary, full-time employees	2.3	1.4	0.086*	1.61
Average number of permanent, full-time employees	23.3	15.3	0.008**	1.52
Average share of skilled production workers (% of production workers)	70.6	84.1	0.000***	0.84
Average experience of the top manager working in the firm's sector (years)	11.4	15.0	0.000***	0.76
% of firms identifying labor regulations as a major constraint	1.2	2.5	0.24	0.49
% of firms identifying labor skill level as a major constraint	1.4	4.0	0.054*	0.36
Regional characteristics: investment climate				
Infrastructure				
Number of power outages in a typical month	1.5	2.5	0.020**	0.62
Duration of power outages (hours)	1.8	2.7	0.008***	0.67
Value lost due to power outages (% of sales)	2.1	2.2	0.908	0.94
Delay in obtaining an electrical connection (days)	9.4	23.5	0.008***	0.40
Average electricity from a generator (%)	2.3	1.5	0.323	1.58
Average number of incidents of water insufficiency in a typical month	3.8	5.5	0.387	0.69
Delay in obtaining a water connection (days)	13.0	30.0	0.151	0.43
Delay in obtaining a mainline telephone connection (days)	20.2	14.0	0.391	1.44
Transport and trade facilitation				
Average time to clear direct exports through customs (days)	2.6	2.0	0.382	1.28
Average time to clear imports from customs (days)	3.5	3.6	0.923	0.97
Average time of inventory of most important input (days)	13.6	14.4	0.673	0.95
% of firms identifying customs & trade regulations as a major constraint	4.3	4.2	0.966	1.02
% of firms identifying transportation as a major constraint	4.8	10.7	0.005***	0.45
Regulations and tax				
Senior management time spent in dealing with requirements of government regulation (%)	2.0	0.9	0.009***	2.09
Average number of visits or required meetings with tax officials	0.2	0.1	0.385	1.26
% of firms identifying tax rates as major constraint	1.2	5.1	0.012	0.24
% of firms identifying tax administration as major constraint	5.0	3.5	0.46	1.41

table continues next page

Table 4.4 Comparison of Firm and Regional Characteristics in Core and Noncore Provinces of Indonesia (continued)

	Core	Noncore	p-value[a]	Core/noncore
Permits and licenses				
Average time to obtain operating license (days)	32.0	9.8	0.008***	3.28
Average time to obtain import license (days)	11.5	9.0	0.337	1.28
Average time to obtain construction-related permit (days)	54.1	22.8	0.203	2.38
% of firms identifying business licensing and permits as major constraint	7.7	4.6	0.179	1.70
Corruption				
% of firms expected to pay informal payment to public officials	18.8	10.7	0.013**	1.76
% of firms expected to give gifts to get an operating license	31.8	12.2	0.059*	2.61
% of firms expected to give gifts in meetings with tax officials	15.8	15.0	0.928	1.05
% of firms expected to give gifts to secure a government contract	42.7	35.5	0.817	1.20
% of firms identifying corruption as a major constraint	14.7	10.9	0.238	1.34
Access to finance				
Finance from internal sources (%)	88.1	87.8	0.951	1.00
Finance from banks (%)	6.3	6.2	0.962	1.03
Finance from trade credit (%)	1.5	0.5	0.502	2.99
% of firms with line of credit or loans from financial institutions	25.4	13.8	0.001***	1.84
% of firms using banks to finance investments	12.3	11.2	0.849	1.10
% of firms using banks to finance expenses	18.0	11.0	0.027**	1.64
% of firms identifying access to finance as a major constraint	16.2	15.4	0.816	1.05

Source: World Bank 2009.
*$p < 0.1$, **$p < 0.05$, ***$p < 0.01$

provinces. In the case of the provinces surveyed in the Indonesia Enterprise Survey (World Bank 2009), "core" includes DKI Jakarta and Java Barat, while "noncore" includes Java Tengah, Java Timur, Banten, Lampung, Bali, Sumatra Utara, and Sulawesi Selatan.

The findings on firm characteristics in table 4.4 are stark. Firms in the core are unambiguously younger, larger, and more foreign owned. They are also much more likely to make use of technology and achieve international quality standards. All of these factors have been shown in previous international research to have a positive association with exporting.

The findings on regional characteristics are also compelling. They suggest that the core provinces have better infrastructure, but suffer from congestion costs, at least in relation to bureaucratic processes like licensing and regulation. Indeed, firms in Jakarta appear to perceive a particularly poor investment environment (relative to firms in other provinces) across virtually all aspects covered in the Enterprise Survey. This finding is in line with the findings presented in chapter 4 of high congestion costs perceived in core regions around the world.

Specifically, we see in table 4.4 that firms in the core report better infrastructure, as measured by fewer disruptions for power outages and a better perception of the transport environment. Firms in the most peripheral province covered in the survey—Sumatra Utara—report more than 67 hours of power outages each month (5.5 times the national average), and more than one-quarter of them report transport as a severe constraint (more than three times the national average). Firms in the core also appear to have much better access to finance, another crucial aspect of being an exporter.

On the other hand, firms in the core appear to face a much worse environment with respect to regulations, licensing, and governance. Again, this is driven primarily by the responses of firms in Jakarta. More than one-third of firms in Jakarta report corruption as a severe problem (three times greater than the national average). They also view the courts system as problematic and report management time spent on dealing with government regulations at three times the national average. By contrast, firms in neighboring Java Barat (also part of the definition of "core") perceive a business environment better than the national average in most areas. At the other end of the spectrum, the most peripheral provinces covered in the survey also report a business environment that is substantially worse than the national average.

Annex 4A Data

Table 4A.1 Provinces and Island Groups in Indonesia

Province name	Census code of province	Island group
Nanggroe Aceh Darussalam	11	Sumatra
Sumatra Utara	12	Sumatra
Sumatra Barat	13	Sumatra
Riau	14 & 21 = "14"	Sumatra
Jambi	15	Sumatra
Sumatra Selatan	16 & 19	Sumatra
Benkulu	17	Sumatra
Lampung	18	Sumatra
Kep. Bangka Belitung	16 & 19	Sumatra
Kepulauan Riau	14 & 21 = "14"	Sumatra
DKI Jakarta	31	Java including Bali
Java Barat	32 & 36	Java including Bali
Java Tengah	33	Java including Bali
DI Yogyakarta	34	Java including Bali
Java Timur	35	Java including Bali
Banten	32 & 36	Java including Bali
Bali	51	Java including Bali
Nusa Tenggara Barat	52	Eastern Islands
Nusa Tenggara Timur	53	Eastern Islands
Kalimantan Barat	61	Kalimantan
Kalimantan Tengah	62	Kalimantan
Kalimantan Selatan	63	Kalimantan
Kalimantan Timur	64	Kalimantan
Sulawesi Utara	71 & 75	Sulawesi

table continues next page

Table 4A.1 Provinces and Island Groups in Indonesia (continued)

Province name	Census code of province	Island group
Sulawesi Tengah	72	Sulawesi
Sulawesi Selatan	73	Sulawesi
Sulawesi Tenggara	74	Sulawesi
Gorontalo	71 & 75	Sulawesi
Maluku	81 & 82	Eastern Islands
Maluku Utara	81 & 82	Eastern Islands
Papua Barat	91 & 92	Eastern Islands
Papua	91 & 92	Eastern Islands

Source: BPS-Statistics Indonesia 2012.
Note: Census code refers to the numeric code linked to each province in the Manufacturing Census. Note that some provinces were separated or merged at various times, which explains the use of multiple codes.

Table 4A.2 Number of Firms and Exporters by Island Group, 1990, 2000, and 2008

	Number of firms			Number of exporters		
	1990	2000	2008	1990	2000	2008
Sumatra	1,891	2,289	1,541	281	534	324
Java (including Bali)	13,575	18,499	14,659	1,452	2,804	2,171
Kalimantan	457	497	310	138	190	93
Sulawesi	382	609	505	45	108	92
Eastern Islands	220	280	177	18	27	24
Indonesia	**16,536**	**22,174**	**17,250**	**1,935**	**3,663**	**2,717**

Source: Calculations based on BPS-Statistics Indonesia 2012.

Table 4A.3 Distribution of Firms across Regions and Sectors, in World Bank Enterprise Surveys

Sector	Bali	Banten	DKI Jakarta	Jawa Barat	Jawa Tengah	Jawa Timur	Lampung	Sulawesi Selatan	Sumatera Utara	All regions
Food	9	11	8	31	31	55	16	9	16	186
Textiles	9	12	11	55	43	38	5	6	4	183
Garments	10	9	31	49	43	15	0	6	5	168
Chemicals	0	21	15	33	32	22	1	3	6	133
Plastics and rubber	0	25	20	37	29	26	3	2	7	149
Non-metallic mineral product	11	14	2	36	27	50	14	21	18	193
Basic metals	0	1	2	1	0	3	0	1	0	8
Fabricated metal products	0	6	3	0	3	3	4	1	3	23
Machinery and equipment	0	1	0	2	1	1	3	0	0	8
Electronics	0	2	0	2	0	1	0	0	1	6
Other manufacturing	12	16	7	16	21	21	8	17	1	119
All manufacturing	51	118	99	262	230	235	54	66	61	1,176

Source: World Bank 2009.

Table 4A.4 Gross Regional Domestic Product per Capita Relative to Indonesia Average

	1990	1996	2000	2008
Sumatra				
Prov. Nanggroe Aceh Darussalam	2.01	1.41	1.51	0.93
Prov. Sumatera Utara	1.00	0.94	0.89	0.89
Prov. Sumatera Barat	0.79	0.82	0.81	0.81
Prov. Riau	3.53	2.25	2.88	2.74
Prov. Jambi	0.66	0.63	0.60	0.77
Prov. Sumatera Selatan	1.18	1.45	1.01	1.02
Prov. Bengkulu	0.64	0.58	0.50	0.48
Prov. Lampung	0.44	0.52	0.52	0.55
Java				
Prov. DKI Jakarta	2.64	3.38	4.09	4.02
Prov. Jawa Barat	0.85	0.85	0.83	0.78
Prov. Jawa Tengah	0.72	0.66	0.55	0.61
Prov. DI Yogyakarta	0.62	0.84	0.65	0.60
Prov. Jawa Timur	0.85	0.85	0.88	0.91
Prov. Bali	1.03	1.11	0.82	0.77
Kalimantan				
Prov. Kalimantan Barat	0.81	0.86	0.72	0.62
Prov. Kalimantan Tengah	0.94	1.18	0.89	0.85
Prov. Kalimantan Selatan	0.85	0.94	0.94	0.72
Prov. Kalimantan Timur	5.40	3.82	5.05	5.53
Sulawesi				
Prov. Sulawesi Utara	0.58	0.52	0.65	0.58
Prov. Sulawesi Tengah	0.53	0.58	0.60	0.63
Prov. Sulawesi Selatan	0.61	0.58	0.57	0.57
Prov. Sulawesi Tenggara	0.58	0.49	0.48	0.58
Eastern Islands				
Prov. Maluku	0.77	0.65	0.35	0.24
Prov. Papua	1.27	1.56	1.52	1.31
Prov. Nusa Tenggara Barat	0.38	0.41	0.46	0.44
Prov. Nusa Tenggara Timur	0.35	0.35	0.31	0.26

Source: Calculations based on BPS-Statistics Indonesia 2012.
Note: Prov. = Province.

Table 4A.5 Index of Structural Change in Output and Exports in Indonesia, 1990–2008

	Output			Exports		
	2 digit	3 digit	4 digit	2 digit	3 digit	4 digit
Bali	0.359	0.419	0.509	0.499	0.517	0.578
Bengkulu	0.140	0.140	0.526	0.120	0.120	0.120
DI Yogyakarta	0.230	0.411	0.447	0.172	0.675	0.683
DKI Jakarta	0.180	0.283	0.327	0.396	0.612	0.723
Jambi	0.646	0.711	0.693	0.533	0.535	0.536
Jawa Barat including Banten	0.206	0.242	0.293	0.263	0.334	0.446
Jawa Tengah	0.088	0.217	0.335	0.127	0.307	0.353
Jawa Timur	0.067	0.144	0.233	0.244	0.286	0.369
Kalimantan Barat	0.459	0.478	0.496	0.402	0.437	0.447
Kalimantan Selatan	0.623	0.647	0.673	0.626	0.661	0.679
Kalimantan Tengah	0.831	0.831	0.831	0.946	0.946	0.946
Kalimantan Timur	0.450	0.488	0.488	0.486	0.492	0.615
Lampung	0.111	0.258	0.389	0.114	0.459	0.503
Muluku	0.817	0.852	0.862	0.994	1.000	1.000
Nanggroe Aceh Darussalam	0.431	0.456	0.515	0.270	0.356	0.410
Nusa Tenggara Barat	0.346	0.348	0.521	0.205	0.419	0.580
Nusa Tenggara Timur	0.625	0.647	0.736	0.988	0.988	1.000
Papua	0.473	0.482	0.556	0.717	0.717	0.717
Riau	0.692	0.694	0.699	0.851	0.846	0.851
Sulawesi Selatan	0.346	0.363	0.539	0.621	0.622	0.738
Sulawesi Tengah	0.502	0.501	0.703	0.391	0.391	0.523
Sulawesi Tenggara	0.793	0.793	0.917	0.971	0.971	0.977
Sulawesi Utara	0.112	0.143	0.297	0.333	0.334	0.374
Sumatera Barat	0.406	0.416	0.679	0.349	0.361	0.376
Sumatera Selatan	0.302	0.309	0.589	0.268	0.352	0.588
Sumatera Utara	0.234	0.263	0.372	0.305	0.351	0.466

Source: Calculations based on BPS-Statistics Indonesia 2012.
Note: Prov. = Province. Data are by province and industry level, ranked by index at 2-, 3-, and 4-digit level. Output is at 2000 prices. ISIC Rev 2 classifications used.

Notes

1. http://www.bps.go.id/eng/index.php.
2. We thank Ana Fernandes for making a cleaned version of the 1990–2005 database available to us.
3. When calculating regional averages, we used weights and strata provided in the database. Firms must be weighted by the inverse of their probability of selection because with stratification the probability of selection of each unit is not the same. When firms answered "do not know," we replaced those answers with "missing." For quantitative variables, we deleted outliers that exceed three standard deviations from the mean. For qualitative variables with several possible answers, we calculated percentages only on the basis of non-missing observations. For example, assume that we have a sample of 100 firms and 60 firms answer "yes," 20 firms "no," and 20 firms show no observations (or "do not know"). In this case, the share of firms saying "yes" would be 75 percent and not 60 percent.

4. This index is made up of two measures capturing remoteness to international ports and major cities: (1) a province's distance to the nearest of four ports (Tanjung Priok, Semarang, Surabaya, or Bandjermasin), and (2) a province's remoteness to the nearest of five major cities (Jakarta, Surabaya, Medan, Makassar, or Batam) weighted by the inverse of the population of the closest city. The latter measure is taken from World Bank (2011, 189). We calculate an index for each of these measures, relating every province to the most remote province (Papua). This results in indices ranging from 0 (no remoteness) to 1 (highest remoteness in Papua). We weight these two measures using two-thirds for the port index, reflecting our focus on trade competitiveness, and one-third for the city index, to also account for domestic market access.

5. Infrastructure is measured as the quality of roads, as measured by surfaced road length as a share of total road length. The measure is taken from World Bank (2011, 189).

6. Note that the Manufacturing Census results report a higher use of imported inputs, on average, than is reported in the Enterprise Surveys. Specifically with Java Timur, the Enterprise Surveys indicate very low use of imported inputs (less than 1 percent), while the Manufacturing Census indicates that firms in Java Timur are the third-highest users of imported inputs (at around 8 percent of inputs).

7. The sectors are defined as agriculture, mining, industry, utilities, construction, trade, transportation, finance, and services & other.

8. This measure was used by Mayer, Butkevicius, and Kadri (2002), Milberg (2004), and Milberg and Winkler (2010).

References

BPS-Statistics Indonesia. 2012. *Indonesian Manufacturing Census 1990–2008*. Jakarta: BPS-Statistics Indonesia.

Deichmann, U., K. Kaiser, S. V. Lall, and Z. Shalizi. 2005. "Agglomeration, Transport, and Regional Development in Indonesia." Policy Research Working Paper 3477, World Bank, Washington, DC.

Dietrich, A. 2011. "Does Growth Cause Structural Change, or Is It the Other Way Round? A Dynamic Panel Data Analysis for Seven OECD Countries." *Empirical Economics*. Published online, September 10. http://zs.thulb.uni-jena.de/servlets/MCRFileNodeServlet/jportal_derivate_00170936/wp_2009_034.pdf.

Handa, S. 2005. "Regional Inequality and Human Capital in Indonesia." *Asia Keizai* 46 (6): 2–15.

Hill, H. 1987. "Concentration in Indonesian Manufacturing." *Bulletin of Indonesian Economic Studies* 23: 71–100.

Mayer, J., A. Butkevicius, and A. Kadri. 2002. "Dynamic Products in World Exports." UNCTAD Discussion Paper 159, United Nations Conference on Trade and Development, Geneva, Switzerland.

Milberg, W. 2004. "The Changing Structure of International Trade Linked to Global Production Systems: What Are the Policy Implications?" *International Labour Review* 143 (1–2): 45–90.

Milberg, W., and D. Winkler. 2010. "Trade, Crisis, and Recovery: Restructuring Global Value Chains." In *Global Value Chains in a Postcrisis World, A Development Perspective*, O. Cattaneo, G. Gereffi, and C. Staritz, eds., 23–72. Washington, DC: World Bank.

Rodríguez-Pose, A. 2011. "Trade and Regional Inequality." Policy Research Working Paper 5347, World Bank, Washington, DC.

Sjöholm, F. 1999. "Exports, Imports and Productivity: Results from Indonesian Establishments Data." *World Development* 27: 705–15.

Stoikov, V. 1966. "Some Determinants of the Level of Frictional Unemployment: A Comparative Study." *International Labour Review* 93 (5): 530–49.

World Bank. 2009. *Enterprise Survey—Indonesia*. World Bank, Washington, DC. http://enterprisesurveys.org.

———. 2010. *World Trade Indicators 2009/10*. Online database. Washington, DC: World Bank. http://info.worldbank.org/etools/wti/1a.asp.

———. 2011. *Boom, Bust and Up Again? Evolution, Drivers and Impact of Commodity Prices: Implications for Indonesia*. World Bank Office, Jakarta.

———. n.d. *Enterprise Survey Indicators*. Online database. Washington, DC: World Bank. http://www.enterprisesurveys.org.

Location and the Determinants of Exporting: Evidence from Manufacturing Firms in Indonesia

Andrés Rodríguez-Pose, Vassilis Tselios, and Deborah Winkler

Introduction

In development circles, Indonesia has often been regarded in recent years as an example to follow. This large and densely populated country that was stuck in low levels of development achieved, after reforms in the late 1980s and early 1990s, a period of high growth that has now lasted two decades. It has also overcome the negative effects of the 1997 Asian crisis, the 2008 Great Recession, civil unrest and armed conflict (Aceh, Timor, Papua), and huge natural disasters such as the 2004 Boxing Day tsunami. Much of the recent economic success has been attributed to reforms that led to an opening of the country to imports and exports and allowed many of its firms to blossom. Indeed, exports have grown at a relatively high pace over the last two decades. Manufacturing exports make up around 50 percent of Indonesian merchandise exports, including high shares of textiles and clothing, office machines and telecom equipment, chemicals, electrical equipment, and semi-manufactures.

However, as discussed in chapter 4, the fruits of this export boom have not been shared equally across the country. Economic activity, and export activity in particular, is becoming increasingly concentrated in certain locations. Chapter 4 provided a valuable description of how the sectoral output and export structures have evolved across Indonesia's provinces in the last two decades. However, such a macro view gives limited insight into the causal links between location and exporting. In this chapter we turn to firm-level data to understand what drives export propensity (that is, the likelihood of exporting) and export intensity (that is, the share of exports in output) across Indonesian firms. Most important, we attempt to explain the role of location in conditioning exporting. Specifically, to what degree is exporting simply a function of firm characteristics versus characteristics of the external environment in which firms are based? And what aspects of this external environment matter most?

These questions will be addressed through two analyses. First, we show that, indeed, firms located in Indonesia's geographical "core" provinces are significantly more integrated in trade than firms in more peripheral areas. We then review some descriptive statistics about the nature of firms and the external environment in the core versus peripheral provinces. Following this, we conduct an econometric analysis using manufacturing census data, covering more than 15,000 Indonesian firms between 1990 and 2005.

Theoretical Framework

Traditionally, research on firm export propensity and intensity has tended to focus on firm-specific characteristics and on national macroeconomic and regulatory settings. Yet the characteristics of the territories where firms are located— and those of neighboring regions—are crucial in order to explain exports, both in developed and in emerging economies. Firms depend on their surrounding geographical environment for qualified labor, information, and knowledge spillovers. Location also determines access to certain economic inputs and trade facilities. And the presence of adequate infrastructure and of agglomeration economies may boost a firm's export potential. In this section we explore the firm-specific and location-bound advantages that allow firms to trade beyond domestic markets.

The Role of Firm Characteristics in Exporting

Firms base their export choices on costs and benefits of production for domestic and foreign markets. Firm-specific characteristics that affect costs and benefits of production and product quality are crucial for explaining firm-level exports (Sjöholm 2003). The key characteristics shaping a firm's potential to export include foreign ownership, the size of a firm, wages, capital stock, productivity, its age, and the sunk entry costs of exporting, among others. This strand of literature typically adds regional dummies along with industry dummies to the firm-level determinants of exporting, since location might account for most of the differences between exporters and nonexporters.

The sunk entry costs of exporting explain a large part of a firm's decision to enter the export market. Studies tend to confirm that sunk entry costs have a strong positive impact on export participation (Aitken, Hanson, and Harrison 1997; Bernard and Jensen 1999; Clerides, Lach, and Tybout 1998; Greenaway and Kneller 2004; Roberts and Tybout 1997). In addition to sunk entry costs, the following firm-level characteristics have been identified as determinants of both export propensity and the percentage of a firm's exports in output.

First, foreign ownership is expected to have a positive effect on export propensity and export intensity. Multinational corporations by definition have an international network (Sjöholm 2003) and thus tend to be better able to produce internationally marketable products and to possess marketing networks (Ramstetter 1999, 45). In addition, transaction costs associated with international trade tend to be lower for multinationals than for local firms (Ramstetter 1999, 45). Emerging and transition economies are no exception. Studies have confirmed that foreign ownership increases the probability of exporting (see, for example, Aitken, Hanson and Harrison 1997; Cole, Elliott, and Virakul 2010). Filatotchev, Stephan, and Jindra (2008) have shown that ownership has an important influence on export intensity in transition economies. In the specific case of Indonesia, it has been reported that foreign-owned firms have a higher export capacity than local firms in sectors such as auto parts, electronics, and garments (Rasiah 2005).

The size of a firm is a second fundamental factor behind export propensity and intensity. Larger firms have been shown to have a greater likelihood of entering the export market (see, for example, Aitken, Hanson, and Harrison 1997; Bernard and Jensen 1999; Cole, Elliott, and Virakul 2010; Greenaway and Kneller 2004). Larger firms also have greater resources and capabilities to export a larger share of their output than smaller firms (Barkema and Vermeulen 1998). Bigger firms may also have more access to, knowledge of, or leverage with overseas suppliers, making the export process easier (Smith and Barkley 1991). By contrast, smaller firms will, by definition, have lower economies of scale and, possibly, a lower degree of specialization, leading to a greater concentration on local markets. The only exceptions are the small subsidiaries of multinational firms, which often have a specialized supplier role within the enterprise, and thus export a large share of its output (Estrin et al. 2008). According to Hill (1992, 249), the main differences between large- and small-scale manufacturing is that the latter has the ability to exploit market niches, to concentrate on activities not characterized by economies of scale, to serve particular markets of commercial interest to larger firms, and to produce goods not easily adapted to mass production technologies.

Two additional factors affecting export propensity and intensity are the real wage of production per worker and the capital stock of a firm. A large proportion of large-scale firm manufacturing in Indonesia is labor-intensive assembly production geared toward export markets (Berry, Rodríguez, and Sandee 2002, 142). These firms, by and large, have a greater capital stock and tend to pay higher wages than equivalent firms targeting the national market. Studies confirm that a higher capital stock increases the likelihood of exporting (see, for example, Clerides, Lach, and Tybout 1998; Roberts and Tybout 1997). Some studies also find a significantly positive impact of wages on exporting (see, for example, Bernard and Jensen 1999; Greenaway and Kneller 2004), although others, such as Cole, Elliott, and Virakul (2010), cannot confirm such a positive relationship.

Productivity also plays a role in firm export propensity and export intensity. Numerous studies have shown that more productive firms (for example, through technological upgrading or through an increase in capital per worker) are more capable of tapping into export markets (see, for example, Aw, Chung, and Roberts 2000; Bernard and Jensen 1999; Cole, Elliott, and Virakul 2010; Delgado,

Farinas, and Ruano 2002; Greenaway and Kneller 2004). These studies argue that firms incur large fixed costs when entering export markets and thus only the more productive and profitable firms are able to export. Hence, exports can be considered a result of increases in productivity, rather than a cause (Blalock and Gertler 2004, 398).

Finally the age of a firm has been also shown to affect export propensity and the share of sales that is exported. However, the impact of firm age on exports is far from clear-cut. On the one hand, it can be envisaged that the involvement of a firm with international markets is a gradual development process (Bilkey and Tesar 1977; Johanson and Vahlne 1977). Firms would export more once they had found their footing in national markets and acquired greater knowledge about foreign markets and operations, leading to an increase of the export propensity (Roberts and Tybout 1997) or export intensity of a firm with age (Jenkins 2006; Moen and Servais 2002).

On the other hand, age can also be a handicap. Many studies have highlighted that export-oriented firms are born that way and not bred into exporting. These firms have been termed the "international new ventures" (McDougall, Shane, and Oviatt 1994), the "born globals" (Knight and Cavusgil 1996), "instant internationals" (Preece, Miles, and Baetz 1998) or "global start-ups" (Oviatt and McDougall 1994), that is, firms that are heavily involved in exporting from the time they are set up (Moen and Servais 2002) and that represent a substantial portion of exports in emerging economies. Due to the balancing of these two offsetting effects, a number of studies tend to find no clear effect of age on exporting (see, for example, Clerides, Lach, and Tybout 1998).

The Role of Regional and Supraregional Characteristics in Exporting

Next to the traditional focus on firm-specific characteristics, the local host environment and the comparative advantages of different locations play a nonnegligible role in the potential of individual firms to export. The growing body of trade literature on the determinants of exports at the firm level typically adds regional dummies along with industry dummies to the firm-level determinants of exports; this is because location might account for most of the differences between exporters and nonexporters and between high and low export intensity, respectively. While such regional dummies might indicate regional differences, they do not reveal which specific characteristics determine the propensity or intensity of exporting.

From a policy perspective, identifying such regional determinants is essential, since regional characteristics influence the costs of exporting, for example, through the availability of skills, transport costs, infrastructure, or institutions in the region. Firms have to rely on locational advantages and regional resources and capabilities, which contribute to their export propensity and intensity (Barney, Wright, and Ketchen 2001). A good location, an adequate sectoral structure, a decent endowment of human capital, knowledge, and infrastructure are all factors that facilitate the capacity of firms to deal with external markets and also to become more successful.

The first source of locational advantages arises from geography—and from what some economists have called first-nature geography. First-nature geography is linked to proximity between economic agents and an adequate natural environment. In spite of the changes brought about by globalization, trade in goods continues to be highly sensitive to transportation costs (Ghemawat 2007). The higher the proximity to export centers—that means ports, in particular, and the coast, in general—the lower the transportation costs. Moreover, firms that are geographically distant from a port are not only likely to export less or not to participate in exporting at all, but, in particular in peripheral regions, they may also face greater barriers to obtaining knowledge about local market opportunities, coordinating sales strategies, and monitoring agents (Ellis 2007; Estrin et al. 2008; Wu et al. 2007). Coastal regions are also likely to enjoy a wider scope of the market and better access to international trade than inland regions (Gallup, Sachs, and Mellinger 1999). However, since Indonesia has a somewhat unique geography, covering more than 17,500 islands, distance to ports might play a less important role compared to other countries, and, in particular, to landlocked ones.

The locational advantages of the host location with respect to inputs into the production process also determine the kind of operations that may be located there (Dunning 1998; Estrin et al. 2008). They emphasize the efficiency gains from proximity between economic agents (Ottaviano and Thisse 2005). Such factors are also known as second-nature geography factors and can be differentiated between agglomeration economies and regional endowments.

Agglomeration economies can have a particularly favorable influence on a firm's propensity and intensity to export as they allow firms to participate profitably and competitively in wide trade networks (Berry, Rodríguez, and Sandee 2002). Agglomeration economies can lower (1) production costs through sharing of resources, mainly social and physical infrastructure, and (2) transportation and transaction costs through increased interaction between suppliers and customers on site (Malmberg, Malmberg, and Lundequist 2000). Regions with high agglomeration economies are expected to attract and retain industries that are primarily oriented to markets outside their own country.

On the other hand, agglomerations may be characterized by congestion costs (Krugman 1991), which can increase (1) production costs through the sharing of resources (for example, power outages), and (2) transportation and transaction costs through increased waiting times (for example, for intermediate inputs or licenses). These effects can counterbalance the gains from agglomerations as described above. The net effect may therefore be ambiguous.

Regional endowments such as the regional sectoral composition, the regional educational endowment, and the physical infrastructure of the regions (for example, electricity, water, and transport infrastructure), among others, are also essential for a firm's export performance. For example, regions with low-cost semiskilled labor or with rich natural resources may attract investments that specifically aim to exploit arbitrage opportunities (Ghemawat 2007).

Firms would also export if their resource endowment made them better suited within a region to serve particular markets. Thus, export propensity and export intensity arise from firm-specific advantages (Rugman and Verbeke 2001) that are grounded in resources that are both firm specific and location bound (Estrin et al. 2008).

However, second-nature geography also depends on the spatial interaction between people and firms in an area (locality, city, and region) (Naudé 2009). According to Marshall (1890), second-nature geography may be explained by mutually reinforcing external effects (Ottaviano and Thisse 2005, 1713). These spatial externalities occur through trade between regions, interregional labor migration and capital mobility, knowledge spillovers, technology transfers and forward and backward linkages, and more generally regional externalities, which lead to geographically dependent localities and regions (Ertur and Le Gallo 2003; Pfaffermayr 2009; Tselios 2009).

These supraregional effects are of capital importance in this study because externalities are primarily intranational in scope, indicating that spillovers are confined within a country (Branstetter 2001). Due to language, cultural, and other institutional differences, regional externalities are more easily captured within national boundaries (Feldman 2000). These interactions and externalities, which cross weak regional boundaries, are important in accounting for the performance of a firm. Consequently, the export propensity and export intensity of a firm are expected to be influenced not only by the specific characteristics of the region in which the firm is located, but also by the characteristics of the neighboring regions.

A first example of the importance of the supraregional effects is the stock infrastructure of the neighboring regions. Good infrastructural endowments in neighboring regions may contribute to output gains and increase the production inputs and outputs of the hosted firms (Abreu, De Groot, and Florax 2005). Another example is that a significant fraction of the total flow of spillovers that affects a firm's research productivity originates from other firms (Jaffe 1986). From a theoretical perspective, spatial externalities and interactions are important themes in the new economic geography theories and the endogenous growth theories (Rey and Janikas 2005).

Estimation Framework

Model Specification

As indicated in the previous section, differences in firms' characteristics and in regional and supraregional endowments determine the differences in the capacity of firms to export. In other words, the export propensity and export intensity of a firm are a function of both firm- and place-based (regional-based and supraregional-based) characteristics. The aim of this chapter is to determine to what extent these factors account for a significant proportion of the observed differences in the export performance of manufacturing firms in Indonesia.

In order to do this, we resort to an econometric specification that considers not only the individual characteristics of a firm, but also the socioeconomic characteristics and endowments of the region where the firm is located and those of the neighboring regions. Based on the theoretical background, the existing empirical studies in the field, and the data availability, the model adopts the following form:

$$exports_{ir,t} = \delta_1 firm_{ir,t} + \delta_2 geography_r + \delta_3 region_{r,t} + \delta_4 extra\_region_{r,t} + v_{ir,t} \quad (5.1)$$

where $exports_{ir,t}$ is the export propensity or export intensity of firm i in region r at time t. The *firm* variable represents a matrix of firm-specific characteristics that may affect *export* propensity and intensity. The *geography* variable indicates how first-nature geography influences the potential of firms to export. Many factors have been used in order to proxy for first-nature geography. In this chapter, we will use what is possibly the most common of all first-nature geography proxies, proximity to the coast. The matrices *region* and *extra_region* control for other factors expected to affect the export propensity and intensity of firms at the regional and supraregional level, respectively. The vectors δ_1, δ_2, δ_3, and δ_4 are vectors of coefficients of the above matrices and $v_{ir,t}$ is the composite error. The *region* and *extra_region* matrices are time variant and are proxies for second-nature geography. We also specifically control for various measures of agglomeration, namely localization effects, urbanization effects, and export spillovers, at the regional and supraregional level.

The supraregional endowments are calculated using a spatial weights matrix that represents the specification of the regional interaction structure (external effects). This spatial weights matrix is equal to 1 in cases where the Euclidian distance between the capital of regions is smaller to a distance threshold δ, and 0 otherwise. This matrix is then row-standardized so the elements in each row add up to 1. The geographical location of the Indonesian major cities and provinces matters for the choice of the fixed cutoff parameter. After pondering a threshold distance 250 km $\leq \delta \leq$ 500 km, we ended up with $\delta = 400$ kilometers as the most appropriate spatial weights scheme, in order to minimize the number of regions that have no neighbors ("islands"), while keeping the threshold level relatively low (see figure 5A.1).

Using these criteria means that each region is not affected by the same number of regions (figure 5.1). Core and small-sized Indonesian regions interact with more regions than peripheral and big-sized ones. For example, the province of Lampung, in Southern Sumatra, interacts with four regions, whereas the province of Nanggroe Aceh Darussalam, in the opposite tip of Sumatra, interacts with only one region. Our spatial weights matrix includes four "islands" (that is, regions where the export performance of their firms is not affected by the interaction with other provinces): these "islands" are the remote provinces of Kalimantan Barat, Kalimantan Timur, Maluku, and Papua.

Figure 5.1 Classification of Indonesian Provinces according to Number of Interactions

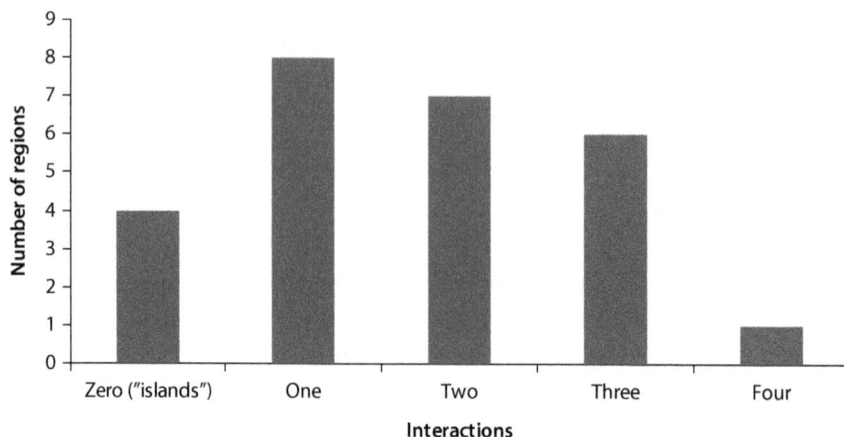

By developing equation 5.1, we obtain the following model:

$$
\begin{aligned}
exports_{ir,t} = {} & \beta_1 ownership_{ir,t} + \beta_2 size_{ir,t} + \beta_3 wage_{ir,t} + \beta_4 capital\_intensity_{ir,t} \\
& + \beta_5 productivity_{ir,t} + \beta_6 age_{ir,t} + \beta_7 prox\_coast_r + \beta_8 localization_{jr,t} \\
& + \beta_9 population_{r,t} + \beta_{10}[W\ population]_{r,t} \\
& + \beta_{11} sector\_concentration_{r,t} + \beta_{12}[W\ sector\_concentration]_{r,t} \\
& + \beta_{13} export\_spillovers_{r,t} + \beta_{14}\left[W\ export\_spillovers\right]_{r,t} \\
& + \beta_{15} sector_{r,t} + \beta_{16}[W\ sector]_{r,t} + \beta_{17} education_{r,t} \\
& + \beta_{18}[W\ education]_{r,t} + \beta_{19} electricity_{r,t} + \beta_{20}[W\ electricity]_{r,t} \\
& + \beta_{21} water_{r,t} + \beta_{22}[W\ water]_{r,t} + \beta_{23} road\_density_r \\
& + \beta_{24}[W\ road\_density]_r + \beta_{25} road\_quality_r \\
& + \beta_{26}[W\ road\_quality]_r + v_{ir,t}
\end{aligned}
\tag{5.2}
$$

where $ownership_{\lambda ir,t}$ measures the percentage of firm i, in region r, in foreign hands at time t. The variable $size_{ir,\ t}$ is a measure of the size of firm i, in region r, at time t, which is calculated as the natural logarithm of the total number of (paid) workers. The variable $wage_{ir,t}$ is measured by the natural logarithm of the real wage of production per worker (base year 2000) of firm i, in region r, at time t, and is an indicator of labor quality (Cole, Elliott, and Virakul 2010). The variable $capital\_intensity_{ir,t}$ represents the natural logarithm of total capital stock (buildings and construction, machines and equipment, land, vehicles, and other capital goods) per worker of firm i, in region r, at time t.

We also include a measure of total factor productivity (TFP). According to the Solow (1957) growth decomposition model, a firm's linearly homogeneous production function can be subdivided into the growth rates of the input factors and the growth rate of some unexplained residual. However, econometric estimates often suffer from simultaneity, because productivity is known to firms when they choose their profit-maximizing input levels. In order to estimate the production function parameters and, thus, TFP consistently, we apply the methodology of Levinsohn and Petrin (2003), who use intermediate inputs as a proxy for unobservable productivity shocks (see Petrin, Poi, and Levinsohn 2004). This is a modified version of the estimator developed by Olley and Pakes (1996), which uses investment as a proxy for productivity shocks. Therefore, $productivity_{i,r,t}$ depicts the productivity of firm i, in region r, at time t, measured as the natural logarithm of the value added per worker.[1] The variable $age_{i,r,t}$ is a measure of the age of firm i, in region r, at time t. It is calculated as the difference between the year of observation and the starting year of commercial production in the region plus one in natural logarithms.

Our first-nature, time-invariant geography variable is $prox\_coast_r$. It indicates the proximity of the capital of province r to the coast and is measured as the natural logarithm of distance (in meters).

We include three types of regional agglomeration economies at the regional and supraregional level. (1) The variable $localization_{j,r,t}$ captures the number of firms within an industry j, in region r, as a percentage of Indonesia's total number of firms within the same industry j, at time t. Since this measure is at both the regional and sectoral level, and not at the regional level only, we cannot include supraregional effects. (2a) The variable $population_{r,t}$ is a region r's natural logarithm of the population (in thousands) to capture *urbanization effects*, while $[W\ population]_{r,t}$ is the average natural logarithm of the population of the neighboring regions of region r, at time t. (2b) The variable $sector\_concentration_{r,t}$ is the Herfindahl-Hirschman index of sectoral concentration by region r, at time t, defined as the sum of squares of an industry's output share to capture *urbanization effects*. The variable $[W\ sector\_concentration]_{r,t}$ accordingly captures supraregional effects of sectoral concentration in the neighboring regions at time t. (3) The variable $export\_spillovers_{r,t}$ is a region's number of exporters as percentage of the region's total number of firms at time t, while $[W\ export\_spillovers]_{r,t}$ measures export spillovers of neighboring regions at time t.

Other regional and supraregional variables in our model are as follows. The variable $sector_{\mu,r,t}$ is a vector of m variables ($\mu = 1,2,3,4$) that capture the sectoral composition of region r, at time t. These variables are measured as the percentage of working people (15 years of age and older) in agriculture ($\mu = 1$: base category), in industry ($\mu = 2$), in services ($\mu = 3$), and in other sectors (mining, utilities, construction, trade, transportation and finance) ($\mu = 4$). The variable $[W\ sector]_{\mu,r,t}$ is the average sectoral composition of neighboring regions of region r, at time t.

The variable $education_{r,t}$ is a proxy for regional educational endowment of region r, at time t, which is measured by the average years of schooling of the adult population (15 and older), and $[W\ education]_{r,t}$ is the average educational endowment of the neighboring regions of region r, at time t. The variable $electricity_{r,t}$ represents the percentage of household access to electricity of region r, at time t, and $[W\ electricity]_{r,t}$ is the access to electricity of the neighboring regions. The variable $water_{r,t}$ denotes the percentage of household access to clean water of region r, at time t, and $[W \, water]_{r,t}$ depicts the access to clean water in the neighboring regions.

Our proxies for transport infrastructure are $road\_density_r$ and $road\_quality_r$. The variable $road\_density_r$ represents the road density of region r, measured by the total length (in kilometers) of national, province, and district roads divided by the size of the region (in square kilometers), and $[W \, road\_density_r]$ is the road density of the neighboring regions. The variable $road\_quality_r$ depicts the road quality of region r, measured by the ratio of roads in good and moderate condition (in kilometers) to total roads (good, moderate, minor damage, severely damaged, in kilometers), and $[W \, road\_quality]_r$ is the road quality of the neighboring regions. Given the limitations of obtaining good-quality road infrastructure data, we have to assume that the road density and quality in any given Indonesian province remains constant over our period of analysis. This implies ignoring the considerable infrastructure effort conducted by the Indonesian government and making the further assumption that any potential changes in road infrastructure endowments are proportional across regions and do not imply significant changes in provincial ranks. The electricity, water, and road variables represent the endowments of the provinces.

Finally, the variable $v_{ir,t}$ is the composite error $[v_{ir,t} = \alpha_i + \varphi_r + \xi_t + \varepsilon_{i,t}$, where α_i represents the fixed effects, φ_r denotes regional dummies (regional specific effects), ξ_t denotes time dummies (time-fixed effects) and $\varepsilon_{i,t}$ is the disturbance term (idiosyncratic error)]. The coefficient β_1, and the elasticity coefficients β_2, β_3, β_4, β_5, and β_6 represent the firm-based effects to exports, while the elasticity coefficients β_7, β_9, and β_{10}, the vector coefficients $\beta_{\mu15}$ and $\beta_{\mu16}$, and the coefficients β_8, β_{11}, β_{12}, β_{13}, β_{14}, β_{17}, β_{18}, β_{19}, β_{20}, β_{21}, β_{22}, β_{23}, β_{24}, β_{25}, and β_{26} represent place-based effects.

Export Propensity

For export propensity, we follow Roberts and Tybout's (1997) theoretical exporting model. The export propensity of firm i at time t depends on the firm's expected revenues R and costs c plus sunk entry costs of exporting, S:

$$\Pr(export\_propensity_{i,t} = 1) = \Pr(R_{i,t} > c_{i,t} + S(1 - export\_propensity_{i,t-1})) \quad (5.3)$$

where $export\_propensity$ denotes an export dummy at the firm level that equals 1 if a firm exports and 0 otherwise. Sunk entry costs of exporting, S, are 1 if a firm exported in period $t-1$ and 0 otherwise. In other words, a firm exports if expected profits $\pi > 0$.

A firm's expected profits π are affected by firm-level characteristics, geography, agglomeration effects, regional characteristics, and supraregional effects, all of which can generate or lower revenues R and/or costs c. Equation 5.3 translates into:

$$\Pr(export\_propensity_{ir,t} = 1) = \Pr(\pi_{ir,t} = \delta_1 firm_{ir,t} + \delta_2 geography_r$$
$$+ \, \delta_3 region_{r,t} + \delta_5 extra\_region_{r,t} + S(1 - export\_propensity_{i,t-1}) > 0) \quad (5.4)$$

Taking into account equation 5.2, equation 5.4 translates into:

$$
\begin{aligned}
exports\_propensity_{ir,t} = {} & \beta_1 export\_propensity_{ir,t-1} + \beta_2 ownership_{irt} \\
& + \beta_3 size_{ir,t} + \beta_4 wage_{ir,t} + \beta_5 capital\_intensity_{ir,t} \\
& + \beta_6 productivity_{ir,t} + \beta_7 age_{ir,t} + \beta_8 prox\_coast_r \\
& + \beta_9 localization_{jr,t} + \beta_{10} population_{r,t} \\
& + \beta_{11}[W\ population]_{r,t} + \beta_{12} sector\_concentration_{r,t} \\
& + \beta_{13}[W\ sector\_concentration]_{r,t} \\
& + \beta_{14}\left[export\_spillovers\right]_{r,t} \\
& + \beta_{15}[W\ export\_spillovers]_{r,t} + \beta_{16}\ sector_{\mu r,t} \\
& + \beta_{17}[W\ sector]_{\mu r,t} + \beta_{18} education_{r,t} \\
& + \beta_{19}\left[W\ education\right]_{r,t} + \beta_{20} electricity_{r,t} \\
& + \beta_{21}[W\ electricity]_{r,t} + \beta_{22}\ water_{r,t} + \beta_{23}[W\ water]_{r,t} \\
& + \beta_{24}\ road\_density_r + \beta_{25}[W\ road\_density]_r \\
& + \beta_{26}\ road\_quality_r + \beta_{27}[W\ road\_quality]_r + v_{ir,t}
\end{aligned} \tag{5.5}
$$

where $export\_propensity_{ir,t-1}$ controls for sunk entry costs of exporting. This model is estimated by a dynamic probit estimator.

Export Intensity
Based on equation 5.2, the export intensity of a firm is modeled in the following way:

$$
\begin{aligned}
exports\_intensity_{ir,t} = {} & \beta_1 ownership_{ir,t} + \beta_2\ size_{ir,t} + \beta_3 wage_{ir,t} \\
& + \beta_4 capital\_intensity_{ir,t} + \beta_5\ productivity_{ir,t} \\
& + \beta_6 age_{ir,t} + \beta_7 prox\_coast_r + \beta_8 localization_{jr,t} \\
& + \beta_9 population_{r,t} + \beta_{10}\left[W\ population\right]_{r,t} \\
& + \beta_{11}\ sector\_concentration_{r,t} \\
& + \beta_{12}\left[W\ sector\_concentration\right]_{r,t} \\
& + \beta_{13}[export\_spillovers]_{r,t} + \beta_{14}[W\ export\_spillovers]_{r,t} \\
& + \beta_{15} sector_{r,t} + \beta_{16}\left[W\ sector\right]_{r,t} + \beta_{17} education_{r,t} \\
& + \beta_{18}\left[W\ education\right]_{r,t} + \beta_{19}\ electricity_{r,t} \\
& + \beta_{20}[W\ electricity]_{r,t} + \beta_{21} water_{r,t} + \beta_{22}[W\ water]_{r,t} \\
& + \beta_{23} road\_density_r + \beta_{24}[W\ road\_density]_r \\
& + \beta_{25} road\_quality_r + \beta_{26}\left[W\ road\_quality\right]_r + v_{ir,t}
\end{aligned} \tag{5.6}
$$

where *export_intensity*$_{i,t}$ denotes the exports of firm i, as a percentage of total output.

The model is estimated by fixed effects in order to control for time-invariant characteristics. It controls (1) for the effects of the omitted variables that are peculiar to each firm and accommodates sectoral heterogeneity (through α_j), and (2) for the unobserved first-nature of geography effects (through φ_r). This estimator wipes out all the sector-specific and space-specific time-invariant variables, but a failure to account for these variables increases the risk that biased estimation results may be obtained (Baltagi 2005).

Given their time-invariant condition, it is impossible to estimate the impact of the proximity to coast (*prox_coast*$_r$) and the road density and quality (*road_density*$_r$ and *road_quality*$_r$) on export intensity by fixed effects. We have to resort in some regressions to random-effects estimators. Hence, we also check the p-values of Hausman's (1978) statistic to test whether the random-effect estimator is an appropriate alternative to the fixed-effects estimator. Finally, our model includes time-dummies (ξ_t) as a means to control for all time-specific spatial-invariant variables.

Data

The microeconomic characteristics are extracted from the Indonesian Manufacturing Census (see description in chapter 4, "Data" section).

All inputs and outputs including exports were deflated using a value added deflator, while net investment flows were deflated using an investment price deflator. The value added deflator was constructed by dividing manufacturing value added in current prices by manufacturing value added in 1995 constant prices. Similarly, the investment price deflator was constructed by dividing the gross capital formation in current prices by gross capital formation in constant 1995 prices. These were available from the World Development Indicator database. Capital stock was then constructed using the perpetual inventory method with depreciation rates taken from Arnold and Javorcik (2009): 3.3 percent for buildings, 10 percent for machinery and equipment, and 20 percent for transport equipment. Land is not assumed to depreciate. Wages were reported in 1995 prices.

This microeconomic information is complemented with data from (National Socioeconomic Survey—SUSENAS) of the Indonesian Bureau of Statistics (Badan Pusat Statistik—BPS[2]); National Labor Force Statistics (BPS), and the Statistical Yearbook of Indonesia (BPS) datasets measuring the regional and supraregional endowments and characteristics of 26 Indonesian provinces (regions). Finally, we used a spatial weights matrix that employs geographic information system (GIS) mapping, which represents the Euclidian distance between the capitals of regions in order to capture the regional interaction structure (external effects).

Our dataset with averages, standard deviations, and minimum and maximum values for each of the variables for 1990, 1997, and 2004 is reported in table 5A.1. The descriptive statistics show that the dataset is unbalanced, which is amenable to estimation methods that manage potential heterogeneity bias (Rodríguez-Pose and Tselios 2009).

Econometric Model: Results for Export Propensity

The regression analysis of firm export propensity covers the period 1990–2005. As mentioned earlier, we apply a dynamic probit estimator. All specifications are robust to heteroscedasticity and include region-fixed effects (26 provinces). We also include sector-fixed effects at the 3-digit International Standard Industrial Classification (ISIC) Rev. 2 level (29 sectors) to each of the specifications. The overall results for the period 1990–2005 are shown in table 5.1.

Table 5.1 Regression Results for Export Propensity in Indonesian Firms, 1990–2005

Dependent variable:	Dynamic probit model				
Export propensity$_{ir,t}$	(1)	(2)	(3)	(4)	(5)
Export propensity$_{ir,t-1}$	1.7000***	1.7421***	1.6828***	1.7000***	1.6839***
	(0.011)	(0.011)	(0.011)	(0.011)	(0.011)
Ownership$_{ir,t}$	0.0047***	0.0045***	0.0046***	0.0046***	0.0045***
	(0.000)	(0.000)	(0.000)	(0.000)	(0.000)
lnSize$_{ir,t}$	0.2862***	0.2683***	0.2810***	0.2808***	0.2834***
	(0.004)	(0.004)	(0.004)	(0.005)	(0.005)
lnWages$_{ir,t}$	−0.0136*	−0.0203***	−0.0191**	−0.0194**	−0.0171**
	(0.007)	(0.007)	(0.008)	(0.008)	(0.008)
lnCapital intensity$_{ir,t}$	0.0620***	0.0582***	0.0621***	0.0621***	0.0640***
	(0.003)	(0.003)	(0.003)	(0.003)	(0.003)
lnProductivity$_{ir,t}$	−0.0610***	−0.0579***	−0.0631***	0.0626***	0.0638***
	(0.005)	(0.005)	(0.005)	(0.005)	(0.005)
lnAge$_{ir,t}$	−0.1197***	−0.1225***	−0.1194***	0.0626***	−0.1223***
	(0.006)	(0.006)	(0.005)	(0.006)	(0.006)
lnProximity to coast$_r$		−0.0130***	−0.1194***	−0.1288***	−0.0005
		(0.003)	(0.006)	(0.006)	(0.007)
Localization$_{r,t}$			−0.0002	0.0021	0.0053***
			(0.005)	(0.005)	(0.001)
lnPopulation$_{r,t}$			0.0051***	0.0037***	−0.0945***
			(0.001)	(0.001)	(0.026)
W lnPopulation$_{r,t}$			−0.0801***	−0.1294***	−0.1604***
			(0.019)	(0.022)	(0.042)
Sector concentration$_{r,t}$			−0.3673***		−0.3001***
			(0.087)		(0.097)
W Sector concentration$_{r,t}$				−0.7216***	−0.6383***
				(0.087)	(0.114)
Export spillovers$_{r,t}$			0.0184***		0.0205***
			(0.001)		(0.001)
W Export spillovers$_{r,t}$				−0.0034***	−0.0030**
				(0.001)	(0.001)
Sector$^{manufacturing}_{r,t}$			−0.0339		0.7196*
			(0.357)		(0.435)

table continues next page

Table 5.1 Regression Results for Export Propensity in Indonesian Firms, 1990–2005 (continued)

Dependent variable: Export propensity$_{ir,t}$	Dynamic probit model				
	(1)	(2)	(3)	(4)	(5)
W Sector$^{manufacturing}_{r,t}$				−3.2482*** (0.509)	−2.2388*** (0.556)
Sector$^{services}_{r,t}$			1.2287*** (0.311)		1.2979*** (0.340)
W Sector$^{services}_{r,t}$				−5.3009*** (0.518)	−2.6312*** (0.574)
Sector$^{other}_{r,t}$			−0.3558 (0.219)		−0.3292 (0.282)
W Sector$^{other}_{r,t}$				−1.8717*** (0.326)	0.8714* (0.377)
Education$_{r,t}$			−0.0673*** (0.022)		0.0013 (0.029)
W Education$_{r,t}$				−0.3041*** (0.035)	−0.0964 (0.062)
Electricity$_{r,t}$			−0.0050*** (0.001)		−0.0060*** (0.001)
W Electricity$_{r,t}$				0.0200*** (0.001)	−0.0033* (0.002)
Water$_{r,t}$			0.0069*** (0.001)		0.0035** (0.001)
W Water$_{r,t}$				0.0196*** (0.001)	0.0047** (0.002)
Road density$_r$			0.8777*** (0.105)		0.6831*** (0.222)
W Road density$_r$				−2.8256*** (0.153)	0.3104 (0.253)
Road quality$_r$			−0.2489*** (0.090)		−0.2198 (0.158)
W Road quality$_r$				1.7208*** (0.198)	1.0406*** (0.282)
constant	−3.3349*** (0.099)	−2.7216*** (0.066)	−2.3153*** (0.289)	−0.7566** (0.385)	−0.2657 (0.658)
Region-fixed effects	Yes	No	No	No	No
Year-fixed effects	Yes	Yes	Yes	Yes	Yes
Sector-fixed effects	Yes	Yes	Yes	Yes	Yes
Observations	201,964	201,964	180,230	177,425	177,425
Pseudo R^2	0.4694	0.4623	0.4685	0.4624	0.4667

Note: Standard errors are in parentheses.
*$p < 0.1$, **$p < 0.05$, ***$p < 0.01$

Firm-Level Determinants

Regression 1 shows the results when we only include firm-level determinants of exporting and control for sector-fixed effects, region-fixed effects, and year-fixed effects, as specified in equation 5.4. Sunk entry costs, foreign ownership, employment, capital intensity, and TFP all have a significantly positive impact on exporting, while the average wage of production workers and firm age have a significantly negative one. The firm-level effects in Regressions 2–6 show similar results in terms of coefficient sign and significance.

First-Nature Geography

Our first-nature geography variable denotes proximity to the sea from the capital of every province. It is expected that having the main city located on the coast would facilitate exports. In Regression 2, we add the proximity of the capital of province r to the coast and exclude region-fixed effects, as specified in equation 5.5. As expected, a higher distance to the coast has a significantly negative impact on exporting, which becomes insignificant in Regressions 3–5.

Agglomeration Effects

In Regression 3, we introduce three types of agglomeration economies, namely localization effects, urbanization effects, and export spillovers. A higher share of firms within the same industry in a province (localization economies) has a significantly positive effect on export propensity. A higher population in a province, our first measure of urbanization economies, has a significantly negative impact on exporting, which might be a consequence of congestion costs in a region. A higher sectoral concentration in a province, our second measure of urbanization economies, also negatively affects exporting, or—in other words—more sectoral diversity in a region increases a firm's export propensity. A higher share of exporting firms in a province (export spillovers) has a significantly positive effect on exporting, clearly indicating the benefits from agglomerations.

Regression 4 only considers firm-level determinants, first-order geography, and supraregional effects on exporting. High population, sector concentration, and export share in a province's neighboring regions all negatively affect a firm's export propensity in a region. The last finding is particularly interesting, as it indicates that a region with a high export activity tends to drain resources from neighboring regions, making it more difficult for firms in such regions to export. The results are confirmed when we combine regional and supraregional effects in Regression 5.

Regional and Supraregional Factors

In Regression 3, we introduce specific regional effects. Firms located in regions with a higher concentration in services have a higher probability of exporting. Surprisingly, the years of schooling of the regional population is negatively associated the propensity to export. Access to water increases a firm's propensity to export, while electricity reduces it. Road density has a positive effect on a firm's export propensity, while road quality has a negative effect.

Regression 4 only considers firm-level determinants, first-order geography, and supraregional effects. A high concentration in manufacturing, services, and other sectors in neighboring regions all have a significantly negative impact on a firm's exporting activity located in region r. Electricity, access to water, and road quality in neighboring regions have positive spillovers on firms' exporting behavior in region r, while education and road density in neighboring areas have a negative effect.

Regression 5 shows the results including both regional and supraregional effects as specified in equation 5.5. The regional effects are similar to the ones already described for Regression 3, with the exception of education and road quality, which no longer have a significantly negative impact on exporting. However, there are some changes in the supraregional effects. Education and road density in neighboring regions no longer show a negative impact on exporting when measured at the supraregional level. Moreover, employment in other sectors in neighboring regions now becomes significantly positive, while electricity in neighboring regions now turns negative.

Controlling for Unobserved Shocks at the Province Level

Table 5A.2 shows the results using clustered standard errors at the province level to allow for the possibility that the error terms are correlated across firms within provinces. The results for all firm-level determinants except for wages on exporting can be confirmed. First-nature geography no longer has a negative effect on export propensity. The effect of regional and supraregional variables depend on whether these are included individually (Regressions 3 and 4) or combined (Regression 5). Almost all individual regional and supraregional effects described above can be confirmed. However, when we combine these variables, many variables become insignificant. In the following, we only interpret the results of Regression 5 in order avoid an omitted variable bias. Regarding agglomeration economies at the regional level, only localization economies and export spillovers show a significantly positive influence on export propensity. At the supraregional level, only population and sector concentration in neighboring regions have a significant impact on exporting, which is negative.

Regarding other regional variables, regions with a higher concentration in services have a higher probability of exporting. The same holds true for access to water, while electricity has a negative impact on export propensity. At the supraregional level, a higher concentration in manufacturing in neighboring regions negatively affects exporting, while a better road quality in neighboring regions has a positive influence.

Econometric Model: Results for Export Intensity

Table 5.2 displays the fixed-effects estimators for firm export intensity as specified in equation 5.6. The fixed-effect estimators are complemented by random effects for those equations where the impact of the proximity to the coast and

Table 5.2 Regression Results for Export Intensity in Indonesian Firms, 1990–2000 and 2004

Dependent variable: export intensity$_{ir,t}$	Static model						
	(1)	(2)	(3)	(4)	(5)	(6)	(7)
Ownership$_{ir,t}$	0.0011*** (0.000)	0.0016*** (0.000)	0.0011*** (0.000)	0.0011*** (0.000)	0.0016*** (0.000)	0.0016*** (0.000)	0.0016*** (0.000)
lnSize$_{ir,t}$	0.0319*** (0.002)	0.0586*** (0.001)	0.0256*** (0.002)	0.0260*** (0.002)	0.0603*** (0.001)	0.0598*** (0.001)	0.0601*** (0.001)
lnWages$_{ir,t}$	−0.0013 (0.001)	−0.0041*** (0.001)	−0.0013 (0.001)	−0.0017 (0.001)	−0.0031*** (0.001)	−0.0036*** (0.001)	−0.0044*** (0.001)
lnCapital intensity$_{ir,t}$	0.0088*** (0.001)	0.0097*** (0.001)	0.0067*** (0.002)	0.0067*** (0.002)	0.0112*** (0.001)	0.0107*** (0.001)	0.0106*** (0.001)
lnProductivity$_{ir,t}$	0.0008 (0.001)	0.0023*** (0.001)	−0.0006 (0.001)	−0.0007 (0.001)	0.0029*** (0.001)	0.0023*** (0.001)	0.0015** (0.001)
lnAge$_{ir,t}$	−0.0288*** (0.002)	−0.0323*** (0.001)	−0.0246*** (0.003)	−0.0247*** (0.003)	−0.0318*** (0.001)	−0.0323*** (0.001)	−0.0296*** (0.001)
lnProximity to coast$_r$		−0.0017** (0.001)			−0.0097*** (0.001)	−0.0077*** (0.001)	−0.0008 (0.001)
Localization$_{r,t}$			0.0004** (0.000)	0.0003 (0.000)			0.0008*** (0.000)
lnPopulation$_{r,t}$			0.0506** (0.022)	−0.0058 (0.028)			−0.0140*** (0.005)
W lnPopulation$_{r,t}$				−0.0164 (0.030)			−0.0180*** (0.007)
Sector concentration$_{r,t}$			−0.0448** (0.018)	−0.0516** (0.020)			−0.0513*** (0.015)
W Sector concentration$_{r,t}$				0.0121 (0.022)			−0.0727*** (0.018)
Export spillovers$_{r,t}$			0.0076*** (0.000)	0.0076*** (0.000)			0.0074*** (0.000)
W Export spillovers$_{r,t}$				0.0000 (0.000)			−0.0002 (0.000)
Sector$^{manufacturing}_{r,t}$			0.1464** (0.063)	0.1850*** (0.066)			0.2110*** (0.059)
W Sector$^{manufacturing}_{r,t}$				−0.0462 (0.068)			−0.1075* (0.065)
Sector$^{services}_{r,t}$			0.0626 (0.055)	0.0953 (0.062)			0.1664*** (0.047)
W Sector$^{services}_{r,t}$				−0.0801 (0.083)			−0.1085 (0.070)
Sector$^{other}_{r,t}$			−0.0892** (0.040)	−0.1273*** (0.046)			−0.0573 (0.038)
W Sector$^{other}_{r,t}$				−0.1023* (0.060)			−0.1194** (0.052)
Education$_{r,t}$			0.0096 (0.008)	0.0006 (0.009)			0.0169*** (0.005)
W Education$_{r,t}$				−0.0085 (0.011)			0.0017 (0.009)
Electricity$_{r,t}$			−0.0010*** (0.000)	−0.0009*** (0.000)			−0.0011*** (0.000)

table continues next page

Table 5.2 Regression Results for Export Intensity in Indonesian Firms, 1990–2000 and 2004 *(continued)*

Dependent variable: export intensity$_{ir,t}$	Static model						
	(1)	*(2)*	*(3)*	*(4)*	*(5)*	*(6)*	*(7)*
W Electricity$_{r,t}$				−0.0008***			−0.0007***
				(0.000)			(0.000)
Water$_{r,t}$			−0.0001	0.0002			0.0006***
			(0.000)	(0.000)			(0.000)
W Water$_{r,t}$				0.0008**			−0.0002
				(0.000)			(0.000)
Road density$_r$					0.3803***	0.4976***	0.2163***
					(0.017)	(0.019)	(0.038)
W Road density$_r$						−0.0799***	0.2336***
						(0.012)	(0.036)
Road quality$_r$					−0.1222***	−0.1399***	−0.1102***
					(0.009)	(0.009)	(0.027)
W Road quality$_r$						−0.1157***	0.1054**
						(0.013)	(0.046)
Constant	−0.0397**	−0.0962***	−0.6142***	0.2618	−0.0468***	0.0328**	0.0079
	(0.020)	(0.012)	(0.204)	(0.437)	(0.014)	(0.016)	(0.092)
FEs or REs estimator	FEs	REs	FEs	FEs	REs	REs	REs
Year-fixed effects	Yes	Yes	Yes	Yes	Yes	Yes	Yes
Sector-fixed effects	No	Yes	No	No	Yes	Yes	Yes
Observations	192,091	192,091	164,574	161,930	192,091	189,009	161,930
R-within	0.0423		0.0628	0.0606			

Note: FE = fixed effect, RE = random effect. Standard errors in parentheses.
*$p < 0.1$, **$p < 0.05$, ***$p < 0.01$

the road density and quality (time-invariant indicators) are considered. More specifically, Regression 1 analyzes the impact of firms' characteristics on export share. We then add the impact of proximity to the coast (Regression 2). Regressions 3 and 4 include agglomeration effects, as well as a set of regional and supraregional time-variant endowments, while Regressions 5 and 6 encompass road density and quality. Regression 7 displays the full econometric specification. Although the *p*-values of Hausman's test in Regressions 2 and 5–7 reject the random-effects estimator as an appropriate alternative to the fixed-effects estimator, and despite the potential drawback linked to the assumption of the random-effects estimator that the α_i are uncorrelated with all explanatory variables across all time periods, it makes sense to treat the α_i as random variables, as our observations are randomly drawn from a large population (Wooldridge 2002). In addition, as $v_{ir,t}$ are serially correlated across time (because α_i is in the composite error in each time period), the random-effects estimator solves the serial correlation problem related to having a very large number of firms (cross-sectional analysis) and relatively short time periods (time-series analysis).

Firm-Specific Results

The results of the microeconomic analysis follow, to a large extent, expectations. Foreign ownership of Indonesian firms is a relatively good predictor of firm export intensity. Private firms with a higher share of foreign ownership tend to export a higher percentage of their output than do firms with lower levels of foreign ownership. Size matters for exports. The size of a firm measured by the number of workers is a decent estimator of export intensity. The coefficient is positive and highly significant (table 5.2). The real wage per worker tends, by contrast, not to matter. Only in the three random-effects regressions (Regressions 2 and 5–7) is the coefficient for the wage of employees negative and significant, but the significance disappears in the fixed-effects regressions. The capital intensity of a firm has a positive and statistically significant impact on export intensity. However, the impact of the level of productivity of a firm tends to be irrelevant in the fixed-effect regressions (Regressions 1, 3, and 4) and only positive and significant in the random-effect ones (Regressions 2 and 5–7). This may be, as already mentioned when analyzing export propensity, a consequence of the tendency of Indonesian firms to specialize in exports at the lower echelons of the value added and technology scale. Older and more established firms do not have an advantage for exports. Indeed, the age of firms is detrimental for export intensity.

Overall, export intensity across Indonesian firms is a function of foreign ownership, size, capital stock, and age of the firm. Larger, more capital-intensive and younger, foreign-owned firms are those more likely to export a larger share of their output. Once these factors are controlled for, productivity and the wage levels of employees become irrelevant for exports. In a country specialized in low- to mid-technology exports, where low labor costs still represent a significant comparative advantage, economies of scale and the outside contacts of owners and managers matter much more for exports than the level of output per worker and their wages.

First-Nature Geography

As in the case of export propensity, Regression 4 in table 5.2 shows that firms in provinces whose capital is located further away from the coast are less likely to export, once the infrastructural endowment of the province and of neighboring provinces is controlled for. However, this effect is not particularly robust, as the coefficient is nonsignificant in Regression 7, the one estimating the whole model. This implies that, although distance from the sea could be, in principle, considered detrimental for exports, in an island country such as Indonesia, it may not be a significant factor. This may be partly because, outside of Java, firms may be located very near the coast but still struggle to access international markets due to uncompetitive ports and shipping service (including the requirement to connect via a main port in Java before going on to international markets).

Agglomeration Effects

Agglomeration effects are also an important determinant of export intensity. In particular, localization and urbanization economies and export spillovers contribute to shape the share of exports in output of Indonesian firms (Regressions 3 and 7). Firms located in areas with a higher than average share of firms in the same industry and with a concentration of other exporting firms consistently export a higher share of their output than firms in other areas. By contrast, urbanization effects seem to have a detrimental influence on export intensity. The greater the sectoral concentration, the lower the export intensity of an average individual firm. Finally, the association between pure population agglomeration and export intensity is ambiguous, with the sign and the significance of the coefficient changing between the fixed-effects model (Regression 3) and the random-effects one (Regression 7). Agglomeration effects in neighboring regions matter much less for a firm's export intensity.

Regional and Supraregional Factors

The regional and supraregional second-nature geography factors are much more pertinent in explaining the export intensity of individual Indonesian firms than access to the sea. A significant majority of the regional and supraregional variables included in the analysis and covering the whole period considered tend to be relevant in determining the capacity of Indonesian firms to export, although their association with firm export intensity does not always have the predicted sign.

In terms of the sectoral composition of the regions, specializations in industry and, to a lesser extent, in services tend to favor the export intensity of individual firms. Being located in areas with a developed manufacturing or service sector facilitates exports, while this is not the case in regions more specialized in agriculture or in other type of activities, such as construction. The overall impact on export intensity of the sectoral characteristics of surrounding regions is, however, relatively limited. Specializations in industry and services in neighboring regions tend to have a negligible—and sometimes negative—effect on the export intensity of local firms.

As already highlighted for the case of firm export propensity, in Indonesia the level of education in the region is not conducive to greater firm-level exports. The years of schooling of the local population are not associated with the presence of firms with a greater capacity to export (Regressions 3, 4, and 7). The coefficients are even negative, implying that human capital endowments at the level of the firm may, once transport infrastructure is considered, be detrimental for exports (Regression 7). This reinforces the idea that the low- to mid-technology exports driving Indonesia's foreign trade do not necessarily require high levels of education. Indeed, higher levels of education will tend to erode one of its main comparative advantages, which are lower labor costs and salaries, thus limiting export intensity.

Access to adequate basic infrastructure, such as water and electricity, also plays a relatively subdued role in a firm's export intensity. Firms in regions with better access to clean water and electricity, and surrounded by other regions with good access to electricity, are not more likely to export more than firms in areas with weaker endowments in basic utilities (Regressions 4 and 6).

Transport infrastructure is, by contrast, the most important second-nature geography determinant for firm exports. Road density is a key driver of individual firm export intensity and matters significantly more for exports than the road quality. Firms in regions with good access to roads tend to export more, while the coefficient for the quality of these roads is negative and significant. However, transport infrastructure does not always generate positive spillovers. In Regression 6, the road density and quality of surrounding regions has a detrimental effect on the export intensity of Indonesian firms. In brief, these results confirm that firms in Indonesia fare better in terms of their export intensity when located in regions with a good overall access to transportation infrastructure. It is, however, unrealistic to expect infrastructural spillovers from neighboring regions in an island country where distances are significant.

Controlling for Unobserved Shocks at the Province Level

Table 5A.3 shows the results using clustered standard errors at the province level to allow for the possibility that the error terms are correlated across firms within provinces. The results for all firm-level determinants on exporting can be confirmed. First-nature geography no longer has a negative effect on export intensity. Regarding agglomeration economies, only export spillovers show a significantly positive influence on export intensity, while regarding regional and supraregional effects, only electricity and transport infrastructure matter for export intensity. More specifically, regional electricity and electricity in neighboring regions have a negative effect. Transport infrastructure is, once more, the most important second-nature geography determinant for firm exports, but only the regional road density is a key driver of individual firm export intensity and not the regional road quality, which has a negative effect on export intensity.

Conclusions

In this chapter, we have looked at the factors that determined the export propensity and intensity of manufacturing firms in Indonesia during the period between 1990 and 2005. We have paid special attention to whether the drivers of firm exports in Indonesia were fundamentally related to firm-specific characteristics or to the environment. We also took note of the conditions of the environment in which the firm is located. By environment, we understand the conditions internal to the region where the firm is located, as well as those in surrounding regions.

The results highlight that both internal and external factors made a difference, but that they matter in ways that may not have always been predicted by the theory. At the internal level of the firm, export propensity and intensity have been fundamentally driven by firm size, the share of foreign ownership, capital intensity, and age of the firm. Younger and larger firms, with a greater capital stock and partially foreign-owned, have been more likely to export and to export a greater share of the output. However, other internal factors that could have been expected to matter are less relevant for exports. Such factors include the productivity of the firm (which is clearly important for the export propensity of a firm, but much less so for its export intensity), but most notably, workers' wages. Manufacturing exporting firms in Indonesia are not those paying the highest wages, as that would erode the cost advantage on which exports by many Indonesian firms are based.

External factors also matter. First-nature geography matters to some degree; for example, distance to the sea is mildly detrimental for the export intensity of Indonesian firms. However, second-nature geography makes a bigger difference. The conditions of the provinces and those of neighboring provinces where a firm is located influence exports. More than pure population agglomeration or human capital, the most relevant factors for exports are those linked to agglomeration effects, sectoral specialization, and transport infrastructure endowment. Firms export when they are surrounded by other firms in the same industry and by other exporting firms. They are also more likely to export and to export a greater share of their output if they specialize in manufacturing than in other sectors. Access to a high-density road system, regardless of its quality, is also key to export participation. These factors have to be in place, as there is very little evidence that spillovers work.

Overall, results highlight that conditions affecting export propensity and intensity in Indonesia are those typical of areas relying on low- to medium-tech manufacturing production. The comparative advantage lies in producing standardized goods at relatively low prices, and factors that would drive a substantial leap in the technology content of exports are relatively absent. These conditions apply both at the firm level and to the geographical context where exporting firms are located. At the firm level, higher wages undermine exports and productivity is not a fundamental determinant of export propensity and intensity, emphasizing the low-cost, low-tech nature of manufacturing exports in Indonesia. At the external level, urbanization, human capital, and some infrastructure endowments, such as access to reliable electricity, seem irrelevant. In brief, the analysis suggests that many exporting Indonesian manufacturing firms have become stuck in a low-tech, low cost trap during the period of analysis, with relatively little potential to advance to a different stage of development. The current export-driven growth may not be sustainable without a radical overhaul of the exporting model.

Annex 5A Data

Figure 5A.1 Number of Neighboring Provinces by Province and Threshold Distance

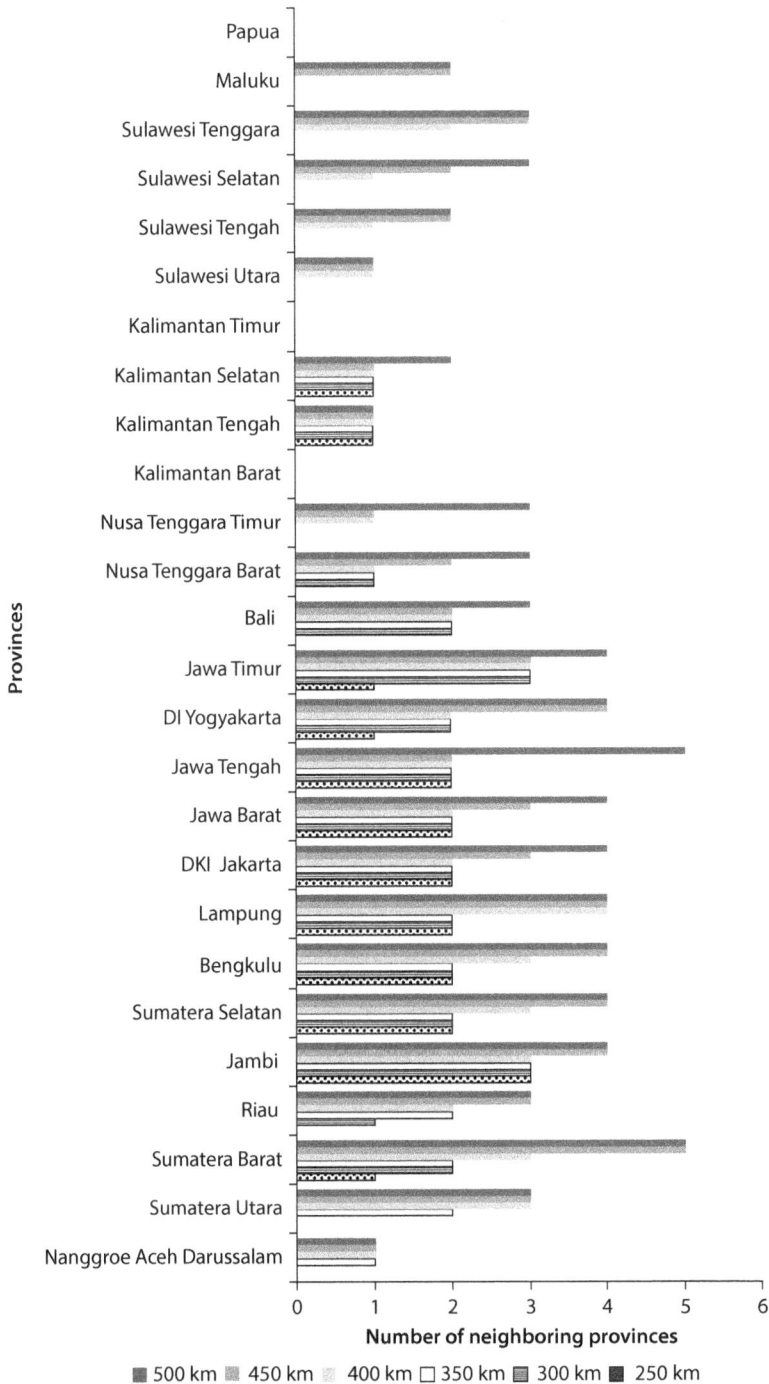

Note: km = kilometer. Bars are neighboring provinces.

Table 5A.1 Descriptive Statistics

Year	Variable	Observations	Mean	Standard deviation	Minimum	Maximum
1990		16,525	0.0783	0.2430	0.0000	1.0000
1997	Export intensity	22,370	0.0996	0.2746	0.0000	1.0000
2004		20,685	0.1153	0.2957	0.0000	1.0000
1990		16,525	2.3316	12.7460	0.0000	100.0000
1997	Ownership	22,370	4.7426	19.1535	0.0000	100.0000
2004		20,685	6.7471	23.5656	0.0000	100.0000
1990		16,515	4.1096	1.1420	1.9459	10.6412
1997	ln*Size*	18,502	4.2581	1.2329	1.9459	10.5610
2004		20,679	4.2542	1.2188	2.9957	10.5959
1990		16,462	7.6288	0.8295	1.6931	14.3257
1997	ln*Wages*	18,383	8.0072	0.8270	−0.5398	11.7806
2004		20,674	8.3373	0.8936	−1.0342	13.2484
1990		14,894	8.4957	1.5617	−0.3357	20.2109
1997	ln*Capital Stock*	16,706	8.5583	1.6006	1.3333	17.8925
2004		17,418	8.4651	1.7621	−4.7124	18.7008
1990		13,728	5.7339	1.1705	−4.0265	12.6471
1997	ln*Productivity*	15,446	5.9462	1.1566	−0.7478	13.4403
2004		15,772	5.8714	1.3043	−3.4443	12.8138
1990		16,524	2.5002	0.9465	0.0000	4.5109
1997	ln*Age*	22,051	2.5222	0.9528	0.0000	4.5850
2004		18,774	2.8251	0.8371	0.6931	4.6540
1990		16,525	9.4396	1.3692	5.3026	11.1302
1997	ln*Proximity to coast*	22,370	9.4725	1.3997	5.3026	11.1302
2004		20,685	9.5295	1.3809	5.3026	11.1302
1990		16,525	22.3038	14.3838	0.0547	57.9605
1997	Localization	22,370	21.8586	13.9163	0.0392	56.7506
2004		20,685	23.4659	15.5271	0.0521	66.6667
1990		16,525	9.7474	0.9084	7.0792	10.4779
1997	ln*Population*	22,370	9.9232	0.8906	7.3038	10.6171
2004		20,685	10.0549	0.8957	7.3454	10.7735
1990		16,201	8.9039	0.5233	7.2138	10.3253
1997	W ln*Population*	21,982	8.9707	0.4957	7.4212	10.3852
2004		20,337	9.0208	0.4780	7.5342	10.4475
1990		16,525	0.1686	0.1214	0.1005	0.9112
1997	Sector concentration	22,370	0.1574	0.1083	0.0878	0.8326
2004		20,685	0.1496	0.0965	0.0922	0.6858
1990		16,201	0.2322	0.0969	0.1590	0.9112
1997	W Sector concentration	21,982	0.2495	0.1035	0.1302	0.8326
2004		20,337	0.2422	0.1068	0.1052	0.6858
1990		16,525	11.7035	5.3258	7.1834	34.3284
1997	Export spillovers	22,370	13.6716	7.8750	4.5455	52.3936
2004		20,685	16.2727	7.4805	10.6061	53.8462
1990		16,201	13.1090	4.0156	7.3300	34.3284

table continues next page

Table 5A.1 Descriptive Statistics (continued)

Year	Variable	Observations	Mean	Standard deviation	Minimum	Maximum
1997	W Export spillovers	21,982	16.8013	6.8921	7.6923	35.4167
2004		20,337	24.5853	8.2040	13.1579	53.8462
1990		16,525	0.4474	0.2084	0.0108	0.8114
1997	Sector ^{agricultural}	22,370	0.3375	0.1446	0.0019	0.6622
2004		20,685	0.3538	0.1494	0.0059	0.7636
1990		16,201	0.5192	0.1000	0.3865	0.7659
1997	W Sector ^{agricultural}	21,982	0.3731	0.0717	0.2961	0.5774
2004		20,337	0.4072	0.0758	0.3379	0.6693
1990		16,525	0.1262	0.0451	0.0247	0.2060
1997	Sector ^{manufacturing}	22,370	0.1484	0.0355	0.0524	0.1884
2004		20,685	0.1451	0.0443	0.0071	0.2088
1990		16,201	0.1053	0.0257	0.0336	0.1283
1997	W Sector ^{manufacturing}	21,982	0.1311	0.0221	0.0598	0.1501
2004		20,337	0.1140	0.0267	0.0334	0.1436
1990		16,525	0.1515	0.0712	0.0774	0.3093
1997	Sector ^{services}	22,370	0.1586	0.0490	0.1019	0.2932
2004		20,685	0.1235	0.0374	0.0682	0.2305
1990		16,201	0.1382	0.0351	0.0864	0.1944
1997	W Sector ^{services}	21,982	0.1679	0.0254	0.1181	0.2293
2004		20,337	0.1299	0.0174	0.0772	0.1493
1990		16,525	0.2749	0.0974	0.0514	0.4739
1997	Sector ^{other}	22,370	0.3556	0.0785	0.1182	0.5165
2004		20,685	0.3777	0.0791	0.1190	0.5549
1990		16,201	0.2373	0.0464	0.0997	0.2947
1997	W Sector ^{other}	21,982	0.3279	0.0348	0.1945	0.3684
2004		20,337	0.3489	0.0399	0.2033	0.3971
1990		0	n.a.	n.a.	n.a.	n.a.
1997	Education	22,370	7.8263	0.8743	6.8300	10.1200
2004		20,685	8.3005	0.7940	7.5100	10.4500
1990		0	n.a.	n.a.	n.a.	n.a.
1997	W Education	21,982	8.1580	0.4246	7.3050	8.6450
2004		20,337	8.7598	0.3922	7.8150	9.1150
1990		0	n.a.	n.a.	n.a.	n.a.
1997	Electricity	22,370	83.5520	10.2347	27.7178	99.6041
2004		20,685	94.2162	8.1276	37.5735	99.5992
1990		0	n.a.	n.a.	n.a.	n.a.
1997	W Electricity	21,982	76.6704	11.3507	44.9895	92.1086
2004		20,337	87.2248	9.6885	58.4240	97.6201
1990		0	n.a.	n.a.	n.a.	n.a.
1997	Water	22,370	42.7290	10.2343	15.3343	60.6448
2004		20,685	51.3765	10.4926	15.9659	71.8216
1990		0	n.a.	n.a.	n.a.	n.a.
1997	W Water	21,982	40.2984	7.1671	18.9721	60.6448
2004		20,337	53.5060	6.9513	33.7206	69.8638

table continues next page

Table 5A.1 Descriptive Statistics *(continued)*

Year	Variable	Observations	Mean	Standard deviation	Minimum	Maximum
1990		16,525	0.1722	0.0665	0.0098	0.4892
1997	Road density	22,370	0.1755	0.0699	0.0098	0.4892
2004		20,685	0.1752	0.0708	0.0098	0.4892
1990		16,201	0.2143	0.1155	0.0188	0.3846
1997	W Road density	21,982	0.2250	0.1172	0.0188	0.3846
2004		20,337	0.2217	0.1156	0.0188	0.3846
1990		16,525	0.6475	0.1752	0.2986	1.0000
1997	Road quality	22,370	0.6265	0.1521	0.2986	1.0000
2004		20,685	0.6183	0.1447	0.2986	1.0000
1990		16,201	0.6725	0.1043	0.3775	0.7861
1997	W Road quality	21,982	0.6826	0.1017	0.3775	0.7861
2004		20,337	0.6886	0.1019	0.3775	0.7861

Note: n.a. = not applicable. The distance threshold considered for all variables is 400 kilometers.

Table 5A.2 Regression Results for Export Propensity, with Standard Errors Clustered at Province Level

Dependent variable: export propensity$_{ir,t}$	Dynamic probit model				
	(1)	(2)	(3)	(4)	(5)
Export propensity$_{ir,t-1}$	1.7000***	1.7421***	1.6828***	1.7000***	1.6839***
	(0.047)	(0.054)	(0.042)	(0.045)	(0.042)
Ownership$_{ir,t}$	0.0047***	0.0045***	0.0046***	0.0046***	0.0045***
	(0.000)	(0.000)	(0.000)	(0.000)	(0.000)
lnSize$_{ir,t}$	0.2862***	0.2683***	0.2810***	0.2808***	0.2834***
	(0.010)	(0.017)	(0.010)	(0.011)	(0.010)
lnWages$_{ir,t}$	−0.0136	−0.0203	−0.0191	−0.0194	−0.0171
	(0.022)	(0.020)	(0.020)	(0.020)	(0.020)
lnCapital intensity$_{ir,t}$	0.0620***	0.0582***	0.0621***	0.0621***	0.0640***
	(0.010)	(0.010)	(0.008)	(0.008)	(0.008)
lnProductivity$_{ir,t}$	0.0610***	0.0579***	0.0631***	0.0626***	0.0638***
	(0.006)	(0.005)	(0.006)	(0.006)	(0.006)
lnAge$_{ir,t}$	−0.1197***	−0.1225***	−0.1194***	−0.1288***	−0.1223***
	(0.010)	(0.013)	(0.012)	(0.013)	(0.012)
lnProximity to coast$_{r}$		−0.0130	−0.0002	0.0021	−0.0005
		(0.025)	(0.013)	(0.015)	(0.018)
Localization$_{r,t}$			0.0051*	0.0037	0.0053*
			(0.003)	(0.003)	(0.003)
lnPopulation$_{r,t}$			−0.0801		−0.0945
			(0.068)		(0.084)
W lnPopulation$_{r,t}$				−0.1294	−0.1604*
				(0.086)	(0.084)
Sector concentration$_{r,t}$			−0.3673		−0.3001
			(0.247)		(0.203)
W Sector concentration$_{r,t}$				−0.7216*	−0.6383***
				(0.379)	(0.201)

table continues next page

Table 5A.2 Regression Results for Export Propensity, with Standard Errors Clustered at Province Level (continued)

Dependent variable: export propensity$_{ir,t}$	Dynamic probit model				
	(1)	(2)	(3)	(4)	(5)
Export spillovers$_{r,t}$			0.0184***		0.0205***
			(0.003)		(0.003)
W Export spillovers$_{r,t}$				−0.0034	−0.0030
				(0.005)	(0.002)
Sector$^{manufacturing}_{r,t}$			−0.0339		0.7196
			(0.752)		(0.747)
W Sector$^{manufacturing}_{r,t}$				−3.2482***	−2.2388**
				(1.152)	(0.912)
Sector$^{services}_{r,t}$			1.2287**		1.2979*
			(0.551)		(0.667)
W Sector$^{services}_{r,t}$				−5.3009***	−2.6312
				(1.825)	(1.637)
Sector$^{other}_{r,t}$			−0.3558		−0.3292
			(0.341)		(0.602)
W Sector$^{other}_{r,t}$				−1.8717**	0.8714
				(0.861)	(0.620)
Education$_{r,t}$			−0.0673		0.0013
			(0.048)		(0.057)
W Education$_{r,t}$				−0.3041**	−0.0964
				(0.141)	(0.129)
Electricity$_{r,t}$			−0.0050**		−0.0060***
			(0.002)		(0.002)
W Electricity$_{r,t}$				0.0200***	−0.0033
				(0.005)	(0.003)
Water$_{r,t}$			0.0069***		0.0035*
			(0.001)		(0.002)
W Water$_{r,t}$				0.0196***	0.0047
				(0.004)	(0.005)
Road density$_r$			0.8777***		0.6831
			(0.300)		(0.455)
W Road density$_r$				−2.8256***	0.3104
				(0.621)	(0.611)
Road quality$_r$			−0.2489		−0.2198
			(0.222)		(0.329)
W Road quality$_r$				1.7208***	1.0406*
				(0.595)	(0.620)
constant	−3.3349***	−2.7216***	−2.3153**	−0.7566	−0.2657
	(0.179)	(0.241)	(1.043)	(1.535)	(1.331)
Region-fixed effects	Yes	No	No	No	No
Year-fixed effects	Yes	Yes	Yes	Yes	Yes
Sector-fixed effects	Yes	Yes	Yes	Yes	Yes
Observations	201,964	201,964	180,230	177,425	177,425
Pseudo R^2	0.4694	0.4623	0.4685	0.4624	0.4667

Note: Standard errors are in parentheses and clustered at province level.

*$p < 0.1$, **$p < 0.05$, ***$p < 0.01$

Table 5A.3 Regression Results for Export Intensity, with Standard Errors Clustered at Province Level

Dependent variable: export intensity$_{ir,t}$	Static model, 1990–2000 and 2004						
	(1)	(2)	(3)	(4)	(5)	(6)	(7)
Ownership$_{ir,t}$	0.0011*** (0.000)	0.0016*** (0.000)	0.0011*** (0.000)	0.0011*** (0.000)	0.0016*** (0.000)	0.0016*** (0.000)	0.0016*** (0.000)
ln Size$_{ir,t}$	0.0319*** (0.003)	0.0586*** (0.003)	0.0256*** (0.003)	0.0260*** (0.003)	0.0603*** (0.003)	0.0598*** (0.003)	0.0601*** (0.003)
ln Wages$_{ir,t}$	−0.0013 (0.002)	−0.0041*** (0.002)	−0.0013 (0.002)	−0.0017 (0.002)	−0.0031 (0.002)	−0.0036* (0.002)	−0.0044** (0.002)
ln Capital intensity$_{ir,t}$	0.0088*** (0.002)	0.0097*** (0.002)	0.0067*** (0.001)	0.0067*** (0.001)	0.0112*** (0.002)	0.0107*** (0.002)	0.0106*** (0.002)
ln Productivity$_{ir,t}$	0.0008 (0.001)	0.0023*** (0.001)	−0.0006 (0.001)	−0.0007 (0.001)	0.0029*** (0.001)	0.0023*** (0.001)	0.0015 (0.001)
ln Age$_{ir,t}$	−0.0288*** (0.010)	−0.0323*** (0.003)	−0.0246** (0.011)	−0.0247** (0.011)	−0.0318*** (0.003)	−0.0323*** (0.003)	−0.0296*** (0.002)
ln Proximity to coast$_r$		−0.0017 (0.006)			−0.0097 (0.006)	−0.0077 (0.005)	−0.0008 (0.003)
Localization$_{r,t}$			0.0004 (0.000)	0.0003 (0.000)			0.0008* (0.000)
ln Population$_{r,t}$			0.0506* (0.025)	−0.0058 (0.036)			−0.0140 (0.015)
W ln Population$_{r,t}$				−0.0164 (0.033)			−0.0180 (0.012)
Sector concentration$_{r,t}$			−0.0448 (0.032)	−0.0516 (0.040)			−0.0513* (0.028)
W Sector concentration$_{r,t}$				0.0121 (0.034)			−0.0727*** (0.026)
Export spillovers$_{r,t}$			0.0076*** (0.001)	0.0076*** (0.001)			0.0074*** (0.001)
W Export spillovers$_{r,t}$				0.0000 (0.000)			−0.0002 (0.000)
Sector$^{manufacturing}_{r,t}$			0.1464 (0.111)	0.1850 (0.112)			0.2110*** (0.079)
W Sector$^{manufacturing}_{r,t}$				−0.0462 (0.079)			−0.1075 (0.094)
Sector$^{services}_{r,t}$			0.0626 (0.066)	0.0953 (0.083)			0.1664** (0.075)
W Sector$^{services}_{r,t}$				−0.0801 (0.098)			−0.1085 (0.079)
Sector$^{other}_{r,t}$			−0.0892 (0.079)	−0.1273 (0.083)			−0.0573 (0.089)
W Sector$^{other}_{r,t}$				−0.1023 (0.084)			−0.1194 (0.100)
Education$_{r,t}$			0.0096 (0.011)	0.0006 (0.011)			0.0169* (0.010)
W Education$_{r,t}$				−0.0085 (0.009)			0.0017 (0.013)
Electricity$_{r,t}$			−0.0010*** (0.000)	−0.0009*** (0.000)			−0.0011*** (0.000)
W Electricity$_{r,t}$				−0.0008*** (0.000)			−0.0007*** (0.000)

table continues next page

Table 5A.3 Regression Results for Export Intensity, with Standard Errors Clustered at Province Level (continued)

Dependent variable: export intensity$_{ir,t}$	Static model, 1990–2000 and 2004						
	(1)	(2)	(3)	(4)	(5)	(6)	(7)
Water$_{r,t}$			−0.0001 (0.000)	0.0002 (0.000)			0.0006 (0.000)
W Water$_{r,t}$				0.0008 (0.001)			−0.0002 (0.001)
Road density$_r$					0.3803*** (0.123)	0.4976*** (0.115)	0.2163*** (0.080)
W Road density$_r$						−0.0799* (0.043)	0.2336*** (0.070)
Road quality$_r$					−0.1222*** (0.037)	−0.1399*** (0.043)	−0.1102** (0.047)
W Road quality$_r$						−0.1157** (0.049)	0.1054 (0.116)
Constant	−0.0397 (0.032)	−0.0962* (0.051)	−0.6142** (0.293)	0.2618 (0.602)	−0.0468 (0.066)	0.0328 (0.082)	0.0079 (0.173)
FEs or REs estimator	FEs	REs	FEs	FEs	REs	REs	REs
Year-fixed effects	Yes	Yes	Yes	Yes	Yes	Yes	Yes
Sector-fixed effects	No	Yes	No	No	Yes	Yes	Yes
Observations	192,091	192,091	164,574	161,930	192,091	189,009	161,930
R-within	0.0423		0.0628	0.0606			

Note: FE = fixed effect, RE = random effect. Standard errors in parentheses and clustered at province level.
*$p < 0.1$, **$p < 0.05$, ***$p < 0.01$

Notes

1. All inputs are deflated using a value added deflator from the World Bank's World Development Indicators (http://data.worldbank.org/data-catalog/world-development-indicators) with 2000 as the base year. Fuels are included as inputs.

2. http://www.bps.go.id/eng/index.php.

References

Abreu, M., H. L. De Groot, and R. J. Florax. 2005. "Space and Growth: A Survey of Empirical Evidence and Methods." *Région et Développement* 21: 13–44.

Aitken, B., G. H. Hanson, and A. E. Harrison. 1997. "Spillovers, Foreign Investment, and Export Behavior." *Journal of International Economics* 43 (1–2): 103–32.

Arnold, J., and B. Javorcik. 2009. "Gifted Kids or Pushy Parents? Foreign Direct Investment and Plant Productivity in Indonesia." *Journal of International Economics* 79 (1): 42–53.

Aw, B. Y., S. Chung, and M. J. Roberts. 2000. "Productivity and Turnover in the Export Market: Micro-level Evidence from the Republic of Korea and Taiwan (China)." *World Bank Economic Review* 14 (1): 65–90.

Baltagi, B. H. 2005. *Econometric Analysis of Panel Data.* Chichester, U.K.: John Wiley.

Barkema, H. G., and F. Vermeulen. 1998. "International Expansion through Start-up or Acquisition: A Learning Perspective." *Academy of Management Journal* 41 (1): 7–26.

Barney, J., M. Wright, and D. J. Ketchen. 2001. "The Resource-Based View of the Firm: Ten Years after 1991." *Journal of Management* 27 (6): 625–41.

Bernard, A. B., and J. B. Jensen. 1999. "Exceptional Exporter Performance: Cause, Effect, or Both?" *Journal of International Economics* 47: 1–25.

Berry, A., E. Rodriguez, and H. Sandee. 2002. "Firm and Group Dynamics in the Small and Medium Enterprise Sector in Indonesia." *Small Business Economics* 18 (1–3): 141–61.

Bilkey, W. J., and G. Tesar. 1977. "Export Behavior of Smaller-Sized Wisconsin Manufacturing Firms." *Journal of International Business Studies* 8 (1): 93–8.

Blalock, G., and P. J. Gertler. 2004. "Learning from Exporting Revisited in a Less Developed Setting." *Journal of Development Economics* 75 (2): 397–416.

Branstetter, L. G. 2001. "Are Knowledge Spillovers International or Intranational in Scope? Microeconometric Evidence from the US and Japan." *Journal of International Economics* 53 (1): 53–79.

Clerides, S. K., S. Lach, and J. R. Tybout. 1998. "Is Learning by Exporting Important? Micro-Dynamic Evidence from Colombia, Mexico, and Morocco." *Quarterly Journal of Economics* 113 (3): 903–47.

Cole, M. A., R. J. R. Elliott, and S. Virakul. 2010. "Firm Heterogeneity, Origin of Ownership and Export Participation." *World Economy* 33 (2): 264–91.

Delgado, M. A., J. C. Farinas, and S. Ruano. 2002. "Firm Productivity and Export Markets: A Non-Parametric Approach." *Journal of International Economics* 57 (2): 397–422.

Dunning, J. H. 1998. "Location and the Multinational Enterprise: A Neglected Factor?" *Journal of International Business Studies* 29 (1): 45–66.

Ellis, P. D. 2007. "Distance, Dependence and Diversity of Markets: Effects on Market Orientation." *Journal of International Business Studies* 38 (3): 374–86.

Ertur, C., and J. Le Gallo. 2003. "An Exploratory Spatial Data Analysis of European Regional Disparities, 1980–1995." In *European Regional Growth*, edited by B. Fingleton, 55–98. Berlin: Springer.

Estrin, S., K. E. Meyer, M. Wright, and F. Foliano. 2008. "Export Propensity and Intensity of Subsidiaries in Emerging Economies." *International Business Review* 17 (5): 574–86.

Feldman, M. P. 2000. "Location and Innovation: The New Economic Geography of Innovation, Spillovers, and Agglomeration." In *The Oxford Handbook of Economic Geography*, edited by G. L. Clark, M. P. Feldman, and M. S. Gertler, 373–94. Oxford, U.K.: Oxford University Press.

Filatotchev, I., J. Stephan, and B. Jindra. 2008. "Ownership Structure, Strategic Controls and Export Intensity of Foreign-Invested Firms in Transition Economies." *Journal of International Business Studies* 39 (7): 1133–48.

Gallup, J. L., J. D. Sachs, and A. D. Mellinger. 1999. "Geography and Economic Development." *International Regional Science Review* 22 (2): 179–232.

Ghemawat, P. 2007. *Redefining Global Strategy*. Boston, MA: Harvard Business School Press.

Greenaway, D., and R. Kneller. 2004. "Exporting and Productivity in the United Kingdom." *Oxford Review of Economic Policy* 20 (3): 358–71.

Hausman, J. A. 1978. "Specification Tests in Econometrics." *Econometrica* 46 (6): 1251–71.

Hill, H. 1992. "Manufacturing Industry." In *The Oil Boom and After: Indonesian Economic Policy and Performance in the Suharto Era*, edited by A. Booth, 204–57. New York: Oxford University Press.

Jaffe, A. B. 1986. "Technological Opportunity and Spillovers of R&D: Evidence from Firms Patents, Profits, and Market Value." *American Economic Review* 76 (5): 984–1001.

Jenkins, M. 2006. "Sourcing Patterns of Firms in Export Processing Zones (EPZs): An Empirical Analysis of Firm-Level Determinants." *Journal of Business Research* 59 (3): 331–34.

Johanson, J., and J. E. Vahlne. 1977. "Internationalization Process of Firm: Model of Knowledge Development and Increasing Foreign Market Commitments." *Journal of International Business Studies* 8 (1): 23–32.

Knight, G. A., and S. T. Cavusgil. 1996. "The Born Global Firm: A Challenge to Traditional Internationalization Theory." In *Advances in International Marketing*, edited by S. T. Cavusgil and T. Madsen, 11–26. Greenwich, CT: JAI Press.

Krugman, P. 1991. "Increasing Returns and Economic Geography." *Journal of Political Economy* 99 (3): 483–99.

Levinsohn, J., and A. Petrin. 2003. "Estimating Production Functions Using Inputs to Control for Unobservables." *Review of Economic Studies* 70 (2): 317–41.

Malmberg, A., B. Malmberg, and P. Lundequist. 2000. "Agglomeration and Firm Performance: Economies of Scale, Localization, and Urbanization among Swedish Export Firms." *Environment and Planning A* 32 (2): 305–21.

Marshall, A. 1890. *Principles of Economics*. London: Macmillan.

McDougall, P. P., S. Shane, and B. M. Oviatt. 1994. "Explaining the Formation of International New Ventures: The Limits of Theories from International Business Research." *Journal of Business Venturing* 9 (6): 469–87.

Moen, O., and P. Servais. 2002. "Born Global or Gradual Global? Examining the Export Behavior of Small and Medium-Sized Enterprises." *Journal of International Marketing* 10 (3): 49–72.

Naudé, W. 2009. "Geography, Transport and Africa's Proximity Gap." *Journal of Transport Geography* 17 (1): 1–9.

Olley, G. S., and A. Pakes. 1996. "The Dynamics of Productivity in the Telecommunications Equipment Industry." *Econometrica* 64 (6): 1263–97.

Ottaviano, G. I. P., and J.-F. Thisse. 2005. "New Economic Geography: What about the N?" *Environment and Planning A* 37 (10): 1707–25.

Oviatt, B. M., and P. P. McDougall. 1994. "Toward a Theory of International New Ventures." *Journal of International Business Studies* 25 (1): 45–64.

Petrin, A., B. Poi, and J. Levinsohn. 2004. "Production Function in Stata Using Inputs to Control for Unobservables." *The Stata Journal* 4 (2): 113–23.

Pfaffermayr, M. 2009. "Conditional Beta- and Sigma-Convergence in Space: A Maximum Likelihood Approach." *Regional Science and Urban Economics* 39 (1): 63–78.

Preece, S. B., G. Miles, and M. C. Baetz. 1998. "Explaining the International Intensity and Global Diversity of Early-Stage Technology-Based Firms." *Journal of Business Venturing* 14 (3): 259–81.

Ramstetter, E. D. 1999. "Trade Propensities and Foreign Ownership Shares in Indonesian Manufacturing." *Bulletin of Indonesian Economic Studies* 35 (2): 43–66.

Rasiah, R. 2005. "Foreign Ownership, Technological Intensity and Export Incidence: A Study of Auto Parts, Electronics and Garment Firms in Indonesia." *International Journal of Technology and Globalisation* 1: 361–80.

Rey, S. J., and M. V. Janikas. 2005. "Regional Convergence, Inequality, and Space." *Journal of Economic Geography* 5 (2): 155–76.

Roberts, M. J., and J. R. Tybout. 1997. "The Decision to Export in Colombia: An Empirical Model of Entry with Sunk Costs." *American Economic Review* 87 (4): 545–64.

Rodríguez-Pose, A., and V. Tselios. 2009. "Education and Income Inequality in the Regions of the European Union." *Journal of Regional Science* 49 (3): 411–37.

Rugman, A. M., and A. Verbeke. 2001. "Subsidiary-Specific Advantages in Multinational Enterprises." *Strategic Management Journal* 22 (3): 237–50.

Sjöholm, F. 2003. "Which Indonesian Firms Export? The Importance of Foreign Networks." *Chapters in Regional Science* 82 (3): 333–50.

Smith, S. M., and D. L. Barkley. 1991. "Local Input Linkages of Rural High-Technology Manufacturers." *Land Economics* 67: 472–83.

Solow, R. 1957. "Technical Change and the Aggregate Production Function." *Review of Economics and Statistics* 39 (3): 312–20.

Tselios, V. 2009. "Growth and Convergence in Income per Capita and Income Inequality in the Regions of the EU." *Spatial Economic Analysis* 4: 347–70.

Wooldridge, J. M. 2002. Econometric Analysis of Cross Section and Panel Data. Cambridge, MA: MIT Press.

Wu, F., R. R. Sinkovics, S. T. Cavusgil, and A. S. Roath. 2007. "Overcoming Export Manufacturers' Dilemma in International Expansion." *Journal of International Business Studies* 38 (2): 283–302.

CHAPTER 6

Trade and Regional Characteristics in India

Deborah Winkler

Introduction and Data

In this chapter, we focus on a descriptive analysis of the relationship between trade and regions in India. It follows the same approach and structure as in the analysis of Indonesia in chapter 4.

Table 6.1 summarizes the main data sources used in the analysis. The Annual Survey of Industries (ASI) covers more than 150,000 firms, with state-level geographical identification (see table 6A.1 for more details on firm coverage by state). This dataset has one fundamental drawback, particularly for a study on trade: although it captures details on firms' output and inputs, it does not differentiate between domestic and foreign sales. (There are also limitations concerning firm size coverage in ASI[1]) Therefore, it is possible to analyze firm-level relationships only between output and location (in the context of trade openness) and not between trade and location directly. In chapter 7, we use another source of firm-level data in India that does provide export and import data—the Prowess database. However, as we were only able to access more recent data from this dataset, it was not fit for the purpose of tracing the evolution of spatial patterns of production over a long time period, which is the purpose of the analysis in this chapter. Data on output from ASI presented in this chapter are deflated using a gross domestic product (GDP) deflator from the World Development Indicators database with 2004 as the base year.

A description of the World Bank Enterprise Surveys can be found in chapter 4 (the "Data" section). We use Enterprise Survey data for India from 2006, which are the most recent data available at the time of this analysis. Most data are obtained from the Enterprise Surveys Indicators Database, and a couple of indicators are retrieved from the Enterprise Surveys Standardized Database. The Indian data are not stratified. The total sample consists of 4,234 firms, 2,218 of which are in manufacturing, 1,949 in services, and 67 other firms. We only include manufacturing firms in the analysis, as this allows for a better comparability with

Table 6.1 Overview of Main Data Sources

Data source	Description/coverage	Main drawbacks
Annual Survey of Industries	Firm-level survey with data on manufacturing sector; data available by state	*No data on exports;* only covers firms with >100 staff in most states (since 2004) and >200 firms (1998–2004)
World Bank Enterprise Surveys	Firm-level survey with data on manufacturing and services sector; data available by province	Limited sample size, particularly at provincial level; limited data on firm characteristics; largely perception-based

Sources: MOSPI; Enterprise Survey Indicators, World Bank.

the ASI data. The Enterprise Surveys data for India differentiate between 16 regions, namely Andhra Pradesh, Bihar, Gujarat, Haryana, Jharkhand, Karnataka, Kerala, Madhya Pradesh, Maharashtra, National Capital Region (NCR), Orissa, Punjab, Rajasthan, Tamil Nadu, Uttar Pradesh, and West Bengal. In presenting the results from the Enterprise Surveys, we organize states into "leading" and "lagging" groups. These are categorized based on a recent World Bank study of India's lagging regions (World Bank 2008), which defines lagging states as those that were in the bottom quarter in terms of per capita income in 2000–01.

Economic Geography and the Evolution of Regional Inequalities in India

In this section, we provide a very brief introduction to the economic geography of India. Specifically, we show (1) the extent of regional inequality (in economic activity and outcomes) and how this has evolved over time; and (2) the relationship between "lagging" regions and geographical factors, including location and density. For more detailed assessment, there is a very large literature on regional disparities in India. Generally, these studies find broad convergence in the period from 1960 up to 1990 and divergence since 1990 (see chapter 9 for an overview of this literature and references).

Snapshot of India's Economic Geography

India faces a relatively high regional Gini index (see chapter 4, table 4.1) measured at the state level. It is likely to be even higher if measured at the district level, given the problem of large inequalities *within* states (World Bank 2008). There is both commonality and heterogeneity in the composition of "leading" and "lagging" states in India. Table 6.2 presents some descriptive comparisons of Indian states on the basis of output, location, and infrastructure. Geographically, most of the lagging states are concentrated in the northeast and north-central parts of the country (the "lagging" states comprise the categories "Low-income states" and "Northeast special category states" in table 6.2). But while many of the lagging states, particularly those in the northeast, are small and have low population densities, others are among the largest and most populous in the country (for example, Uttar Pradesh, Bihar, Madhya Pradesh, and Rajasthan). Similarly, while most of the lagging states are landlocked, Orissa is not, and some

Table 6.2 The Links between Distance, Density, and Lagging Regions in India

	Remoteness	Population	Infrastructure	Output per capita vs. India average
Low-income states				
Bihar	0.3110	103,804,637	0.6174	0.57
Chhattisgarh	0.4077	25,540,196	0.3220	0.79
Jharkhand	0.1881	32,966,238	0.1259	—
Madhya Pradesh	0.4094	72,597,565	0.2674	0.48
Orissa	0.1761	41,947,358	0.1968	0.71
Rajasthan	0.1637	68,621,012	0.3611	0.68
Uttar Pradesh	0.4257	199,581,477	0.8405	0.49
Uttarakhand	0.5991	10,116,752	0.3775	0.97
Northeast special category states				
Arunachal Pradesh	—	1,382,611	0.1165	0.73
Assam	0.4442	31,169,272	0.3393	0.62
Jammu and Kashmir	1.0000	12,548,926	0.0456	0.65
Manipur	0.5400	2,721,756	0.2993	0.56
Mizoram	—	1,091,014	0.2452	0.79
Meghalaya	0.4442	2,964,007	0.2440	0.71
Nagaland	0.5476	1,980,602	0.5754	0.56
Tripura	0.5629	3,671,032	1.1617	0.74
Middle-income states				
Andhra Pradesh	0.1759	84,665,533	0.4912	1.06
Himachal Pradesh	0.6144	6,856,509	0.3807	1.07
Karnataka	0.0631	61,130,704	0.7985	1.08
Kerala	0.1053	33,387,677	2.9963	1.12
Sikkim	—	607,688	0.1998	1.00
West Bengal	0.0000	91,347,736	2.3861	0.85
High-income states				
Delhi	0.3415	16,753,235	1.8477	2.10
Goa	0.2546	1,457,723	2.0702	2.82
Gujarat	0.2039	60,383,628	0.6746	1.22
Haryana	0.5861	25,353,081	0.6266	1.81
Maharashtra	0.0081	112,372,972	0.5786	1.26
Pondicherry	0.0704	1,244,464	4.9353	2.26
Punjab	0.5861	27,704,236	0.7444	1.35
Tamil Nadu	0.0000	72,138,958	1.1329	1.20

Correlation coefficient	Remoteness	Population	Infrastructure	Output per capita vs. India average
Remoteness	1	−0.391**	−0.1111	−0.2506
Population		1	0.0520	−0.2540
Infrastructure			1	0.5113***
Output per capita vs. India average				1

Sources: Data on geographical distances for remoteness calculations from the World Bank Development Economics Vice Presidency; data on population from MOSPI 2012; data on infrastructure from MORTH 2008; data on output per capita from Database on India's Economy, RBI (2008–09 per capita net state domestic product at factor cost).
Note: — = not available.
** indicates significance at 0.05 level and *** indicates significance at 0.01 level.

of the richest states in the country have no direct access to seaports (for example, Delhi, Haryana, Punjab).

Table 6.2 suggests that remoteness[2] is associated with lower outcomes in Indian states, with remoteness related to lower populations, lower-quality infrastructure, and lower per capita GDP (although the correlation is not significant in the latter two). But more important than remoteness is infrastructure,[3] which shows a strong correlation with GDP per capita.

Evolution of Regional Inequalities

Regional inequalities have grown even faster in India than in Indonesia, as can be seen in figures 6.1 and 6.2.[4] The Gini index of regional inequality has risen by more than 30 percent in just the past 15 years, with divergence particularly strong since the early 2000s (figure 6.1). The percentage point difference between mean per capita income of the group of leading and lagging states doubled between 2003 and 2009 (figure 6.2). Growing regional inequality corresponded with a period of steadily growing trade openness (merchandise trade share of India's GDP more than doubled over the past 15 years). On the whole, lagging states experienced the slowest increases in GDP per capita over the past decade, leading to further erosion in their relative positions. Middle-income states fared best over the period, with many high-income states also extending their output gap relative to the national average.

While there is much heterogeneity in the story, there are few "winners" among the traditional lagging states (see table 6.3). The main exceptions here are Orissa, which rose from 64 percent of the national average to 71 percent, and

Figure 6.1 Gini Index of Regional Income Inequality and Trade Openness in India, 1993–94 to 2008–09

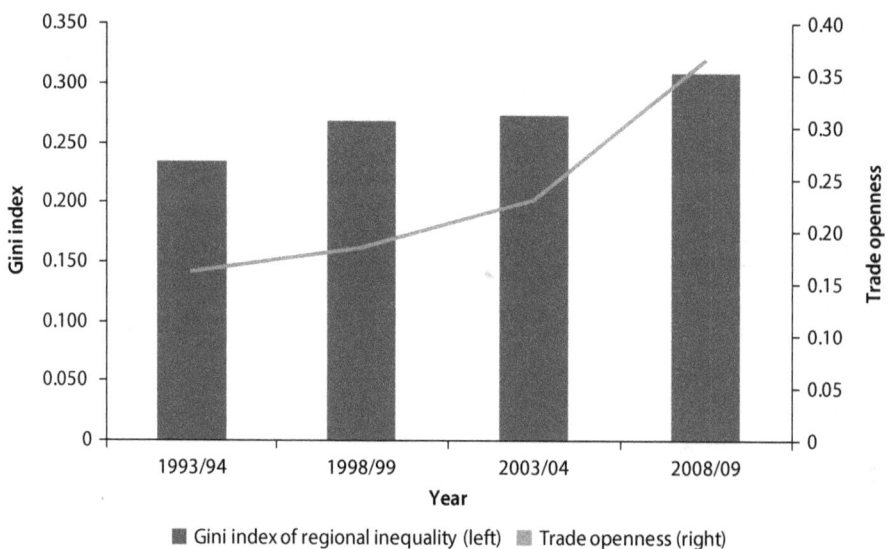

■ Gini index of regional inequality (left)   ■ Trade openness (right)

Source: Calculations based on data from Database on India's Economy, RBI.

Figure 6.2 Percentage Difference between Mean per Capita Income of Leading and Lagging States in India, 1993–94 to 2008–09

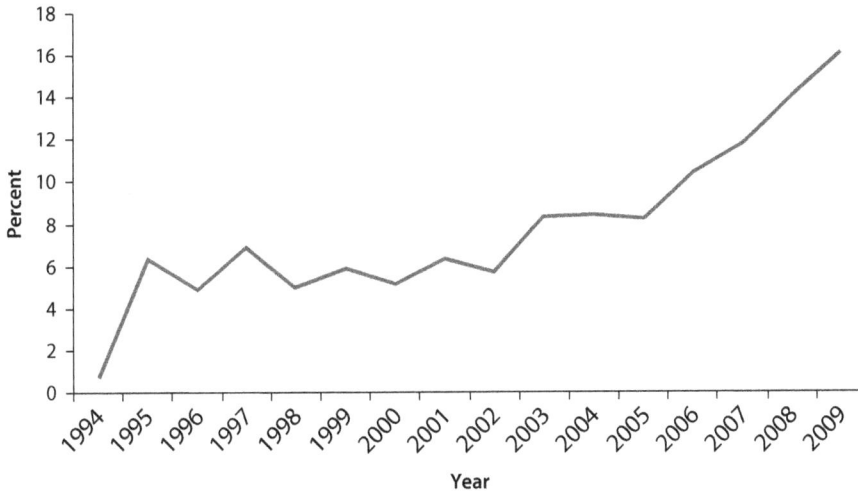

Source: Aggarwal and Archa 2012.

Uttarakhand, which rose from 90 to 98 percent of the national average. On the other hand, there are many examples of lagging states that have fallen much further behind over the past 15 years. Most notable are Nagaland, whose relative position fell by more than half, from almost 120 percent of the national average GDP per capita to just 56 percent, and Arunachal Pradesh, which declined from 114 to 73 percent. Madhya Pradesh also experienced major decline from 86 percent of the national average to just 48 percent, making it the second poorest state (after Bihar) as measured by state GDP per capita. Interestingly, the high-income states include both states that were major winners over the past decade (Haryana, Goa, and Pondicherry) as well as states that have declined substantially in relative terms (Maharashtra, Punjab, and Delhi).

Trade Participation and Structural Change in Indian States

Trade Participation

Figure 6.3 gives perspective on the relative export participation and intensity of firms across geographies in India, based on the limited number of states available from the Enterprise Surveys. It suggests that, with some exceptions (particularly Rajasthan and Maharashtra, but also Uttar Pradesh and Karnataka), firms in leading states are much more likely to be exporters than those in lagging states. They are also somewhat more likely to export a larger share of their output. Geographically, figure 6.3 indicates that firms located in central-east and northeast states are less likely to be exporters than those in the north-central, south, and west. These same patterns hold true for use of imported inputs

Table 6.3 Gross State Domestic Product per Capita Relative to India Average

	1993–94	1998–99	2003–04	2008–09
Low-income states				
Bihar	0.395	0.312	0.328	0.337
Chhattisgarh	0.850	0.699	0.743	0.790
Jharkhand	0.767	0.744	0.621	0.573
Madhya Pradesh	0.856	0.742	0.685	0.481
Orissa	0.637	0.609	0.683	0.707
Rajasthan	0.804	0.859	0.791	0.684
Uttar Pradesh	0.659	0.588	0.549	0.486
Uttarakhand	0.897	0.754	0.973	0.974
Northeast special category states				
Arunachal Pradesh	1.136	0.900	0.926	0.731
Assam	0.743	0.613	0.742	0.622
Jammu and Kashmir	0.851	0.805	0.862	0.646
Manipur	0.760	0.677	0.706	0.562
Mizoram	1.082	0.936	1.052	0.789
Meghalaya	0.896	0.828	0.944	0.710
Nagaland	1.187	0.862	0.998	0.562
Tripura	0.720	0.765	1.013	0.741
Middle-income states				
Andhra Pradesh	0.964	0.970	1.056	1.056
Himachal Pradesh	1.023	1.121	1.358	1.071
Karnataka	1.019	1.069	1.001	1.075
Kerala	1.038	1.137	1.246	1.115
Sikkim	1.093	0.991	1.029	1.002
West Bengal	0.879	0.948	1.000	0.846
High-income states				
Delhi	2.362	2.385	2.348	2.099
Goa	2.153	2.796	2.615	2.816
Gujarat	1.274	1.320	1.290	1.221
Haryana	1.441	1.343	1.634	1.811
Maharashtra	1.584	1.399	1.396	1.255
Pondicherry	1.272	1.998	2.289	2.257
Punjab	1.653	1.472	1.498	1.349
Tamil Nadu	1.164	1.207	1.154	1.202

Source: Calculations based on data from Database on India's Economy, RBI.

(figure 6.4), adding further support to the link between trade integration and patterns of leading and lagging states.

Changes in Sectoral Specialization

As discussed in chapter 4, the relationship between trade and regional inequalities is likely to work through a number of channels, an important one of which is specialization and the corresponding structural change this induces in regions.

Figure 6.3 Export Propensity and Intensity in Indian States, 2006

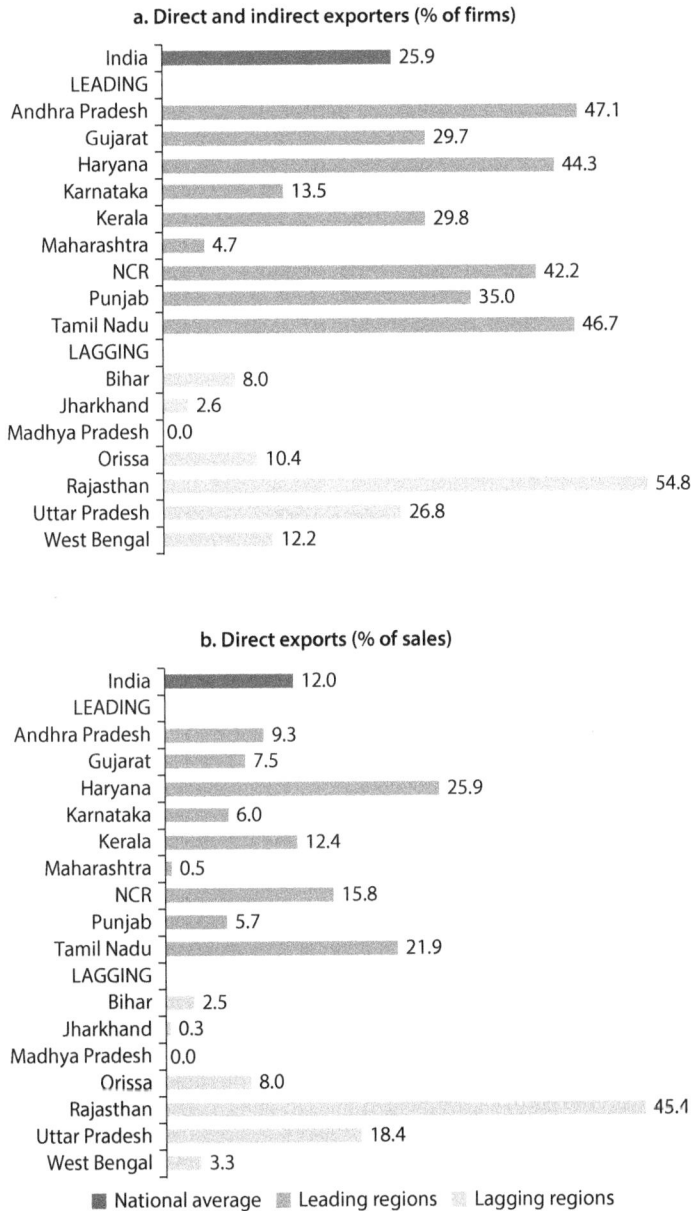

a. Direct and indirect exporters (% of firms)

India	25.9
LEADING	
Andhra Pradesh	47.1
Gujarat	29.7
Haryana	44.3
Karnataka	13.5
Kerala	29.8
Maharashtra	4.7
NCR	42.2
Punjab	35.0
Tamil Nadu	46.7
LAGGING	
Bihar	8.0
Jharkhand	2.6
Madhya Pradesh	0.0
Orissa	10.4
Rajasthan	54.8
Uttar Pradesh	26.8
West Bengal	12.2

b. Direct exports (% of sales)

India	12.0
LEADING	
Andhra Pradesh	9.3
Gujarat	7.5
Haryana	25.9
Karnataka	6.0
Kerala	12.4
Maharashtra	0.5
NCR	15.8
Punjab	5.7
Tamil Nadu	21.9
LAGGING	
Bihar	2.5
Jharkhand	0.3
Madhya Pradesh	0.0
Orissa	8.0
Rajasthan	45.1
Uttar Pradesh	18.4
West Bengal	3.3

■ National average ▦ Leading regions ▨ Lagging regions

Source: World Bank 2006.

In this section, we look briefly at the link between trade and structural changes in the regional economies of India. We apply the same index of structural change (ISC) used to analyze Indonesia, and described in detail in chapter 4. The analysis of structural change in Indian states is based on output only, as no state-level data are available on exports across a sufficient time period. Moreover, the data

Figure 6.4 Offshoring Intensity in Indian States, 2006

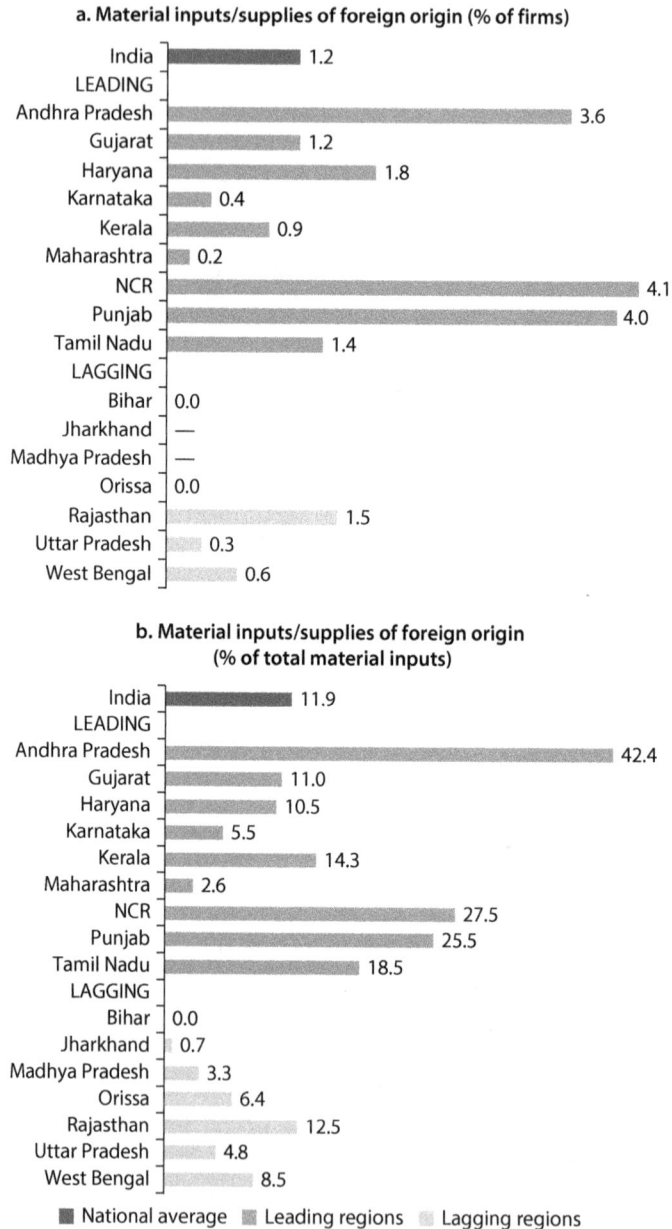

a. Material inputs/supplies of foreign origin (% of firms)

India	1.2
LEADING	
Andhra Pradesh	3.6
Gujarat	1.2
Haryana	1.8
Karnataka	0.4
Kerala	0.9
Maharashtra	0.2
NCR	4.1
Punjab	4.0
Tamil Nadu	1.4
LAGGING	
Bihar	0.0
Jharkhand	—
Madhya Pradesh	—
Orissa	0.0
Rajasthan	1.5
Uttar Pradesh	0.3
West Bengal	0.6

b. Material inputs/supplies of foreign origin (% of total material inputs)

India	11.9
LEADING	
Andhra Pradesh	42.4
Gujarat	11.0
Haryana	10.5
Karnataka	5.5
Kerala	14.3
Maharashtra	2.6
NCR	27.5
Punjab	25.5
Tamil Nadu	18.5
LAGGING	
Bihar	0.0
Jharkhand	0.7
Madhya Pradesh	3.3
Orissa	6.4
Rajasthan	12.5
Uttar Pradesh	4.8
West Bengal	8.5

■ National average   ■ Leading regions   ▨ Lagging regions

Source: World Bank 2006.
Note: — = not available.

available from ASI only allows us to measure change over a single decade (1998–2007), rather than the nearly two decades we were able to trace in Indonesia. As a result, structural changes resulting from the shift to openness in the late 1980s and early 1990s may already be captured at the starting point of our data. On the other hand, as noted earlier, India's trade share of GDP rose dramatically only after 1998, so trade-induced changes in regional output structure should be captured in the data presented here. Finally, like with most of the analysis of Indonesia, the data used for India focus only on the manufacturing sector.[5]

Figure 6.5 shows the ISC for output across the Indian states, which are grouped according to their status as "leading" and "lagging" states. We use

Figure 6.5 Index of Structural Change in Output in India, 1998–2007

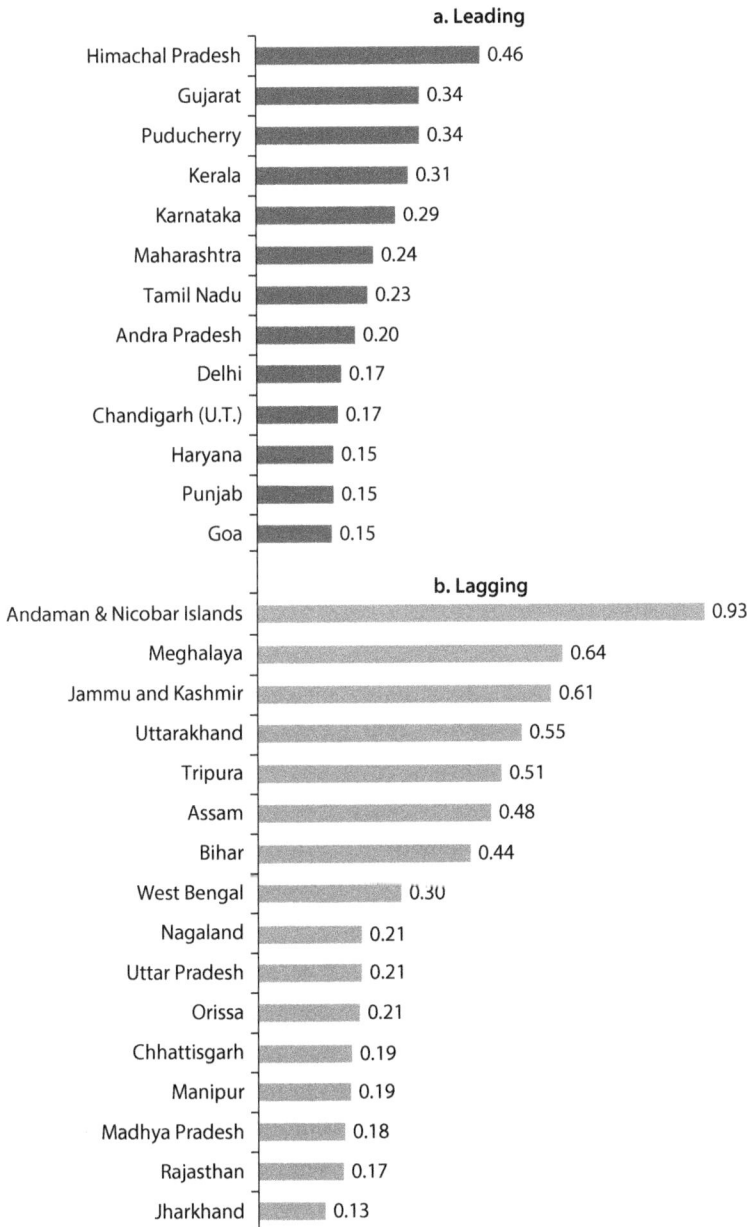

a. Leading

Himachal Pradesh	0.46
Gujarat	0.34
Puducherry	0.34
Kerala	0.31
Karnataka	0.29
Maharashtra	0.24
Tamil Nadu	0.23
Andra Pradesh	0.20
Delhi	0.17
Chandigarh (U.T.)	0.17
Haryana	0.15
Punjab	0.15
Goa	0.15

b. Lagging

Andaman & Nicobar Islands	0.93
Meghalaya	0.64
Jammu and Kashmir	0.61
Uttarakhand	0.55
Tripura	0.51
Assam	0.48
Bihar	0.44
West Bengal	0.30
Nagaland	0.21
Uttar Pradesh	0.21
Orissa	0.21
Chhattisgarh	0.19
Manipur	0.19
Madhya Pradesh	0.18
Rajasthan	0.17
Jharkhand	0.13

Source: Calculations based on Data from MORTH 2008, 2-digit ISIC Rev. 3.
Note: ISIC = International Standard Industrial Classification. Index for output based on 1998 and 2007 values.

1998/99 and 2007/08 as the two points in time and calculated the ISC at the 2-digit (26 sectors) industry level using the International Standard Industrial Classification (ISIC) Rev. 3 classification. Overall, the results indicate that, like in Indonesia, India's lagging states experienced significantly more structural change in output than the traditionally leading states (on an unweighted basis, lagging states had an ISC of 0.33 versus 0.25 for leading states). From a geographical perspective, states in the most peripheral regions—in the northeast and far north—experienced the greatest change, followed by those in the far south and then the west. Like in Indonesia, the lowest rate of structural change occurred in the traditional leading, core states, here mainly in the north. But interestingly, the band of low-income states in the center of the country—including Madhya Pradesh, Chhattisgarh, Jharkhand, and Orissa—also experienced limited structural change in output. States with the highest output shares, namely, Maharashtra and Gujarat, but also Andhra Pradesh, Tamil Nadu, and Uttar Pradesh, all show a medium structural change in output.

As was the case in Indonesia, most of the Indian states that experienced the greatest structural change over the decade were, initially at least, concentrated in natural resources–based sectors. However, in contrast to the peripheral provinces in Indonesia, India's peripheral states were by 1998 already much more diversified and industrialized. Most of these states experienced diversification away from mainly food processing to a wider set of industries, in particular chemicals, metals, and machinery. Interestingly, the pattern in many of the lagging states indicates a diversification toward more capital-intensive production, and not necessarily toward sectors that are particularly export oriented. For example, Jammu and Kashmir's top two manufacturing sectors in 1998 were food manufacturing and textiles; by 2008, they were chemicals and basic metals. Himachal Pradesh produced textiles, minerals, and food as its top three product groups in 1998; by 2008, chemicals was its top product group, followed by minerals and textiles.

Industrial Relocation: Changing Spatial Patterns of Industry

Here we present high-level, descriptive data on the regional location patterns of manufacturing in order to support further understanding of the factors that help shape the regional divergence observed.

Figure 6.6 provides a summary assessment of the patterns of geographical concentration and dispersion (at the state level) of manufacturing output in India across sectors between 1998 and 2008. As in the analysis for Indonesia in chapter 4, we use a modified version of the Herfindahl-Hirschman index (HHI) calculated for each product category by taking the total sum of the squared market shares of all regions producing that good:

$$HHI_j = \sum_i (S_{ij})^2 \qquad (6.1)$$

Figure 6.6 Herfindahl-Hirschman Index in Output by Industry in India, 1993–94 to 2008–09

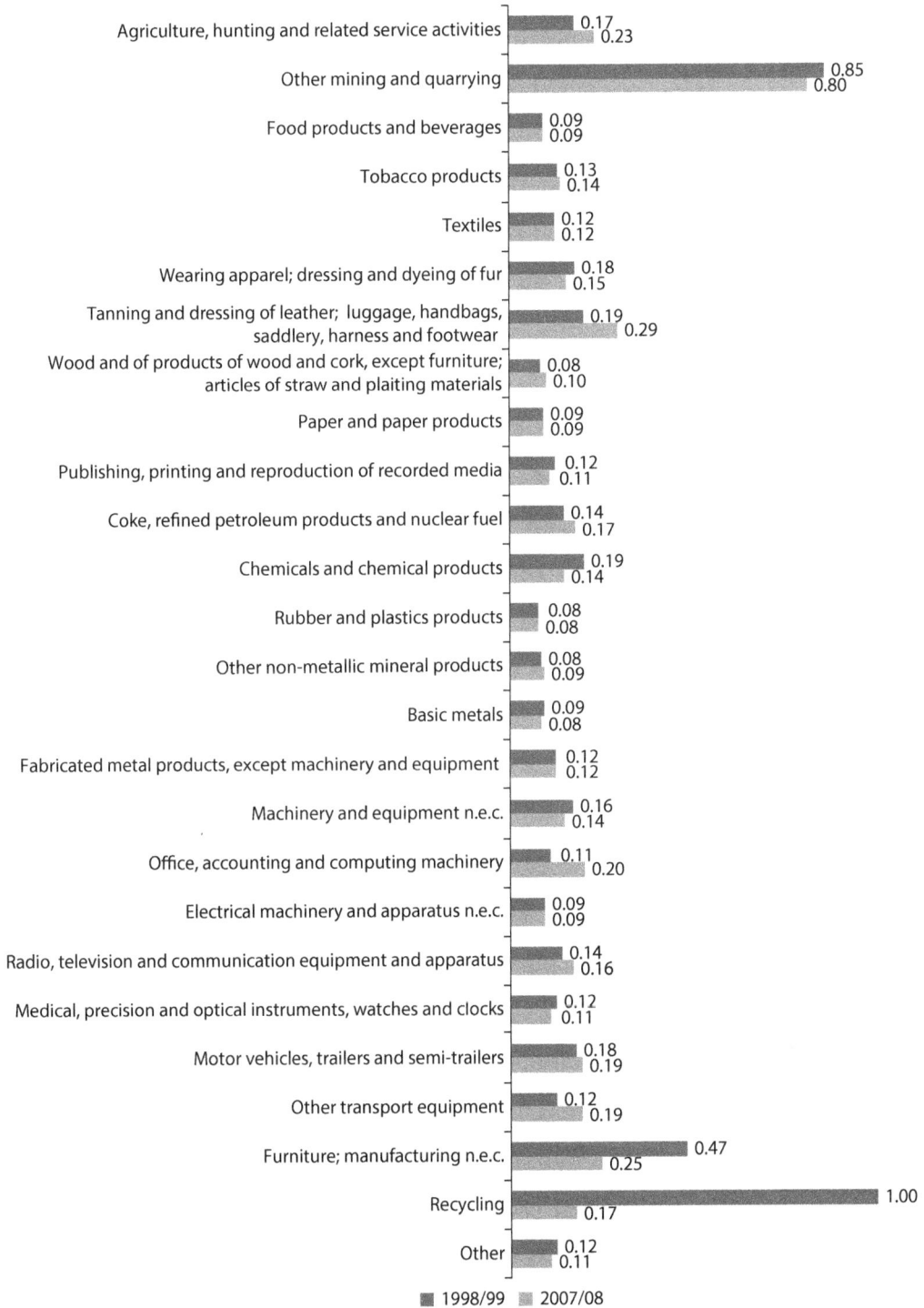

Agriculture, hunting and related service activities — 0.17 / 0.23
Other mining and quarrying — 0.85 / 0.80
Food products and beverages — 0.09 / 0.09
Tobacco products — 0.13 / 0.14
Textiles — 0.12 / 0.12
Wearing apparel; dressing and dyeing of fur — 0.18 / 0.15
Tanning and dressing of leather; luggage, handbags, saddlery, harness and footwear — 0.19 / 0.29
Wood and of products of wood and cork, except furniture; articles of straw and plaiting materials — 0.08 / 0.10
Paper and paper products — 0.09 / 0.09
Publishing, printing and reproduction of recorded media — 0.12 / 0.11
Coke, refined petroleum products and nuclear fuel — 0.14 / 0.17
Chemicals and chemical products — 0.19 / 0.14
Rubber and plastics products — 0.08 / 0.08
Other non-metallic mineral products — 0.08 / 0.09
Basic metals — 0.09 / 0.08
Fabricated metal products, except machinery and equipment — 0.12 / 0.12
Machinery and equipment n.e.c. — 0.16 / 0.14
Office, accounting and computing machinery — 0.11 / 0.20
Electrical machinery and apparatus n.e.c. — 0.09 / 0.09
Radio, television and communication equipment and apparatus — 0.14 / 0.16
Medical, precision and optical instruments, watches and clocks — 0.12 / 0.11
Motor vehicles, trailers and semi-trailers — 0.18 / 0.19
Other transport equipment — 0.12 / 0.19
Furniture; manufacturing n.e.c. — 0.47 / 0.25
Recycling — 1.00 / 0.17
Other — 0.12 / 0.11

■ 1998/99   ▨ 2007/08

Source: Calculations based on Annual Survey of Industries, MOSPI.
Note: n.e.c. = not elsewhere classified.

where S_{ij} is the share of region i expressed as a percentage of a country's total output of product j. The HHI can range between $1/n$ (if each of the n regions has the same output share) and 1 (if one region produces all) where n designates the total number of regions producing this good. A decline reflects a greater degree of spatial dispersion of output in that sector, while an increase reflects a greater degree of regional concentration.

Taken as a whole, the manufacturing sector experienced almost no change in the relative concentration of activity. At the sector level, approximately half of sectors became more concentrated geographically and half less concentrated. For the majority of these sectors, however, the change was modest. The only significant increases in concentration were in leather, office equipment, other transport equipment, and perhaps most importantly, agriculture. In contrast, significant dispersion of output is observed only in recycling, furniture, and chemicals.

The data available for this analysis of geographical sectoral structures limits us to the manufacturing sector. However, there is evidence that geographical structural transformation in India goes well beyond manufacturing. In fact, perhaps the most significant change has been the shift in some leading states away from manufacturing and toward greater reliance on services. Similarly, some of the lagging regions, particularly in the northeast and hill areas, have seen a shift from primary to manufacturing activity. Table 6.4 shows the movement in the share of manufacturing and services contribution to gross state domestic product (GSDP) over almost three decades.

Indeed, this structural shift may be playing an important role in determining the levels of regional inequality in India. Table 6.5 shows the disparities in per capita value added in manufacturing, services, and agriculture, showing the coefficients of variation in total and sectoral per capita net GSDP as provided by Khomiakova (2008) up to 2004–05 and calculated by Aggarwal and Archa (2012) (chapter 9 of this book) after that. While it confirms the trend of overall divergence, table 6.5 also indicates that the manufacturing sector, which has been the single largest contributor to regional imbalances, has been converging of late. Conversely, the service sector divergence has shown upward movement.

Firm and Regional Characteristics: Descriptive Analysis Using Enterprise Survey Data

In this section, we provide a descriptive overview of the relationship between trade participation and firm and regional characteristics. It relies mainly on the Enterprise Survey data discussed previously, which restricts our coverage of provinces. Table 6.6 follows the same analytical approach used in chapter 4 for Indonesia and in chapter 3 (see the section "Descriptive Analysis") for the cross-country dataset, comparing the differences in mean outcomes of various indicators for firms based in core versus noncore provinces. In the case of the provinces surveyed for the India Enterprise Survey, "core" includes Maharashtra, Karnataka,

Table 6.4 Share of Manufacturing in GSDP by State in Selected Years, 1980–81 to 2008–09
percent

State	Share of manufacturing				Share of services			
	1980–81	1990–91	2000–01	2008–09	1980–81	1990–91	2000–01	2008–09
Andhra Pradesh	13.86	15.32	13.69	12.05	39.26	41.71	46.54	51.25
Bihar	9.92	12.56	3.73	2.50	28.02	31.95	43.39	51.28
Gujarat	18.92	26.14	30.41	29.94	33.22	37.34	44.18	44.38
Haryana	13.65	19.10	20.59	20.00	25.39	29.81	40.18	46.43
Karnataka	15.25	18.63	17.26	19.85	31.59	39.17	46.13	54.53
Kerala	9.52	11.11	11.68	9.96	40.92	50.35	56.09	60.73
Madhya Pradesh	11.11	15.50	15.35	12.73	27.99	33.36	40.55	39.71
Maharashtra	24.92	26.08	23.93	23.46	39.94	43.86	53.36	57.20
Orissa	9.08	11.29	12.13	17.04	27.16	34.76	43.38	45.07
Punjab	9.21	13.61	15.96	16.05	36.18	33.48	36.92	41.27
Rajasthan	12.43	12.36	16.5	15.63	33.94	35.12	41.15	41.90
Tamil Nadu	31.47	28.54	24.36	23.32	36.73	39.98	47.93	57.1
Uttar Pradesh	9.01	13.87	14.02	14.01	33.94	37.9	40.34	42.440
West Bengal	20.31	17.8	17.28	16.37	40.38	43.34	49.35	53.50
Arunachal	3.80	2.60	3.43	2.03	29.04	23.08	34.24	23.31
Assam	9.55	9.17	7.67	10.74	31.57	35.34	44.58	51.05
Manipur	6.41	13.53	7.93	7.48	23.13	41.59	46.24	41.03
Meghalaya	1.80	2.42	2.07	8.49	42.46	49.88	53.45	50.79
Mizoram	1.49	2.87	1.73	2.13	59.10	46.15	64.42	62.46
Tripura	3.44	2.78	4.85	2.82	39.37	49.84	59.23	58.42
Himachal	3.01	7.32	15.02	13.64	33.65	38.69	41.57	40.95
Jammu and Kashmir	—	—	5.86	8.1	—	—	51.44	48.76
Mean	11.0568	13.0114	12.46	12.5974	35.7164	39.811	46.875	48.36
Coefficient of variation	0.68869	0.59505	0.6426	0.6143	0.23899	0.2025	0.1567	0.1800

Source: Aggarwal and Archa 2012.

Note: GSPD = gross state domestic product, — = not available.

Tamil Nadu, and Gujarat; "noncore" includes 12 other provinces.[6] The results from table 6.6 show very clear differences in both the firm characteristics and the reported business environment of firms in core and noncore regions.

Like in Indonesia, firms in India's core tend to be larger and more foreign owned (although not significantly in India), and tend to make greater use of technology, training, and quality certification. This same pattern generally holds true if grouping states into the traditional leading and lagging categories.

The results from table 6.6 with regard to the business environment in core versus noncore regions are powerful. The table shows that, like in Indonesia, firms in India's core regions have better infrastructure, as measured by electricity quality, and better transport (although customs clearance times are much worse in the core). They also have significantly better access to finance. Again, like in

Table 6.5 Coefficient of Variation of per Capita Income by Sector, 1993–2004

Year	GSDP	Agriculture	Industry	Services
1993–94	0.4450	0.4315	0.5951	0.7168
1994–95	0.4577	0.4359	0.5869	0.7455
1995–96	0.4676	0.4388	0.5661	0.7662
1996–97	0.4990	0.4523	0.6307	0.7991
1997–98	0.5072	0.4334	0.6860	0.7886
1998–99	0.5364	0.4239	0.7466	0.7813
1999–2000	0.5303	0.4436	0.7382	0.7646
2000–01	0.5391	0.4709	0.7633	0.7528
2001–02	0.5479	0.4462	0.8025	0.7517
2002–03	0.5707	0.4685	0.8509	0.7562
2003–04	0.5403	0.4675	0.8216	0.7431
2004–05	0.5504	0.4847	0.8228	0.7484
2005–06	0.5725	0.4515	0.9122	0.7708
2006–07	0.5938	0.4486	0.8999	0.7918
2007–08	0.6129	0.4759	0.8811	0.8100
2008–09	0.6222	0.4774	0.8929	0.8291

Sources: Khomiakova 2008; Aggarwal and Archa 2012.
Note: GSDP = gross state domestic product.

Indonesia, core regions appear to suffer some "congestions costs," particularly with respect to management time spent dealing with regulations. However, firms in core regions appear to have a significantly better business environment than those in noncore regions on many other factors, including licensing, tax administration, and, most critically, corruption. This is in stark contrast to the results from Indonesia, where firms in the core perceived a substantially worse business environment in these areas.

Of course, beneath these broad findings lies heterogeneity across states, with firms in both leading and lagging states performing both better and worse than the national average. On electricity, the situation appears to be particularly bad in Jharkhand and Bihar, where firms experience outage-related losses at more than twice the national average. In terms of transport, only one (Kerala) of the eight leading states considered it a greater obstacle than did firms across India as a whole. In contrast, in several lagging states it was identified as a major obstacle at rates two to four times the national average. On the other hand, other lagging states (Orissa, West Bengal) rated transport as not being a significant concern. Although transport is seen as much more an issue by firms in landlocked than in coastal lagging states, the same pattern is not apparent in leading states (where landlocked states like Punjab and Haryana rate transport as not being a major constraint). Customs also is perceived as a more severe constraint, on average, by firms in lagging states. Here, with minor exceptions (see, for example, Jharkhand), both lagging and leading landlocked states perceived customs as a bigger obstacle than do firms in coastal states. With regard to business licensing, the overall situation is more heterogeneous; however, four of the seven lagging states performed worse here than any of the leading states.

Licensing, regulation, and governance issues show much less clarity in terms of core versus noncore or leading versus lagging categorizations; the outcomes appear to be very state-specific, with surprisingly little correlation with development levels. Geographically, states in the east, west, and south are all among the worst performers.

Table 6.6 Comparison of Firm and Regional Characteristics of Core and Noncore States in India, 2006

Characteristics	Core	Noncore	p-value[a]	Core/noncore
Export and trade outcomes				
Direct exports (% of sales)	11.5	12.1	0.656	0.95
% of firms that export directly	22.3	18.3	0.057*	1.22
% of firms that use material inputs and/or supplies of foreign origin	11.5	12.0	0.771	0.96
Firm characteristics				
Ownership				
Private domestic ownership (%)	97.9	97.1	0.201	1.01
Private foreign ownership (%)	1.1	0.9	0.526	1.33
Technology				
% of firms with internationally recognized quality certification	26.8	21.0	0.007**	1.27
% of firms using technology licensed from foreign companies	6.4	4.9	0.188	1.32
% of firms using their own website	37.6	31.3	0.007**	1.20
% of firms using email to communicate with clients/suppliers	71.2	57.0	0.000***	1.25
Workforce				
% of firms offering formal training	21.2	13.8	0.000***	1.54
Average number of seasonal/temporary, full-time employees	5.7	3.5	0.025**	1.60
Average number of permanent, full-time employees	79.9	53.4	0.000***	1.50
% of firms identifying labor regulations as a major constraint	16.4	14.0	0.173	1.17
% of firms identifying labor skill level as a major constraint	15.3	14.0	0.454	1.09
Investment climate				
Infrastructure				
Duration of power outages (hours)	4.5	3.8	0.538	1.19
Value lost due to power outages (% of sales)	5.6	6.6	0.01**	0.84
Delay in obtaining an electrical connection (days)	27.5	24.5	0.519	1.12
Average electricity from a generator (%)	7.7	12.3	0.000***	0.63
Delay in obtaining a water connection (days)	42.2	18.3	0.059*	2.31
Delay in obtaining a mainline telephone connection (days)	11.1	9.6	0.393	1.16
Transport and trade facilitation				
Average time to clear direct exports through customs (days)	23.0	12.2	0.000***	1.87
Average time to clear imports from customs (days)	18.1	14.1	0.1	1.28
Average time of inventory of most important input (days)	25.5	23.5	0.09*	1.09
% of firms identifying customs and trade regulations as a major constraint	11.6	16.2	0.005**	0.72
% of firms identifying transportation as a major constraint	6.2	7.4	0.297	0.83
Regulations and tax				
Senior management time spent in dealing with requirements of government regulation (%)	11.5	10.2	0.008**	1.12
Average number of visits or required meetings with tax officials	1.9	2.9	0.000***	0.66

table continues next page

The Internal Geography of Trade • http://dx.doi.org/10.1596/978-0-8213-9893-7

Table 6.6 Comparison of Firm and Regional Characteristics of Core and Noncore States in India, 2006 *(continued)*

Characteristics	Core	Noncore	p-value[a]	Core/noncore
% of firms identifying tax rates as major constraint	24.5	38.8	0.000***	0.63
% of firms identifying tax administration as major constraint	19.2	30.5	0.000***	0.63
Permits and licenses				
% of firms identifying business licensing and permits as major constraint	7.4	9.6	0.092*	0.77
Corruption				
% of firms expected to pay informal payment to public officials	28.9	41.0	0.000***	0.70
% of firms expected to give gifts to get an operating license	34.0	68.7	0.000***	0.50
% of firms expected to give gifts in meetings with tax officials	34.3	61.0	0.000***	0.56
% of firms expected to give gifts to secure a government contract	11.4	28.7	0.000***	0.40
% of firms identifying corruption as a major constraint	21.5	29.6	0.000***	0.73
Access to finance				
Finance from internal sources (%)	50.0	53.6	0.1	0.93
Finance from banks (%)	44.1	26.0	0.000***	1.70
Finance from trade credit (%)	1.0	6.4	0.000***	0.15
% of firms using banks to finance investments	63.0	48.9	0.000***	1.29
% of firms using banks to finance expenses	64.0	61.8	0.368	1.04
% of firms identifying access to finance as a major constraint	7.9	16.9	0.000***	0.47

Source: Calculations from Enterprise Survey Indicators, World Bank.
a. t-test of difference in means.
*$p < 0.1$, **$p < 0.05$, ***$p < 0.01$

Annex 6A Data

Table 6A.1 Number of Firms Covered in Each ASI Survey Year in Indian States, 1998–2009

Number	State	1998–99	2003–04	2007–08	2008–09
	Total	131,707	129,074	146,385	155,320
1	Andaman and Nicobar Islands	22	21	12	12
2	Andhra Pradesh	13,455	14,802	16,741	16,903
3	Assam	1,424	1,570	1,859	2,211
4	Bihar	1,528	1,460	1,783	1,775
5	Chandigarh (UT)	337	263	294	278
6	Chhattisgarh	1,259	1,295	1,854	1,919
7	Dadra and Nagar Haveli	725	960	1,014	1,151
8	Daman and Diu	988	1,386	1,487	1,443
9	Delhi	3,619	3,197	3,198	3,026
10	Goa	423	549	522	519
11	Gujarat	15,455	12,795	15,107	14,863
12	Haryana	3,786	4,265	4,707	4,450
13	Himachal Pradesh	428	530	1,160	1,294
14	Jammu and Kashmir	351	342	672	649
15	Jharkhand	1,457	1,447	1,615	1,846
16	Karnataka	7,442	7,067	8,443	8,451
17	Kerala	4,703	5,491	5,584	5,868
18	Madhya Pradesh	3,216	2,982	3,165	3,345

table continues next page

Table 6A.1 Number of Firms Covered in Each ASI Survey Year, by State, India (1998–2009)
(continued)

Number	State	1998–99	2003–04	2007–08	2008–09
19	Maharashtra	19,390	17,474	18,304	20,450
20	Manipur	65	45	69	72
21	Meghalaya	25	47	90	95
22	Nagaland	145	120	104	91
23	Orissa	1,539	1,678	1,822	1,930
24	Pondicherry	404	610	703	675
25	Punjab	7,003	6,853	10,178	10,065
26	Rajasthan	4,778	5,452	6,337	6,352
27	Tamil Nadu	20,434	20,246	21,042	26,122
28	Tripura	206	269	340	363
29	Uttar Pradesh	10,508	9,237	10,717	10,935
30	Uttaranchal	713	679	1,474	1,907
31	West Bengal	5,879	5,942	5,987	6,260

Source: Annual Survey of Industries, MOSPI.
Note: ASI = Annual Survey of Industries.

Notes

1. Between 1997–98 and 2003–04, only firms with 200 or more workers were included in the census, along with some other "significant units." In 12 states with lower industrial development, all firms were covered (Goa, Himachal Pradesh, Jammu and Kashmir, Manipur, Meghalaya, Nagaland, Tripura, Andaman and Nicobar Islands, Chandigarh UT, Dadra and Nagar Haveli, Daman and Diu, and Pondicherry). Between Annual Survey of Industries (ASI) 2004–05 and 2008–09, firms with 100 or more workers were included, with the exception of five states with lower industrial development (Manipur, Meghalaya, Nagaland, Tripura, and Andaman and Nicobar Islands), where all firms were included (MOSPI 2008).

2. As in Indonesia (chapter 4), the remoteness index is made up of two measures capturing remoteness to international ports and major cities: (1) a state's distance to the nearest of seven major ports (Chennai, Cochin, Jawaharlal Nehru, Kolkata, Mundra, Pipavav, and Tuticorin), and (2) a state's remoteness to the nearest of seven largest cities (Ahmedabad, Bangalore, Chennai, Delhi, Mumbai, Hyderabad, and Kolkata) weighted by the inverse of the population of the closest city. We calculate an index for each of these measures, relating every state to the most remote state (Jammu and Kashmir). This results in indices ranging from 0 (no remoteness) to 1 (highest remoteness in Jammu and Kashmir). We weight these two measures using two-thirds for the port index, reflecting our focus on trade competitiveness, and one-third for the city index to also account for domestic market access.

3. Infrastructure is proxied by road quality, as measured by surfaced road length as a share of total road length.

4. The analysis is confined to 21 states for which comparable data used in the study are available for the period of analysis. The states studied are Andhra Pradesh, Assam, Bihar, Gujarat, Himachal Pradesh, Haryana, Karnataka, Kerala, Madhya Pradesh, Maharashtra, Orissa, Punjab, Rajasthan, Tamil Nadu, Uttar Pradesh, Jammu and Kashmir, Manipur, Tripura, Arunachal Pradesh, Meghalaya and West Bengal. These

states are categorized as leading and lagging on the basis of the region's relative income in the base period 1992–94, with national average equal to 100. Due to wide fluctuation in data, a single-point base year is avoided; rather, a three-year average is considered. Lagging states consist of regions with per capita income less than 90 percent of the national average and leading regions with income greater than or equal to 90 percent of the national average in the base period. This results in Andhra Pradesh, Gujarat, Haryana, Himachal Pradesh, Karnataka, Kerala, Maharashtra, Punjab, Tamil Nadu, Meghalaya, Arunachal Pradesh, Jammu and Kashmir, and West Bengal being categorized as leading states, with the others as lagging states.

5. The ASI data cover activities related to manufacturing processes, repair services, gas, and water supply, and cold storage.

6. Andhra Pradesh, Haryana, Kerala, National Capital Region, Punjab, Bihar, Jharkhand, Madhya Pradesh, Orissa, Rajasthan, Uttar Pradesh, and West Bengal.

References

Aggarwal, A., and P. S. Archa. 2012. "Regional Development Policies in India." Unpublished background paper to chapter 9 of this book, World Bank, Washington, DC.

Khomiakova, T. 2008. "Spatial Analysis of Regional Divergence in India: Income and Economic Structure Perspectives." *The International Journal of Economic Policy Studies* 3: 137–61.

Ministry of Road Transport and Highways (MORTH). 2008. *Basic Road Transport Statistics of India, 2007–08*. Government of India, New Delhi.

Ministry of Statistics and Programme Implementation (MOSPI). n.d. *Annual Survey of Industries (ASI)*. Government of India, New Delhi. http://mospi.nic.in/mospi_new/upload/asi/ASI_main.htm.

———. 2008. *ASI Manual*. Government of India, New Delhi.

———. 2012. *2011 Indian Census*. Government of India, New Delhi. http://mospi.nic.in/Mospi_New/site/home.aspx.

Reserve Bank of India (RBI). n.d. *Database on India's Economy*. Online database. http://dbie.rbi.org.in/DBIE/dbie.rbi?site=statistics.

World Bank. 2006. "Enterprise Survey—India." World Bank, Washington, DC. http://enterprisesurveys.org.

———. 2008. "Accelerating Growth and Development in the Lagging Regions of India." Poverty Reduction and Economic Management South Asia, March 11. World Bank, Washington, DC.

———. n.d. *Enterprise Survey Indicators*. Online database. Washington, DC: World Bank. http://www.enterprisesurveys.org.

Location and the Determinants of Exporting: Evidence from Manufacturing Firms in India

Megha Mukim

Introduction

Public policy makers, at national and at subnational levels, have set aside resources to provide domestic firms with an impetus to enter foreign markets—that is, to start exporting. These investments are also often made in lagging regions with the intention of encouraging economic activity, firms, and employment to locate in areas they hadn't previously favored. Developing countries are no different in this regard. Indeed, while there is a large and burgeoning literature on firm characteristics and trade, there remains little understanding of how locational factors shape trade participation and, in turn, performance, and even less research on how these effects affect less-developed countries. This chapter will study the decision of firms in India to export and will analyze the factors that determine the extensive and the intensive margin of exporting. In other words, it will identify to what extent characteristics of the firm, industry, and the location determine export participation.

In this chapter, export participation has been defined in two ways—the propensity of firms to start exporting, and the intensity with which they export. First, the chapter tests what sorts of factors affect the probability that the firm will start to export. Firm-level factors are examined, such as productivity; type, age, and the size of the firm; or whether agglomeration also plays a role in reducing the sunk costs of entry. Then, the analysis asks whether these factors also play an important role in firm performance, conditional on entry. The chapter will also disentangle the cross-sectional variation across firms and the time-series variation within firms. While the former reveals how the factors of interest affect firms within a given industry, the latter reveals how these factors affect any given firm.

There are two strands of literature that are relevant to the question at hand—that of sunk entry costs in exporting, and of positive externalities associated with agglomeration. Theoretical models developed by Baldwin and Krugman (1989) and Dixit (1989) describe the presence of fixed costs faced by firms to enter into export markets. These sunk costs of entry might relate to information on foreign markets, the establishment of distribution channels, the costs of complying with new or more developed product standards, and so forth. Theoretical models have described the scope of the benefits from industrial clustering at different levels, including at the own-industry level (Arrow 1962; Marshall 1890; Romer 1986), the interindustry level (Venables 1996), and through industrial diversity (Chinitz 1961; Jacobs 1969). This chapter is mainly concerned with the intersection of the predictions from these theoretical models, in particular how the presence and scope of agglomeration economies lower the sunk costs of export entry. The follow-up question is to what extent the performance of the firm is affected at the margin after entry when it continues to export.

Duranton and Puga (2004) describe microeconomic mechanisms, such as sharing, matching and learning, and so forth, through which the benefits of agglomeration could flow to individual firms at a particular location. There is also a lively empirical literature on measuring export spillovers. Aitken, Hanson, and Harrison (1997) find that the presence of multinational firms affects the probability of entry into export markets for Mexican firms by a factor of 0.035. In their study of Italian firms, Becchetti and Rossi (2000) find that geographical agglomeration significantly increases export intensity and export participation. Greenaway and Sousa (2004) find a similar result for firms in the United Kingdom. Lovely, Rosenthal, and Sharma (2005) find that domestic firms cluster in response to exports to countries with higher barriers to entry, suggesting the presence of export spillovers. Konig (2009) studies export spillovers by destination for French firms and finds that exporter agglomeration positively affects the probability of starting to export to a given country and that these effects are destination specific.

However, the findings of the literature are not conclusive and there are papers that find little or no evidence of export or other spillovers. Barrios, Gorg, and Strobl (2003) find no evidence of export spillovers between exporters or multinationals for domestic firms in Spain, and Bernard and Jensen (2004) find no evidence that export or agglomeration spillovers affect export entry for firms in the United States.

This chapter will directly test for these hypotheses to understand what factors might affect the decision of the firm to start exporting. The chapter will use a panel of heterogeneous firms, wherein firms differ with regard to characteristics such as productivity, size, age, type, and participation in export markets. There are two distinct types of spillovers: (1) those generated by agglomeration of more general economic activity within a location, and (2) those generated by exporter-specific clustering within a location. The chapter will also study the effect of the business environment more generally proxied by variables relating to levels of general infrastructure and by institutional variables. Controlling for attributes of a firm and for attributes of a location, the model will identify the effect of factors specific to the firm, those associated with Krugman's (1991) first- and second-nature geography,[1] and the general investment climate. The empirical analysis is carried out using districts as a geographical unit of study—equivalent to a county in the United States or in China, or a *municipo* in Brazil, a unit that coincides reasonably well with Marshall's notion of agglomeration.

The remainder of the chapter is organized as follows: The next section provides a descriptive overview of the clustering of economic activity, general and export-oriented, across districts in India. The third section outlines the theoretical model and the estimation framework. It also describes the variables used and lists the sources of data. The fourth section presents the results of the model for the extensive margin, and for the intensive margin of export participation in the fifth section. The last section concludes.

Descriptive Analysis

An important focus of this chapter is to ascertain what part of firms' exporting behavior can be explained by the effects of agglomeration—in other words, if spillovers between firms can lower the sunk costs of export entry. The chapter later will consider the various effects of infrastructure and institutions at a location, but this section tries to establish if there is any evidence of clustering. In later sections, the analysis will focus on disentangling second-nature effects from the natural geography and the more general sources of business-oriented advantages.

There are two phenomena that would indicate that agglomeration and exporting go hand-in-hand—if exporters are drawn to other exporters, and/or if exporters are drawn to industrial activity more generally. Different methods can be used to ascertain whether firms are uniformly distributed across various locations in the country, or if they show patterns of spatial concentration. Clustering in its simplest form can be shown through a bird's eye view of where economic activity is located by means of geographical maps. Figure 7.1 provides maps that represent, by district, (1) all firms, exporting and nonexporting, as a percentage of the population,[2] and (2) firms that export as a percentage of the population. Since the figures are generated as a proportion of population size, the actual percentages are very small. The maps are presented in three shades of gray, illustrating whether districts host any economic activity at all, whether the percentage of economic activity hosted lies below the median, or whether it lies above the median. In other words, clustering of all firms and that of exporters is presented after having controlled for the size of the district.

What is immediately clear is that there is much concordance between the districts hosting general and export-oriented economic activity. Not only do firms and exporters show evidence of clustering in a few districts, but they also seem to cluster in the same districts. However, while maps provide a general visual representation, there are not very useful for isolating the differences across exporter clusters and other activity. Table 7.1 lists districts in descending order of the economic activity hosted. Although economic activity, whether exporting or not, seems to be located in the same districts, there is evidence that some locations host much higher proportions of export-oriented activity.

Having identified that there is evidence of clustering of exporters and economic activity in the country, this chapter will now examine to what extent the characteristics of the location affect the propensity of firms to start exporting and other attributes of their exporting behavior more generally. The effect of second-nature clustering will be identified separately from that of first-nature geography and the investment climate. The latter are particularly interesting, in so far as public policy makers can directly affect the provision of infrastructure and affect institutional variables within a location.

Estimation Framework

Econometric Model

The decision to start exporting is estimated using a logit model that controls for the specific characteristics of firms, locations, and years. Consider a firm i that makes a decision to start exporting. The associated profits are π_i and the sunk cost

Figure 7.1 Density of Firms and Exporter Firms in India, 2004

a. All firms, exporting and nonexporting, as a percentage of the population

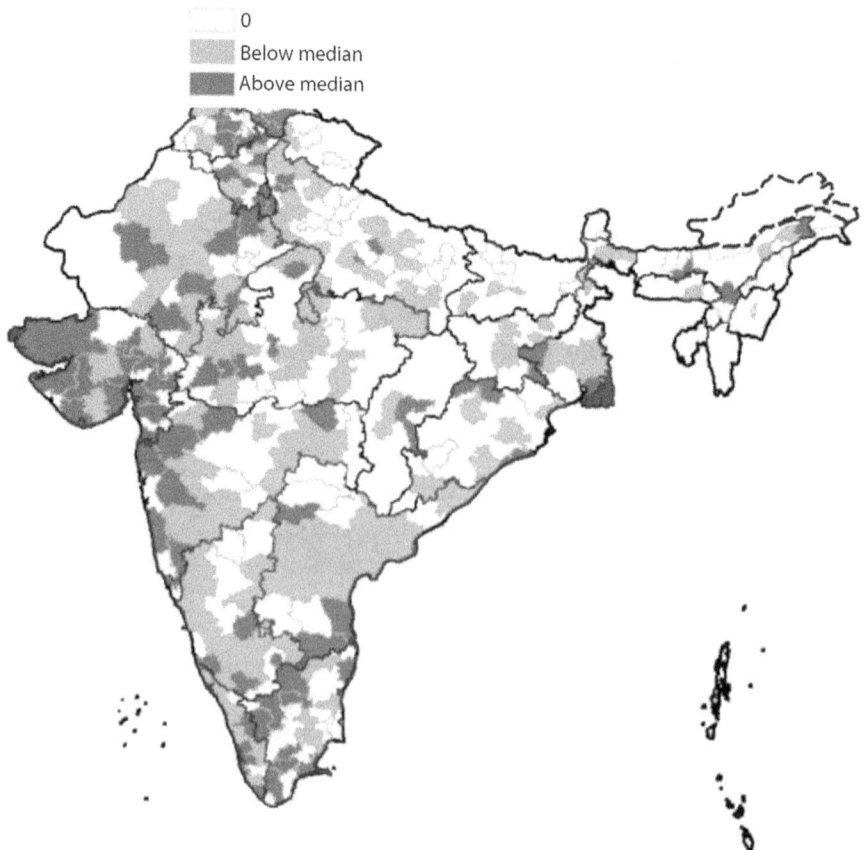

figure continues next page

Figure 7.1 Density of Firms and Exporter Firms in India (Controlling for District Size), 2004
(continued)

b. Firms that export as a percentage of the population

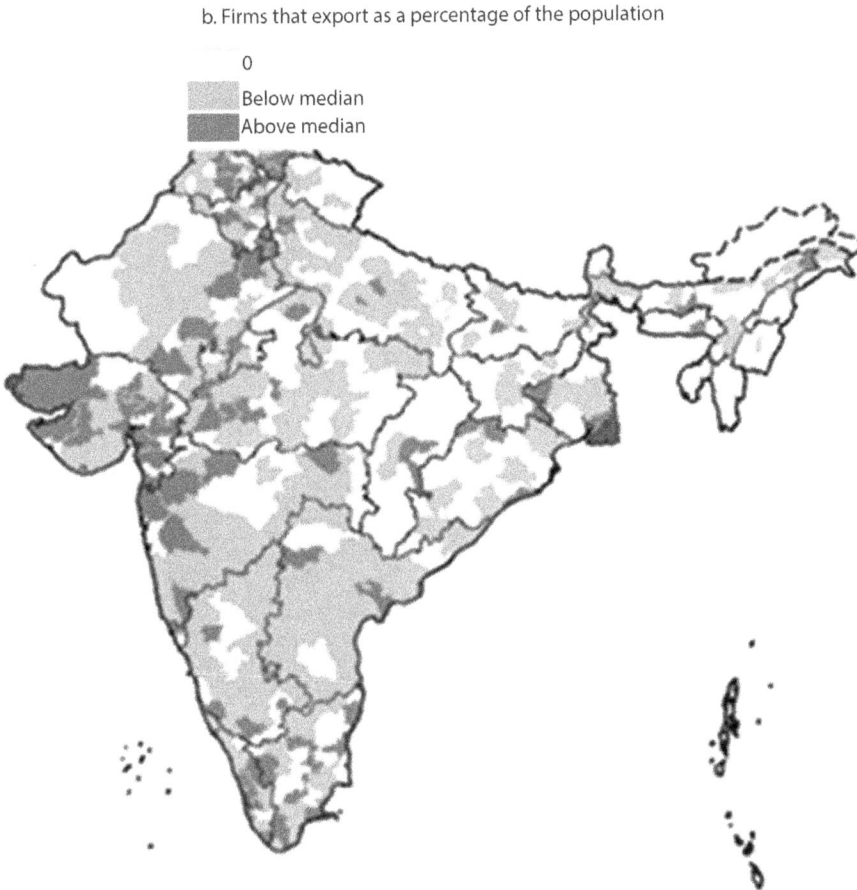

Source: Calculations based on CMIE 2012.

Table 7.1 Top 10 Districts in India by Activity, 2004

Rank	Exporter	Nonexporter	All	Proportion of exporters
1	Mumbai	Mumbai	Mumbai	Sirmaur
2	Delhi	Delhi	Delhi	Hassan
3	Chennai	Kolkata	Kolkata	Mahbubnagar
4	Kolkata	Chennai	Chennai	Chandrapur
5	Hyderabad	Hyderabad	Hyderabad	North 24 Parganas
6	Bangalore	Ahmedabad	Ahmedabad	Bundi
7	Ahmedabad	Bangalore	Bangalore	Shajapur
8	Pune	Coimbatore	Pune	Shimoga
9	Thane	Vadodara	Coimbatore	BaraBanki
10	Coimbatore	Pune	Thane	Chittaurgarh

Source: Calculations based on CMIE 2012.

of entering export markets is f_i. Since we are mainly interested in firms that begin to export for the very first time, in this model we do not consider firms that continue to export. Because there is no need to account for export experience of a given firm, this approach has the added benefit that there is no endogeneity bias owing to the introduction of lagged export status (see Bernard and Jensen 2004; Roberts and Tybout 1997).

Following Konig (2009), it is assumed that a firm will start to export if profits associated with entry exceed the cost of entry, that is, $\pi_i > f_i$. Thus, the probability that a firm i starts to export at time t is given by equation 7.1:

$$\Pr(Y_{it} = 1) = \Pr(\pi_{it} > f_{it}) \tag{7.1}$$

Profits of a firm are assumed to be a function of productivity and other characteristics of the firm, and the sunk cost of entry is assumed to be a function of local exporting activity and agglomeration specific to a given industry k in a location j. Rewriting equation 7.1, the probability of starting to export is given by equation 7.2:

$$\Pr(Y_{it} = 1) = \Pr(\beta_1 X_{it} - \beta_2 Z_{jkt} + \varepsilon_{ijkt} > 0), \tag{7.2}$$

where firm characteristics are included in the vector X_{it} and characteristics affecting the sunk cost of entry specific to the location and industry are included in Z_{jkt}. This expression can be estimated using a logit model under the assumption that the error term is distributed logistically. Thus, the dependent variable Y_{it} is a dummy variable describing whether the firm i starts to export at time period t. The regressions include only those firms that have entered the export market at least once—in other words, firms that have never exported over the sample period are excluded. Additionally, the dependent variable equals 1 for the year in which the firm first starts exporting and equals 0 for all other years leading up to that year. If firms continue to export, or if they switch status after having entered the export market for the first time, these observations are not included in the regressions.

Specification of the Variables

The deterministic component of the function consists of the various attributes of the location that can influence the propensity of a firm to start exporting. The random component consists of the unobserved characteristics of the location and measurement errors. As mentioned above, the dependent variable is a dummy variable at time t that equals 1 if the firm starts to export and 0 for all years leading up to t. The explanatory variables in the model are defined at time $t - 1$, and as indicated, for National Industrial Classification (NIC) 2-digit industry (k) and at the spatial unit of the district (j) or the state (J). The sources of data are described in the next subsection.

Firm-specific characteristics include ω_{it}, which represents the productivity of the firm; age_{it}, which represents the age of the firm; $size_{it}$, which represents the size of the firm; and $type_i$, which represents the type of firm (private domestic, private foreign, public, or mixed). Agglomeration (or second-nature geography) is described by exp_{jt}, which represents the count of other exporters found in district j weighted by district population; exp_{jkt}, which represents the count of other exporters by industry found in district j weighted by district population; σ_{jkt}, which represents localization economies, represented by the share of employment in industry k found in district j; Λ_{jkt}, which represents interindustry trading relations measured by the strength of buyer-supplier linkages; and U_{jt}, which represents urbanization economies in district j. Other economic geography variables getting at first-nature geography include MA_{jt}, which summarizes access to markets in neighboring districts; and $Port_j$, which summarizes distance for a given district from the closest port.

Infrastructure variables are given by $Road_j$, which measures the density of roads (primary and secondary) in district j; Ed_{jt}, which measures the level of human capital in district j; X_{jt}, which captures the quality and availability of infrastructure (electricity and communications); W_{jt}, which is a vector of factor input price variables in district j; and WE_{jt}, which captures the level of wealth in district j. And lastly, institutional variables are given by $flex_J$, which is an indicator of the flexibility of labor regulations in state J; and $riots_{jt}$, which is an indicator of social institutions and unrest.

The remainder of this section provides a detailed description of each of the variables used in the model—firm-specific variables, second-nature geography, first-nature geography, infrastructure, and institutional. For easy reference, a summary of the variables is provided in table 7.3 (see page 190).

Firm-Specific Controls

Firm-specific controls include the productivity, size (sales), age, and the type of firm (private domestic, private foreign, public, or mixed). There is a lively literature that suggests that exporters are usually more productive than nonexporters because of two distinct mechanisms: self-selection into export markets and learning-by-exporting. Exporters may be more productive than their counterparts, who only supply the domestic market, simply because more productive firms are able to engage in export activity and compete in international markets. The second mechanism is post-entry productivity benefits, because when firms enter into export markets they gain new knowledge and expertise, which allows them to improve their level of efficiency. Although this chapter is not concerned with the causal impact of exporting on productivity, it is important to control for the self-selection of more productive firms into exporting. Lagging productivity by one period effectively controls for possible endogeneity, since the decision to "start" exporting takes place only once.

To obtain consistent production function estimates, we follow Olley and Pakes (1996) to compute firm-level total factor productivity (ω_{jt}). This approach controls for two distinct sources of bias: (1) simultaneity between outputs and inputs, which would bias the labor coefficient upward, and (2) endogenous exit of firms from the sample, which would bias the capital coefficient downward.

Under fairly general assumptions, Levinsohn and Petrin (2003) show that with simple ordinary least squares (OLS) estimations, the labor coefficient will be upward biased and the capital coefficient will be downward biased. This would imply that productivity estimates would be upward biased for more capital-intensive firms, such as exporters. We compute the labor and capital coefficients under simple OLS assumptions using the Olley-Pakes procedure and report these in table 7A.2. We use data on the firm's total wage bill as a proxy for the labor input, and on its fixed assets[3] as a proxy for capital. These nominal values are deflated using NIC 2-digit-level output and input-specific price indices.[4]

Agglomeration Variables

The count of other exporters within the district ($\exp_{jt}$) and the count of other exporters by industry within the district ($\exp_{jkt}$) are weighted by the district population, which captures the effect of export spillovers. The idea is that proximity to other exporters could result in knowledge spillovers that might help nonexporters to start exporting. In addition, more general industrial agglomeration within a location would also increase the likelihood for denser interactions between exporters, no matter what the proportion of exporters in the overall cluster. Thus, not only does the specification control for the effect of other exporters, by industry and otherwise, within a district, but it also includes measures of own-industry and input-output agglomeration and industrial diversity. Note that clustering could also be associated with diseconomies such as congestion or increased competition. Thus, the estimations will capture the net effect of the positive and negative impacts on export participation.

Localization economies (σ_{jkt}) can be measured by own-industry employment in the district, own-industry establishments in the district, or an index of concentration, which reflects disproportionately high concentration of the industry in the district in comparison to the country. We measure localization economies as the proportion of industry k's firms in district j as a share of all of all industry k firms in the country for a given year t. The variable takes a different value for each industry in a given district, across districts. It identifies spillovers that are associated with within-industry clustering, regardless of the final markets that these firms serve. The higher this value, the higher the expectation of intra-industry concentration benefits in the district, as expressed in equation 7.3:

$$\sigma_{jkt} = \frac{E_{jkt}}{E_{kt}} \qquad (7.3)$$

There are several approaches for defining interindustry linkages: input-output based, labor skill based, and technology flow based. Although these approaches represent different aspects of industry linkages and the structure of a regional economy, the most common approach is to use the national-level input-output accounts as templates for identifying strengths and weaknesses in regional buyer-supplier linkages (Feser and Bergman 2000). The strong presence or lack of nationally identified buyer-supplier linkages at the local level can be a good indicator of the probability that a firm is located in that region. To evaluate the strength of buyer (supplier) linkages for each industry, a summation of regional (here district) industry firms weighted by the industry's input (output) coefficient column (row) vector from the national input-output account is used in equation 7.4:

$$\Lambda_{jkt} = \sum_{k=1}^{n} w_k n_{jkt},$$ (7.4)

where Λ_{jk} is the strength of the buyer (supplier) linkage, w_k is industry k's national input (output) coefficient column (row) vector and n_{jk} is the total number of firms in industry k in district j in year t. The measure examines local-level interindustry linkages based on national input-output accounts. The national input-output coefficient column vectors describe intermediate goods requirements for each industry, whilst the input-output coefficient row vectors describe final good sales for each industry. Assuming that local industries follow the national average in terms of their purchasing (selling) patterns of intermediate (final) goods, national-level linkages can be imposed to the local-level industry structure for examining whether district j has a right mix of buyer-supplier industries for industry k. By multiplying the national input-output coefficient vector, which is time invariant, for industry k and the size of each sector in district j, simple local firm numbers can be weighted based on what industry k purchases or sells nationally.

We use the Herfindahl-Hirschman index (HHI) to examine the degree of economic diversity in each district. We refer to this index as urbanization economies (U_{jt}) in each district in a given year t. Urbanization economies are a reference to large urban areas, which are industrially diverse and enjoy access to large labor pools with multiple degrees of specialization, financial and professional services, better physical and social infrastructures, and so forth. The HHI, although it captures only the level of industrial diversity within a region, is a proxy for these larger urbanization economies. The HHI of a district j (U_{jt}) is the sum of squares of firm shares of all industries in district j (equation 7.5):

$$U_{jt} = \sum_k \left(\frac{E_{jkt}}{E_{jt}} \right)^2.$$ (7.5)

Unlike measures of specialization, which focus on one industry, the diversity index considers the industry mix of the entire regional economy. The largest value for U_j is one when the entire regional economy is dominated by a single industry. Thus a higher value signifies a lower level of economic diversity.

First-Nature Geography Variables
In principle, improved access to consumer markets (including interindustry buyers and suppliers) will increase the demand for a firm's products, thereby providing the incentive to increase scale and invest in cost-reducing technologies.

The proposed model will use the formulation proposed initially by Hanson (1959), which states that the accessibility at point A to a particular type of activity at area B (say, employment) is directly proportional to the size of the activity at area B (say, number of jobs) and inversely proportional to some function of the distance separating point A from area B. Accessibility is thus defined in equation 7.6 as the potential for opportunities for interactions with neighboring districts:

$$MA_{jt} = \sum_j \frac{S_{mt}}{d_{j-m}^b},\qquad(7.6)$$

where MA_{jt} is the accessibility indicator estimated for location j in year t; S_m is a size indicator at destination m (in this case, district population) in a given year; d_{j-m} is a measure of distance between origin j and destination m; and b describes how increasing distance reduces the expected level of interaction.[5] The size of the district of origin j is not included in the computation of market access—only that of neighboring districts is taken into account. Thus, the accessibility indicator is constructed using population (as the size indicator) and distance (as a measure of separation), and is estimated without exponent values. The measure of distance is travel time (in number of minutes) between any given pair of districts. Origin and destination points are located at the geographic center of each district, and the travel-time estimate is based on the least time-consuming path between the two. Time is computed[6] using geographic information system (GIS) data as the length of the road between two points with assumptions about the speed of travel according to different road categories.[7] The same travel-time measure is also used to compute $Port_j$, which is the distance of a given district to the closest of the 13 largest trading ports in the country. Access to a major merchandise shipping port should, in theory, positively impact the probability of starting to export.

Infrastructure Variables

The next set of variables deals with the general quality of infrastructure within a district, since one would expect that the general business environment would have a positive impact on the probability of a firm to enter export markets. Such variables are also particularly interesting to policy makers since, unlike agglomeration, targeted investments within a location can help to better infrastructure and make a location more business friendly. We include the density of roads, defined as the length of roads per square kilometer within a district, as a proxy for transport infrastructure. These values were computed using ArcGIS data,[8] and the density data is time invariant.[9] We assess quantitatively the role of human capital by including the proportion of the population within the district with a high-school education in a given year, captured by the education variable Ed_{jt}. We define X_{jt} as a measure of "natural advantage" through the embedded quality and availability of infrastructure in the district. We use the availability of power (proxied by the proportion of households with access to electricity) at a district level as an indicator of the provision of infrastructure. In addition, we also use the proportion of households within a district with a telephone connection as an indicator of communications infrastructure.

W_{jt} is an indicator of labor costs in location j, and is given by nominal district-level wage rates (that is, nonagricultural hourly wages). The expected effect of this variable is hard to pin down theoretically. On the one hand, if wages were a measure of input costs, then one would expect export activity to be inversely related to wages. However, it is also important to control for the skill set of the workers because a positive coefficient on wages could be proxying for more skilled labor. Although we are unable to directly control for the ability of the worker, we include "education" as a proxy for the level of human capital within the district. And thus, the proportion of high-income households (WE_{jt}) within a district is an indicator of the general level of wealth, or more specifically, consumer expenditure within a district. The variable is constructed using household consumption data and refers to those households that belong to the expenditure group with the highest monthly per capita consumption.[10]

Institutional Variables

We also control for the quality of institutions within the location. We include a dummy variable, which is set equal to one for states with labor laws rated as pro-business by Besley and Burgess (2004). Although labor regulations are mainly legislated and enforced by state governments, they also have an important effect on the cost of contracts at the district level. We also include a district-level variable on the frequency of riots and social unrest per capita across different years as a proxy for social institutions. This information is drawn from Marshall and Marshall (2008) (table 7.2).

In summary, the firm characteristics and economic geography variables are supplemented with controls for infrastructure (transport, education, electricity, and telephone), input costs (wages), and institutional variables (flexibility of labor regulations and social unrest).

Sources of Data

Firm-level data on export behavior (including when a firm starts to export, and, following entry into export markets, the value of exports as a proportion of sales) and on output and inputs are drawn from the Prowess database. Prowess is a corporate database that contains normalized data built on a sound understanding of disclosures of over 20,000 companies in India. The database provides financial statements, ratio analysis, fund flows, product profiles, returns and risks on the stock market, and so forth. The Centre for Monitoring the Indian Economy (CMIE), which collects data from 1989 onward, assembles the Prowess database. The database contains information on 23,168 firms for the years 1989–2008.[11] After cleaning the data, the final dataset contains 6,296 firms. Since there are limited data for other district-level variables, the analysis is restricted to fewer years (1999–2004). The analysis is also limited to the manufacturing sector (that is, NIC 2-digit units 14–36). We also exclude firms for which data on sales, gross

Table 7.2 Summary of Variables

	Logs?	Variable	Unit of analysis	Expected sign	Definition
Firm characteristics	Yes	Productivity	Firm, year	+	TFP calculated using Olley-Pakes (1996) methodology
	No	Age	Firm, year	−	Age of the firm
	Yes	Sales	Firm, year	+	Sales (deflated)
	No	Type	Firm		Private domestic, private foreign, public or mixed
Agglomeration	Yes	Exporters	District, year	+	Count of other exporters per capita
	Yes	Exporters by industry	District, industry, year	+	Count of other exporters within the same industry per capita
	Yes	Localization	District, industry, year	+	Agglomeration of firms with other firms within the same industry
	Yes	Input	District, industry, year	+	Agglomeration of firms with their suppliers (that is, those who they buy from)
	Yes	Output	District, industry, year	+	Agglomeration of firms with their buyers (that is, those that they sell to)
	Yes	Industrial diversity	District, year	−	Industrial diversity within a district (higher values mean lower industrial diversity)
First-nature geography	No	Market access	District, year	+	Accessibility indicator measuring access to neighboring regions
	No	Port	District	−	Travel time (in minutes) to the closest port
Infrastructure	Yes	Roads	District, year	+	Road density per square kilometer
	Yes	Electricity	District, year	+	Proportion of households with access to electricity
	Yes	Telephone	District, year	+	Proportion of households with a telephone connection
	Yes	Education	District, year	+	Proportion of population with a high school degree
	Yes	Wages	District, year	±	Nonagricultural hourly wages
	Yes	Wealth	District, year	+	Proportion of high-income households
Institutional	No	Labor regulations	State	−	Besley and Burgess (2004) classification (pro-employer = 0, pro-labor = 1)
	Yes	Riots	District, year	−	Incidents of social unrest per capita

Note: TFP = total factor productivity.

assets, and wages are missing, since these are crucial to the computation of firm-level productivity. Of the firms in the final dataset, 3,638 firms enter the export market at least once over the period of study. There is also a large degree of firm heterogeneity in terms of size and age.

Some caveats should be mentioned here. It is not mandatory for firms to supply data to the CMIE, and one cannot tell exactly how representative of the industry is the membership of the firms in the organization. Prowess covers 60–70 percent of the organized sector in India, 75 percent of corporate taxes, and 95 percent of excise duties collected by the Government of India (Goldberg et al. 2010[12]). Large firms, which account for a large percentage of industrial production and foreign trade, are usually members of the CMIE and are more likely to be included in the database. Therefore, the analysis is based on a sample of firms that is, in all probability, taken disproportionately from the higher end of the size distribution. As Tybout and Westbrook (1994) point out, a lot of productivity growth comes from larger plants, which are also more likely to be exporters, providing confidence in the comprehensive scope of the study.

Measures of agglomeration are constructed using unit-level data for the years 1999–2004 from the Annual Survey of Industries (ASI), conducted by the Ministry of Statistics and Programme Implementation (MOSPI) of the Government of India. The ASI covers all factories registered under the Factories Act of 1948 that employ 20 or more workers, or that employ 10 or more workers and use electricity. Although the ASI has a large sample size, certainly larger than Prowess, and it contains data on firm-level characteristics, it cannot be used to study firm-level export behavior. This is because even though the ASI provides information on whether a firm exports or not, the database does not follow firms over time. In other words, firms are sampled afresh every year and it is not possible to create a panel of firms over time. Data on the number of units (that is, the plant or the factory) are used in the analysis since employment-level data is often scarce or missing. As ASI collects data for primarily the manufacturing sector, agglomeration measures do not account for the activities of services enterprises. This is a shortcoming of the analysis as service sector activity and clustering within a location might be strongly associated with the availability of essential inputs that might reduce entry costs into export markets. The data set on market access is constructed using district-level population figures drawn from various surveys of the National Sample Survey Organisation[13] (NSSO), an organization under MOSPI.

Data on measures of infrastructure, such as education, electricity, and communications infrastructure, and on wages and wealth within the district are also drawn from the household surveys of the NSSO. These data are only available for three rounds of the survey: Round 55.10 (July 1999–June 2000), Round 60.10 (June 2004), and Round 61.10 (July 2004–June 2005). The specifications with infrastructure variables thus refer to fewer years than those for firm-level and economic geography variables. Finally, as mentioned previously, Besley and Burgess (2004) and Marshall and Marshall (2008) are the main sources for the data on the flexibility of labor regulations and of measures of social unrest, respectively. A tabular summary of the data is provided in table 7A.1.

Econometric Results: Extensive Margin

Results across Firms

The results of the econometric specification are provided in table 7.3. The dependent variable is "start"—that is, a dummy variable that equals 1 if the firm starts exporting and 0 otherwise. All columns include year and industry (2-digit NIC level) controls. From left to right, the columns present estimations that include an increasing number of variables and then finally also include location-specific effects. Model specification (1) controls for firm-level characteristics only; in addition to these, model (2) includes agglomeration variables; model (3) adds first-nature geography variables; model (4) adds further infrastructure

Table 7.3 Decision to Start Exporting (Across-Firm Logit)

Variable	(1)	(2)	(3)	(4)	(5)	(6)
Productivity	0.0840**	0.0801**	0.0789**	0.0913	0.0046	0.0125
	[0.037]	[0.039]	[0.039]	[0.130]	[0.170]	[0.185]
Age	−0.0002	−0.0010	−0.0008	0.0024	0.0049	0.0050
	[0.002]	[0.002]	[0.002]	[0.007]	[0.009]	[0.009]
Size	−0.1280***	−0.1303***	−0.1327***	−0.0455	−0.0256	−0.0105
	[0.031]	[0.035]	[0.036]	[0.060]	[0.093]	[0.104]
Exporter count		0.0422	0.0551	−0.1350	−0.1733	−0.2857*
		[0.041]	[0.044]	[0.103]	[0.133]	[0.173]
Exporter count (India)		0.0275	0.0244	0.0166	0.0569	0.0971
		[0.044]	[0.042]	[0.127]	[0.142]	[0.148]
Localization		−0.0019	0.0142	−0.1750***	−0.9611	−0.9169
		[0.028]	[0.034]	[0.064]	[2.046]	[2.171]
Input economies		0.3357***	0.3423***	0.0153	−0.5117	−0.6113
		[0.123]	[0.123]	[0.263]	[0.657]	[0.693]
Output economies		−0.3609***	−0.3815***	0.0676	1.3390	1.3776
		[0.113]	[0.114]	[0.262]	[2.673]	[2.837]
Diversity		−0.0577	−0.0219	−0.0247	−0.2156	−0.1450
		[0.075]	[0.089]	[0.190]	[0.234]	[0.296]
Market access			0.0000	−0.0000	−0.0000	0.0000
			[0.000]	[0.000]	[0.000]	[0.000]
Port			0.0000	−0.0003	−0.0006	−0.0005
			[0.000]	[0.000]	[0.000]	[0.001]
Road density				0.1674	0.1720	0.2985
				[0.153]	[0.185]	[0.317]
Telephone				−0.0104	−0.0031	−0.2274
				[0.219]	[0.226]	[0.300]
Electricity				0.3126	0.1813	0.0855
				[0.470]	[0.534]	[0.720]
Education				0.5746*	0.4870*	0.6845*
				[0.342]	[0.413]	[0.502]
Wages				0.1035	0.0748	0.1809
				[0.555]	[0.575]	[0.617]
Wealth				0.0143	−0.0792	−0.2822
				[0.213]	[0.224]	[0.255]
Flex					−0.0625	0.0000
					[0.288]	[0.000]
Riots					−0.1233**	−0.1321**
					[0.053]	[0.067]
Population	0.0466	0.0184	−0.0488	0.0495	0.0876	−0.4675
	[0.033]	[0.059]	[0.096]	[0.241]	[0.458]	[0.774]

table continues next page

Table 7.3 Decision to Start Exporting (Across-Firm Logit) *(continued)*

Fixed effects	Year and industry	Year and industry	Year and industry	Year and industry	Year and industry	Year and industry and state
Number of observations	2,519	2,300	2,272	679	478	478
Pseudo	0.0181	0.0192	0.0191	0.0481	0.0689	0.0753

Note: All specifications control for the type of the firm (that is, private domestic, private foreign, public, and mixed). Lagged values ($t-1$) of explanatory variables are being used. Robust errors are in brackets, clustered at the district level.
*$p < 0.1$, **$p < 0.05$, ***$p < 0.01$

variables, and model (5) adds institutional variables. Model (6), which includes all variables (firm, second and first nature, infrastructure and institutional), also includes state-fixed effects. Owing to limited data availability for infrastructure variables, as described earlier, the number of observations is considerably reduced in model (4). Due to missing data, this loss of observations is exacerbated in models (5) and (6).

As one would expect, firm-level productivity is strongly and positively associated with the decision of the firm to enter export markets, providing some evidence for self-selection of the most productive firms into the export market. Additionally, the size of the firm seems to effect the export decision negatively, suggesting that smaller firms are more likely to start exporting. Interestingly, once productivity is controlled for, the age of the firm has no statistically significant effect on the log odds of entry. Also, once infrastructure variables are included in the regressions, these effects are no longer statistically significant.

The count of existing exporters per capita, by industry and in total, within a district seems to have little or no discernible effect on the propensity of the firm to export. For example, the magnitude of the coefficient of "exporter count" in model (6) can be interpreted as follows: a unit increase in the percentage of exporters within a district decreases the log odds of starting to export by 0.2857, although this variable is only significant at the 10 percent level.

Other aspects of more general agglomeration within a district—that is, localization, input-output economies and industrial diversity—have a stronger impact on the odds of entering export markets. In fact, the coefficient on localization is negative, suggesting that this variable might be capturing some aspects of competition across firms within the same industry—although the coefficient is not significant in any specifications barring the one in model (4). Input linkages–that is, access to suppliers—have a positive effect before infrastructure controls are introduced. On the other hand, proximity to buyers—that is, those that firms sell to—seems to have a negative effect. The effect of industrial diversity is stable and negative, but statistically insignificant, across different specifications.

In model (3), first-nature economic geography variables are introduced— market access and access to the closest port. Neither variable seems to have any effect on the probability of starting to export.

Model (4) introduces infrastructure variables into the specifications, and finds that most of these variables seem to have little or no effect on the odds of a firm entering export markets. Interestingly however, the effect of education (that is, the proportion of the population with a high-school education) is positive and significant at the 10 percent level. In, lengthier checks (not shown here) the introduction of road density reduces the significance of the education variable, suggesting that some of the effect of more skilled labor is explained by the availability of better transport infrastructure. Lower wages seem to reduce the costs of entry, but the effect is not significant across specifications.

Finally, institutional variables at the state level (that is, the flexibility of labor regulations) and at the district level (that is, social unrest per capita) are introduced in model (5). The effect of business-friendly labor regulations is insignificant. The impact of riots per capita, however, is negative and significant, suggesting that more social unrest within a district lowers the odds of a firm's entry into export markets.

The last column, model (6) introduces location (that is, state[14]) fixed effects in an attempt to control for any unobserved characteristics of the location that are not captured by the first-nature geography variables. In summary, firm-specific characteristics, namely productivity and size of the firm, have a significant effect on the odds of entry into exporting. Additionally, the agglomeration of same-industry firms within a district seems to have a negative effect, although that of exporter-specific clustering within the district is harder to pin down. Access to suppliers has a positive effect on entry, whereas access to buyers does not. The level of skilled labor within a location has a positive effect, and social unrest is associated with lower odds of entry.

Results within Firms

The previous regressions have been estimated at the industry level. Including industry dummies implies that the coefficients are averaged for all firms within a given industry (and year and/or state). However, it could also be the case that a change in industry-level (or state-level) characteristics could affect firms in that industry differently, depending on the individual characteristics of the firm. For instance, Bown and Porto (2010) study the effect of a change in preferential market access for the Indian steel industry and find that some firms within the industry, such as those with past ties to developed markets, responded more quickly than others in order to increase their exports. Indeed, as their analysis shows, aggregating variables at the industry level fails to capture the differences across firms, some of which are large producers that were active for a number of years prior to the shock and others that were relatively new entrants to the market.[15] And since ultimately the analysis is concerned with studying the effects of agglomeration and other characteristics of a location on the propensity of *a given firm* to enter export markets, this section re-runs the regressions with the introduction of firm-level fixed effects.

Taking firm-level fixed effects not only constrains the coefficient to be averaged within firms and not across firms, but it also provides the most stringent control. It effectively controls for any possible endogeneity running from unobservables at the level of industries and locations, and the coefficients describe the effects at the level of firms over time. It is then redundant to take account of industry or location unobservables, and the introduction of firm dummies provides a much cleaner analysis of effects at the level of the firm. Table 7.4 reports the results from the specifications that include firm-level fixed effects. Since convergence was not reached with the inclusion of infrastructure variables, the models were run without them.[16]

Controlling for all characteristics of a given firm, the size of the firm has a negative effect on its odds of entry. Just as in the previous results on across-firm estimations, this suggests that smaller firms are more likely to start exporting.[17] However, the coefficient on productivity is not only larger in magnitude, but is also highly significant across all specifications. Since productivity has been lagged, this is robust evidence to support the theory that more productive firms are more likely to self-select into exporting.

Table 7.4 Decision to Start Exporting (Within-Firm Logit)

Variable	(1)	(2)	(3)	(4)
Productivity	7.2029***	8.2003***	8.0641***	8.1679***
	[1.253]	[1.067]	[1.028]	[1.029]
Age	−0.0253	−0.0188	−0.0383	−0.0283
	[0.029]	[0.027]	[0.027]	[0.029]
Size	−7.6330***	−8.5703***	−8.5851***	−8.6132***
	[0.985]	[0.811]	[0.882]	[0.935]
Exporter count		−10.2220**	−6.5037**	−5.6270**
		[4.478]	[2.591]	[2.292]
Exporter count (India)		−1.5294	−1.0657	−1.1338
		[0.976]	[0.909]	[0.916]
Localization		2.5703***	3.8538**	3.5649**
		[0.634]	[1.858]	[1.740]
Input economies		−1.3971	2.8879	2.0964
		[3.000]	[3.294]	[7.144]
Output economies		−1.8025	−7.4212**	−7.2446
		[3.196]	[3.664]	[6.390]
Diversity		−0.3300	0.8929	−0.6864
		[2.862]	[2.248]	[2.529]
Market access			0.0000148*	0.0000157*
			[0.000]	[0.000]
Riots				0.1012
				[0.143]
Population	14.3365**	5.1065	−15.1162	−14.6737
	[7.230]	[7.833]	[9.344]	[9.859]
Fixed effects	*Firm*	*Firm*	*Firm*	*Firm*
Number of observations	1,850	1,586	1,566	1,462
Pseudo	0.298	0.390	0.478	0.503

Note: Lagged values ($t − 1$) of explanatory variables are being used. Robust standard errors are in brackets, clustered at the firm level.
*$p < 0.1$, **$p < 0.05$, ***$p < 0.01$

The Internal Geography of Trade • http://dx.doi.org/10.1596/978-0-8213-9893-7

There are some marked differences compared to the results of the across-firms analysis. The effect of clustering of exporters within the district has a strong negative and significant effect on the probability of a given firm to enter export markets. In other words, being surrounded by other exporting firms, irrespective of industry type, seems to discourage entry. On the other hand, the effects of more general industrial agglomeration are much more noteworthy than in earlier models. For instance, within-industry clustering of firms seems to have a strong positive effect on the log odds of entry into export markets. Additionally, local industrial diversity seems to have no effect on the log odds of entry. Compared to earlier results, now access to larger neighboring markets positively affects the odds that a firm will enter the export market.

Although these specifications shed much light about the effect of geography- and firm-level variables on the decision of the firm to start exporting, they do not say much about how these same variables might affect export participation conditional on entry. The next subsection will explore these effects in greater detail.

Econometric Results: Intensive Margin

There is evidence (Das, Roberts, and Tybout 2007) to show that entry costs are substantial not just with regard to the decision to export—that is, the extensive margin—but also with regard to how much to export—that is, the intensive margin. Thus, it could be argued that characteristics of the location affect not only the probability that a firm might start to export, but that they also have an effect on the continued success of the firm in export markets. Firms seeking to enter foreign markets might face fixed costs of participation for every additional year of exporting. Indeed, there is some evidence (Arkolakis 2009) to show that firms begin by exporting small quantities and increase their volume of exports quickly over time. Thus, export performance could also be measured as the intensity with which firms export.

To identify the effect of geography- and firm-level variables on the intensity of export participation, we proceed in equation 7.2 to regress the log of the value of exports on a set of firm-, industry-, and location-specific characteristics:

$$\ln \exp_{it} = \gamma_1 + \beta_1 X_{it} - \beta_2 Z_{jkt} + \varepsilon_{ijkt} \qquad (7.7)$$

Equation 7.7 is estimation using OLS regressions.[18] Firm characteristics are included in the vector X_{it}, and characteristics specific to the location and industry are included in Z_{jkt}. As with the extensive margin, we identify below the effects of geography and firm characteristics for firms within a given industry and location, and then for a given firm.

Results across Firms

The first set of results is presented in table 7.5, wherein the model specifications are the same as those in table 7.3. However, the dependent variable is now the log of total exports of the firm, since we are mainly interested in understanding the factors that affect the intensity of participation in export markets.

Table 7.5 Export Intensity (Across-Firm OLS)

Variable	(1)	(2)	(3)	(4)	(5)	(6)
Productivity	−0.3294***	−0.3170***	−0.3131***	−0.3354***	−0.2985***	−0.2938***
	[0.039]	[0.037]	[0.037]	[0.054]	[0.059]	[0.063]
Age	−0.0101***	−0.0103***	−0.0105***	−0.0086***	−0.0101***	−0.0093***
	[0.001]	[0.001]	[0.001]	[0.002]	[0.003]	[0.003]
Size	0.9618***	0.9538***	0.9580***	0.9446***	0.9451***	0.9469***
	[0.021]	[0.023]	[0.023]	[0.026]	[0.032]	[0.033]
Exporter count		−0.0943**	−0.1016**	−0.0136	−0.0726	0.0004
		[0.045]	[0.045]	[0.076]	[0.076]	[0.060]
Exporter count (India)		0.1680***	0.1687***	0.0768	0.0863	0.0949
		[0.058]	[0.060]	[0.085]	[0.087]	[0.086]
Localization		0.1112***	0.1004***	0.1419***	0.0906*	0.0962**
		[0.027]	[0.028]	[0.048]	[0.068]	[0.068]
Input economies		0.3095***	0.3213***	0.2234	−0.2376	−0.3222
		[0.116]	[0.114]	[0.270]	[0.348]	[0.362]
Output economies		−0.3991***	−0.4000***	−0.3275	−1.1736	−1.359
		[0.124]	[0.120]	[0.274]	[0.697]	[0.712]
Diversity		−0.0092	−0.0092	−0.0419	0.0022	0.1827
		[0.066]	[0.076]	[0.085]	[0.097]	[0.111]
Market access			0.0000	0.0000	−0.0000	−0.0000***
			[0.000]	[0.000]	[0.000]	[0.000]
Port			−0.0001	−0.0003*	−0.0002	−0.0011**
			[0.000]	[0.000]	[0.000]	[0.000]
Road density				0.1251*	0.0141	−0.2107
				[0.100]	[0.113]	[0.137]
Telephone				−0.1337	−0.0451	−0.0373
				[0.113]	[0.117]	[0.102]
Electricity				−0.1037	−0.1346	−0.2857
				[0.200]	[0.192]	[0.205]
Education				−0.2087	−0.0851	0.1853
				[0.144]	[0.133]	[0.151]
Wages				0.0977	0.0712	−0.0273
				[0.132]	[0.137]	[0.150]
Wealth				0.0459	0.0825	0.0875
				[0.088]	[0.091]	[0.085]
Flex					0.1410***	0.0000
					[0.132]	[0.000]
Riots					0.0458	−0.0193
					[0.030]	[0.030]
Population	−0.0080	0.0114	−0.0325	−0.1334	0.0702	0.3068
	[0.044]	[0.053]	[0.083]	[0.146]	[0.207]	[0.215]

table continues next page

Table 7.5 **Export Intensity (Across-Firm OLS)** *(continued)*

Fixed effects	Year and industry	Year and industry	Year and industry	Year and industry	Year and industry	Year and industry and state
Number of observations	13,695	12,397	12,243	3,312	2,622	2,622
	0.405	0.405	0.408	0.406	0.424	0.432

Note: OLS = ordinary least squares. All specifications control for the type of the firm (that is, private domestic, private foreign, public and mixed). Lagged values $(t - 1)$ of explanatory variables are being used. Robust errors are in brackets, clustered at the district level.
$*p < 0.1, **p < 0.05, ***p < 0.01$

The first striking result is that lagged productivity has a negative effect on value of exports: in fact, a 1 percent increase in productivity seems to lower exports by between 29 and 33 percent. Age is also negatively associated with export intensity, indicating that younger firms tend to export more. And, intuitively, the size of the firm is positively associated with exports.

The clustering of exporters within the district seems to affect export intensity negatively, while the clustering of exporters of the same industry within the district has a positive effect. A percentage increase in the number of same-industry exporters within the district increases the value of exports by 16 percent. In the same vein, more general clustering—that is, clustering of firms within the same industry—has a positive and significant coefficient. Thus, there is some evidence of positive externalities of within-industry clustering on the intensity of a firm's participation in export markets. Access to suppliers has a positive effect, and access to buyers has a negative effect, although these coefficients are not statistically significant once infrastructure and other variables are controlled for.

Market access has a negative effect, although the magnitude of the effect is small. Access to the closest port has a negative effect, suggesting that firms closer to large trading ports are more likely to export more. In fact, a 1 minute increase in the travel-time distance to the closest port decreases exports by 0.11 percent (see model 6). It seems that being located close to a port does not affect the odds of starting to export (see the result in table 7.3), but that it does positively affect the intensity of export participation. Firms close to a large trading port are not more likely to start exporting, but once they do start exporting, they are more likely to export more.

Infrastructure variables seem to be statistically insignificant in all cases, except for road density, which seems to suggest that higher density is associated with more intensive exporting, although the effect is insignificant and negative with the introduction of institutional variables and location-level fixed effects. Finally, although social unrest might negatively affect the propensity of firms to turn to foreign markets, once they do start exporting, it is no longer statistically significant. In fact, the flexibility of labor regulations now seems to be much more important: more pro-business regulations are associated with higher intensity of exports.

Results within Firms

Just as in the case of the extensive margin, this chapter will now concentrate on how the factors discussed above affect the intensity of participation in export markets for *a given firm*. As before, the introduction of firm-level fixed effects will help to convincingly deal with any omitted variables bias and will indicate the true effect of locational and other factors for firms. Additionally, variables that are time invariant are not included in the analysis, because the coefficients on these would be zero; these include distance to the closest port, road density, and labor regulations (denoted by "flex"—short for flexibility).

In table 7.6, columns (1)–(5) introduce the different sets of variables, and column (6) also includes year dummies along with firm-level fixed effects. When the coefficient is averaged within firms and not across firms—that is, after controlling for firm-level fixed effects—some of the earlier results remain stable. Productivity continues to have a negative impact on export intensity, and the size of the firm has a strong positive impact. However, the age of the firm seems to have little or no impact on export intensity.

Interestingly, the count of exporters within a district affects export intensity positively, as compared to the across-firm specifications presented earlier. Although the result is not statistically significant once infrastructure and other variables are controlled for, this does seem to suggest that accounting for the effect of firm unobservables might be important to estimate the average impact of exporter agglomeration. It appears that aggregating the coefficients within firms seems to reverse the impact of spillovers from exporter clustering. The impact of within-industry export clustering is now statistically insignificant.

The remaining economic geography variables do not have any statistically significant effects on the intensity of exports. Market access has a small and negative effect on export intensity, which disappears once year dummies are introduced. Additionally, neither the infrastructure nor the institutional variables have any impact on the intensity of exports for a given firm. The introduction of firm-level fixed effects effectively seems to absorb most of the variation in the data, especially for those variables that vary only by district and year.

Conclusions

This chapter investigates the factors that affect the decision of a firm to start exporting and its performance thereafter, using India as a case study. In particular, it studies the impact of firm-specific characteristics and those of the location within India—agglomeration, infrastructure, and institutional. It separates the effect of these factors across firms and within firms. When comparing firms within the same industry and year, we find that the impact of local agglomeration of exporting firms seems to negatively affect the odds of entry into export markets; and with the introduction of firm-level fixed effects, the impact is negative and significant across all specifications. Within-industry clustering of firms seems to have little or no impact on the odds of entry when the coefficient is averaged across firms, but after controlling for unobservables at the level of

Table 7.6 Export Intensity (Within-Firm OLS)

Variable	(1)	(2)	(3)	(4)	(5)	(6)
Productivity	−0.3871***	−0.3547***	−0.3588***	−0.1212	−0.0428	−0.0333
	[0.079]	[0.095]	[0.095]	[0.166]	[0.182]	[0.177]
Age	0.0000	0.0011	0.0013	−0.0065	−0.0120	−0.0121
	[0.002]	[0.002]	[0.002]	[0.009]	[0.007]	[0.007]
Size	1.2604***	1.2760***	1.2871***	1.1570***	1.1926***	1.1623***
	[0.081]	[0.083]	[0.081]	[0.089]	[0.117]	[0.113]
Exporter count		0.3902***	0.3661***	0.1574	0.1352	0.1004
		[0.138]	[0.138]	[0.328]	[0.355]	[0.368]
Exporter count (India)		0.0039	0.0127	0.1152	0.1628	0.1476
		[0.081]	[0.080]	[0.196]	[0.239]	[0.231]
Localization		−0.0299	−0.0290	0.0410	−0.3063	−0.7747
		[0.047]	[0.044]	[0.068]	[0.272]	[0.785]
Input economies		0.0788	0.0813	0.0654	0.0354	0.0367
		[0.056]	[0.055]	[0.075]	[0.058]	[0.035]
Output economies		0.0256	0.0387	0.0155	0.3320	0.7779
		[0.189]	[0.103]	[0.104]	[0.256]	[0.775]
Diversity		−0.0610	−0.0648	−0.2321	−0.0205	−0.0908
		[0.140]	[0.140]	[0.254]	[0.308]	[0.297]
Market access			−0.0000	−0.0000	−0.0000**	−0.0000
			[0.000]	[0.000]	[0.000]	[0.000]
Telephone				0.1874	0.0902	−0.0826
				[0.120]	[0.135]	[0.204]
Electricity				0.4281*	0.1611	0.1979
				[0.239]	[0.271]	[0.262]
Education				0.2018	0.1169	−0.0563
				[0.244]	[0.246]	[0.231]
Wages				−0.0481	−0.0041	0.0307
				[0.156]	[0.171]	[0.188]
Wealth				0.0132	0.0283	0.0548
				[0.069]	[0.090]	[0.091]
Riots					−0.0047	−0.0317
					[0.028]	[0.027]
Population	−0.1562***	0.2629	0.2617	0.3136	0.4723	0.2219
	[0.038]	[0.161]	[0.175]	[0.401]	[0.422]	[0.450]
Fixed effects	Firm	Firm	Firm	Firm	Firm	Firm
Number of observations	13,695	12,397	12,243	3,312	2,622	2,622
	0.899	0.903	0.904	0.932	0.934	0.935

Note: OLS = ordinary least squares. All specifications control for the type of the firm (that is, private domestic, private foreign, public and mixed). Lagged values ($t − 1$) of explanatory variables are being used. Robust errors are in brackets, clustered at the district level.
*$p < 0.1$, **$p < 0.05$, ***$p < 0.01$

the firm, it positively affects the log odds of entry. Educational attainment and institutional factors seem to matter. We also find compelling evidence of self-selection of more productive firms into the export market. The effect of other location-specific factors, such as infrastructure and institutional controls, varies by model specification. This chapter also showed how these factors affect the intensity of participation once firms have started exporting. More productive firms are less likely to export intensively, and the size of the firm is an important determinant of its export participation. Controlling for unobservables at the firm level seems to indicate that clustering of other exporters might affect participation positively, but there is little evidence that other factors affect export intensity.

The policy implications of these findings are relevant, not just for those wishing to encourage export participation by firms in India, but also more generally for policy makers in developing countries. The across-firm results provide indications on the sorts of factors that affect firms within given industries. Indeed, if one were interested in providing incentives that encouraged a particular domestic industry to export, these results would be particularly relevant. Better education and better institutions are the most important factors. On the other hand, if one were hoping to give certain kinds of firms within particular industries a boost into export markets, then the within-firm results would be important. In other words, if all that mattered was that the best, or the most productive, firms within given industries and locations accessed foreign markets, then more general agglomeration within a location would be an important factor.

In summary, these findings suggest that if, in fact, there are positive externalities from clustering of export-oriented activity, then governments could provide incentives to encourage such co-location. However, the existence of spillovers from more general economic clustering suggests that governments might have limited ability to create incentives, because their effect on generating agglomeration economies is unclear. Finally, investment in more general education infrastructure and in improving institutional characteristics of regions might also help to reduce the sunk costs of export entry.

Annex 7A Data

Table 7A.1 Data Availability

		Availability					
Variable	Source(s)	1999	2000	2001	2002	2003	2004
Productivity	Prowess	✓	✓	✓	✓	✓	✓
Age	Prowess	✓	✓	✓	✓	✓	✓
Sales	Prowess	✓	✓	✓	✓	✓	✓
Type	Prowess	✓	✓	✓	✓	✓	✓
Exporter count	Prowess	✓	✓	✓	✓	✓	✓
Localization	ASI	✓	✓	✓	✓	✓	✓
Input-output	ASI	✓	✓	✓	✓	✓	✓
Industrial diversity	ASI	✓	✓	✓	✓	✓	✓

table continues next page

Table 7A.1 Data Availability *(continued)*

Variable	Source(s)	Availability					
		1999	*2000*	*2001*	*2002*	*2003*	*2004*
MA	NSSO/travel-time distance	✓	✓	✓	✓	✓	✓
Road density	ArcGIS	✓	✓	✓	✓	✓	✓
Electricity	NSSO	✓	—	—	—	✓	✓
Telephone	NSSO	✓	—	—	—	✓	✓
Education	NSSO	✓	—	—	—	✓	✓
Wages	NSSO	✓	—	—	—	✓	✓
Wealth	NSSO	✓	—	—	—	✓	✓
Labor regulations	Besley and Burgess (2004)	✓	✓	✓	✓	✓	✓
Riots	Marshall and Marshall (2008)	✓	✓	✓	✓	✓	✓
Population	NSSO/census	✓	✓	✓	✓	✓	✓

Source: See column 2.
Note: — = not available, ASI = Annual Survey of Industries, NSSO = National Sample Survey Organisation. The values assigned to different states regarding their labor regulations, and those for road density assigned to districts, do not vary over year, and the value does not vary over time.

Table 7A.2 Capital and Labor Coefficients by Industry

NIC	NIC sector name	Olley-Pakes			OLS		
		Capital	*Labor*	*#*	*Capital*	*Labor*	*#*
15	Manufacture of food products and beverages	1.0256***	0.2055***	3,012	0.7470***	0.3182***	3,531
16	Manufacture of tobacco products	0.7768**	0.2802***	78	0.7828***	0.3638***	86
17	Manufacture of textiles	0.7123***	0.3469***	2,785	0.6441***	0.3858***	2,964
18	Manufacture of wearing apparel; dressing and dyeing of fur	0.7421***	0.3848***	418	0.6738***	0.4743***	457
19	Tanning and dressing of leather; manufacture of luggage, handbags and footwear	0.1178	0.4476***	243	0.4740***	0.5791***	284
20	Manufacture of wood and of products of wood and cork, except furniture	0.5592***	0.4966***	125	0.4338***	0.7010***	144
21	Manufacture of paper and paper products	0.3629**	0.4996***	735	0.3609***	0.5891***	764
22	Publishing, printing and reproduction of recorded media	0.6958***	0.3982***	222	0.5495***	0.4679***	286
23	Manufacture of coke, refined petroleum products and nuclear fuel	0.6992***	0.4302***	265	0.5686***	0.5638***	295
24	Manufacture of chemicals and chemical products	0.7428***	0.4490***	5,100	0.5286***	0.5308***	5,466
25	Manufacture of rubber and plastic products	0.8023***	0.4534***	1,546	0.5484***	0.5463***	1,740
26	Manufacture of other non-metallic mineral products	0.5144***	0.4920***	879	0.5274***	0.5773***	1,024
27	Manufacture of basic metals	0.8639***	0.2580***	2,098	0.5827***	0.3569***	2,575
28	Manufacture of fabricated metal products, except machinery and equipments	1.0148***	0.2689***	802	0.6635***	0.3629***	855
29	Manufacture of machinery and equipment n.e.c.	1.0025***	0.3401***	1,365	0.6799***	0.3958***	1,770
30	Manufacture of office, accounting and computing machinery	0.9153***	0.6034***	198	0.3873***	0.6965***	233

table continues next page

Table 7A.2 Capital and Labor Coefficients by Industry (*continued*)

NIC	NIC sector name	Olley-Pakes			OLS		
		Capital	Labor	#	Capital	Labor	#
31	Manufacture of electrical machinery and apparatus n.e.c.	1.1370***	0.3449***	876	0.6669***	0.4295***	991
32	Manufacture of radio, television and communication equipment and apparatus	0.9436***	0.6574***	634	0.4887***	0.6974***	695
33	Manufacture of medical, precision and optical instruments, watches and clocks	1.0387***	0.4980***	310	0.5121***	0.6117***	333
34	Manufacture of motor vehicles, trailers and semi-trailers	0.7570***	0.5300***	1,254	0.4936***	0.5983***	1,484
35	Manufacture of other transport equipment	1.0306***	0.4041***	208	0.5877***	0.4551***	251
36	Manufacture of furniture; manufacturing n.e.c.	1.2380***	0.1309***	398	1.0892***	0.1825***	500

Note: n.e.c. = not elsewhere classified, NIC = National Industrial Classification. The table reports production function estimates using Olley and Pakes (1996) and simple OLS methodologies, by each 2-digit NIC industry. With constant returns to scale the sum of the coefficients should equal 1, and if higher, this implies increasing returns to scale for the given industry.
$*p < 0.1, **p < 0.05, ***p < 0.01$

Notes

1. First-nature geography is when the characteristics of the natural geography determine clustering. Second-nature geography is when interactions between economic agents and increasing returns to scale determine clustering.

2. Proportions instead of absolute counts are presented since it could be argued that clustering in these districts is simply a factor of the size of the district.

3. Fixed assets include plant and machinery, computers, electrical installations, transport and communication equipment and infrastructure, fittings and furniture, social amenities, and other fixed assets.

4. Since more productive forms are likely to have a lower-than-average firm-specific price, the use of industry price indices might systematically underestimate the output of more productive firms and therefore underestimate their productivity. On the other hand, if exporters were more likely to use better-quality inputs and materials, then using industry-specific deflators would overestimate productivity. The converse would be true for less-productive firms. In the absence of firm-specific prices, we are unable to overcome this bias.

5. In the original model proposed by Hanson (1959), b is an exponent describing the effect of the travel time between the zones.

6. The author is grateful to Brian Blankespoor of the World Bank for carrying out the computations and for making the data available for this analysis.

7. Some examples of road types are motorways, primary roads, secondary roads, trunk links, tertiary roads, residential roads, and so forth.

8. http://www.esri.com/software/arcgis.

9. This is a strong assumption, and with the availability of better data we can attempt to update these results at a later stage.

10. The actual consumption category differs depending on the year of the survey, the type of district (rural or urban), and the population of the district.

11. More recent data are also available, but the data extracted for this chapter stop at 2008.

12. Quoted in earlier version of NBER working paper No. 14127, available: http://www.nber.org/papers/w14127.

13. http://pib.nic.in/newsite/erelease.aspx?relid=80823.

14. Convergence is not reached when district fixed effects are introduced.

15. For instance, when aggregated across all firms, it seems that the share of sales associated with the preferential products seems to fall in response to the increase in market access. This could be because new entrants in the market sell only a small share of preferential products, compared to more established firms, which brings down the aggregate average for all firms.

16. The author also tried the model with the inclusion of firm and year fixed effects but convergence was not reached.

17. Keep in mind that this model says nothing about the intensity with which a firm might export, and looks exclusively at the decision to enter the export market. The next subsection will look more closely at the effect of continued and more intensive export participation.

18. We also had the choice of regressing exports of the firm as a proportion of sales on the explanatory variables. In this case, the dependent variable would be a fraction that varies between 0 and 1, and using OLS would lead to incorrectly identified coefficients. This is because the effect of any explanatory variable cannot be constant through its entire range. Additionally, the predicted values from an OLS regression often produce figures outside the range of 0–1. Papke and Wooldridge (1996) examine potential econometric alternatives and support using quasi-likelihood methods. Accordingly, we try and use fractional logit regressions, but find that these models do not converge with the introduction of firm-level fixed effects.

References

Aitken, B., G. H. Hanson, and A. E. Harrison. 1997. "Spillovers, Foreign Investment, and Export Behaviour." *Journal of International Economics* 43: 103–32.

Arkolakis, K. 2009. "Market Penetration Costs and the New Consumers Margin in International Trade." NBER Working Paper 14214, National Bureau of Economic Research, Cambridge, MA.

Arrow, K. 1962. "The Economic Implications of Learning by Doing." *Review of Economic Studies* 29 (3): 155–73.

Baldwin, R. E., and P. R. Krugman. 1989. "Persistent Trade Effects of Large Exchange Rate Shocks." *Quarterly Journal of Economics* 104 (4): 635–54.

Barrios, S., H. Gorg, and E. Strobl. 2003. "'Explaining Firms' Export Behavior: R&D, Spillovers and the Destination Market." *Oxford Bulletin of Economics and Statistics* 65: 475–96.

Becchetti, L., and S. P. S. Rossi. 2000. "The Positive Effect of Industrial District on the Export Performance of Italian Firms." *Review of Industrial Organisation* 16: 53–68.

Bernard, A., and J. B. Jensen. 2004. "Why Some Firms Export." *Review of Economics and Statistics* 86 (2): 561–69.

Besley, T., and R. Burgess. 2004. "Can Labor Regulation Hinder Economic Performance? Evidence from India." *Quarterly Journal of Economics* 119 (1): 91–134.

Bown, C., and G. Porto. 2010. "Exporters in Developing Countries: Adjustment to Foreign Market Access as a Trade Policy Shock." Working Paper, World Bank, Washington, DC.

Chinitz, B. 1961. "Contrasts in Agglomeration: New York and Pittsburgh." *American Economic Review* 51: 279–89.

Centre for Monitoring the Indian Economy (CMIE). 2012. *Prowess.* Online database. Mumbai: Centre for Monitoring the Indian Economy. http://prowess.cmie.com.

Das, S., M. J. Roberts, and J. R. Tybout. 2007. "Market Entry Costs, Producer Heterogeneity, and Export Dynamics." *Econometrica* 75 (3): 837–73.

Dixit, A. 1989. "Entry and Exit Decisions under Uncertainty." *Journal of Political Economy* 97 (3): 620–38.

Duranton, G., and D. Puga. 2004. "Micro-foundations of Urban Agglomeration Economies." In *Handbook of Regional and Urban Economics*, edited by J. V. Henderson and J. F. Thisse, Vol. 4. Amsterdam: North-Holland.

Feser, E. J., and E. M. Bergman. 2000. "National Industry Cluster Templates: A Framework for Applied Regional Cluster Analysis." *Regional Studies* 34 (1): 1–20.

Goldberg, P., A. Khandelwal, N. Pavcnik, and P. Topalova. 2010. "Multiproduct Firms and Product Turnover in the Developing World: Evidence from India." *Review of Economics and Statistics* 92 (4): 1042–49.

Greenaway, D., and W. K. Sousa. 2004. "Do Domestic Firms Learn to Export from Multinationals?" *European Journal of Political Economy* 20: 1027–43.

Hanson, G. H. 1959. "How Accessibility Shapes Land Use." *Journal of the American Institute of Planners* 25: 73–76.

Jacobs, J. 1969. *The Economy of Cities.* Cambridge, MA: MIT Press.

Konig, P. 2009. "Agglomeration and the Export Decisions of French Firms." *Journal of Urban Economics* 66 (3): 186–95.

Krugman, P. 1991. "Increasing Returns and Economic Geography." *Journal of Political Economy* 99 (3): 483–99.

Levinsohn, L., and A. Petrin. 2003. "Estimating Production Functions Using Inputs to Control for Unobservables." *Review of Economic Studies* 70 (2): 317–41.

Lovely, M., S. Rosenthal, and S. Sharma. 2005. "Information, Agglomeration and the Headquarters of US Exporters." *Regional Science and Urban Economics* 35 (2): 167–91.

Marshall, A. 1890. *Principles of Economics.* London: Macmillan.

Marshall, M. G., and D. R. Marshall. 2008. *Crime in India: Annual Series, 1954–2006.* Electronic Dataset and Codebook, Center for Systemic Peace, Vienna, VA, USA. http://www.systemicpeace.org/inscr/inscr.htm.

Ministry of Statistics and Programme Implementation (MOSPI). n.d. *Annual Survey of Industries (ASI).* Government of India, New Delhi. http://mospi.nic.in/mospi_new/upload/asi/ASI_main.htm.

Olley, G. S., and A. Pakes. 1996. "The Dynamics of Productivity in the Telecommunications Equipment Industry." *Econometrica* 64 (6): 1263–97.

Papke, L. E., and J. M. Wooldridge. 1996. "Econometric Methods for Fractional Response Variables with an Application to 401(K) Plan Participation Rates." *Journal of Applied Econometrics* 11 (6): 619–32.

Roberts, M. J., and J. R. Tybout. 1997. "The Decision to Export in Colombia: An Empirical Model of Entry with Sunk Costs." *American Economic Review* 87 (4): 545–64.

Romer, P. M. 1986. "Increasing Returns and Long-Run Growth." *Journal of Political Economy* 94 (5): 1002–37.

Tybout, J. R., and M. D. Westbrook. 1994. "Trade Liberalization and the Dimensions of Efficiency Change in Mexican Manufacturing Industry." *Journal of International Economics* 39: 53–78.

Venables, A. J. 1996. "Equilibrium Locations of Vertically Linked Industries." *International Economic Review* 49: 341–59.

PART 3

Policies to Promote Trade and Investment in Lagging Regions: Are They Aligned and Effective?

Introduction

Background

One thing that becomes clear from the analysis in part 2 of this book is that, while distance and density are "endowments" that cannot, at least in the short term, be changed, regional trade participation and economic outcomes also depend on factors that should not inherently bias peripheral regions. Competitiveness is strongly impacted by the collective policy choices and implementation arrangements at the regional and national levels. In this regard, lagging regions are not only affected by policy choices that are common to all regions, but they are often subject to targeted interventions designed expressly to reduce spatial disparities, justified by the existence of both government and market failures (see Hon, Rojchaichaninthorn, and Schmidt 2009), and a wide range of government policies have been deployed globally to promote agglomeration in lagging areas and to close the gap between leading and lagging regions, including infrastructure investments, wage policies, deregulation, promotion of clusters, development of industrial parks and special economic zones, and, most commonly, fiscal incentives to encourage investment. While some of these policies have at least implicit emphasis on trade, for the most part trade integration of lagging regions has not been at the forefront of regional policies.

Evaluations of Regional Development Policy

There exist several well-known examples of poor regional development policy choices leading to inefficient or even perverse development outcomes at the subnational level, such as Italy's infrastructure and industrial policy in the Mezzogiorno and India's use of the Licensing Raj (World Bank 2009). For truly remote and sparsely populated regions, spatially targeted growth policies have for the most part been expensive failures, subsidizing inefficient investment, aggravating the leakage of the best firms and most talented workers, and contributing to unfavorable institutional environment.

More often, the issue is not so much that interventions have had negative results, but rather that their impact has been minimal relative to their cost. This was the case with targeted interest rate subsidies in Brazil, for example, where the policies did succeed in attracting some firms into lagging regions, but at a cost of several billion dollars annually (Carvalho, Lall, and Timmins 2006). Similarly in Mexico, significant fiscal incentives to promote industrial development outside of the three largest metropolitan areas was found to have, at best, an insignificant impact on decentralization (Deichmann et al. 2008).

Impact evaluations of policies based on fiscal incentives have generally found that the level of grants and subsidies made available for investing in peripheral regions has been insufficient to offset the benefits to firms of their existing agglomerations (Devereux, Griffith, and Simpson 2007), or put another way, to offset the higher costs of operating in the peripheral region. This was the case, for example, in Thailand, where efforts to promote investment in regions outside of Bangkok during the 1970s and 1980s failed in part because the fiscal incentive—a deduction on corporate taxes—became irrelevant when the cost structure of operating in the peripheral regions made it difficult to turn a significant profit in any case (Deichmann et al. 2008).

Overall, there is now widespread recognition that past attempts to use blunt instruments to get investment in lagging regions has failed and that more nuanced approaches are needed.

Ongoing Theoretical Debate

Yet an intense debate remains over whether and how governments should intervene to support investment and growth in lagging regions. This can be seen in the contrast between the "place-based" approach of the European Union and the "place-neutral" approach outlined in the World Bank's *World Development Report 2009* (WDR 2009) (Barca, McCann, and Rodríguez-Pose 2012). Briefly, the approach outlined in the WDR (World Bank 2009) argues against policies that attempt to move economic activity into lagging regions, and instead focuses on promoting economic integration between leading and lagging regions through "spatially blind" improvements in institutions, spatially connective infrastructure, and spatially targeted incentives, built around well-defined comparative advantage. The "place-based" approach, however, argues for the endogeneity of institutions, and therefore the critical importance of context-specific interventions (including the provision of public goods) that must be inherently made at the local level.

Overview of Part 3

Putting the theoretical debate aside, it is clear that the political imperative remains for national governments to remain engaged in policies that aim to promote growth of lagging regions. In this last main section of the book, we present examples from our two case study countries: Indonesia and India. Both countries have a long history of attempts to address the "lagging region problem," covering a wide range of policies and programs, with limited success. The case examples here provide a history of the diagnoses and policy responses in each country, including some discussion on the effectiveness of these policies. Note that no detailed impact evaluations have been carried out as part of this book, but such studies have been undertaken in both countries and are referenced in the relevant chapters.

References

Barca, F., P. McCann, and A. Rodríguez-Pose. 2012. "The Case for Regional Development Intervention: Place-Based versus Place-Neutral Approaches." *Journal of Regional Science* 52 (1): 134–52.

Carvalho, A., S.V. Lall, and C. Timmins. 2006. "Regional Subsidies and Industrial Prospects of Lagging Regions." World Bank Policy Research Working Paper 3843, World Bank, Washington, DC.

Deichmann, U., S.V. Lall, S.J. Redding, and A.J. Venables 2008. "Industrial Location in Developing Countries." *World Bank Research Observer* 23 (2): 219–46.

Devereux, M., R. Griffith, and H. Simpson. 2007. "Firm Location Decisions, Regional Grants and Agglomeration Externalities," *Journal of Public Economics* 91 (3–4): 413–35.

Hon, V., J. Rojchaichaninthorn, and E. Schmidt. 2009. "A Framework for Bank Engagement in Lagging Areas." Spatial and Local Development Team Finance, Economics and Urban Department Sustainable Development Network, Washington, DC: World Bank, May 20, 2009.

World Bank. 2009. *World Development Report 2009: Reshaping Economic Geography.* Washington, DC: World Bank.

CHAPTER 8

Policies to Promote Development and Integration of Lagging Regions: The Indonesian Experience

Della Temenggung

Introduction

Uneven patterns of spatial economic development have contributed to increasing inequalities across various territorial scales in Indonesia, including at the broad regional level (western versus eastern Indonesia), across provinces within these regions, as well as between urban and rural areas within some provinces. To address the problem, Indonesia's government has introduced a wide range of policies and programs over the past 40 years. Beginning in the late 1960s, the government initiated the First Five-Year Development Plan (Rencana Pembangunan Lima Tahun I, Repelita I 1969–1973). This was followed by other policies such as investment and financial reforms, decentralization and interregional fiscal transfers (the Inpres program), a migration program (Azis 1990; Uppal and Budiono 1986), Integrated Economic Development Zone (Kawasan Pengembangan Ekonomi Terpadu, KAPET) program, and, more recently, special economic zones (SEZs). Despite these efforts, there has been no significant change in the concentration of economic activity across the country. Economic activities remain concentrated in western Indonesia—particularly in Java, Bali, and Sumatra, with an increasing role of Kalimantan recently (Hill, Resosudarmo, and Vidyattama 2008)—and, indeed, evidence suggests that inequalities are growing.

This chapter provides a brief outline of the recent history of regional policies on investment in Indonesia. The focus of the case study is to discuss what has been the history of efforts to promote investment in peripheral or "lagging" regions over the course of Indonesian development, covering two aspects: summary of the main policies and the types of incentives offered and result to date. The chapter starts with a brief history on efforts to promote investment in lagging regions through investment incentives. The next section discusses the implementation of KAPET, followed by a discussion of the local investment climate after decentralization. A further section discusses some recent development on the integrated efforts to promote inclusive development and to reduce the development gap between eastern and western Indonesia through the Master Plan of Economic Transformation. The chapter ends with some brief conclusions.

Efforts to Promote Investment in Lagging Regions: Investment Incentives

National Investment Incentives (1967–84)

Starting in the early period of the New Order government, in 1967, government granted a set of incentives to investors. The aim was to support industrial policy and thereby attract investment in manufacturing, and to signal to foreign investors that the country had shifted from a closed to an open investment regime. In addition, the incentives had a clear aim of improving the country's foreign exchange position, either through promoting export-oriented or import-substituting activities. Following the issuance of a new law for foreign investment (Law No. 1 of 1967, extended to domestic investors through Law No. 6 of 1968), the government granted a five-year holiday from corporate tax, duty exemptions on the import of capital goods and equipment, and accelerated depreciation.[1] Incentives were granted after considering the priority fields of activity. In practice, however, the incentives were almost automatic, as long as the projects met basic requirements in terms of size and foreign exchange earnings (Ikhsan 2006). See table 8.1 for a summary of these requirements.

Table 8.1 Summary of Investment Incentives in Indonesia, 1967–84

Year	Law	Major provisions/changes
1967/68	Law No. 1 of 1967 on Foreign Investment and Law No. 6 of 1968 on Domestic Investment	Five-year tax holiday from corporate tax, duty exemptions on the import of capital goods and equipment, and accelerated depreciation, based on following criteria: • Provisions would apply to investment in the first two years for projects greater than US$2.5 million, which would save or earn foreign exchange. • An additional year would be granted for such investment if it was located outside Java, or in infrastructure, or if considered risky. • An additional year could be given to investment made in 1967 and 1968 if it was "pioneer" or valued more than US$15 million.
1970/71	Law No. 12 of 1970	Reduction of basic tax holiday to two years for all firms in priority sectors, with one additional year exemption possible for each of the following: • a project that saves a significant foreign exchange • large or "risky" projects • location outside Java • "special priority" projects
1983/84	Law No. 7 of 1983 on Income Tax	Income tax holiday on investments eliminated

The criteria and incentives were slightly modified in 1970, most notably in reducing the standard tax holiday from five years to two years, with longer periods linked to meeting objectives (see table 8.1). While location (outside of Java) was maintained, the eligible additional tax incentive remained only one year.

Finally, in 1984, the income tax holiday was eliminated. The main reasons for this were to increase the efficiency of tax collection and advocate for a simple and neutral tax regime (Pangestu and Bora 1996), given the limited administrative capacity of the Indonesian tax authorities. Since then, there have been various attempts by different groups to lobby for the reintroduction of the tax incentives for investment. Proponents argue that the incentive is crucial to attract investment in the eastern part of Indonesia and to promote certain sectors in Indonesia that offer high potential for economic growth.

In summary, during the early period of development, government focused largely on attracting investment into Indonesia in general, rather than to lagging areas in particular. Although an effort to attract investment to regions outside Java was introduced in the regulations, the incentive offered was not significant; it provided only one additional year to the tax holiday that was available to investors in Java. Moreover, although there was an incentive linked to foreign exchange, the structure of the incentives regime could not be seen as "export oriented." As a result, through the 1980s, the investment incentives had little to no impact on the location of investment in the country, which tended to concentrate in Java and, to a lesser extent, Sumatra.

Targeting Incentives for Lagging Regions (1990–2000)

The early 1990s saw more targeted efforts to address investment and economic development in lagging regions. However, these initial efforts remained primarily focused on using the instrument of investment incentives. In 1990, a ministerial decree[2] offered special incentives—in the form of fiscal loss compensation (loss carry forward) for up to eight years—in 13 eastern Indonesian provinces.[3] The incentive was made available for new investment and expansion in a wide range of sectors, including agriculture, farming, fisheries, mining, forestry, industry, real estate or industrial estates, hotels and tourism, and transportation.

This initial effort was expanded to a more strategic program called the Acceleration of Eastern Indonesian Development (Percepatan Pembangunan Kawasan Timur Indonesia, PPKTI) in 1993. In 1996, government introduced an Integrated Economic Development Zone (Kawasan Pengembangan Ekonomi Terpadu, KAPET) program as a further attempt to accelerate development in lagging regions, especially in eastern Indonesia. Special incentives were provided in KAPET based on Government Regulation No. 20 of 2000. This initiative is discussed separately in the next section of this chapter.

In addition, the national investment incentives regime became more focused on lagging regions during this period. For example, in the 1994 incentives program, lagging regions were specifically defined, although somewhat ambiguously, as regions with "feasible economic potential" but "lacking in economic facilities and cannot be reached by public transportation,"[4] therefore requiring investors to face higher risk and potentially a longer time to obtain a return on their investment. The incentive program included three main components:

- depreciation and accelerated amortization
- fiscal loss compensation (loss carry forward) for the following fiscal year for a maximum of 10 consecutive years
- 20 percent reduction of income tax on profits.

The incentive program was again revised in 1996.[5] Under this new regime, the primary emphasis was on attracting investment in specific industry sectors, for example, electronics. The main incentive was a 10-year tax holiday for eligible investments. Lagging regions were targeted through the provision of an additional two-year holiday for investments made outside Java and Bali. Selection of industries eligible for the incentive was made by the president, based on input from a "National Team for Tax Incentives for Certain Industries," a body formed through a Presidential Decree (Keputusan Presiden, Keppres). Incentives were granted on case-by-case basis, with no automaticity and no transparent criteria. The tax incentives were granted by an interministerial team led by the Coordinating Minister for Economic Affairs; the team consisted of the Finance Minister, the Industry and Trade Minister, and the Chairman of the Indonesia's Investment Coordinating Board (Badan Koordinasi Penanaman Modal, BKPM).

Finally, the 1994 and 1996 regimes were revised once more in 2000, with minor changes to the previous incentives, including greater flexibility in applying depreciation and/or accelerated amortization, increasing the net income tax reduction incentive from 20 to 30 percent of total invested capital, and reducing foreign dividend taxes.

Again, in this period, the effort to attract investment to lagging regions outside Java was considered to be ineffective. The incentive offered failed to attract significant investment to those regions (Wuryan 1996). Following the 1996 regulation, only one of six projects was located outside Java and Bali area and only one of them was awarded to electronic investment (Ikhsan 2006).

The Introduction of Law No. 25 of 2007

As one of the implementing regulations of Law No. 25 of 2007 on Investment, the government of Indonesia issued Government Regulation No. 1 of 2007 on Fiscal Incentives for Investment in Certain Sectors and Certain Regions. "Certain Regions" here was defined more broadly than the previous regulations, although equally ambiguously. Specifically, in addition to regions previously identified as lagging, the new regulations also targeted regions that were deemed to have "economic potential for development." In practice, this meant that although most of the incentives provided were for regions located outside Java, some of the incentives were applicable for investment in provinces in Java.

In contrast to the previous regulations in 1996 and 2000, where decisions to grant incentives were made discretionarily through an interministerial body, the new regulation stated clearly the sectors and regions where the incentive would be applicable. This was in line with the message of transparency and simplicity that government delivered when the Law on Investment of 2007 and the Negative Investment List were introduced.[6]

The incentive regime included the same main instruments that were available under previous regimes: net income tax reduction of 30 percent of total invested capital (now for a period of six years); depreciation and/or accelerated amortization; a 10 percent income tax on dividend for foreign taxpayers; and fiscal loss compensation (loss carry forward) for at least five, and up to 10 years. Again, the regime offered an additional one year of incentive for investments meeting certain criteria with regard to size, infrastructure requirements, research and development investment, use of local raw materials, and, of course, location. In this case, the regional targeting became linked to certain sectors, with the intention of promoting investments in sectors that leveraged the comparative advantages of each region. Table 8.2 provides a sample of how this sector/region incentive scheme was mapped.

Following the announcement of Law No. 25 of 2007 on Investment, the private sector response was not enthusiastic. The Indonesian Chamber of Commerce (KADIN) considered that the incentive would not be effective in attracting investment in Indonesia. A similar response came from the Indonesian Association of Employers (APINDO). Their arguments rested on three main concerns, which underline the weaknesses of the government's approach to using investment incentives to encourage development of lagging regions over the previous two decades. First, they argued that the incentive provided was half-hearted, as it was not enough to overcome the many barriers to operating profitably in lagging regions, particularly given the relatively demanding requirements to become eligible and actually be granted the incentive. Second, and more broadly, they argued that tax incentives were not the main requirement for investors; more important were issues like law enforcement, having a business-friendly tax system, and adequate infrastructure. Third, there was also concern that the implementation of

Table 8.2 Sectors and Provinces Eligible for Incentives under Indonesia's 2007 Law on Investment

Sectors	Provinces
Food packaging (fish and others)	Maluku, North Maluku, Papua, West Irian Jaya, North Sulawesi, South Sulawesi, Central Sulawesi, Southeast Sulawesi, West Sulawesi, and Gorontalo
Agri-based industries (cooking oil, flour, sugar, and others)	Provinces in Sulawesi and outside Java for sugar
Textile yarn	Provinces in Sulawesi and Nusa Tenggara
Packaging industries (box and plastic)	Outside Java
Cement	Papua, West Irian Jaya, Maluku, North Maluku, North Sulawesi, and West Nusa Tenggara
Furniture (wood and rattan)	Outside Java
Fishery and integrated food processing and packaging (certain fishes, lobster, prawn, crab, and so forth)	Provinces located in the Indian Ocean

the package would face significant obstacles. The private sector asked government to revise the package soon after the announcement (Business Indonesia 2008).

Another issue that impacted the implementation of this new investment law was lack of effective international coordination among the relative units of government. Although some of the officials (DG of Tax System and Deputy CMEA on Industry and Trade) argued that the incentive package provided a better and more transparent system (Kompas 2008), the Minister of Finance was also concerned with the potential effectiveness of the incentive and asked for further study before putting in place the necessary implementing regulations to enable the new regime to take effect.[7] This led to some delays in implementation.

In response to the concerns raised by the private sector, the government revised the regulations and issued Government Regulation No. 62 of 2008. The new regulation provided similar tax incentives for investment, but included more sectors and regions in the list, specifically food farming, horticulture, leather industries, shipping industries, and transshipment ports. The implementation of the new regime was also not without problems. Some have argued that the inclusion of these additional industries and regions on the list was not fully transparent, and was instead based primarily on the private sector's lobby. Moreover, the Minister of Industry argued that the fiscal incentive would not attract the significant investment that Indonesia needed, and argued instead that Indonesia needed to introduce a tax holiday system to simplify the incentive package (Business Indonesia 2010).

As of late 2011, the government is in the process of revising the incentives law. The Ministry of Industry (MoI) is playing a more active role and proposes including 62 sectors on the list. Moreover, MoI has proposed more flexible criteria for investors to be eligible for the tax incentive, in particular by reducing the employment requirement.[8]

The Integrated Economic Development Zone (KAPET)

Brief History of KAPET

To address uneven development between the west of the country (Java, Bali, and Sumatra) and the east, in 1993 the government implemented a program called Acceleration of Eastern Indonesian Development (Percepatan Pembangunan Kawasan Timur Indonesia, PPKTI), and established the Development Council for Eastern Indonesia (Dewan Pengembangan Kawasan Timur Indonesia). Following this, in 1996, the government introduced the KAPET program. As stated in Presidential Decree No. 89 of 1996,[9] a KAPET is designed as a growth center or growth pole for a peripheral region. As in previous programs, KAPET established vague criteria for eligible regions, including

- having potential for rapid growth
- having leading sectors capable of boosting the economic growth of hinterland areas
- offering potential for large investment return.

However, unlike previous programs, the KAPET program outlined very specific objectives, which included not only investment, but also exports, growth, and broader development. In the short term (up to 2004), the objectives for the program overall were to bring the per capita gross domestic product (GDP) and the HDI (Human Development Index[10]) of KAPET regions closer to the national average; to achieve 20 percent share of total national investment in these regions; and to achieve a 20 percent share of national exports in these regions. Long-term targets (up to 2010) were to increase the purchasing power in these regions to the national level; bring HDI up to the national average; and maintain at least 20 percent of total national export and investment.

Most important, KAPET for the first time went beyond simply investment incentives and took a much more comprehensive approach to increasing economic growth in lagging regions. A list of 31 priority programs in human resources, economic and natural resources, facilities and infrastructure, and institutional development were developed to achieve the targets. Of course, fiscal incentives were part of the program, but these were in line with the investment laws outlined earlier in this chapter.[11] More important were the nonfiscal incentives, which included investment facilitation (specifically information, guidance for establishing investments, and so forth) and a "one-stop-shop" integrated licensing system.

KAPET were managed by Managing Bodies (Badan Pengelola), which consisted of central and local governments (provincial and district levels). Following decentralization, the management of the KAPET programs was divided into two bodies. At the central level, management of the program was conducted by the Developing Body of KAPET, responsible for policy implementation and coordination and chaired by the Coordinating Minister of Economic Affairs. To manage the program at the regional level, individual KAPET were assigned a Managing Body with the local governor as chairman and headed by an executive director.

Since the program was launched, 14 KAPET have been launched: 12 have been established in eastern Indonesia and two in western Indonesia. The distribution by province is as follows:

- four in Kalimantan (Batulicin, Khatulistiwa, Das Kakab, and Sasamba)
- four in Sulawesi (Pare-pare, Bitung, Bukari and Batui)
- two in Nusa Tenggara (Bima and Mbay)
- one in Maluku (Seram)
- one in Papua (Biak)
- two in Sumatra (Natuna and Sabang later become Banda Aceh).

In total, the 12 KAPET in eastern Indonesia cover 51 districts or municipalities.

Performance of the KAPET Program

The KAPET program has been implemented for more than 15 years, covering different eras in Indonesian development (specifically, the New Order, Reformasi, and Post-Reformasi eras). It was started before decentralization and has undergone several adjustments due to changes in central and local governments' arrangement following decentralization.

At the early stage of its implementation, the Ministry of Acceleration of Eastern Indonesia reported in 2003 that the program overall had not performed to expectation. According to the joint report of the Development Council of Acceleration of Eastern Indonesia and the Developing Body of KAPET in the same year, six KAPET (Sasamba, Batulicin, Pare-pare, Bukari, Bitung, and Biak) showed a better performance compared to the remaining six KAPET (Bima, Mbay, Seram, Batui, Das Kakab, and Khatulistiwa) (Soenandar 2007).

In 2011, during an evaluation and consultative meeting with parliament, government concluded that the KAPET program had failed to attract investment to lagging regions. According to Gita Wirjavan,[12] the head of the BKPM, from 2005 to 2010 KAPET attracted only a total of Rp 27.5 trillion, equivalent to 3.4 percent of national investment—far from the initial target of a 20 percent share of national investment. Among the 14 KAPET, three attracted almost all of the investment: Banda Aceh (Rp 22.3 trillion), Batu Licin-South Kalimantan (Rp 3.1 trillion), and Bitung-Manado (Rp 3.5 trillion), while the other 11 KAPET received no investment (Kompas 2011a, 2011b). According to government,[13] several factors contributed to the failure of the KAPET program, including the following:

- *Weak management:* For example, lack of capacity of local governments in many KAPET areas meant that "one-stop-shop" facilities were not fully implemented and, more broadly, that the investment facilitation service was unable to be delivered effectively.

- *Poor institutional coordination:* Coordination between central and local government and coordination among related departments in both levels of government was one key element that needed to be significantly improved. This was particularly problematic after decentralization, which not only shifted management to the local level, but also required much greater coordination across districts (most KAPET encompassed several districts).

- *Poor infrastructure and facilities:* Poor infrastructure and facilities have also been cited as a major constraint faced by many KAPET (Ministry of Public Works 2004; Samosir and Wibowo 2004; Soenandar 2007). Availability of roads, ports, and electricity, as well as social infrastructure such as housing, transportation, public health facilities, security, water supply, and education, was seen as a prerequisite condition for investors, for which the modest tax incentives offered could not compensate.

- *Lack of funding to promote and develop KAPET:* Again, decentralization was one of the factors here, as management of both KAPET and funding was shifted from central to local government. This became a significant problem as many regions lacked sufficient funding to support the programs adequately. In part because of this lack of funding and institutional capacity, KAPET could not deliver the required infrastructure or the investor facilitation and support that formed a crucial part of the nonfiscal incentive package.

• *Lack of market access:* Most KAPET were located far from key markets and ports, making it particularly difficult for large-scale investments, particularly export-oriented ones, to be viable. This was exacerbated by the lack of sufficient investment in connecting infrastructure.

• *Tax incentives not sufficient:* Given the challenges noted above, the relatively modest tax incentives offered in the KAPET were far from sufficient to attract investors who had more attractive investment options within and outside Indonesia.

The Local Investment Environment after Decentralization

During the 1990s, the disparity of income per capita across regions in Indonesia became a crucial topic. Regions that fell behind started to show their dissatisfaction with the central government, demanding larger income transfers and greater authority in managing their development. The 1997–98 Asian economic crisis provided momentum for political change. After the collapse of the New Order regime, the demand for a more democratic environment was granted. This democratization also reshaped the relationship between central and local government. Indonesia drastically shifted from highly centralized to highly decentralized government with the "big bang" decentralization of 2001 (see Balisacan, Pernia, and Asra 2002; Tadjoeddin, Suharyo, and Mishra 2001).

Based on early lessons from Indonesian decentralization, it has been argued in several studies that the investment climate did not improve. Indeed, local regulations often hindered investment and trade (Oktaviani and Irawan 2009; Saad 2003). Prior to decentralization, local government acted as a mere "implementing agency" of central government regulation. The only remaining authority left to the local government was the Local Revenues (Pendapatan Asli Daerah, PAD), which was exercised through the issuance of local regulations. Some studies reveal that the implementation of decentralization at the beginning was dominated by the euphoria of exercising control over local revenue. Most regulations issued by local governments were levy related and created a high-cost economy and harmed the investment climate (LPEM-FEUI 2002; Saad 2003; SMERU 2001).[14] The National Trade and Industry Chamber (Kamar Dagang dan Industri, KADIN) reported the list of more than a thousand local regulations (Peraturan Daerah, Perda) that were considered to be not business friendly (Simarmata 2002).

There is also evidence that following decentralization, some investment projects have not been implemented due to conflicting regulation between central and regional governments. For example, local government of East Nusa Tenggara approved a US$700 million investment in the cultivation of a raw material used for biofuel. The central government opposed the project, arguing that it could have an adverse impact on national foreign policy (Oktaviani and Irawan 2009).

This problem highlights the need for clearly separated regulatory authorites among different levels of government to prevent any overlap or conflict between regulations.

In addition to unclear business regulations, corruption was another issue that arose from decentralization (Patunru and Wardhani 2008). Henderson and Kuncoro (2004) argue that the significant additional bureaucracy created by the need to increase local fiscal capacity opened the opportunity for corruption. In addition, they found that the local districts with high transfers from central government were less likely to impose red tape. Their study also found that the largest amounts of red tape appeared in the form of licenses, which were imposed in two areas: the application and monitoring processes. Business owners or managers bribe the officials to "ease up" the application process and/or to avoid spending a significant amount of time to deal with a harassment visit by the local officials in the monitoring process.

With several exceptions, costly, lengthy, and complicated procedures to start a business remain with decentralization. But there is now significant variation across locations. For example, according to a KPPOD study (2007), it takes up to 108 days in Trenggalek (East Java) and 57 days in Karimun (Kepri) to obtain a Business Registration Certificate. However, some districts in Sulawesi island (Gorontalo, North Luwu, Pinrang, Luwu, and East Luwu) require only two days to issue the license. Although the evidence should be looked at more carefully due to the methodological issues, it suggests that some districts located in Eastern Indonesia have used the opportunity offered by decentralization to attract investment.[15]

While decentralization has had some adverse effect on the investment climate, it also has the potential to create competition among districts. It forces the local government to think carefully about implementing regulations that are unfriendly toward investors (Patunru and Wardhani 2008). One of the examples is local government initiatives to establish One Stop Services (OSS) (Asian Development Bank and World Bank 2005). The most striking example was that of Sragen, Central Java. In a district dominated by agricultural sectors and small and medium enterprises, the establishment of OSS in 2001 by the new head of district has significantly improved the time to obtain local licenses. This has contributed, over time, to improvements in the local economy. A study by Von Luebke (2007) argues that the leadership of mayor or *bupati* as the head district plays a key role in introducing a business-friendly attitude to the district level. His study shows a strong positive impact of leadership of the head district toward local regulations, license administration, and fairness in public tendering process. On the other hand, there is a strong negative impact toward bribery related to permits.

Recent Developments

Law on SEZs

Indonesia has a long history of developing a "special zone," with Batam island (and later Bintan and Karimun) as one important example. The development of Batam dated back to 1971 when Batam was designated as an industrial zone by a presidential decree. To facilitate the industrial development, the Batam Industrial Development Authority (BIDA) was established. In November 1978, Batam was declared as a bonded zone to support the development of export-oriented industries. At the end of 1970s, a master development plan was introduced for Batam to be developed as an industrial, commercial, and tourism centre in Indonesia.

On October 29 1989, the law on the management of industrial estates by private companies was passed. About 1,700 hectares of land was allocated for eight industrial estates in Batam. By 1990, the scope and geographical coverage of regional development extended beyond Batam to neighboring islands and provinces. The whole of Batam Islands were declared a Bonded Zone in 1992. In July 2005, the status of the Batam Industrial Bonded Zone, together with Bintan Industrial Estate and Karimun Industrial Cooperation Zone, were upgraded to "Bonded Zone Plus" to give investors more legal certainty. The Minister of Finance confirmed Batam's status as a "Bonded Zone Plus" and issued a package of reforms to improve the island's investment climate. This was supported further by the signing of a framework agreement between Singapore and Indonesia on Economic Cooperation in the islands of Batam, Bintan, and Karimun in June 2006. In June 2007, Batam was granted Free Trade Zone status while Bintan and Karimun were granted enclave status (Wong and Ng 2009).

After a long process and consultation, Law No. 39 of 2009 on SEZs was passed by parliament on September 15, 2009. Following the introduction of the new law, government, through Coordinating Minister of Economic Affairs, promised that the implementing regulation required to support the law would be released within 100 days (Tempo 2009). Later, 48 districts applied to be selected for SEZs, including some districts in eastern Indonesia. In June 2010, the Coordinating Minister of Economic Affairs announced that only five SEZs would be developed and would be part of the Economic Corridors plan designed by the government (see below). The groundwork for these SEZs is expected to be ready in 2014 (Republika 2010). Currently, government is in the process of incorporating development of SEZs into a broader development agenda of Economic Corridors discussed in the next section.

Master Plan of Economic Corridors

In May 2011 the president launched a new Master Plan for the Acceleration and Expansion of Indonesian Economic Growth, 2011–2025 (Master Plan Percepatan dan Perluasan Pembangunan Ekonomi Indonesia, MP3EI). Among the key challenges the program was designed to address was the continuing development gap between western and eastern Indonesia.[16] As such, the program is designed to promote investments outside of Java and improve the integration of western and eastern Indonesia. The main features of the new Master Plan are summarized in figure 8.1.

The Master Plan focuses on development of six economic corridors (covering 8 programs[17] and 22 activities) and the national connectivity to spur inclusive growth. The economic corridors approach is intended to build a more integrated

Figure 8.1 Master Plan for the Acceleration and Expansion of Indonesian Economic Growth

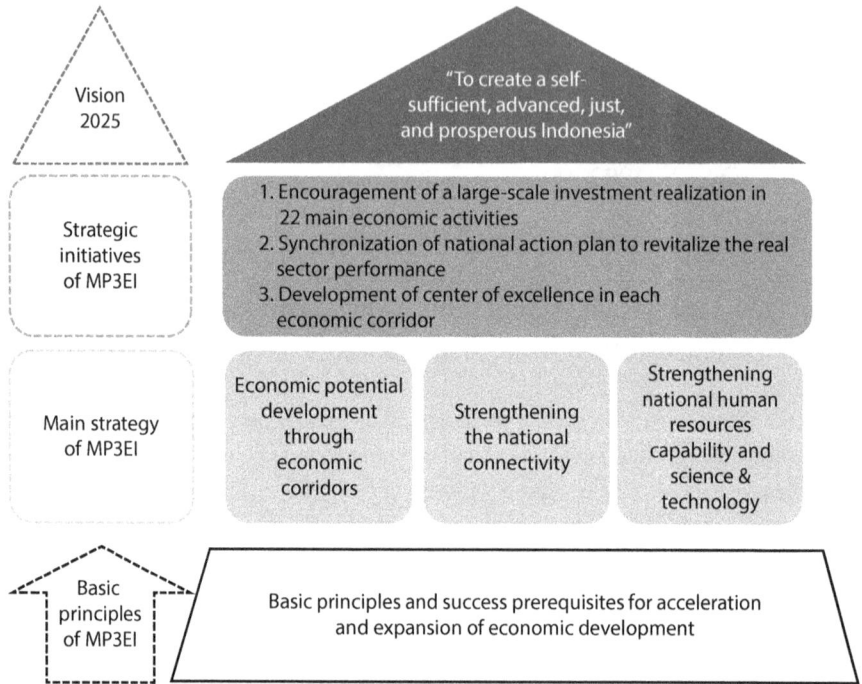

Source: Coordinating Ministry for Economic Affairs 2011.
Note: MP3EI = Master Plan Percepatan dan Perluasan Pembangunan Ekonomi Indonesia.

development across Indonesia, including the lagging regions. Learning from the failure of previous programs to reduce economic gap between and within regions, the economic corridors approach is intended to connect lagging regions to appropriate corridors and economic activities. The six economic corridors and their associated regions are as follows:

1. *Sumatra:* Plantations Production and Processing Center and National Energy Reserve.
2. *Java:* National Industry and Services Booster.
3. *Kalimantan:* Mining Production and Processing Center and National Energy Reserve.
4. *Bali and Nusa Tenggara:* National Tourism Gate and National Food Support.
5. *Sulawesi:* National Plantation, Agriculture, and Fisheries Production and Processing Center.
6. *Papua:* Abundant Natural Resources Processing and Prosperous Human Resources.

The new Master Plan is considered to be a bold attempt to bring provincial and local government, business leaders, and state-owned enterprises into one integrated national development framework. It also provides for better coordination of line ministries and regional governments and facilitates putting pressure on them to support industrial and infrastructure development. In addition, the Master Plan outlines a strategic direction for investors, who need to know where the government's industrial emphasis will be in the next 15 years. However, the key to a successful implementation will always be execution and enforcement.

The private sector and opinion makers have given the program a mixed response. Government has made a significant effort to involve the private sector and academics in preparation of the Master Plan. As a result, the private sector, as represented by KADIN and APINDO, support the introduction of the Master Plan. However, there are concerns from the private sector and opinion makers about implementation. Specifically, the issue of financing and how to strategically allocate funding to the highest potential areas has been mentioned on several occasions (Seputar Indonesia 2011). Indonesia has been trying to boost investment in its badly needed infrastructure through a series of Infrastructure Summits, but these have failed to attract significant investment.

More attention should be given to the importance of regional government planning in fostering an enabling business climate, because uncoordinated regional and national policies can frustrate efforts of the central government to promote investments throughout the country. Moreover, it is important in the early stage of implementation to identify the institutional arrangements required for high-level coordination between the different ministries and agencies involved in the design and implementation of the reforms. The Master Plan will also require in-depth monitoring by a team that has the mandate to make adjustments if necessary (World Bank 2011).

Moreover, regulatory reform is needed to solve current problems related to investment climate. The government has listed a number of regulations that have become bottlenecks for investment and has promised to revise those regulations (Kompas 2011b). Some regulations would require approval from parliament, which could in some cases take years to conclude. One example is Law No. 13 of 2003 on Labor, revisions to which have been in discussion for at least eight years.

Finally, the nature of the political system in Indonesia has also become a concern for the implementation of Master Plan. Some opinion makers argued that the private sector should push government on the implementation up until election 2014, because the newly elected president might not fully support implementation.[18] Academics and opinion makers also raise the possibility of a new administration simply using the Master Plan as a tool for business and political interests, while abandoning the idea of inclusive development and narrowing development gap.

Conclusions

The Indonesian government has introduced and implemented various policies over the past four decades to reduce the development gap between leading and lagging regions. Common to all of these programs—from the first in 1967 to the most recent launched in 2011—has been a focus on *attracting investment* to lagging regions, rather than focusing on trade integration or on broader issues of growth. Overall, the efforts have failed to attract significant investment to truly lagging regions, especially in Eastern Indonesia. As figure 8.2 illustrates, absolute levels of investment are dramatically higher in Java and, secondly, Sumatra and Kalimantan, than in more peripheral provinces. On a per capita basis, Kalimantan, buoyed by the mining sector, has seen higher levels of investment with Java following (although for foreign direct investment [FDI], Java remains far ahead of Kalimantan, even on a per capita basis). As seen elsewhere in the statistics on trade, Sulawesi appears to be pulling away from the eastern islands, which remain the true lagging region of Indonesia.

Figure 8.2 Average Realized Investments by Island Group: Three-Year Averages, 1997–2010

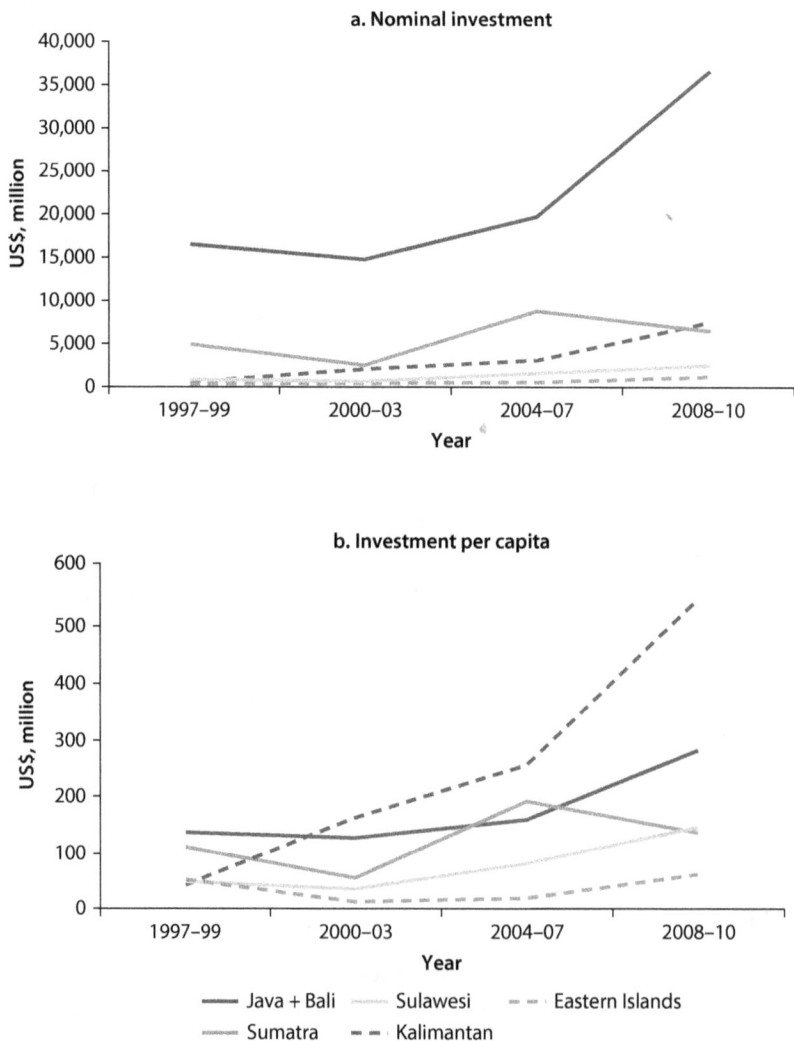

Note: FDI = foreign direct investment.

One reason these efforts failed to stimulate investment in lagging regions is likely the excessive focus on narrow and insufficiently fiscal incentives. For the most part, the incentives regime offered only one additional year of tax breaks for firms investing in lagging regions. The underlying assumption of such an approach is that fixed costs and/or risks of investment would be higher than in core regions, but that profitability in "steady state" operations would not be appreciably different. Given the gaps in infrastructure, worker skills, and the investment in climate in many of the country's lagging regions, however, it is highly unlikely that firms—particularly those competing in national and international markets—could operate effectively.

But the problems with Indonesia's lagging region policies go beyond the overemphasis on fiscal incentives. The KAPET program, at least in design, is an example of a targeted and comprehensive approach to improving the investment and business operating environment in lagging regions. After 15 years of implementation, however, government has recently acknowledged the program's failure. This is due to a range of factors, including, poor infrastructure, lack of coordination among institutions, low capacity of local government, lack of consistency between policy and implementation, and insufficient financial support.

An alternative potential opportunity for addressing the regional gap arose with the "big bang" decentralization of 2001, which gave local authorities much greater control not only over development policies, but, critically, also over the local investment climate. Overall, however, early evidence suggests that the local investment climate has worsened following decentralization. This is the result of poor design and implementation of local regulations, and of overlap and coordination problems between national and local regulations. With a few exceptions, most local government have not used the opportunity offered by decentralization to facilitate an improved local investment climate and to attract greater investment in the regions. In 2008, the central government issued a regulation that push local governments to provide local incentives for investment. However, the implementation of this regulation has not yet been seen as a significant incentive by investors.

Another path to boost investment in the regions, initiated by the long history of development of Batam, is the Law on SEZs, passed in 2009. Despite much interest from district governments, recent updates signaled that development of SEZs will be delayed and incorporated into the broader agenda of the Master Plan for Economic Transformation. The government's recently launched Master Plan focuses on development of six economic corridors and national connectivity to spur inclusive growth. Although it is considered to be a strategic move to attract investment in lagging regions, the key to a successful implementation will always be good execution and enforcement.

Notes

1. Specifically, exemptions included: exemption from corporate taxes on profits; exemption from dividend taxes on some of the accrued profits paid to shareholders; exemption from corporate taxes on profits accruing to capital subtraction of taxes and

other financial obligations in Indonesia that are reinvested in the enterprise in Indonesia; exemption from import duties on fixed assets such as machinery, tools, or instruments needed; and exemption from capital stamp duties. Relief incentives were also granted, including: corporate tax relief through a proportional rate of not more than 50 percent for a period not exceeding five years after expiration of the exemption period; offsetting losses suffered during the period of exemption; and allowing accelerated depreciation of fixed assets.

2. Finance Minister Decree No. 747/KMK.04/1990.

3. The 13 provinces are East Kalimantan, West Kalimantan, South Kalimantan, Central Kalimantan, North Sulawesi, South Sulawesi, Central Sulawesi, Southeast Sulawesi, East Nusa Tenggara, West Nusa Tenggara, Timor-Leste, Maluku, and Irian Jaya.

4. Government Regulation No. 34 of 1994 on Tax Incentive for Investment in Selected Sectors and or Selected Regions.

5. Government Regulation No. 45 of 1996 on Income Tax for Business Units in Certain Industries.

6. Source: presentation of Coordinating Minister of Economic Affairs and Minister of Trade to private sectors (KADIN and Foreign Chambers).

7. Personal meeting with Minister of Finance as Head of Working Group 4 on Incentive, National Team for the Enhancement of Export and Investment 2008.

8. Specifically, whereas the previous regulation required industry to employ at least 1,000 workers to receive incentive, the new criteria would be as follows: (1) for labor-intensive industries, an initial investment of 50 billion rupiah and employment of at least 300 workers; and (2) for capital-intensive industries, an initial investment of 100 billion rupiah and employment of at least 100 workers (Seputar Indonesia 2011).

9. Later replaced by Presidential Decree No. 150 of 2000.

10. http://hdr.undp.org/en/statistics/hdi/.

11. Specifically: net income tax reduction of 30 percent of total invested capital; flexibility in applying depreciation and/or accelerated amortization; fiscal loss compensation (loss carry forward) for up to 10 consecutive years; a 10 percent income tax on dividend for foreign taxpayers.

12. Who was, later in 2011, appointed as the new Minister of Trade.

13. Media interview with Ministry of Finance and Head of BKPM (Kompas 2011a, 2011b).

14. For further discussion on initial experiences and problems of decentralization, see Usman (2001).

15. Note, however, that according to Subnational Doing Business in Indonesia, the best-performing city within Indonesia represented in the survey would rank in 117th and 143rd positions globally (if they were countries) for cost and day to start a business, respectively (World Bank and IFC 2010).

16. Other key challenges the program is designed to address are lack of value added and manufacturing, poor infrastructure, low-quality human capital, rapid urbanization, and climate change (CMEA 2011).

17. The eight programs are: Agriculture, Mining, Energy, Industrial, Marine, Tourism, Telecommunication, and Development of Strategic Areas.

18. These observations came from personal discussion with Dr. Chatib Basri of the National Economic Committee, and from discussions with members of private sector business associations.

References

Asian Development Bank and World Bank. 2005. "Improving the Investment Climate in Indonesia." Joint Report. Asian Development Bank, Indonesia.

Azis, I. J. 1990. "'Inpres' Role in the Reduction of Interregional Disparity." *Asian Economic Journal* 4 (2): 3–27.

Balisacan, A. M., E. M. Pernia, and A. Asra. 2002. "Revisiting Growth and Poverty Reduction in Indonesia: What Do Subnational Data Show?" ERD Working Paper Series 25, Economics and Research Department, Asian Development Bank, Manila.

Business Indonesia. 2008. "Insentif PP No.1/2007 Segera Dikaji Ulang." Jakarta, January 3. http://pajak.com/index.php?option=com_content&task=view&id=19&Itemid=48.

———. 2010. "Menperin: Hapus saja PP 62/2008." Jakarta, February 23. http://www .ikpi.or.id/content/menperin-hapus-saja-pp-622008.

Coordinating Ministry of Economic Affairs (CMEA). 2011. *Masterplan for Acceleration and Expansion of Indonesia Economic Development.* CMEA, Jakarta.

Henderson, J. V., and A. Kuncoro. 2004. "Corruption in Indonesia." NBER Working Paper 10674, National Bureau of Economic Research, Cambridge, MA.

Hill, H., B. P. Resosudarmo, and Y. Vidyattama. 2008. "Indonesia's Changing Economic Geography." *Bulletin of Indonesian Economic Studies* 44 (3): 407–35.

Ikhsan, M. I. 2006. "FDI and Tax Incentives in Indonesia." Paper presented at the International Symposium on FDI and Corporate Taxation: Experiences of Asian Countries and Issues in the Global Economy, Hitotsubashi University, Tokyo, February 17–18, 2006.

Komite Pemantauaan Pelaksanaan Otonomi Daerah (Committee Monitoring the Implementation of Regional Autonomy, KPPOD). 2007. *Daya Saing Investasi Kabupaten/Kota di Indonesia* [Investment Competitiveness of Indonesian Districts]. KPPOD, Jakarta.

Kompas. 2008. "Bidang Berfasilitas PPh Bertambah" [More Sectors Receiving Income Tax Facility]. Jakarta, October 7. http://www.kompas.com.

———. 2011a. "Hanya Rp 27, 5 Triliun: Kapet Minim Himpun Investasi" [Only 27.5 Trillion: KAPET Collect Minimum Investment]. Jakarta, February 23. http://www .kompas.com.

———. 2011b. "Tak Jelas Dasar Hukum: Kapet Jalan Ditempat" [Unclear Legal Basis: KAPET Stagnant]" Jakarta, February 23. http://www.kompas.com.

Lembaga Penyelidikan Ekonomi dan Masyarakat (Institute for Economic and Social Research, LPEM FEUI). 2002. *Construction of Regional Index of Doing Business.* Universitas Indonesia, Jakarta.

Ministry of Public Works. 2004. *Evaluasi Kinerja dan Rencana Penanganan Kawasan Pengembangan Ekonomi Terpadu* [Performance Evaluation and Management Plan for Integrated Economic Development Zones]. Directorate General of Spatial Planning, Ministry of Public Works, Jakarta.

Oktaviani, R., and T. Irawan. 2009. "Does Decentralization Foster a Good Trade and Investment Climate? Early Lessons from Indonesian Decentralization." Policy Brief 20, Asia-Pacific Research and Training Network on Trade, Bangkok, Thailand. http:// www.unescap.org/tid/artnet.

Pangestu, M., and B. Bora. 1996. "Evolution of Liberalization Policies Affecting Investment Flows in the Asia Pacific." Policy Discussion Paper 96/01. Centre for International Economic Studies, University of Adelaide, Adelaide, Australia.

Patunru, A. R., and S. B. Wardhani. 2008. "Political Economy of Local Investment Climates: A Review of the Indonesian Literature." PAPI background paper for the Political Economy of the Local Investment Climate in Indonesia Project, Institute of Development Studies, Brighton, U.K. http://www2.ids.ac.uk/gdr/cfs/pdfs/ PatunruLitRev.pdf.

Republika. 2010. "Pemerintah Hanya Prioritaskan Lima Kawasan Ekonomi Khusus" [Government Prioritizes Five Special Economic Zones]. Jakarta, June 22. http://www .republika.co.id.

Saad, I. 2003. "Implementasi Otonomi Daerah Sudah Mengarah Pada Penciptaan Distorsi dan High Cost Economy" [The Implementation of Regional Autonomy Leads to Distortion Creation and High Cost Economy]. Working Paper, SMERU Research Institute, Jakarta.

Samosir, A. P., and T. Wibowo. 2004. "Analisis Efektivitas Pemberian Insentif Fiscal di Kawasan Timur Indonesia (Studi kasus: KAPET Pare-pare)" [Analysis of the Effectiveness of Fiscal Incentive Program in Eastern Indonesia (Case Study: KAPET Pare-Pare)]. *Kajian Ekonomi dan Keuangan* 8 (1): 1–18.

Seputar Indonesia. 2011. "Yang Dibangun Banyak, Dana Terbatas" [Many Things Need to be Developed, Funding Limited]. Jakarta, May 30. http://www.seputar-indonesia.com.

Simarmata, R. 2002. "Regional Autonomy and the Character of Local Government Laws and Regulations: New Pressures on the Environment and Indigenous Communities." Perkumpulan Pembaharuan Hukum Berbasis Masyarakat dan Ekologis [Community and Ecological Based Society for Law Reform, HuMA], Jakarta. http://huma.or.id.

SMERU Research Institute. 2001. "Otonomi Daerah dan Iklim Usaha" (Regional Autonomy and the Business Climate). Paper presented to the Conference on Globalization, Domestic Trade and Decentralization. Organized by the Partnership for Economic Growth, the United States Agency for International Development, and Department of Industry and Trade, the Republic of Indonesia, Jakarta, April 3.

Soenandar, E. S. 2007. "Government Policy in Solving Uneven Regional Development between West and East Indonesia: Case Study on KAPET." *Economic Journal of Hokkaido University* 34: 171–92.

Tadjoeddin, Z., W. I. Suharyo, and S. Mishra. 2001. "Regional Disparity and Vertical Conflicts in Indonesia." *Journal of the Asia Pacific Economy* 6 (3): 283–304.

Tempo. 2009. "Rancangan Undang Undang Kawasan Ekonomi Disetujui" [Draft Law Approved for Economic Zones]. Jakarta, September 15. http://www.tempo.co/read/ news/2009/09/15/090198115/Rancangan-Undang-Undang-Kawasan-Ekonomi-Disetujui.

Uppal, J. S., and S. H. Budiono. 1986. "Regional Income Disparities in Indonesia." *Ekonomi dan Keuangan Indonesia* 34 (3): 287–304.

Usman, S. 2001. "Indonesia's Decentralization Policy: Initial Experiences and Emerging Problems." Working Paper 123, East Asian Bureau of Economic Research Governance, Australian National University, Canberra.

Von Luebke, C. 2007. "Local Leadership in Transition: Explaining Variation in Indonesian Subnational Government." Unpublished PhD thesis, Crawford School of Economic and Governance, Australian National University, Canberra.

Wong, P. K., and K. K. Ng. 2009. "Batam, Bintan and Karimun: Past History and Current Development Towards Being a SEZ." Working Paper, Asia Competitiveness Institute, Lee Kwan Yew School of Public Policy, National University of Singapore.

World Bank. 2011. *Indonesia Economic Quarterly June 2008: Current Challenges, Future Potential.* World Bank, Jakarta.

World Bank and International Finance Corporation. 2010. *Doing Business in Indonesia 2010: Comparing Regulations in 14 Cities and 183 Economies.* Washington, DC: World Bank and International Finance Corporation.

Wuryan, H. 1996. "Pemberian Insentif bagi Perusahaan PMA yang Melakukan Investasi di Kawasan Timur Indonesia dan Kaitannya dengan Perpajakan" [Providing Incentive for PMA Companies to Invest in Eastern Indonesia and its Relation to the Taxation]. Gema Stikubank, December, Jakarta. http://jurnal.pdii.lipi.go.id/index.php/search .html?act=tampil&id=15712&idc=72.

CHAPTER 9

Regional Development Policies in India

Aradhna Aggarwal and Prakash Singh Archa

Introduction

Achieving balanced regional development has been a critical component of India's development strategy since the commencement of planning in 1950–51. The first five-year plan noted with concern that "greater attention will have to be paid to the development of those states and regions which have remained backward" (GoI 1951, 442).

The second plan ushered in a new development phase with a well-rounded planning framework and adopted "modernization through state-led heavy industrialization" as the centerpiece of India's development strategy. However, it recognized that industrialization could benefit the economy of the country as a whole if disparities in the level of development between different regions were progressively reduced. The second plan observed:

Only by securing a balanced and co–ordinated development of the industrial and the agricultural economy in each region, can the entire country attain higher standards of living. (GoI 1956a, 48)

The concern over uneven development rose even more in the third plan. It contained a full chapter on balanced regional development, noting:

A balanced development of different parts of the country, the extension of benefits of economic progress to less developed regions, and widespread diffusion of industry are among the major aims of planned development. (GoI 1961, 44)

This spirit has been carried forward in all the subsequent plans. Economic reforms of the 1990s systematically modified the trade, industrial, investment, and macroeconomic regimes. Economic policies, institutions, and role of the state and markets all have undergone a fundamental transformation. But "balanced regional development" remains one of the declared objectives of the national policy.

In the federal democratic framework of the country, the primary responsibility for regional development policy has been assigned to the central government; the state governments largely take care of the execution and implementation. However, the nature of federalism has been changing ever since the economic reforms of the 1990s. The Industrial Policy Statement of July 1991 eliminated many of the controls earlier exercised by the central government and thereby increased the role of state governments in many areas that are critical for economic development. Further, in the most ambitious attempt at political decentralization, the government passed in 1993 a series of constitutional reforms designed to democratize and empower local political bodies—the Panchayats. This has made local administration responsible for the development needs to overcome regional and local dimensions of poverty and inequality. As a result, strategic programs driven by local and state government have grown in prominence. Several policy initiatives are being introduced at the state level to attract investment, both domestic and foreign, in order to ensure a more participatory growth. India's federal democracy has thus been increasingly characterized by regionalization of politics and decentralization of economic powers to the regional levels, with economic development at the state level being driven by subnational economic policies rather than national policies. This makes the economic performance of individual states subject to their own policies and their implementation.

Against this backdrop, this chapter *outlines the history* and *evolution* of India's industrial policy for tackling the problem of investment in lagging regions since independence. It aims to explore the effect of new regionalism on the process of regional convergence. We also try to identify the critical policy issues that need to be addressed if the slow-growing states are to achieve more respectable growth rates in future.

The rest of the chapter is organized into five sections. The next three sections examine how the substance and approaches of government policy have evolved over the years since independence, first during the period 1948–80, then in the early reform period of the 1980s, and finally in the post-reform era since 1991. We then review the findings on the evolution and nature of regional inequalities, from both existing literature and quantitative statistics. The last section offers some conclusions.

India's Highly Centralized Approach to Regional Policy: 1948–80

The first Industrial Policy Resolution of independent India was announced in 1948. But for technical and constitutional reasons, it was the industrial policy of 1956 that molded industrial development of India for the next few decades. Inspired by and based on the Mahalanobis Model[1] of import substitution driven growth, the Industrial Policy Resolution of 1956 emphasized industrial development with greater stress on heavy industries in the public sector (GoI 1956b). To tackle the issue of spatial disparities, the Industrial Policy Resolution proposed to ensure the provision of facilities such as power, water supply, transport and communications, training institutions, and so forth to areas that lagged industrially, provided the location was otherwise suitable. Following this, several state governments took steps to establish industrial areas and provide basic facilities at suitable focal points in order to encourage the growth of industries on a wider scale. In the federal framework of India, states were dependent primarily upon the central government for funding these programs. Under the Indian Constitution, the central government convenes a Finance Commission every five years to recommend principles for governing the federal-state financial relations. The general goal is to correct resource and expenditure imbalances between the center and the states, and, in particular, reduce the regional disparities in development. The Planning Commission (established in 1950)[2] has also been an important institution for the transfer of resources to promote balanced regional development. The disbursement criteria assign poorer states proportionately more funds for development than rich states (Ghosh, Marjit, and Neogi 1998).

In addition, major initiatives were launched at the national level based on the following instruments as provided for in the industrial policy:

- *Industrial licensing:* Industrial licensing is governed by the Industries (Development and Regulation) Act of 1951. Licensing was envisaged as an instrument to control the establishment and operation of private enterprises to achieve planned industrial development. In order to achieve the objective of balanced regional development, government used this as a tool to regulate the location of private sector units. The underlying message was to grant more licenses to industrial units in backward regions and at the same time control the industrial expansion of the already developed regions.

- *Location of public sector units:* Several of the large industrial complexes in the public sector were established in mineral-rich backward areas. These areas included, for instance, Hardwar, Bhilai, Kota, and Ranchi.

- *Promotion of small-scale units:* The industrial policy supported the role of cottage, village, and small-scale industries in growth and equality. Policy support included measures such as restricting production in large-scale industries, differential taxation, and direct subsidies.

- *Distribution and price policies:* To promote regional equality, the government pursued the policy of equalizing prices and controlling distribution of key production inputs throughout the country through railway freight charges and retention prices. The policy was intended to facilitate dispersal of industry by negating the locational advantages of proximity with raw materials.

The Third Five-Year Plan (1961–65) recognized the crucial role of infrastructure in economic development of backward regions to complement the location and price policies (GoI 1961, 149). To enact the plan, industrial corporations were set up in each state in the 1960s to promote industrialization in backward regions. The corporations acquired suitable tracts of land at focal points where good communications existed or could easily be developed; developed factory sites thereon; provided basic facilities like power, water, and sewage; and then offered the land for sale or on a long lease to prospective entrepreneurs. The plan also addressed the need for education and training in less-developed areas where new industrial projects were located. About

The Internal Geography of Trade • http://dx.doi.org/10.1596/978-0-8213-9893-7

346 industrial estates had been completed by the end of March 1969, as compared to 66 estates in 1960–61.

In 1965, the government set up the first industrial estate for export-oriented production when an export processing zone (EPZ) was established in Kandla in Gujarat. The site of Kandla was selected with multiple objectives, including a primary goal of developing an industrially backward region of the Kutch (Aggarwal 2004). From 1965 to 1974, this remained the only operating zone in India; another EPZ was set up in 1974 in the Santa Cruz area of Mumbai.

Finally, in order to give a further push to small industries, a Rural Industries Planning Committee was set up within the Planning Commission in 1962. Further, a centrally sponsored scheme for Rural Industries Projects was taken up in 1962–63. To start with, 45 areas were selected for intensive development of small industries in rural areas. These locations were in the states and some union territories (UTs), and each comprised 3–5 development blocks (each block with a population of 300,000–500,000). In 1965, more development areas near large-scale projects of Durgapur, Bhilai, Bhadravati, and Ranchi in lagging regions were also added. The scope of the project was extended in subsequent plans.

In 1967, the Planning Commission examined the impact of Third Five-Year Plan programs on interstate and interregional inequality, including variations in consumption, unemployment, land holding, rural investment and debt, agricultural development, educational and health facilities, roads, and so forth. In another attempt at assessment, in July 1967 the government appointed the Industrial Licensing Policy Inquiry Committee (ILPIC) to examine the operation of the licensing system in reducing regional disparities. Several scholars also undertook independent studies to analyze the central government's approach to balanced development. These studies and committees raised serious doubts about the effectiveness of the program. Major findings were as follows:

- First, the licensing system did not succeed in bolstering backward areas. Mitra (1965) found that between 1953 and 1961, 35.8 percent of the total licenses issued went to the top three industrial centers: Bombay, Calcutta, and Madras. According to the ILPIC Report (GoI 1967), the primary reason for the licensing system's ineffectiveness was that no economic criteria had been developed for the identification of backward areas.

- Second, the policy of locating large public sector enterprises in backward areas met with limited success. Contrary to the general belief, most of these location decisions were based on the economic consideration of resource availability. Yet, the large public sector enterprises could not establish linkages with the regional economies to generate multiplier effects and had only marginal impact on these economies (Goyal 1975; Nair 1980; Patnaik 1974; Prasad 1976; Sarma 1982). Some researchers found that locating large public sector firms in backward regions indeed reduced regional disparities (Gupta 1973; Pathak 1971). Alagh et al. (1983) and Sekhar (1983) found the policy to be regressive due to changes in sectoral priorities.

- The policy of induced industrialization through industrial estates also proved to be a failure due to poor infrastructural facilities. Some of the most successful estates were concentrated around the urban areas, but even those estates could not forge linkage with the regional economies (Alexander 1963; Nagia 1971; Sanghvi 1979; Sekhar 1983).

- The performance of the only EPZ in Kandla was hampered by several handicaps, including poor industrial climate in the region (GoI 1982). This was perhaps the reason that the second EPZ was set up in Mumbai, a commercial hub of India.

- The rural industries program could not be integrated with the block and the district programs. The program faced several constraints due to unavailability and high turnover of trained staff, and poor industrial and training infrastructure (GoI 1968).

- The policy of equalizing freight facilitated the location of industry near market centers rather than near the sources of raw materials (Raina 1969). In contrast to the objectives of the policy, it actually facilitated agglomeration in developed regions with large markets at the cost of backward but resource-rich regions such as Bihar, Madhya Pradesh, and Orissa, aggravating regional imbalances further.

The rather limited success of the policies of industrial dispersal led the government to constitute a study group with the Planning Commission in 1966, which asked state governments to pay special attention to the development of backward areas and coordinate their efforts with central government programs. The government also suggested 11 parameters to identify underdeveloped areas and classified the areas into five types: desert, hill, drought prone, high-density population, and tribal. In 1968, the Planning Commission formed two committees: one under the chairmanship of B. D. Pande to formulate guidelines for the identification of backward areas; and the other under the chairmanship of N. N. Wanchoo to suggest fiscal and tax concessions to encourage investment in backward areas.

The Planning Commission—in consultation with financial institutions and the state governments, and following recommendations of the Pande Committee—identified and notified 238 districts as backward during the Fourth Five-Year Plan (1969–74). This was the first systematic endeavor to identify industrially backward regions.[3] Further, following the recommendations of the Wanchoo Committee, major incentives were proposed to be offered by the central government for the promotion of industries in backward areas. These were as follows:

- concessional finance from all-India financial institutions (AIFIs)
- investment subsidy to the extent of one-tenth of the total capital cost for projects costing up to Rs 5 million both in the private and public sectors (grant of subsidy to be considered on merits)

- central transport subsidy
- deduction of income under Section 80 HH of the Income Tax Act of 1961.

Thus, the spectrum of policy instruments for influencing industrial location was broadened to include fiscal incentives during the Fourth Five-Year Plan period. State governments designed their own incentive packages. According to Godbole (1978, 79–86), there was cutthroat competition among state governments in offering concessions and incentives. Consequently, the promotional measures and concessions were not very different across states. In terms of the major initiatives undertaken, the Fourth Five-Year Plan is considered a watershed.

The Fifth Five-Year Plan (1975–79) recognized that backwardness was a long-term problem and that financial incentives needed to be reinforced by other incentives and development programs based on local strategies and participation. During this time, a majority of programs were implemented in areas of structural impoverishment, including drought-prone, Western Ghats hill, northeast, and tribal areas. The main thrust of the Industrial Policy Statement of 1977 had been on effective promotion of cottage and small industries that were widely dispersed in rural areas and small towns. The scheme of "District Industrial Centre"—offering a package of single-window customs clearance, financial assistance, and tax incentives—was conceived for the promotion of small and cottage industries in backward regions. In each district, one agency was set up to deal with all requirements of small and village industries. The central government also took steps to discourage more industrial growth in developed areas. Its Industrial Policy Statement of 1977 stipulated that no more licenses would be granted to industrial units in and around metropolitan cities, or in urban areas with a population of 500,000 and above. Furthermore, the government decreed that industrial units that did not require licenses would be denied financial assistance if they located in these areas. It was also decided that the large industries would be provided assistance in order to shift from congested metropolitan cities to backward areas. Finally, special allocations were made to reinforce the programs for hill, tribal, and drought-prone areas.

Cautious Deregulation and Export Promotion: 1980–91

The early 1980s marked the beginning of deregulation of industries. The government initiated the process of relaxation in the licensing regime, albeit cautiously. In the run up to the Sixth Five-Year Plan (1980–85), a National Committee for the Development of Backward Areas (NCDBA) was constituted under the chairmanship of B. Sivaraman in 1981 to analyze the performance of government programs, in particular subsidies and concessions for combating regional imbalance. The Sivaraman Committee (GoI 1981b) found that concessional finance and subsidies had not been a significant motivating factor in persuading entrepreneurs to locate their units in backward districts, due to the lack of integrated planning of related facilities and coordination between the different agencies involved. These programs had benefited a small number of districts, mostly near the industrially developed states. Of the total subsidy disbursed between 1971 and 1976, as much as 59 percent was directed to developed states. Of the total subsidy granted to developed states, more than one-fifth was cornered by Maharashtra alone. According to Dua (1980), more than 55 percent of the capital investment subsidy granted until 1978–79 went to only 25 eligible districts of well-off states. It was also observed that financial assistance provided by nonbank financial institutions were primarily accessed by backward regions in the developed states. This may have been the result of the Planning Commission's insistence on the availability of a minimum level of infrastructure in the district for concessional finance (Awasthi 1991). Plausibly, the policy helped reduce intraregional inequalities, but its role in addressing interregional disparities was not evident.

The Committee also highlighted weaknesses in the coordination of planning at the local level with poorly developed and indifferently staffed administrative systems. It observed that improvements in local planning and coordination were essential if the special programs were to succeed, and emphasized the importance of coordinating central and state planning. In a move toward local planning, the Committee recommended the concept of "Growth Centres" in various backward regions. Under this concept, an industrial development authority within the region would have the charter to develop and provide necessary infrastructural support, as well as to mobilize funds from The Industrial Development Bank of India (IDBI) Bank Ltd.,[4] the Housing and Urban Development Corporation (HUDCO),[5] and other financial institutions. State governments were given responsibility for providing requisite infrastructure at these selected locations. The underlying message was that the central and state governments would have to work together to promote industrial development (GoI 1981a). States would need to build in preferences in their own concession schemes for areas identified as industrially backward in the central schemes. The concept of Growth Centres could not be implemented during the Sixth Five-Year Plan. However, in the early 1980s, the government decided to give overriding priority to backward areas in granting industrial licensing for industry dispersal. A list of "no industry" districts was introduced in March 1982. In April 1983, the government also introduced a scheme of assistance to subsidize infrastructural development in these areas (Bandyopadhyay and Datta 1989).

Further, the Industrial Policy Statement of 1980, in coherence with the Sixth Five-Year Plan, addressed the need for a more vibrant and dynamic industrial environment, including an increased role for small-scale industry in the growth process. Steps were taken to improvise an overall culture of small-scale industry, which involved streamlining of licensing procedures, allowing for automatic growth beyond the licensed capacity, and raising the cap on the investment limits. Policies helping small-scale industries were a reaffirmation of government commitment to growth with equity, and a continuation of previous industrial policy, including restraints on more industrial development in metropolitan cities and large urban areas.

To reduce migration from small towns and rural areas to cities in search of better employment opportunities, the Integrated Development of Small and Medium Towns (IDSMT) program was initiated in 1979–80 with central government sponsorship. IDSMT aimed to further support decentralized economic growth in small and medium-size towns.

An important policy initiative during the 1980s was expansion of the export-oriented sector. India's trade balance situation had started deteriorating in the late 1970s, and by 1981–82, the trade deficit had become unmanageable. In 1981–82, it was placed at Rs 5.9 billion. India's share in world exports had declined sharply from 2.42 percent in 1948 to 0.37 percent by 1981. To promote exports, the government launched a new scheme of "100 percent export oriented units" (EOUs) in 1981 as a complement to the EPZ scheme. EOUs can be established anywhere in India. They function under the administrative control of the Development Commissioner of the EPZ (now called special economic zones, SEZs), whose jurisdiction is established by the Ministry of Commerce. EOUs undertake to export their entire production, except a fixed percentage of sales in the domestic tariff area (DTA) as may be permissible under the policy. EOUs can locate their units in places of their choice, subject to the overall location policy of the central government. By March 31, 1988, there were 111 EOUs across the country. Of them, 67 (60 percent) were in five states: Andhra Pradesh, Gujarat, Karnataka, Tamil Nadu, and Maharashtra. These states also accounted for two-thirds of total EOU exports. All but one (Andhra Pradesh) were industrially advanced.

In 1982, the government set up a task force on free trade zones and EOUs (GoI 1982) to recommend measures to improve the functioning of EPZs and EOUs. The task force recommended that in a country of India's size, it was important to establish four or five more EPZs in addition to EOUs, to provide a boost to the country's export promotion efforts. Following the report, in 1984, four new EPZs were set up at Noida (northern India), Falta (eastern India), Cochin (southern India), and Chennai (southeast India). Thereafter, Visakhapatnam EPZ in Andhra Pradesh EPZ (southeast India) was established in 1989 (it started functioning in 1994). Thus, this period witnessed establishment of five zones. With the exception of Chennai, all were established in backward regions.

The Seventh Five-Year Plan (1985–90) acknowledged the need to consolidate development achievements, and to initiate policies to prepare Indian industry to respond effectively to emerging challenges, including new political power dynamics and growing international development. The industrial policy of 1988 exempted all but 26 industries from licensing. (The exempted industries, however, were subject to investment and location-specific limitations.) The delicensing facility was barred for industries within 50 kilometers of cities with population more than 250,000, 30 kilometes from cities with population between 150,000 and 250,000, and 15 kilometers from cities with population between 0.75 and 1.5 million outside the municipal limits of all other cities and towns. The Industrial Policy Statement of 1988 also considered promoting nonpolluting industries by delicensing new units with up to Rs 250 million investment in nonpolluting industries (such as electronics, computer software, and printing) and nonbackward/metropolitan areas.

The process of delicensing reduced the policy space for the national government to address the issue of regional imbalance. However, the Seventh Five-Year Plan did express concern over growing regional disparity and reiterated its emphasis on the promotion of industrialization in backward areas. To achieve its stated objective of "industrialization with regional balance," the plan emphasized the role of infrastructure development. The Industrial Policy Statement of 1988 announced the "Growth Centre" Scheme simultaneously with the NCDBA. Under the scheme, 71 Growth Centres were proposed to be set up throughout the country. These Growth Centres were to be endowed with basic infrastructure facilities, including power, water, telecommunications, and banking services, to attract and encourage new industry. By 2002, 68 Growth Centres were in operation. As of March 31, 2002, the total fund released under the scheme was a little more than 32 percent of the approved amount of Rs 19,888 billion. Of this amount, the central government contributed 35.4 percent, the state government contributed around 44 percent, and the balance was raised from banks and financial institutions. The scheme failed to attract enough industrial entrepreneurs, due to the inability of project authorities to develop the infrastructure facilities, and thus did not generate significant employment. According to a study conducted by the Planning Commission, by March 2002, the land acquired was 14,959 hectares, well short of a target of 23,197 hectares. Similarly, 3,232 (31.2 percent) plots were actually developed and allotted as against the target of 10,367 plots; 1,733 plots (53.6 percent) were occupied (GoI 2011). Accessibility of other physical infrastructure for the Growth Centres was also lagging. Only 24 Growth Centres had been provided water connections for industrial purposes, and only nine were provided water connections for domestic purposes. There was also insufficient development of other infrastructure, such as drainage facilities, power distribution, street lights, and telecom facilities. Finally, 385 units out of 837 (46 percent) were reported to be closed or otherwise nonviable.

The Hill Area Development Program (HADP), in operation since the inception of the Fifth Five-Year Plan, was redesigned in the Seventh Five-Year Plan to meet the aim of balanced regional development. The improved program provided support for the growth of industries suited to the hill area, such as electronics, watchmaking, optical glass, and collapsible furniture, as well as cottage industries like carpet manufacture and handlooms. To accelerate the pace of industrial development, the central government declared the whole northeastern region as industrially backward and brought it under the purview of the Central Investment Subsidy Scheme at the maximum permissible rate. The transport subsidy for raw materials and end products was also made available at 75 percent and covered all modes of transport.

Period of Economic Reforms: 1991 to the Present

A marked change in development strategy took place in 1991. Focus shifted from an inward-oriented, centrally planned, heavy industrialization to export-led, private sector–driven industrial growth. Although the process of change was initiated in the early 1980s and was somewhat accelerated in the mid-1980s, it was not until 1991 that the government signaled a systemic shift to a more open economy with greater reliance upon market forces; a larger role for the private sector, including foreign investment; and a restructuring of the role of government. The Industrial Policy Statement of 1991 aimed at attaining international competitiveness and maintaining a sustained growth in productivity and gainful employment. It emphasized entrepreneurship, development of technology through investment in research and development and technology transfers, dismantling of the regulatory system leading to increased competitiveness, and development of the financial sector to increase availability of capital at an unregulated rate.

To achieve these objectives, the Industrial Policy Statement of 1991 announced major policy changes, such as reducing industrial licensing, relaxing industrial location policy, encouraging private sector initiatives in core industries (which were so far reserved for the public sector), and allowing entry of large enterprises into the small-scale industry sector under certain conditions. The policy did not lose sight of regional disparities and noted that "The spread of industrialisation to backward areas of the country will be actively promoted through appropriate incentives, institutions and infrastructure investments" (GoI 1991, 2). However, the process of liberalization has restricted national policy space in terms of the number of available instruments due to decontrols, a larger role for private investment, and emphasis on fiscal discipline. The approach of the Finance Commission, while defining the distribution criteria and principles for distributing grants, also changed with a focus on fiscal reforms and fiscal discipline. A Reserve Bank of India (RBI) study observes that the degree of equalization effect was the highest in the case of the Eleventh Finance Commission of India (2000–05); thereafter it has been declining continuously (RBI 2011). In view of the limited availability of the regulatory tools of industrial location, the central government has adopted a targeted approach to address the problem of regional imbalance with a focus on bolstering certain regions and sectors designated as target groups. A greater role has been assigned to state governments for the creation of the right conditions for rapid growth, and for attracting private sector investment. Thus the two major features of the policy are (1) a targeted approach (by region and sector) at the national level, and (2) the increasingly important role of subnational strategies. These are discussed in more detail below.

Targeted Approach by Region and Sector
The Northeast
The northeast region of India is characterized by climatic and biological diversity and ecologically complex environmental characteristics. In terms of socioeconomic characteristics, the region has the problem of a low level of accessibility.

The scope for land development is restricted, there are rich water resources and hydro potential, and it is ethnically and culturally diverse. In addition, the region has geopolitical complexity, as it shares boarders with China, Myanmar, Bhutan, and Bangladesh directly and gives access to other Association of Southeast Asian Nations (ASEAN) countries also. Considering the strategic position of the region in protecting India's political interests and harnessing natural resources, in 1997, government approved the North East Industrial Policy (NEIP) (GoI 1997) primarily to develop the industrial infrastructure in the region. In general, NEIP measures included the promotion of Growth Centres, subsidies, fiscal incentives, and relaxation in licensing and other rules. Other highlights of NEIP included the following:

- central government assistance for the promotion of growth centres, subject to a ceiling of Rs 150 million extension of the Transport Subsidy Scheme for seven years—up to March 31, 2007
- designation of the North East Development Financial Corporation (NEDFI) as a nodal agency for release of transport subsidy in northeastern states
- conversion of the Growth Centres and Integrated Infrastructure Development Centres (IIDCs) into total tax free zones for a period of 10 years from the commencement of production
- capital investment subsidies for industries located in Growth Centres
- setting up of dedicated branches/counters of commercial banks and NEDFI
- an interest subsidy of 3 percent on working capital loans
- extension of similar benefits to the new industrial units or their substantial expansions in other Growth Centres/IIDCs/industrial estates/parks/EPZs set up by states in any zone
- expansion of the Prime Minister's *Rozgar Yojana* [Universal Rural Employment] scheme to cover areas of horticulture, piggery, poultry, fishing, small tea gardens, and so forth so as to cover all economically viable activities
- promotion and strengthening of small and micro village enterprises
- strengthening the Weaver's Service Centres in the northeast and the Indian Institute of Handloom Technology at Guwahati so that technology and training support could be provided to the weavers
- provision of a new design center for development of handicrafts to upgrade the skill of artisans.

In 2007, the state of Sikkim was included in NEIP (GoI 2007a), which earlier covered the states of Arunachal Pradesh, Assam, Manipur, Meghalaya, Mizoram, Nagaland, and Tripura. NEIP of 2007 carried forward most of the provisions of the earlier industrial policy for the region. Fiscal incentives were extended to cover more industries, including the following:

- hotels (not below the two-star category)
- adventure and leisure sports including ropeways
- medical and health services, including nursing homes with a minimum capacity of 25 beds and old-age homes

- vocational training institutes such as institutes for hotel management, catering and food crafts, entrepreneurship development, nursing and paramedical, civil aviation–related training, fashion, design, and industrial training
- IT-related training centers and IT hardware units
- biotechnology industry
- power generating industries.

To establish a monitoring mechanism for implementation of NEIP 2007, a High-Level Committee and Advisory Committee would be established. The committees would be chaired by the Department of Industrial Policy and Promotion Secretary, and members would include secretaries of the Ministries/Departments of Revenue, the Department of Development of North Eastern Region, Banking and Insurance, a representative of Planning Commission, the Chairman and Managing Director of NEDFI, and other major stakeholders, including the industry associations of the northeastern region. In addition, an Oversight Committee would be constituted and chaired by the Minister of Union Commerce and Industry, with industry ministers of northeastern states as its members.

Since northeast India is a natural bridge between India and southeast Asia, economic integration with its transnational neighbors is expected to open up new opportunities for the region in particular and the nation as whole. To harness more benefits in terms of trade and to improve infrastructure in the region, India under its "look east" policy concluded a number of bilateral and multilateral projects, aimed at enhancing connectivity between the northeast region and southeast Asia. The first outcome of the "look east" policy was the Indo-Myanmar Trade Agreement, signed on January 31, 1994.[6] Efforts have also been underway to improve infrastructure, particularly road links, as well as a rail link from Jiribam in Manipur to Hanoi in Vietnam, passing through Myanmar. India and Myanmar have also recently agreed on the Multi–Modal Transit Transport Facility. To start cross-border trade, the agreement initially identified 22 products, mostly agricultural and primary commodities produced in the trading countries. In 2001, more products were added to the list of tradable items. As a result of India's trade with bordering countries, the northeast has seen dramatic expansion, with its share of Indian exports going up almost five times from 1.7 percent in 1992–93 to 8 percent in 2003–04.

Jammu and Kashmir

With a view to accelerating industrial development in the state of Jammu and Kashmir, the Central Capital Investment Subsidy Scheme was initiated for industrial units in 2002 and remains in force up to and inclusive of June 2012. Under the provision of the scheme, interest subsidies would be provided on working capital loans for industrial units. The grant or subsidy under the scheme is available to the following types of units:

- all industrial units in the Growth Centres approved for Jammu and Kashmir

- new industrial units or existing units on their substantial expansion in Growth Centres or IIDCs
- industrial estates, EPZs, and commercial estates set up by the state.

Himachal Pradesh and Uttarakhand

To attract investment to the industrial sector for Himachal Pradesh and Uttarakhand, both of which are Special Category States,[7] tax and excise concessions were announced in 2002. To qualify for the incentives, the industry must satisfy the condition of having environmentally friendly production processes and should generate employment for the local people and use local resources. The incentives provided under the scheme were as follows:

- Commercial production gets up to 100 percent exemption from excise duty for a period of 10 years from the date production commences.
- Commercial production gets a 100 percent exemption from income tax for an initial period of five years. Thereafter, companies get a 30 percent income tax exemption and entities other than companies get a 25 percent exemption for a further period of five years. These exemptions apply to new industrial and existing industrial units set up in Growth Centres, IIDCs, industrial estates, EPZs, and themed industrial parks (food processing parks, software technology parks, and so forth).
- All new units in the notified location get a capital investment subsidy, as do existing units on their substantial expansion, as defined.
- Growth Centres are promoted with central government assistance.
- IIDCs get financial support.
- Handlooms get special assistance from the Ministry of Textiles.
- Food processing industries get special assistance from the Ministry of Agro and Rural Industries.
- Small-scale industries receive various incentives, including exemptions from excise duties and licensing registration controls.

Small-Scale Sector

The government has the long-standing and consistent policy of encouraging small-scale units to improve their competitive capacity compared to large manufacturing units. Thus, in 1978, the government provided major relief by granting a full exemption from central excise duties on a specified output until 1986, after which only units having turnover less than Rs 20 million were eligible for concessions.

The central government's 1995–96 budget increased the limit further from Rs 20 million turnover to Rs 30 million for a small-scale industry to be eligible for exemption from excise duty. The current turnover excise tax exemption limit is Rs 40 million. Initially, the prerequisite for receiving the excise duty exemption was that the small industry should be registered with the State Directorate of Industries or Development Commissioner (Small-Scale Industries). In 1994, the registration prerequisite was also abolished. Small industries are also exempt from maintaining any statutory records for excise purposes (GoI 2007b).

Micro, Small, and Medium Enterprises

In 2006, the government passed the Micro, Small, and Medium Enterprises Development Act to facilitate promotion, development, and enhancing competitiveness of these enterprises. The act contains the following provisions:

- establishment of specific funds for promotion
- technologies and support for quality upgrading, marketing support, and support for entrepreneurial and managerial development for enhancing competitiveness
- progressive credit policies and practices
- preference in government procurements for products and services of micro and small enterprises
- simplification of the process of closure of business.

The RBI has issued guidelines to public sector banks to ensure 20 percent year-on-year growth in credit to the micro, small, and medium enterprises. Government has provided grants to the Small Industries Development Bank of India to augment its portfolio risk fund, and thereby to scale up and strengthen its credit operations for micro enterprises (GoI 2007b).

The Role of Subnational Strategies

Liberalization in India has comprised both deregulation and changes in the federal democratic framework, with subnational strategies and processes playing an increasingly important role. Decentralization has emerged as a strong trend in India's federal framework. It is part of the broader process of liberalization, privatization, and other market reforms aimed at transferring decision making to the lowest possible level, where the costs and benefits of actions can be internalized. Economic reforms of 1991 enabled regional governments to introduce their own "liberalization policies," including a greater role for private sector–led development and avenues for the participation of foreign investment. These were followed by institutional and administrative changes, such as one-window customs clearance agencies. Each state has evolved its policy framework in order to respond to region-specific policy dilemmas.

Two constitutional amendments (the 73rd in 1992 and the 74th in 1993) established mandatory provisions for decentralization of administrative powers to local governments in India. The subsequent state and municipal acts created a policy conducive to decentralized governance, and these are being strengthened through devolution of resources from the center. The acts further enhanced the role of the local planning and strategies.

In a major initiative to promote export-based industrialization, the government of India announced an SEZ policy in 2000 to replace the then-existing policy of EPZs. India was the first country in Asia to set up a free trade zone (in Kandla) in 1965, and six more EPZs had been set up by the central government by 1994. However, the Indian economy failed to emerge as a leading producer and successful exporter of manufactured goods, unlike several other developing countries. The new policy was intended to make SEZs an engine for economic growth with the support of quality infrastructure, an attractive fiscal package at both the center and state levels, and the minimum possible regulations. Under the old policy, EPZ could be set up and managed only by the central government, but the new policy allows SEZs to be set up by private, public, and joint sectors and by state governments. The central government refrains from developing new zones; it is largely responsible for policy making.

Between 2000 and 2005, 12 new SEZs were set up; the majority of them were established by state governments. However, the policy failed to evoke interest among the private investors. To instill confidence in investors and signal the government's commitment to a stable SEZ policy regime, an SEZ Act was passed in May 2005. The 2005 SEZ Act envisages key roles for state governments in export promotion and creation of related infrastructure. SEZ applications recommended by the respective state governments/UT administration are considered by the 19-member interministerial SEZ Board of Approval for approval. State governments are also responsible for promotion and implementation of the policy. They have been asked to design their own SEZ acts and policies to cover state-level subjects. Six states have passed their own SEZ act: Gujarat, Haryana, Madhya Pradesh, Punjab, Tamil Nadu, and West Bengal. In addition, Karnataka, Kerala, Jharkhand, Maharashtra, and Uttar Pradesh and have their own SEZ policy. Madhya Pradesh, Punjab, and West Bengal have established SEZ policies to work in concert with the SEZ Act.

Since 2005, there has been proliferation of SEZs. As of January 2011, there were 582 formally approved SEZs spread across 23 states, and 380 have been notified in 20 states; that is, they have obtained all final clearances for initiating authorized operations. As table 9.1 shows, notified SEZs are highly concentrated in a small number of states; indeed, nearly 60 percent of SEZs and 90 percent of SEZs by area are located in five high-income states in India. Among the bottom-rung states, only Madhya Pradesh and West Bengal have performed relatively well, with over 475 hectares of notified land (1,212 hectares of approved land) and 17 SEZs (37 approvals) shared between them. The rest of the states have remained untouched by the SEZ wave.

The Impact of Regional Policy: Reviewing the Evidence

As the previous sections show, the policy approaches for the pre- and post-reform periods may clearly be distinguished. The pre-reform period approach involved top-down identification of lagging areas and targeting them with interventionist and regulatory measures designed to address their structural deficiencies. In the initial years of planning, industrial licensing, direct investment in public sector units, and price and distribution policies to reduce regional disparities were seen as the best way to achieve equality. In the mid-1960s, the existing instruments were reinforced by infrastructure support in backward areas. In the 1970s, the scope was further widened to include incentives and concessions. In the 1980s, when structural reforms were initiated, the major thrust was

Table 9.1 Distribution of Notified SEZs by State and Status

State category[a]	State	No. of SEZs	Share in total (%)	Share in area (%)
Top-rung states	Gujarat	29	7.8	27.6
	Andhra Pradesh	74	19.8	26.7
	Maharashtra	63	16.8	20.0
	Tamil Nadu	57	15.2	10.1
	Karnataka	36	9.6	4.8
Middle-rung states	Haryana	34	9.1	3.1
	Orissa	6	1.6	1.7
	Rajasthan	8	2.1	1.5
	Kerala	17	4.6	1.4
	Uttar Pradesh	20	5.4	0.9
Bottom-rung states	Madhya Pradesh	6	1.6	0.6
	Goa	3	0.8	0.5
	West Bengal	11	2.9	0.5
	Chhattisgarh	1	0.3	0.2
	Chandigarh	2	0.5	0.1
	Nagaland	1	0.3	0.1
	Punjab	2	0.5	0.1
	Jharkhand	1	0.3	0.1
	Uttarakhand	2	0.5	0.1
	Dadar and Nagar Haveli	1	0.3	0.0
Total		374	100	100

Source: Aggarwal 2012.
Note: SEZ = special economic zone.
a. States are classified as top, middle, and bottom rung according to their performance in terms of area covered under SEZ.

on infrastructure development for both domestic and export-oriented production. With the opening up of the economy and removal of controls in the 1990s, the era of state-led industrialization ended. The post-reform policy approach has been much more "bottom-up." It has been focused both on securing sufficient policy space for states and localities to work out their own strategies of development, and on improving the overall environment for the economic growth of targeted states/sectors through a combination of major infrastructure interventions, institutional reforms, and appropriate incentive structures. In the next sections, we consider the impact on the ground of these varying approaches.

Conclusions from the Literature

As noted in chapter 6, there exists a huge literature on the subject of regional inequalities in India, mostly focused on the post-reform (post-1990) period. Among the works covering the period from 1960 to 1990, no clear consensus emerges, with studies finding absolute convergence (Cashin and Sahay 1996; Dholakia 1994), limited convergence (Bajpai and Sachs 1996), and no convergence (Marjit and Mitra 1996) in income among states. Mohan (1997), on the other hand, found industrial policy successful, with more than a three-fold increase in the number of industrial centers and a decline in the relative share of industry in the industrially advanced states. Overall, regional policies were seen to have had a marginal impact. Large interstate disparities were attributed to the level of agricultural development (which influenced the industrial development as well), human capital, infrastructure, agglomeration economies, ineffectiveness of the centrally planned approach that neglected spatial dimensions, and interstate differences in the central government grants.

Research on the period since 1990, however, shows a strong consensus that the ongoing economic reforms since 1991 have been associated with higher growth across states, but they have further aggravated the interstate disparities (see Ahluwalia 2000, 2002; Bhattacharya and Sakthivel 2004; Dasgupta et al. 2000; Gaur 2010; Ghosh 2008; Ghosh, Marjit, and Neogi 1998; Kar and Sakthivel 2007; Krishna 2004; Kurian 2000; Maiti and Marjit 2009; Mathur 2001; Rao, Shand, and Kalirajan 1999; Sachs, Bajpai, and Ramiah 2002; Shand and Bhide 2000; Shetty 2003). While explaining the trend, most studies find that institutional quality and investment climate matter (for instance, Chakravorty 2003; Goswami et al. 2002; Mitra, Varoudakis, and Veganzones-Varoudakis 2002; among several others). Critically, from the perspective of trade, several studies also show that trade participation is associated with growth and with growing inequalities across Indian states. Maiti and Marjit (2009), using regional openness indices, suggest that the states that are more open have grown faster than others by 1–1.5 percent per year. Bajpai and Sachs (1999) observe that states that have been able to shift production patterns toward more exportable production due to favorable institutions and investment climate have accelerated their growth rates.

Although policies have tended to converge over time, differing structural and political economy factors at the state level may lead to divergent patterns of performance. States that were most aggressive in attracting foreign direct investment (FDI) not only gained competitively in manufacturing output and export, but also lead in reform of other sectors (infrastructure, social development and demographic dividend) and thus in investment. While examining the performance of Gujarat and West Bengal, for example, Sinha (2004) concludes that despite policy *convergence*, institutional *divergence* and different political responses by political and social groups continue to persist, which is driving the regionally diverse pattern of investment flows and corresponding growth patterns.

Quantitative Evidence since 1990

As discussed in Chapter 6, there is clear evidence of growing disparities in the post-reform period, with particularly strong diversion since the early 2000s (the period in which India's trade openness grew rapidly), as shown in figures 9.1 and 9.2.[8]

Data on FDI and export-oriented investment, which show strong concentration in a small set of leading states, suggest that trade and investment may be a major driving force behind divergence. Figure 9.3 shows the percentage share of FDI inflows by states for states having at least 1 percent of aggregate inflows. Unfortunately, the state-level actual FDI data are available only for 1991–2002 (figure 9.3). Since then, the Department of Industry Policy and Promotion has been releasing the amount of FDI flows by regional centers (figure 9.4). From the

Figure 9.1 Movement in Mean per Capita Income in Selected States, 1993–94 to 2008–09

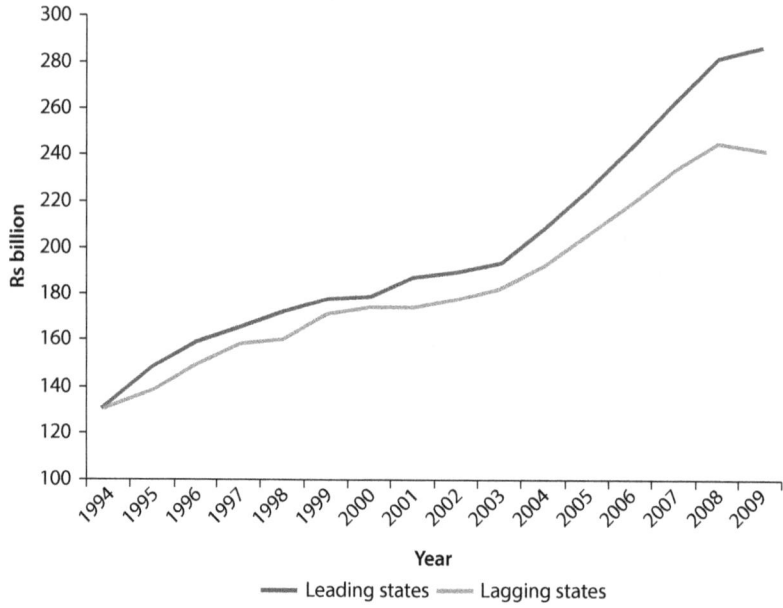

Source: Calculation based on Database on India's Economy, RBI.

Figure 9.2 Percentage Difference between Mean per Capita Income of Selected Leading and Lagging States, 1993–94 to 2008–09

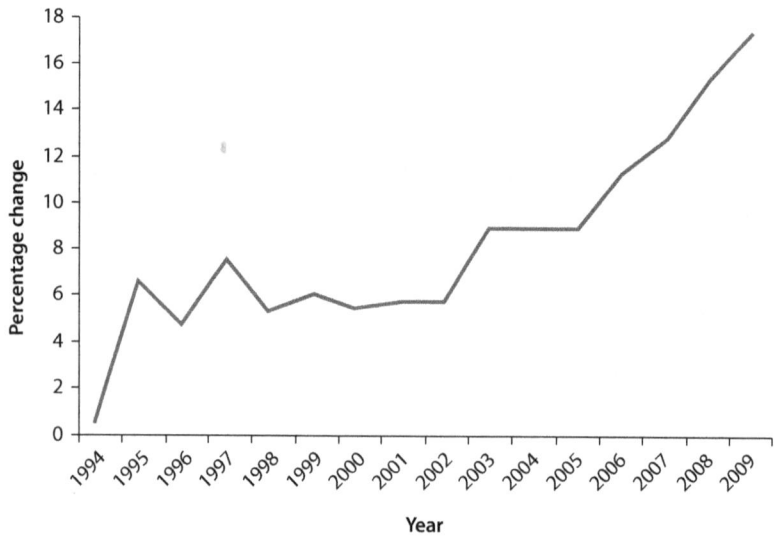

Source: Calculation based on Database on India's Economy, RBI.

Figure 9.3 Percentage of FDI Inflow in Selected Cities, 1991–2002

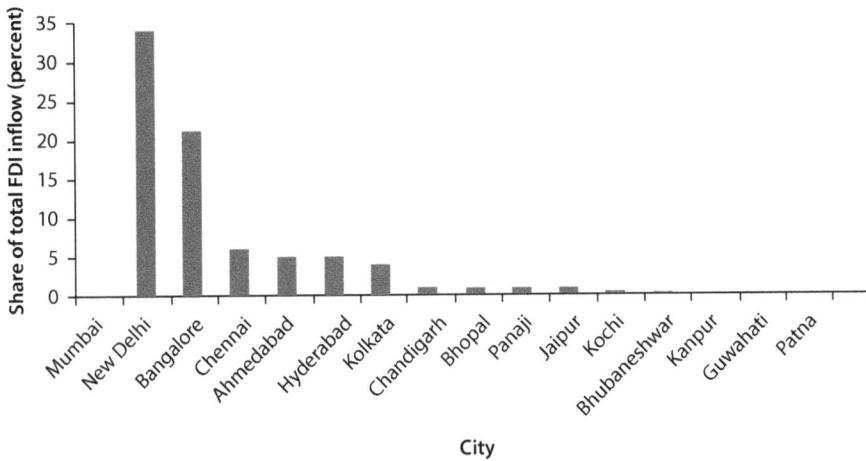

Source: Pal and Ghosh 2007.
Note: FDI = foreign direct investment.

Figure 9.4 Percentage of FDI Inflow to Total FDI Inflow, July 2000 to July 2011

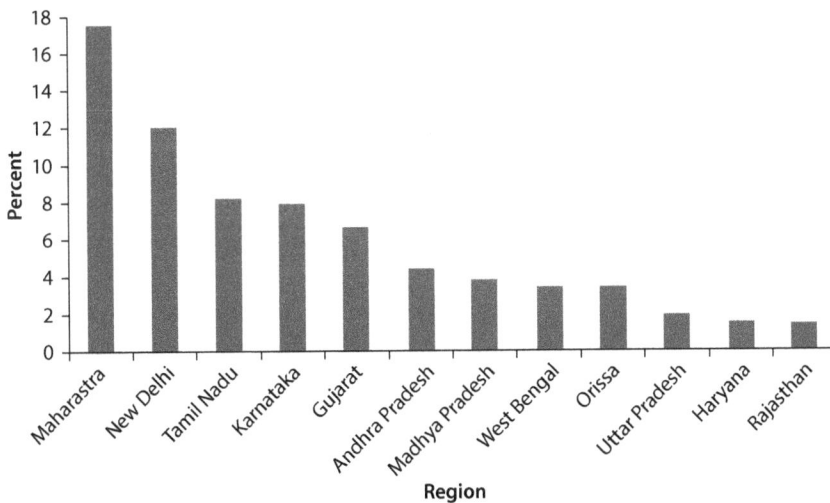

Source: FDI Statistics, Department of Industry Policy and Promotion.
Note: FDI = foreign direct investment.

figures, it can be seen that the top 10 Indian states attracted more than 63 percent of total FDI in India. In contrast, the bottom 10 states together received less than 1 percent of total FDI. The distribution of FDI depicts a strong regional bias, with the southern and western states faring much better than the other parts of the country.

Similarly, data on investment and employment in SEZs show a heavy and growing concentration in five leading states. Table 9.2 presents a disaggregated analysis of the performance of these SEZs. Substantial expansion of the SEZ

Table 9.2 State-Wise Performance of SEZs before and after Passage of the 2005 SEZ Act

| State | Employment number | | | Investment (Rs million) | | |
	Before 2005 SEZ Act	2011	Share in total	Before 2005 SEZ Act	2011	Share in total
Andhra Pradesh	2,650	83,911	12.4	367	16,857	8.3
Gujarat	16,995	40,322	6.0	570	83,188	41.0
Maharashtra	48,562	159,841	23.6	280	16,683	8.2
Tamil Nadu	27,362	161,630	23.9	1,274	24,103	11.9
Karnataka	—	91,978	13.6	—	26,216	12.9
Subtotal	*95,569*	*537,682*	*79.5*	*2,491*	*167,047*	*82.4*
Haryana	—	19,278	2.8	—	4,599	2.3
Uttar Pradesh	21,398	47,520	7.0	660	7,228	3.6
Rajasthan	331	9,573	1.4	55	1,105	0.5
Kerala	6,449	19,865	2.9	541	4,244	2.1
Orissa	—	3,069	0.5	—	12,635	6.2
Subtotal	*28,178*	*99,305*	*14.7*	*1,256*	*29,811*	*14.7*
Madhya Pradesh	1,476	8,746	1.3	230	2,646	1.3
West Bengal	4,481	26,170	3.9	357	2,058	1.0
Other states	—	4,705	0.7	—	1,249	0.6
Grand total	**129,704**	**676,608**	**100.0**	**4,335**	**202,811**	**100.0**

Source: Aggarwal 2012.
Note: — = not available. Data cover period up to March 31, 2011.

sector is evident in all 16 states after the 2005 SEZ Act became effective in February 2006, but SEZ expansion in the top-rung states has been the most spectacular. As a result, their share in total SEZ employment and investment between 2006 and 2011 increased from 73 and 57 percent to 79 and 82 percent, respectively.

Finally, data on the state-wise distribution of export units shows the same pattern as with SEZs, confirming that five leading states are reaping the benefits of openness and are likely to grow faster than the others (table 9.3).

On the other hand, table 9.4, which presents average investment implemented through the Industrial Entrepreneurs Memorandum (IEM) in selected periods as the ratio of state domestic product,[9] suggests that for industrial activity—including both foreign and domestic investment—there has been fairly strong convergence across states over the past decade.

Conclusions

Achieving growth while redressing regional imbalances has been the fundamental tenet of planned development in India. From the very beginning, the national planning strategy incorporated the locational concepts in industrial policies. The approach of successive governments for tackling the regional imbalance relied on regulatory instruments, fiscal transfers, fiscal incentives, location of public investment in backward areas, and infrastructure support.

Table 9.3 State-Wise Distribution of Export-Oriented Units in Selected Years, 2000–06

State	2000 Number of units	2000 Exports (Rs miilion)	2003 Number of units	2003 Exports (Rs million)	2006 Number of units
Andhra Pradesh	156	567.3	110	1,452.7	197
Gujarat	168	1,013.2	233	2,448.3	231
Karnataka	175	2,131.6	244	4,162.5	330
Maharashtra	184	2,485.2	268	3,100.1	305
Tamil Nadu	278	2,600.0	313	4,195.3	391
Haryana	53	333.0	59	750.0	69
Rajasthan	75	353.1	78	700.0	86
Uttar Pradesh	75	817.2	78	2,019.0	84
West Bengal	43	230.7	82	457.4	81
Madhya Pradesh	68	864.8	26	850.0	27
Kerala	25	490.7	40	695.3	52
Orissa	6	441.4	4	2.2	6
Punjab	40	762.0	42	800.0	42
Assam	—	—	2	—	1
Bihar	1	0.1	1	—	0
Chhattisgarh	—	—	4	50.0	4
Himachal Pradesh	8	146.2	9	160.0	9
Jammu and Kashmir	—	—	1	2.0	1
Jharkhand	—	—	6	37.0	6
Total	1,438	13,700.9	1,701	22,728.9	2,037

Source: Ministry of Commerce and Industry, Government of India.
Note: — = not available.

Despite sustained efforts, regional disparities have continued to grow and the gaps have accentuated between lagging and leading regions, with the benefits of economic growth largely confined to the more-developed regions. Liberalization and laissez fair policy has contributed to and has exacerbated inter- and intra-state disparities. In their initial phases, the programs were criticized for being controlled by the central government, and for the lack of state participation at the level of policy formulation. Programs were formulated and implemented with little understanding of the strengths and weaknesses of the local area.

The government approach toward closing the gap between lagging and leading states has changed significantly over recent decades In the late 1990s, the focus shifted to a targeted approach and subnational strategies. The government began to focus on structural impoverishment of areas, including the northeast region and the hilly states of Himachal Pradesh, Jammu and Kashmir, and Uttarakhand. The belief was that decentralization of decision making would strengthen competition among the states, triggering higher efficiency and productivity. However, the advanced industrial states have tended to accrue all the benefits in the reform years, and the other states have continued to lag behind.

The growing regional disparity in the post-reform period is a matter of serious concern. The period is characterized by deregulation of private investment, in the

Table 9.4 IEM Investment per Unit of Gross State Domestic Product in Selected Periods, 1997–2009

State	1997–99	2002–04	2007–09
Andhra Pradesh	0.0453	0.0233	0.0009
Arunachal Pradesh	0.0000	0.0000	0.0001
Assam	0.0008	0.0006	0.0002
Bihar	0.0014	0.0052	0.0002
Gujarat	0.1132	0.0361	0.0012
Haryana	0.0326	0.0123	0.0007
Himachal Pradesh	0.0010	0.0007	0.0002
Jammu and Kashmir	0.0013	0.0038	0.0002
Karnataka	0.0062	0.0054	0.0002
Kerala	0.0128	0.0055	0.0003
Madhya Pradesh	0.0581	0.0262	0.0009
Maharashtra	0.0255	0.0068	0.0003
Manipur	0.0000	0.0000	0.0000
Meghalaya	0.0003	0.0003	0.0001
Orissa	0.0012	0.0027	0.0002
Punjab	0.0401	0.0131	0.0008
Rajasthan	0.0187	0.0067	0.0003
Tamil Nadu	0.0136	0.0059	0.0003
Tripura	0.0000	0.0000	0.0000
Uttar Pradesh	0.0322	0.0094	0.0005
West Bengal	0.1788	0.0465	0.0013
Coefficient of variation	1.5933	1.2701	0.9111

Source: Calculations based on Department of Industrial Policy and Promotion.
Note: IEM = Industrial Entrepreneurs Memorandum.

hope that faster growth would induce more investment, and this in turn would reduce regional disparity. Unfortunately, backward states have been unable to catch up for a variety of reasons, including preexisting conditions, poor infrastructure, weak socioeconomic institutions, and ineffective local political leadership. that characterize their economic environment. There appears, however, to be some convergence in industrial investment across states.

In light of these findings, there is a strong case for proactive public policy to promote social and economic infrastructure in backward states through public investment in social and industrial infrastructure. However, the quality of governance, in particular at the state level is of utmost importance. Creation of enabling institutions that address the "investment environment" affects both the realities of operating as well as the perception of businesses. This role of political leaders in instigating this reform is critical. Narender Modi in Gujarat, Naveen Pattnaik in Orissa, and Nitish Kumar in Bihar are examples of regional leaders who have been instrumental in attracting businesses through their personal charisma and leadership. Much depends on the spirit of experimentation in policy making informed by strategic medium- to long-run vision and commitment. A crucial ingredient of strategic approach is strong political commitment that reflects intense focus on growth, knowledge of the necessary and sufficient conditions for growth, and belief in the strategy adopted for growth.

Notes

1. Komiya 1959. See also http://en.wikipedia.org/wiki/Mahalanobis_model.

2. http://planningcommission.nic.in. The Planning Commission was set up to promote a rapid rise in living standards through efficient exploitation of the resources, increased production, and opportunities for employment in the service of the community.

3. In addition, areas characterized by structural impoverishment were also identified, including drought-prone areas (1971), the Western Ghats hill area (1972), northeast India (1972), and tribal areas (1974).

4. http://www.idbi.com.

5. http://www.hudco.org.

6. The cross-border trading post at Moreh and Tamu was formally opened on April 12, 1995.

7. The special category status has been given to 11 states. These include the eight northeastern states: Arunachal Pradesh, Assam, Manipur, Meghalaya, Mizoram, Nagaland, Sikkim, and Tripura; along with Himachal Pradesh, Jammu and Kashmir, and Uttarakhand. They have been given preferential treatment in the Union government's resource allocation because of harsh terrain, backwardness, and other social problems.

8. The analysis in figures 9.1 and 9.2 is confined to 21 states for which comparable data used in the study are available for the period of analysis. The states studied are Andhra Pradesh, Arunachal Pradesh, Assam, Bihar, Gujarat, Haryana, Himachal Pradesh, Jammu and Kashmir, Karnataka, Kerala, Madhya Pradesh, Maharashtra, Manipur, Meghalaya, Orissa, Punjab, Rajasthan, Tamil Nadu, Tripura, Uttar Pradesh, and West Bengal. These states are categorized as leading and lagging on the basis of the region's relative income in the base period 1992–94, with national average equal to 100. Due to wide fluctuation in data, a single-point base year is avoided; rather, a three-year average is considered. Lagging states consist of regions with per capita income less than 90 percent of the national average and leading regions with income greater than or equal to 90 percent of the national average in the base period. This results in Andhra Pradesh, Arunachal Pradesh, Gujarat, Haryana, Himachal Pradesh, Jammu and Kashmir, Karnataka, Kerala, Maharashtra, Meghalaya, Punjab, Tamil Nadu, and West Bengal being categorized as leading states, with the others as lagging states.

9. Large-scale industries (having investment more than Rs 100 million in the manufacturing sector and more than Rs 50 million in the service sector), which are outside the purview of the licensing provisions, have to file an application for IEM for investment. The same is true of items not exclusively reserved for manufacture by small-scale industry sector.

References

Aggarwal, A. 2004. "Export Processing Zones in India: Analysis of the Export Performance." Working Paper 148, Indian Council for Research on International Economic Relations, New Delhi.

———. 2012. *Social and Economic Impact of SEZs in India*. New Delhi: Oxford University Press.

Ahluwalia, M. S. 2000. "Economic Performance of States in Post-Reforms Period." *Economic and Political Weekly* 35 (19): 1637–48.

———. 2002. "State-Level Performance under Economic Reforms in India." In *Economic Policy Reforms and the Indian Economy*, edited by A. O. Krueger, 91–128. New Delhi: Oxford University Press.

Alagh, Y. K., S. P. Kashyap, J. V. Shah and D. N. Awasthi. 1983. "Indian Industrialisation: Regional Structure and Planning Choices." *Man and Development* 5 (1): 62–83.

Alexander, P. C. 1963. *Industrial Estates in India*. Bombay: Allied Publishing House.

Awasthi, D. N. 1991. *Regional Patterns of Industrial Growth in India*. New Delhi: Concept Publishing.

Bajpai, N. and J. D. Sachs. 1996. "Trends in Inter-State Inequalities of Income in India." Development Discussion Paper 528, Harvard Institute for International Development, Harvard University, Cambridge, MA.

———. 1999. "The Progress of Policy Reform and Variations in Performance at the Subnational Level in India." Development Discussion Paper 730, Harvard Institute for International Development, Cambridge, MA.

Bandyopadhyay, R., and S. Datta. 1989. "Strategies for Backward-Area Development: A Systems Approach." *The Journal of the Operational Research Society* 40 (9): 737–51.

Bhattacharya, B. B., and S. Sakthivel. 2004. "Regional Growth and Disparity in India." *Economic and Political Weekly* 39 (10): 1071–77.

Cashin, P., and R. Sahay. 1996. "International Migration, Centre-State Grants, and Economic Growth in the States of India." *IMF Staff Papers* 43 (1): 123–71.

Chakravorty, S. 2003. "Industrial Location in Post-Reform India: Patterns of Interregional Divergence and Intraregional Convergence." *The Journal of Development Studies* 40 (2): 120–52.

Dasgupta, D., P. Maity, R. Mukherjee, S. Sarkar, and S. Chakroborty. 2000. "Growth and Interstate Disparities in India." *Economic and Political Weekly* 35 (27): 2413–22.

Department of Industry Policy and Promotion, Government of India. n.d. *FDI Statistics*. Online database. Ministry of Commerce and Industry, New Delhi. http://dipp.nic.in/English/Publications/FDI_Statistics/FDI_Statistics.aspx.

Dholakia, R. H. 1994. "Spatial Dimensions of Accelerations of Economic Growth in India." *Economic and Political Weekly* 29 (35): 2303–09.

Dua, A. 1980. "Capital Investment Subsidy Scheme as an Instrument for Industrialization of Backward Areas: An Exploratory View." Industrial Development Bank of India. http://www.idbi.com.

Gaur, A. K. 2010. "Regional Disparities in Economic Growth: A Case Study of Indian States." Paper prepared for the 31st General Conference of The International Association for Research in Income and Wealth, St. Gallen, Switzerland, August 22–28.

Ghosh, M. 2008. "Economic Reforms, Growth and Regional Divergence in India." *Margin: The Journal of Applied Economic Research* 2 (3): 265–85.

Ghosh, B., S. Marjit, and C. Neogi. 1998. "Economic Growth and Regional Divergence in India, 1960 to 1995." *Economic and Political Weekly* 33 (26): 1623–30.

Godbole, M. D. 1978. *Industrial Location Policies*. Mumbai, India: Himalaya Publishing House.

Governemnt of India (GoI). 1951. *The First Five Year Plan, Chapter VII.* Planning Commission, GoI, New Delhi.

——. 1956a. *The Second Five Year Plan, Chapter II.* Planning Commission, GoI, New Delhi.

——. 1956b. *Ministry of Industry Industrial Policy Resolution.* GoI, New Delhi.

——. 1961. *The Third Five Year Plan, Chapter III.* Planning Commission, GoI, New Delhi.

——. 1967. *Industrial Licensing Policy Inquiry Committee Report,* chaired by Subimal Dutta. Ministry of Industrial Development, International Trade and Company, GoI, New Delhi.

——. 1968. *Evaluation of Rural Industries Projects PEO Study No. 69.* Planning Commission, GoI, New Delhi. http://planningcommission.nic.in/reports/peoreport/ cmpdmpeo/volume1/evofru.pdf.

——. 1981a. *Report on General Issues Relating to Backward Areas Development.* Planning Commission, GoI, New Delhi. http://planningcommission.nic.in/reports/publications/ pb80_NCDBAgn.pdf.

——. 1981b. *Report on Industrial Dispersal by National Committee on Development of Backward Areas (NCDBA),* chaired by B. Sivaraman. Planning Commission, GoI, New Delhi.

——. 1982. *The Committee on Free Trade Zones and 100 Percent Export Oriented Units,* chaired by Tondon. Ministry of Commerce, GoI, New Delhi.

——. 1991. *Statement on Industrial Policy.* Ministry of Industry, GoI, New Delhi.

——. 1997. *Ministry of Commerce & Industry Department of Industrial Policy & Promotion.* The North East Industrial Policy (NEIP). GoI, New Delhi. http://dipp.nic .in/incentive/discontinuation_NEIP_1997.pdf.

——. 2007a. *Ministry of Commerce & Industry Department of Industrial Policy & Promotion.* North East Industrial and Investment Promotion Policy. GoI, New Delhi. http://dipp.gov.in/incentive/NEIIPP_2007.pdf.

——. 2007b. *Ministry of Small Scale Industries and Agro & Rural Industries Package for Promotion of Micro and Small Enterprises.* GoI, New Delhi. http://www.dcmsme.gov .in/publications/circulars/GazNot/promotion_package_english.pdf.

——. 2011. *Report of the Committee on Restructuring of Centrally Sponsored Schemes (CSS).* Government of India, New Delhi, September 2011.

——. n.d. *Ministry of Commerce and Industry.* Online database. Government of India, New Delhi. http://commerce.nic.in.

Goswami, O., A. K. Arun, S. Gantakolla, V. More, A. Mookherjee (Confederation of Indian Industry) and D. Dollar, T. Mengistae, M. Hallward-Driemier, and G. Iarossi (World Bank). 2002. "Competitiveness of Indian Manufacturing: Results from a Firm-Level Survey." A Confederation of Indian Industry (CII) Study in Collaboration with the World Bank, CII, New Delhi.

Goyal, V. 1975. "Area Development Strategy: Diffusion of Growth Process." *Economic Times,* December 17.

Gupta, S. P. 1973. "The Role of the Public Sector in Reducing Regional Income Disparity in India." *Journal of Development Studies* 9 (2): 243–60.

Kar, S., and S. Sakthivel. 2007. "Reforms and Regional Inequality in India." *Economic and Political Weekly* 42 (47): 69–77.

Komiya, R. 1959. "A Note on Professor Mahalanobis' Model of Indian Economic Planning." *Review of Economics and Statistics* 41 (1): 29–35.

Krishna, K. L. 2004. "Patterns and Determinants of Economic Growth in Indian States." Working Paper 144, Indian Council for Research on International Economic Relations, New Delhi.

Kurian, N. J. 2000. "Widening Regional Disparities in India: Some Indicators." *Economic and Political Weekly* 35 (7): 538–55.

Maiti, D., and S. Marjit. 2009. "Regional Openness, Income Growth, and Disparity across Major Indian States during 1980–2004." Development Economics Working Papers 22927, East Asian Bureau of Economic Research, Australian National University, Canberra.

Marjit, S., and S. Mitra. 1996. "Convergence in Regional Growth Rates: Indian Research Agenda." *Economic and Political Weekly* 31 (33): 2239–42.

Mathur, A. 2001. "National and Regional Growth Performance in the Indian Economy: A Sectoral Analysis." Paper presented at the National Seminar on Economic Reforms and Employment in the Indian Economy, Institute of Applied Manpower Research, New Delhi.

Mitra, A. 1965. *Levels of Regional Development in India.* Census of India, 1961, New Delhi.

Mitra, A., A. Varoudakis, and M. Veganzones-Varoudakis. 2002. "Productivity and Technical Efficiency in Indian States Manufacturing: The Role of Infrastructure." *Economic Development and Cultural Change* 50 (2): 395–426.

Mohan, R. 1997. "Industrial Location Policies and Their Implications for India." In *Urbanization in Large Developing Countries: China, Indonesia, Brazil and India*, edited by G. W. Jones and P. Visaria, 289–314. Oxford and New York: Clarendon Press.

Nagia, D. 1971. *Industrial Estates Programme: The Indian Experience.* Hyderabad, India: Small Industrial Extension Training Institute.

Nair, D. P. 1980. "Efficiency of State Enterprises Investment in Kerala." *Lok Udyog* 14 (5).

Pal, P., and J. Ghosh. 2007. "Inequality in India: A Survey of Recent Trends." DESA Working Paper 45, Department of Economic and Social Affairs, United Nations, New York.

Pathak, M. 1971. "Impact of a Public Sector Project on a Backward Economy." *ARVIK* 7 (2).

Patnaik R. C. 1974. "Regional Economic Development with Special Reference to Orissa." *IEJ* 22 (5).

Prasad, P. H. 1976. "Industrial Policies in Developing Country. The Indian Case." *IEJ* 24 (5): 177–78.

Raina, M. K. 1969. "Railway Rates and Regional Development." Paper presented at 52nd Indian Economic Association Conference, Patna, India.

Rao, M. G., R. T. Shand, and K. P. Kalirajan. 1999. "Convergence of Incomes across Indian States." *Economic and Political Weekly* 34 (13): 769–78.

Reserve Bank of India (RBI). 2011. "Finance Commissions in India: An Assessment." http://rbidocs.rbi.org.in/rdocs/Publications/PDFs/7CHSF280311.pdf.

———. n.d. *Database on India's Economy.* Online database. Mumbai: Reserve Bank of India. http://dbie.rbi.org.in/DBIE/dbie.rbi?site=statistics.

Sachs, J., N. Bajpai, and A. Ramiah. 2002. "Why Some Indian States Have Grown Faster than the Others." *Rediff Money Special*, February 26.

Sanghvi, R. L. 1979. *Role of Industrial Estates in a Developing Economy.* Mumbai, India: Multi-Tech Publishing Co.

Sarma, A. 1982. "Public Enterprise: Policy Goals in India." *State Enterprise* 1 (3).

Sekhar, U. A. 1983. "Industrial Location Policy: The India Experience." World Bank Staff Working Paper 620, World Bank, Washington, DC.

Shand, R. T., and S. Bhide. 2000. "Sources of Economic Growth: Regional Dimensions of Reforms." *Economic and Political Weekly* 35 (42): 3747–57.

Shetty, S. L. 2003. "Growth of SDP and Structural Changes in State Economies: Interstate Comparisons." *Economic and Political Weekly* 38 (49): 5189–200.

Sinha A. 2004. "Ideas, Interests, and Institutions in Policy Change: A Comparison of West Bengal and Gujarat." In *Comparing Politics Across India's States: Case Studies of Democracy in Practice*, edited by R. Jenkins, 66–108. New Delhi: Oxford University Press.

PART 4

Conclusions and Policy Implications

CHAPTER 10

Summary of Main Conclusions

Thomas Farole

Introduction

Trade is a critical driver of growth for nations and regions, in both the short and long term. By enabling the realization of static and dynamic gains (specialization and knowledge spillovers, respectively), trade integration helps drive investment and raise productivity, contributing to long-term growth. But not all countries, or regions within a country, are in the same position to take advantage of the opportunities of trade integration, due to a variety of factors including those that are geographical, historical, demographical, political, and institutional in nature. And as trade is also both a catalyst and an accelerator of agglomeration, it has the potential to deepen already-existing disparities in economic activity, output, and income across regions.

As pointed out in the *World Development Report 2009*, regional inequality is not necessarily a problem; indeed, if it contributes to greater absolute growth on a national level, there may be greater political and economic scope to deal with regional disparities, for example through tax and transfer policies (World Bank 2009). Moreover, if labor and capital flow smoothly across regions and factor prices adjust effectively to demand, it is possible to make significant progress in equalizing differential rates of regional growth. However, in the absence of substantial redistribution mechanisms, or where significant barriers to factor movement exist, disparities in growth can lead to entrenched inequalities in income across regions. This, in turn, can become politicized, particularly when income disparities coincide with existing social, religious, and ethnic differences. At worst, this could result open conflict. But even in a relatively "best case" scenario, spatial disparities are likely to contribute to pressure for policies that are redistributive in nature. In either case, it brings a serious risk of undermining long-term growth.

With that in mind, this book has aimed to contribute to a better understanding of the relationship between subnational regions and trade. The results of our analysis can help inform the policy challenges of addressing regional divergence in general and lagging regions in particular. The remainder of this chapter summarizes the conclusions of the book on its three main dimensions: (1) how trade integration has affected regions within countries; (2) how the characteristics of a region affect the trade competitiveness of firms located there (or, put another way, what factors determine the locational choices of export-oriented firms); and (3) how effective traditional regional policy has been in addressing the particular challenges that trade brings to the problem of lagging regions.

How Trade Affects Regions within Countries

The standard models of economic geography can be taken to predict both convergence and divergence of regions in the context of trade opening, depending on the centrifugal and centripetal forces included in the model and, critically, on the assumption of the relative level of trade costs. Although much of the empirical literature to date finds divergence within countries, particularly in the past 10–20 years, the relationship between trade and regional divergence in this work remains somewhat ambiguous.

Developing Countries More Likely to Experience Divergence in the Context of Trade Expansion

In the analysis presented in chapter 2, we find that regional inequalities are growing in 18 of the 28 countries studied, with only 3 countries experiencing regional income convergence. The results from a comprehensive econometric model show that trade, *in combination with other factors*, may have a significant impact on regional inequality. Critically, the findings show clearly that trade openness is more likely to lead to divergence in developing countries than in developed countries. Moreover, we find that economic growth has on average been less polarizing in developing countries than in developed ones, strengthening the case for the link between trade openness and divergence in developing countries. Several factors turn out to interact with trade openness to determine patterns of divergence. Specifically, countries with lower government expenditure, higher variations in regional sector structures, a spatial structure dominated by high internal transaction costs, and a higher degree of coincidence between prosperous regions and foreign market access are likely to experience greater rises in regional inequality when opening to foreign trade. In addition, what matters most is, unsurprisingly, past levels of regional inequality. The point is not that trade causes increasing inequalities per se, but rather that it is likely to exacerbate existing inequalities, particularly when those are linked to structural deficiencies.

These findings suggest we are likely to see further growth in regional inequalities within developing countries in the future, for the following reasons: (1) they tend to be characterized by the structural features (discussed above) that potentiate the polarizing effect of trade openness; (2) many of them already have significant, preexisting spatial inequalities; and (3) their level of trade openness is, on average, still only a fraction of the level in most developed countries.

Heterogeneity within the Overall Trends

Evidence from our two case studies (Indonesia and India) supports these findings, showing that greater trade openness seems to coincide with increasing regional inequality. Both countries have experienced increasing regional inequalities in the decades since they substantially increased their openness to regional and global trade and investment. Regional divergence has been particularly strong during the 2000s. The case studies indicate that export participation has grown substantially across almost all regions in both countries. Thus, it is not the case that firms in lagging regions have been unable to access foreign markets at all; rather, on average, they are growing exports, just at a slower pace than in many of the leading regions. In fact, the findings suggest there is significant heterogeneity both in regional outcomes and in the regional response to trade openness in these countries, with no obvious pattern of winners and losers among core versus periphery. Indeed, in Indonesia, intermediate regions (that is, those that are neither in the core on Java nor in the remote eastern islands) appear to have benefited from trade more than both core and peripheral regions. This is partly a function of the role of natural resources–based sectors in some of these regions, and their export intensity.

A Link with Structural Transformation and Shifting Location of Firms

Another explanation may be found in the structural transformation of regional economies that is, in part, induced by trade integration. Evidence from both Indonesia and India shows that the relative change in sectoral output and export structures is much higher in peripheral regions than it is in the core. This is unsurprising, as these regions have been (and generally remain) concentrated in a narrow set of natural resources sectors. This shift, however, brings with it adjustment costs and geographical shifts in production that may contribute to growing regional inequalities.

Interestingly, however, our case study countries exhibit only moderate geographical concentration of their manufacturing sectors, on average, in the post-openness era, with substantial heterogeneity across sectors. Overall, capital-intensive sectors seem to have become more dispersed. Indeed, in India, the manufacturing sector has experienced some dispersion and appears, on the whole, to contribute (very marginally) to convergence in recent years. This may be a function of active regional policies in India to disperse manufacturing activity, but more likely indicates the natural progression of industry and regional lifecycles, with many leading core regions beginning to shift their comparative advantage toward services, and more basic manufacturing functions shifting to lower-cost locations within the country. Finally, in both Indonesia and India, the geographical structure of sectors with strong preexisting clusters appears to have changed little during the period of growing trade openness, suggesting an important territorial embeddedness of these clusters.

How Location Affects the Trade Competitiveness of Firms

Firms in the Core Are More Likely to Export

The findings in this book show clear evidence that firms located in core regions of countries are more likely to be exporters than those located outside the core regions. On the other hand, once a firm becomes an exporter, there is no significant difference across countries in the share of output that is exported. This is perhaps explained by the sectoral composition of exports in core and noncore regions (for example, in natural resources sectors, there is a greater likelihood of firms exporting virtually all of their output). It may also be a function of the lack of a local market in peripheral regions and poor access to core regions within the country, so that firms in peripheral regions that reach a certain scale beyond what can be absorbed locally are indifferent to selling to core regions or internationally.

Firms in the Core Are Also More Likely to Import

Even more so than exporting, findings from our case study countries show that firms in the geographical core tend to make significantly greater use of imports than firms in more peripheral regions. This again is likely to be at least partly a function of sectoral specialization. But it also suggests that divergence in regional incomes might not be the result of imports hurting the domestically oriented firms of lagging regions, as much as it is of imports facilitating the competitiveness of exporting firms in leading regions. Put another way, importing might indicate the potential for firms to participate in global value chains, but this potential may not be the same in different regions.

Firms in the Core Are More Competitive

Basic descriptive statistics using Enterprise Survey data indicate that these differences in trade participation may, in part, be related to differences in the characteristics of firms located in core versus noncore regions. We find striking differences in a number of firm-related factors that have, in previous research, been associated with exporting. Specifically, relative to firms in noncore regions, firms in the core are on average larger, have a greater share of foreign ownership, have a top manager with more experience, make greater use of technology, have an international quality certification, and provide formal training for their workers. And the findings that firms in the core are more likely to import also means they are in a better position to take advantage of technology and knowledge spillovers, giving them a further productivity boost. What is not clear is whether these firm characteristics are endogenous to the core, or if firm characteristics are a case of spatial sorting. In other words, do core regions have an environment that allows firms to become more competitive and export ready, or do export-ready firms choose to locate in the core while firms serving domestic markets choose to locate outside it?

Higher Competitiveness in the Core Comes despite Significant Congestion Costs

It is perhaps unsurprising that firms located in the core are more productive than those outside it. They are able to reach a larger (domestic) market more easily, lowering transport and transactions costs and enabling them to operate at larger scale. They also have access to deep pools of labor and other inputs. And they are likely to face greater competition from other firms, which acts as a constant driver of increasing productivity. On the other hand, one striking finding from chapter 3 of this book is that, across developing countries, firms in the core perceive in general a worse investment environment than those in the periphery, indicating the presence of congestion costs. This does not appear to be a function of infrastructure, however, where the results indicate that firms in the core benefit from better transport and access to finance. Instead, it is primarily a function of regulation, bureaucracy, and governance. For example, firms in the core report more visits by tax officials; wait longer to obtain permits, licenses, utility connections, and customs clearance; spend more of their management time dealing with regulation; and report greater problems with corruption. Although the findings in Indonesia are in line with the international findings, this is not the case in India, where there is greater heterogeneity in the experience of firms across states and where, overall, firms in noncore regions report even greater obstacles in relation to tax inspection and corruption.

Clearly, there is something in the core that not only offsets, but also overcomes these congestion costs. The results from our econometric exercises in Indonesia and India support and help unpack these findings.[1]

Firms and Agglomeration Matter Most

Overall, firm characteristics have the most significant association with export behavior. Specifically, we find that, regardless of where they are located, larger, younger, foreign-owned, and more productive firms are more likely to export and to export a greater share of their output. In India, however, some of the findings go against these regularities. For example, smaller firms in India are *more* likely to start exporting than larger ones, and productivity is *negatively* associated with export intensity. But the general findings on the predominate importance of firm characteristics highlight again the importance of self-selection into exporting, and raise yet again the question of whether core regions breed export-ready firms or whether export-ready firms seek out core regions.

The other strong finding of the study is that outside of individual firm characteristics, agglomeration has the strongest effect on exporting, with different forms of agglomeration having opposing impacts. Location in an area of high general economic or population density makes it less likely that a firm will be an exporter. This may indicate the presence of congestion costs, but it may also be that access to a large local market enables the sustainability of large number of small and medium firms without the compulsion to export. In contrast, firms located in regional economies where there is substantial diversity of firms across sectors (urbanization economies) as well as density of firms in a specific sector (localization economies) are more likely to become exporters. Similarly, in the cross-country and Indonesia analyses, the existence of a large number of existing exporters (regardless of sector) makes it more likely that a firm exports (although in India the these factors worked against the probability of a firm starting to export). These findings on localization, diversity, and export agglomerations all point to the potential importance of having diverse industrial districts and more widely of the benefits of shared resources in overcoming the fixed-cost barriers to export entry.

Location and the Investment Climate Have More Nuanced Impacts on Firm Export Behavior

In both Indonesia and India, first-order geography, in particular proximity to port infrastructure and connectivity to domestic markets, affects the decision to export, but its impact is minor. Overall, location seems to matter more for facilitating export participation than export intensity, indicating that location and distance are important fixed-cost barriers to exporting. So-called "second-order geography"—regional endowments and the investment climate—appears to have relatively weaker, but still in some cases important, impacts on exporters. Overall, infrastructure (as measured by transport and electricity) is found to be associated with greater export participation and intensity, although the results are not unambiguous. Access to finance is positively associated with exporting for firms in the core. On the other hand, there is no strong evidence for the role of education or of institutions on export competitiveness, although in the case of India, good institutions (proxied by law and order) have a strong association with the decision to export. Interestingly, in the cross-country analysis, regional characteristics appear to have a much stronger influence on export performance for firms located in the core than for those outside it, where firm-level factors are more significant.

The Competitiveness of Neighboring Regions Also Matters

Finally, the Indonesian case study revealed some interesting findings on the possible impact of regional spillovers—that is, how export participation and intensity of a firm in one region may be affected by the characteristics of neighboring regions. Greater sector concentration (in industry and services) and export participation in one region tends to be associated with lower levels of exporting in neighboring regions. This indicates specialization and agglomeration, and therefore competition, for mobile factors of production. On the other hand, for the most part, there appear to be positive spillovers of infrastructure across regions, suggesting that infrastructure investment is not a zero-sum game.

Implications Are Positive for the Urban Fringe, Less So for Sparsely Populated Rural Regions

What do these findings mean for noncore and lagging regions? While we find evidence of significant congestion costs in the core, the power of agglomeration appears to be strong enough to overcome these costs. For peripheral regions, this suggests that the forces for dispersion will, in most cases, not be sufficient to shift exporters (and exporting) to regions without significant additional incentives, or at least without some substantial economic endowments (for example, natural resources). On the other hand, for regions on the fringe of the core and in secondary cities with the potential to support agglomeration, the possibilities of building export clusters are much more realistic, particularly in sectors that are in the stages of their industrial lifecycle in which the endowments of the metropolitan core are becoming less critical sources of comparative advantage.

The Effectiveness of Regional Policies in the Context of Trade

Our two case studies illustrate how difficult and entrenched is the problem of lagging regions. Both Indonesia and India have spent decades and substantial sums to address the problem, yet divergence is growing. As our earlier findings suggest, trade openness is likely to have accelerated this trend. Of course, it is impossible to know the counterfactual in these countries in the absence of active regional industrial policies, but it is difficult to imagine that they could be considered effective, and certainly not cost effective. The two cases also suggest that to address the problem requires not only designing good policies, but also implementing them effectively, and doing so over a long period of time. The governance and political economy challenges of this should not be underestimated.

Trade Is Generally Not an Explicit Objective of Regional Industrial Policy

As a starting point, it is important to note that facilitating trade or even exports is typically not a primary objective of regional industrial policies. Instead, the main objectives, rightly, tend to focus on relative growth in economic (and sometimes social and other human development) outcomes. For example, in India, the objective from the beginning has been to achieve "balanced regional development." More important, perhaps, is that the main channel through which regional policies usually hope to achieve these outcomes is investment. Trade tends to be derivative of these policies. And even where it is part of the objectives, the emphasis is squarely on exporting rather than trade in general.

This said, where national industrial policies became export oriented, the export objective often came through into regional policy. When India shifted to promoting exports more widely, some of these instruments—export-oriented units (EOUs) and export processing zones (EPZs)—became part of the toolkit of regional policy; but even then, exporting was not explicitly part of the program's objectives. In Indonesia, export-led growth policies did actually translate into regional policy in the Integrated Economic Development Zone (Kawasan Pengembangan Ekonomi Terpadu, KAPET) program, where an explicit target for export growth sat alongside targets for investment and gross domestic product (GDP) growth.

Narrow and Weak Policy Instruments Deployed in Indonesia

Indonesia's efforts at regional policy have suffered through the years from an excessive emphasis on investment attraction over virtually all other objectives. And, in line with the experiences of many other countries around the world, Indonesia has attempted to achieve these objectives. There has been an overemphasis on fiscal incentives for investment, too little focus on addressing the local investment climate and improving infrastructure, and virtually no efforts to improve firm-level competitiveness. What makes matters worse is that the incentives offered to investors to locate in peripheral regions have been far too weak to make a significant impact on their location decisions, particularly in light of the relative differences in the locational competitiveness of regions.

This is not to say there have been no efforts at more comprehensive approaches to the problem in Indonesia. The KAPET program in particular attempted to combine fiscal incentives with infrastructure and the establishment of "one-stop" investment facilitation. Unfortunately, here poor implementation got in the way. More recently, plans to broaden the use of special economic zones (SEZs) and the growth corridor program offer some potential for a more integrated and comprehensive spatial policy.

In India, Almost Everything Has Been Tried

In contrast to Indonesia, over the long history of its program, India has constantly evolved and adjusted its policy instruments. By now, an extremely wide range of instruments has been deployed, from the counterproductive and distortive to those that should play a positive role in facilitating local competitiveness. Even from the beginning, India's program went beyond just investment incentives (in fact, fiscal incentives only came in during the second decade of regional policy). However, early efforts focused too heavily on using central regulatory power—through licensing restrictions, price equalization, and the location of state-owned enterprises—in an attempt to force a more desired economic geography. But even these early efforts also included provision of industrial infrastructure and efforts to address skills. Like the KAPET in Indonesia, India's Growth Centres aimed to combine fiscal incentives with other support for investment, including improvement of the investment climate and of the capacity of local firms.

The top-down efforts were abandoned over time and efforts have shifted to greater use of instruments like Growth Centres and national industrial policy instruments like EPZs and EOUs. However, the introduction of EPZs and EOUs, whereby the availability of incentives is for the first time delinked from location in a lagging region, has resulted in a heavy concentration of investment in leading regions. The evidence from India's regional program seems to indicate (as has been the experience in many other countries) that the regions benefitting most from regional policies are not the most peripheral or the greatest laggards, but rather those regions or districts that are located in very close proximity to core or leading regions.

The Critical Importance of Implementation and Governance

In both Indonesia and India, implementation of regional policy has been poor. One of the arguments has been that this was the inevitable result of central design and implementation for problems that are local in nature. However, regional policy in both countries has become substantially more bottom up since decentralization efforts in the 1990s (India) and 2000s (Indonesia). Unfortunately, the findings more recently suggest that the implementation problem remains. This is partly related to capacities of regional government, but also to the challenges of coordination, both between national and regional government as well as across various local government units within a region.

Finally, political leadership at the subnational level plays an increasingly important role in regional outcomes. Innovative and outgoing state leaders in India have been successful at reforming the local investment climate, accessing critical funding and infrastructure from the central government, and directly attracting large-scale investment. There is some evidence that similar innovative local leaders are beginning to emerge in Indonesia. Although this is a positive development, differing local capacities and governance also seems to result in more heterogeneous results—that is, a greater distinction between winners and losers. Therefore, regional policy itself may now be increasingly a driver of divergence.

Note

1. An important caveat here is that due to data limitations, we were restricted in the econometric exercise mainly to measuring infrastructure and endowments as indicators of the regional investment environment. We were unable to measure factors like regulation, licensing, and governance, which were shown in the descriptive work to be more problematic in core regions (at least in Indonesia).

Reference

World Bank. 2009. *World Development Report 2009: Reshaping Economic Geography.* Washington, DC: World Bank.

CHAPTER 11

Policy Implications

Thomas Farole

The findings of this book suggest a number of important considerations for the design and implementation of policies to promote trade integration, investment, and growth of peripheral and lagging regions. In this chapter, we organize these recommendations around five broad categories:

1. Principles of policy design for the integration and growth of peripheral regions
2. Policies targeting factors of production
3. Policies facilitating connectivity
4. Policies promoting agglomeration
5. Coordination and implementation

Note that the focus of these policy recommendations is on how to facilitate trade integration of lagging regions, and how to use trade as an instrument to facilitate investment, growth, and job creation. This is, of course, just one dimension of the policy program that would be required to support comprehensive growth and integration of lagging regions. The *World Development Report 2009* (WDR 2009) provides a comprehensive policy framework for lagging regions (World Bank 2009).

Principles of Policy Design for the Integration and Growth of Lagging Regions

Focus on the Core for Efficiency while Building Capacity in the Periphery

One of the clear findings in this book is that interventions focused primarily on core regions are likely to have a bigger impact on aggregate competitiveness than interventions targeting peripheral ones. This is particularly true of efforts designed to improve the external environment for competitiveness, such as reducing regulatory and bureaucratic burdens, improving hard and soft trade infrastructure (including transport, energy, and customs), and facilitating better access to finance. A related implication is that policies designed to improve the competitiveness of existing agglomerations, for example policies targeted to existing clusters, may be particularly effective in raising national competitiveness.

As discussed above, such policies will of course have consequences for regional inequalities, potentially exacerbating already growing disparities. But in the context of a spatially aware approach to competitiveness, more effective targeting of policies for peripheral areas (see the remainder of this chapter), and most importantly, a societal agreement on redistribution, the net result should be positive. This is, broadly, the position outlined in the WDR 2009.

On the other hand, it is also recognized that the unequal distribution of economic activity—particularly when it also comes with restraints on labor mobility and variable quality of infrastructure, public services, and institutions—can have detrimental social and political consequences and can also constrain growth in the long run. As a result, it remains critical that a balance is struck between improving aggregate competitiveness through interventions in the core and building the endogenous capacity for improved competitiveness and economic growth in peripheral regions.

Carving Out the Opportunities for Lagging Regions: Industrial and Regional Lifecycles

In the context of increasingly powerful agglomeration forces (which appear to be even more important for export-oriented sectors than for sectors that largely serve domestic markets) and the related historical processes of cumulative causation, is there a possibility for peripheral regions to support export-oriented activity? Or should firms with growth and internationalization ambitions simply pack their bags and leave the periphery for the core? For policy makers in the core, is there any hope of leveraging the benefits of international trade and investment?

The findings in this book indicate that truly peripheral regions, particularly those with low economic density, are likely to struggle to attract investment away from core regions, except where investments are based on location-specific resource endowments like in the tourism, mining, and agricultural sectors. However, our findings also provide clues to some opportunities for noncore regions. First, consider the findings on congestion costs in the core, combined with the fact that many of the regions which have grown exports fastest in recent years have been "intermediate" (neither the metropolitan core nor the remote periphery). These data suggest there may be a migration of some industrial activity to secondary cities and the fringe regions around the core (to be replaced by services). Second, the findings from Indonesia and India suggest that many of the factors associated positively with manufacturing exporting (for example, in relation to skills and wages) are in line with the comparative advantage of noncore regions. These findings are also in line with concepts of industrial and technological lifecycles, where over time the sources of competitive advantage for an industry (or a task or step in a value chain) shift from technological innovation to standardization (and therefore cost). The spatial corollary to this—regional lifecycles—suggests that the most competitive location for these industrial activities will shift from locations that offer advanced technological inputs and urbanization economies to those that offer low-cost production, scale, and possibly clusters of specialized inputs.

From a policy perspective, this means that at least some noncore regions—those on the fringe of core regions, those with existing industrial specializations, and those with density and infrastructure to support agglomerations—might target investment in direct export-oriented manufacturing, or specialize in supplying less skill- and knowledge-intensive components to exporters in the core. Even then, however, the process of transition of industrial activities to noncore regions may take many years. Within this framework of industrial and regional lifecycles, it is clear is that even these intermediate regions, and certainly lagging, peripheral regions, should focus on the opportunities that are in line with their comparative advantage. These are likely to be sectors linked to location specific endowments (such as mining, agriculture, and tourism) and where the benefits of agglomeration economies are of relatively less importance. Such an approach argues against attempting to build specialized clusters "from scratch" or to develop advanced sectors like high technology and life sciences without an existing base on which to anchor them.

One caveat to the regional lifecycles story outlined here is that the opportunities for peripheral regions to benefit may be greater in sectors that are primarily domestic oriented. Those sectors that are more outward focused and integrated into regional and global production networks are more likely to view location choices also in the regional and global context. Therefore, the decision is not core versus peripheral region in a single country, but rather a wide range of regions across a broad set of countries.

Fiscal Incentives Should Only Be a Complementary Policy Tool

Attracting (foreign) investment has always been the most common strategy of regional policies, and fiscal incentives have been the most common tool. But what is clear from past experiences of regional policy, and can be inferred from the quantitative findings of this book, is that while fiscal incentives may be effective at the margin, in most cases they are little more than a transfer of rents from lagging regions to international and domestic investors. The structural factors that determine the competitiveness of location have a far greater impact on a firm's long-run profits (and risks). The case of Indonesia supports previous findings that the level of incentives that most countries offer falls far short of what it would take to tip the balance of firm's decision; and the level that would be required to do so would be simply unaffordable for most lagging regions. By implication, investment incentives should be considered as part of the policy arsenal only *after* structural and investment climate issues have been addressed to the point at which incentives can be cost-effective.

A Framework for Different Types of Lagging Regions

As already discussed in this chapter, this book shows clearly that not all lagging regions are the same. Some have greater potential to support agglomeration, others may benefit from cross-border integration, while others may have few realistic opportunities to integrate into global or even national production networks. Table 11.1—inspired by the WDR 2009 and incorporating the

Table 11.1 A Framework for Competitiveness Policies in Different Types of Lagging Regions

Region type	Nature of policies
Near the core	• Many traditional regional policies may be effective, including investment incentives and export-oriented incentives • Promotion and facilitation of agglomeration, including industrial parks/SEZs and cluster policies • Investment climate reforms
Peripheral but with economic mass	• Targeted FDI attraction (following comparative advantage and industry lifecycles) • Support to competitiveness of existing industry clusters • Transport connectivity and infrastructure • Investment climate reforms • Firm-level competitiveness interventions (training, finance, and so forth) • Critical importance of governance
Peripheral and without density	• Limited prospects for export-oriented investment—focus on endowment-based opportunities is applicable (such as mining, agriculture, tourism) • Focus on social infrastructure and connectivity • Firm-level competitiveness interventions

Note: FDI = foreign direct investment, SEZ = special economic zone.

recommendations made throughout this chapter—provides a very basic framework for the regional policies that may be most effective in addressing trade competitiveness and growth in different types of lagging regions.

Policies Targeting Factors of Production

The Importance of Firm-Level Interventions in Lagging Regions

The findings of this book show clearly that there is a gap in the competitiveness of firms in the periphery relative to those in the core. They also indicate that firm-level characteristics are more strongly associated with trade outcomes for firms in noncore regions than regional investment climate characteristics and agglomeration (the opposite of the findings for firms in core regions). There is clearly significant endogeneity here with respect to other regional factors like endowments, infrastructure, and the regulatory environment. But these findings does suggest that any short- and medium-term efforts to raise the competitiveness of lagging regions and to expand export participation of firms in these regions must go beyond the external environment to address firm-level competitiveness. This means introducing new tools and instruments into regional policy beyond simply investment and export promotion, including vocational development and training (which has been implemented in some programs, for example in India), access to technology, and addressing management skills and capacity and access to finance.

In addition, where there is an explicit emphasis on export participation, export promotion programs will need to be "re-tooled" to be able to deliver more effectively at the regional level. Across most countries, export promotion support tends to have a bias toward core regions, partly because the majority of firms are based there, but also because access to information and the delivery of support programs tend to be much easier in the core, where most export promotion agencies are based. A starting point for more regional focus may be improving information dissemination to peripheral regions, and possibly partnering with other national agencies that have better local coverage. For example, support agencies for small and medium businesses often have very good coverage across core and peripheral regions.

Attracting and Linking Foreign and Domestic Capital

Foreign direct investment (FDI) tends to attract the greatest attention of policy makers engaged in lagging regions. If the intention is to support export-led growth, then FDI is likely to be critical, particularly in terms of seeing a short-term impact. On the other hand, evidence shows that foreign investors are much more likely to establish their operations in the core (again, with the exception of resource-seeking investment). Therefore, efforts to attract FDI should consume a limited share of resources devoted to lagging regions and be highly targeted to those sectors in which a region has clear comparative advantage. Findings from this book also indicate that domestic investors may be more likely to invest outside core areas than foreign investors, all other things being equal. This is not surprising, as domestic investors may have advantages of information, experience, and established networks that can help offset some of the costs of establishing and operating in peripheral regions. In fact, the existence of information asymmetry is the often the argument used to justify subsidizing FDI to invest in lagging regions. Yet, the research presented in this book indicates that investment promotion efforts and incentives for investment should, at the very least, avoid bias against domestic investors.

The experiences of Indonesia and India also show that unless there is a preexisting local cluster within the same industry, large foreign and domestic investments in lagging regions often fail to integrate with local economy. As a result, the economic impact tends to be limited to employment; and indeed, where these investments are relatively capital intensive, even that benefit is minimal. Therefore, FDI attraction policies should be careful to target sectors and firms where there exist reasonable prospects for backward integration, particularly if fiscal incentives are being offered. Moreover, where FDI attraction is a fundamental component of a regional development agenda, an explicit program to facilitate forward and backward linkages between investors and the local economy should be developed.

Developing and Empowering Labor

If too much attention has been paid to fiscal incentives to attract investment in lagging regions, then too little has been paid to the local labor force. Indeed, policies have tended to reinforce the asymmetry of highly footloose international capital and largely immobile local labor. As recommended in the WDR 2009, policies to promote labor mobility are important. These policies both support "people centered" development (allowing individuals to take advantage of employment opportunities, wherever those opportunities may be located) and empower lagging regions to attract labor scale and skills to underpin investment potential. Of course, the reality is that with mobile labor markets, the former is more likely than the latter, and many lagging regions will, at least in the short term, experience some "brain drain." Therefore, it is important for regional policy to focus also on education and training to build local skills. Investment incentives under European Union regional policies, for example, tend to focus almost exclusively on supporting training and skills development rather than on underwriting risk.

Policies Facilitating Connectivity

Facilitating Imports and Value Chain Integration

Competitiveness in exporting is also linked to importing. This is partly because having access to the highest-quality and most cost-effective imports allows firms to leverage dynamic gains of trade to improve competitiveness and profitability. It is also because, increasingly, becoming a competitive manufacturing exporter is about participating in integrated regional and global value chains.

This has two possible implications for regional policy. First, it raises yet another question mark over the practicality of aiming to attract export-oriented manufacturing investment in peripheral regions. In the context of just-in-time global production networks, adding additional time and costs on both inbound and outbound legs of the production process will seriously impede the competitiveness of firms located in peripheral regions.

Second, where the opportunity to attract (value-chain-oriented) investment to lagging regions is realistic, governments must identify and address location-specific barriers to importing. This is likely to include connective transport infrastructure, which is critical for both importing and exporting. However, from an export perspective, the transport solution may be focused simply on getting products out through a port or airport as quickly and cost effectively as possible. But access to service inputs for production may equally require effective connectivity between the peripheral regions and the metropolitan core, as many firms (particularly smaller ones) in peripheral regions will import indirectly through agents and distributors who will most likely be based in the core. Addressing barriers to customs clearance of imports in lagging regions may also be an important part of the policy agenda, as firms in peripheral regions may face bigger hurdles (if not necessarily more time) in accessing goods cleared through the national port, requiring them to take on the extra costs of hiring a freight agent to facilitate clearance and delivery. Among the solutions to address these barriers may be inland dryports, location of customs facilities within peripheral regions, and/or electronic clearance procedures.

Connecting and Integrating Domestic, Regional, and Global Markets

In addition to connecting regions, through trade gateways, to global markets, facilitating exports actually relies on improved connectivity of peripheral regions with *national* markets. National-level connectivity is particularly important, because firms located in the periphery may naturally play a role in producing or servicing for the domestic core. However, even when focusing on exports alone, connectivity to the core is important for several reasons. First, it offers exporters access to agents and distributors, mainly based in the core, who can act as sources of indirect exporting (firms in the core are often not only physically disconnected from global markets, but also lack the information and commercial relationships necessary to export). Second, improved connectivity to the core offers peripheral regions the opportunity to benefit from the regional product cycle patterns discussed previously. Third, and more specifically, better connectivity makes it more likely that a firm based in the core or abroad will locate part of their operation in a peripheral region to take advantage of a lower cost base or access to certain endowments.

Connectivity policies are particularly difficult when it comes to lagging regions. Indeed, one of the main lessons learned from the failed Mezzogiorno policies in Italy in the 1950s and 1960s is the problem of the "two-way road." That is, if connective infrastructure precedes by too much the reforms on other critical factors that determine competitiveness, then local firms will be unable to compete with newly arriving domestic and foreign competitors (who benefit from the now-lower market access costs) and valuable resources will be more likely to move out of the region (brain drain). From the perspective of international trade and investment, another factor to consider is the nature of FDI. As pointed out by Sjöholm (1999) in his research on Indonesia, for market-seeking FDI, improved accessibility within a country allows investors to concentrate in one location (which will most likely be the core). This is much less the case for efficiency-seeking FDI, where accessibility to the core and to international trade gateways will be important for a region to have a chance to attract investment.

Given these challenges, improving domestic connectivity must be a critical component of the policy agenda to improve a region's competitiveness and prospects for taking advantage of regional and global market opportunities. This requires investment in hard infrastructure—not only roads, but also as in the case of Indonesia, domestic ports, as well as airports. But improved connectivity also requires investment in soft infrastructure (for example, customs) and, critically, efforts to address regulatory and competition barriers that hinder market access. For example, domestic trade in India has long been hampered by a wide range of interstate barriers, including standards and licensing requirements. Furthermore, poor barriers to competition in the transport sector raise the cost of domestic connectivity in many countries. This tends to hit peripheral regions hardest, as they already suffer from lower levels of competition and lack of scale in transport markets.

Finally, beyond domestic connectivity, integration with regional markets is also critical, particularly for border regions, which may be located much closer to the core of a neighbor than their own domestic core. Peripheral border regions may in fact have significant, unexploited trade-related opportunities to build economic agglomeration thwarted by closed cross-border goods and factor markets (think of the northeast and far north of India). In these cases, addressing trade policy barriers is likely to have a dramatically bigger impact on growth and convergence prospects than traditional regional industrial policy.

Policies Promoting Agglomeration

Leveraging Agglomeration—A Balancing Act

The powerful role of agglomerations in potentiating exports has important policy implications. However, these must be considered carefully to avoid the inclination of policy makers to attempt to "build" agglomerations where they have not developed organically. Both core and noncore regions should remove barriers to natural agglomeration. These include physical and social infrastructure, but also regulatory barriers, distorting land markets and spatial planning, as well as poorly integrated goods and factor markets (this latter point is particularly critical for regions located along relatively closed international borders). Beyond the removal of these barriers, regional policies to support the development and competitiveness of existing clusters—but not in creating them from "scratch"—may have a positive impact.

Special Economic Zones Are Better to Accelerate than to Catalyze

Special economic zones (SEZs) are increasingly being adopted by developing countries as tools of export-oriented development policy. In many, if not most of these countries, they also become considered as a tool for attracting investment into lagging regions. The international experience with using SEZs as a tool of regional development has been, almost without exception, a failure.

On the other hand, this book highlights the importance of agglomeration (as well as infrastructure and the local investment climate), and in this sense SEZs, and industrial estates more broadly, may have a role to play. But this role will be mainly for lagging regions with economic density and those located in close proximity to leading regions, where SEZs may offer the missing ingredients to accelerate slowly developing agglomerations. It is far less likely to make a difference in low-density, geographically peripheral regions, where agglomerations have not yet emerged.

Coordination and Implementation

Spatially Aware Trade Policy and Trade-Aware Spatial Policy

Policies designed specifically to expand trade, as opposed to growth policies in general, may have the consequence of increasing spatial inequalities, particularly for developing countries. Thus, governments focusing on export-led growth, and more broadly on policies designed to attract mobile capital, should be aware up front of the potential spatial implications, and should consider what policies may be required to mitigate the negative consequences of such implications. As discussed in this book, the degree to which trade policy will have significant spatial impacts will vary from country to country. Partly, this is because of different sectoral structures across countries. But more important, it is because mechanisms that mitigate the development of widening spatial *income* disparities—tax and transfer policies and fluid factor markets—differ considerably from country to country.

Governments must also recognize the powerful spatial forces that operate in the trade and investment environment and take a realistic approach to regional industrial policy. This means recognizing in what types of regions spatial policy has a greater potential to tip the balance on location decisions, and what types of regional policies may be more or less effective over the short and long term. One of the clear findings from this research presented in this book is that regional experiences are heterogeneous in the face of increasingly open trade and investment environments. Thus, context matters: one-size-fits-all regional policies risk being poorly targeted, and quite likely being detrimental to many peripheral regions.

Coordinating Regional Policies with National Trade and Industrial Policies
As is clear from the policy recommendations outlined in this chapter, for regional policies to have an impact in the context of increasingly mobile factors of production, they must be comprehensive. This means combining simple measures to attract investment with policy interventions that actually make a territory an attractive investment location over the long term: broadly addressing infrastructure, connectivity, the regulatory and bureaucratic environment, governance, and competitive firms. The latter point, of course, has an element of circularity to it, but the point is that the existence of clusters of competitive firms is among the most effective ways to attract other firms. Although many countries do have some of all of these elements in their national trade industrial policies, they often do not translate effectively to regional policy. The translation is difficult enough under top-down approaches to regional policy that could (in theory) derive from the national industrial policy. But with increasing emphasis on locally developed solutions, coordination becomes more important, and more crucial to the success of both sets of policies.

Decentralization: Exploiting Opportunities and Addressing Challenges
In both Indonesia and India, and increasingly in many other developing countries, the political responsibility for regional policy has shifted in recent years from the national to the regional or local level. As discussed in chapter 10, this opens up the potential for more targeted, context-specific interventions and for greater policy innovation.

Taking advantage of these opportunities, however, will require addressing three main challenges. First, there is the availability of financial resources, which may no longer be coming (at least not at the same level) from the central government. Regions must establish clear financial agreements with central governments on funding for regional policy. They should also take advantage of opportunities to tap into national industrial policy initiatives to support aligned regional policies. Second, improving coordination of policies among localities and between regions and the national government is likely to be critical both to avoid inefficiency and improve effectiveness. Third, the role of innovative and active local political leadership in driving the regional development agenda will be critical to success going forward. In the context of a trade- and investment-oriented regional growth strategy, leadership may be particularly important. On the other hand, of even greater importance is establishing a stable governance environment that is not dependent on any one individual.

Addressing all of these challenges requires a multilevel approach to governance. Such an approach will combine incentives to promote experimentalism among local actors with greater accountability, backed up by effective monitoring and evaluation.

References

Sjöholm, F. 1999. "Exports, Imports and Productivity: Results from Indonesian Establishments Data." *World Development* 27: 705–15.

World Bank. 2009. *World Development Report 2009: Reshaping Economic Geography.* Washington, DC: World Bank.

Environmental Benefits Statement

The World Bank is committed to reducing its environmental footprint. In support of this commitment, the Office of the Publisher leverages electronic publishing options and print-on-demand technology, which is located in regional hubs worldwide. Together, these initiatives enable print runs to be lowered and shipping distances decreased, resulting in reduced paper consumption, chemical use, greenhouse gas emissions, and waste.

The Office of the Publisher follows the recommended standards for paper use set by the Green Press Initiative. Whenever possible, books are printed on 50% to 100% postconsumer recycled paper, and at least 50% of the fiber in our book paper is either unbleached or bleached using Totally Chlorine Free (TCF), Processed Chlorine Free (PCF), or Enhanced Elemental Chlorine Free (EECF) processes.

More information about the Bank's environmental philosophy can be found at http://crinfo.worldbank.org/crinfo/environmental_responsibility/index.html.

www.ingramcontent.com/pod-product-compliance
Lightning Source LLC
Chambersburg PA
CBHW080606270326
41928CB00016B/2941